THE CALIFORNIA IDEA
and
AMERICAN HIGHER EDUCATION

1850 to the 1960 Master Plan

JOHN AUBREY DOUGLASS

STANFORD UNIVERSITY PRESS
Stanford, California

Stanford University Press
Stanford, California

Printed in the United States of America
CIP data appear at the end of the book

To Chancellor Broad:

In admiration and appreciation for your past and future deeds in higher education.

With warm regards,

[signature] Dorfuss

May 9, 2001

THE CALIFORNIA IDEA
and
AMERICAN HIGHER EDUCATION

1850 to the 1960 Master Plan

To my parents,

Malcolm Paul Douglass and Enid Hart Douglass

CONTENTS

FIGURES

PREFACE

There are few studies on how states have grappled with the issue of expanding educational opportunity. Scholarship has focused largely on the general development of the American college and the research university or on individual institutions, ignoring the intricacies and influence of regional and state politics.[1] However, the regional context of policymaking, as well as the interplay between the academy and state and local governments, and ultimately with the taxpayer, is historically one of the most important influences on the organization, funding, and mission of American higher education.

This book is the first attempt at a comprehensive history of public higher education in California.[2] Hence, the following narrative does not simply chronicle the founding and building of colleges and universities. Bricks and mortar and the difficulties of hiring faculty and creating management structures are, in fact, a relatively small part of this effort. The story of California's pioneering public higher education system is inseparable from the political, social, and economic landscape from which it grew. I have attempted to provide the reader with a sense of the contextual influences and the actions of individuals that drove policymaking. The exigencies of segregated schools, capitalist conspiracies (both real and imagined), reform movements, depressions, world wars, the perceived threat of Communist subversives, tax revolts, and more generally philosophical debates over the role of higher education in socioeconomic mobility and American economic development all play an important part in this narrative.

In writing this book, I readily admit to the difficulty of trying to do justice to such an expansive subject. The saliency of higher education in the modern world has led to a proliferation of books, essays, and archival collections. But the lack of previous attempts to analyze the movement toward mass higher education at the core level of policymaking has made this effort a perplexing assignment.

I received guidance and encouragement along the way from a number of people, foremost Elliot Brownlee at the University of California—Santa Barbara, who has been both a mentor and friend. Other important influences include Clark Kerr, Dean McHenry, Vernon Cheadle, Kevin Starr, Hugh Graham, Nancy Diamond, Barry Munitz, Suzanne Ness, A. Alan Post, Hubert Semens, Dorothy Knoell, Martin Trow, Sheldon Rothblatt, Burton Clark, Patrick Callan, Lyman Glenny, Howard Bowen, Duncan Mellichamp, Calvin Moore, Richard Jensen, and my colleagues at the Center for Studies in Higher Education (University of California—Berkeley), in particular Arnie Leiman, and also Marian Gade, Diane Harley, Carroll Brentano, and Anne Maclachlan. More distantly, yet still influential, have been people such as David Riesman, Roger Geiger, David Gardner, Richard Atkinson, Verne Stadtman, Eugene Lee, Neil Smelser, Jack Smart, Clive Condren, Jurgen Herbst, and Daniel Aldrich. Each has, through conversation or writing, influenced my effort at one time or another.

Indeed, perhaps the most gratifying aspect of the entire experience has been the opportunity to talk with and listen to those who have shaped American higher education, understood its complexities and challenges over time, and articulated its intellectual and social raison d'être. Clark Kerr in particular—one of the intellectual giants of American higher education in the twentieth century—has often offered not only his unique insights into the trials and tribulations of California's higher education system but also a kind ear and a gentle manner.

I am also deeply grateful for the financial support provided by the Spencer Foundation in the form of a two-year postdoctoral fellowship, which partially relieved me of my duties as a university administrator at a critical juncture in my research. In association with the National Academy of Education, the Spencer Fellowship offered me new venues and new people to meet. In retrospect, this experience was essential for completing this book in addition to a series of publications. I also must credit my fortunate circumstance of working for the university-wide Academic Senate as an administrator and policy analyst. The Academic Senate is a community of scholars who, on the whole, saw worth in my research and writing. My arrival at the Center for Studies in Higher Education provided a final and current environment of support and encouragement.

As the reader will undoubtedly notice, archival materials provide the most important sources of information for this book. The librarians and archivists who have helped me are too numerous to mention. However, I must note the assistance and guidance of William Roberts, the UC archivist, along with the staff at Bancroft Library (UC-Berkeley), the California State Archives, the California State Library, and Karen Jean Hunt at the California State University Archives located at CSU-Dominguez Hills.

I extend my thanks as well to Norris Pope at Stanford University Press, and I appreciate the hard work and patience of Kate Washington, Stacey Lynn, and Lisl Hampton in helping to produce the final manuscript.

Last but not least, I must thank my family and friends. Perhaps my focus on higher education policy has genetic routes? I prefer to think it has more to do with my general interest in using history to understand contemporary policies and politics. The reader may sense that it is the latter since my grandfather, whom I never met, was an education advisor to California Governor Earl Warren and headed the state teachers colleges in the immediate post–World War II era. He was also a protégé of G. Stanley Hall, the psychologist and president of Clark University. I am grateful to my father and mother, Malcolm and Enid Douglass, for constant support and conversations about the world of Hall and John Dewey, my grandfather's encounters in the state capitol, and the political world of higher education. My sister Susan, an oral historian at University of California–Los Angeles, has also helped to broaden my knowledge of California, as has my brother who teaches at San Jose State University. Dario Caloss, Larry Martinez, and Tye Simpson have always been ready to share their thoughts on the pitfalls and triumphs of the sometimes lumbering, sometimes innovative, and always largest system of public higher education in the nation. To end this inadequate list of influences and sources of support, I want to thank my wife, Jill, and our two great kids, Claire and Aubrey, for their patience, understanding, and help.

John Aubrey Douglass
Center for Studies in Higher Education
UC Berkeley, November 1999

THE CALIFORNIA IDEA
and
AMERICAN HIGHER EDUCATION

1850 to the 1960 Master Plan

Introduction: California and a Great American Movement

> We almost owe more of our economic gains in the last seven decades to investment in people than to saving and the amassment of capital. And the margin in favor of people is increasing.
>
> —JOHN KENNETH GALBRAITH, 1960

> California can and will, as in both the past and the present, provide adequate support for an efficient program of public higher education designed to meet fully the changing needs of society.
>
> —CALIFORNIA MASTER PLAN FOR HIGHER EDUCATION, 1960

To a degree unmatched by any other state in the twentieth century, California embraced public higher education as a tool of socioeconomic engineering, and with dramatic results. As early as the 1920s, when the state ranked only eleventh in total population, California had the largest enrollment in public education of any state. By the 1930s, 24 percent of California's college-age population matriculated to an institution of higher education, while the national average was closer to 12 percent. Only New York, with its vast network of private colleges, rivaled California in the college-going rate of high school graduates. By 1960, California's college-going rate was 55 percent, while the national average was close to 45 percent.[1]

In 1959, before a gathering of the AFL-CIO in San Diego, Clark Kerr, president of the University of California and a labor economist by training, reflected on this remarkable record. "[California] comes closer than any nation or any other state to the achievement of universal education of young people," explained Kerr. "It provides equality of educational opportunity, it stimulates an unusually high proportion of high school graduates to seek further training, and it offers those students perhaps the richest and most varied opportunities for advanced training to be found anywhere in the nation."[2] Access to a public higher education had become an important facet in the lives of Californians. It profoundly shaped their aspirations and, ultimately, their views on what it meant to be a Californian.

The pivotal role of public and private colleges and universities in the state's economy added to the centrality of higher education in California. From the growth of the state's agricultural economy to the cold war dependence on high technology and, more recently, to the arrival of the microchip and the burgeoning world of biotechnology, institutions such as the University of California, Stanford University, and Caltech, as well as the California State University system have been the major sources of trained labor and research expertise; they have been the catalysts for new technologies and new businesses.

Here, I attempt to tell why and how Californians created their network of public colleges and universities. I also attempt to decipher California's place within the historical landscape of American higher education. California was not alone in its effort to nurture higher education as both a tool for socioeconomic mobility and an engine for economic growth. Yet the state chose a path that reflected its unique and evolving political culture. On the far side of the western frontier, California at first emulated great experiments in higher education of other states. By the turn of the century, however, California was a leader in a movement toward mass higher education that would engulf America and fundamentally reshape society. In the twentieth century, the Golden State has offered an aggressive and influential model for both increasing access and creating high quality institutions of higher education: a model that I have called the *California Idea*.

A Great American Movement

The stimulus for expanding higher education in the United States emerged from a complex matrix of sources.[3] In the earliest years of the republic, the college filled an important gap in America's social structure,[4] but it was, in large part, a devoutly sectarian effort, steeped in missionary purposes and structured to create America's clergy. Institutions such as Harvard and Yale would transform themselves beyond this singular purpose, becoming homes for classical training and for educating the sons of America's elite. New experiments also blossomed in the post-Revolutionary period, notably the publicly funded and nondenominational University of Virginia—the direct outgrowth of the passions of Thomas Jefferson and his acceptance of the Enlightenment. It was, however, the advent of the nation's network of "land grant" universities in the mid-1800s that formed the first dramatic period of transformation and growth in American higher education—a transformation linked to the ethos of the common school and the arrival of the industrial revolution.

The passage of the Morrill Act is a watershed in the history of American higher education. Signed into law during the Civil War by Abraham Lincoln in July 1862, the utilitarian focus of the act was a triumph of Whig-Republicanism that advocated the use of public institutions, such as the university, to shape America's political, economic, and social experiment. The act led to the establishment of some sixty-eight land grant colleges and universities. It also provided a federal subsidy and incentive that forced the expansion of higher education toward an education and research model suitable for a changing national economy.

The academy had resisted this broadening of its charge. Scientism, along with the call of America's farmers and an emerging business and professional class for applied training, had been met with severe skepticism. Sectarian-controlled private colleges, which dominated American higher education, looked at the teaching of modern science and the creation of "godless" public institutions as not only a threat to their way of life but as gateways for moral decay. The Morrill Act provided a turning point. The federal government became a critical instigator for change, offering an endowment in the form of federal land for possible use by both public and private institutions of higher education. The largess came with a number of stipulations. Income generated by federal scrip could be used for expanding existing institutions and for the creation of new colleges and universities, but only if the institutions included programs in "agriculture and mechanical arts" and only if they adopted two relatively new concepts beyond teaching: scientific research and public service.

Under the Morrill Act and all other federal legislation intended to support America's colleges and universities, it remained the responsibility of state governments to organize education in their respective states and to charter institutions of higher education. This key interpretation of the U.S. Constitution has fundamentally shaped America's multifaceted and decentralized brand of education. The Morrill Act placed the burden on state lawmakers to manage and disburse the profits generated by the land grants. Although federal land scrip for education had been provided in the immediate post-Revolutionary era, the Morrill Act remains the largest single allocation of resources for higher education and is closely matched only by the surge of federal funding in the immediate post-Sputnik era.

The Morrill Act provided a grand vision of a network of colleges and universities tied to local economies and needs. It was a catalyst for states to establish one or more land grant institutions, and it significantly influenced the growth of institutions that began to call themselves research universities. Yet the income generated by this seminal legislation and managed by state governments was largely exhausted by the 1890s. In most states, land grant funds had been spent on a relatively small number of public and private institutions that could not possibly meet the appetite of a growing American population for higher education.[5] The burden of funding America's public research universities and expanding higher education opportunities fell to state governments, many of which had earlier assumed that federal grants would prevent the need for large state investments—at least for the foreseeable future.

At the turn of the century, state lawmakers began a more concerted effort to establish and expand existing public colleges and universities. On the one side, the drive of individuals to succeed in an increasingly complex and technical marketplace created a new demand for postsecondary education. On the other side, state lawmakers and business interests increasingly recognized higher education as a means to improve the skills of the nation's labor force and the productivity of major sectors of its economy. This widely recognized link—of investment in higher education to socioeconomic mobility and economic prosperity—drove one of the most important social engineering experiments in American society. No longer should postsecondary education be reserved for the affluent or for a restrictive definition of an intellectual elite; it should train, accredit, and impart social status to a larger mass of students, irrespective of social and economic class, and it should create knowledge to serve the needs of society. As with the common school of the 1800s, the concept of broad access to higher education eventually became an accepted part of the American political landscape and increasingly occupied the time and thoughts of lawmakers and the public.

Older, prestigious private institutions, such as Harvard and Yale, considered this change in societal values and incorporated more expansive admission practices. Though these institutions developed more applied curricula and expanded their research activities, they remained largely divorced from this profound public sector movement toward mass higher education.

Writing in 1903 and after serving for twelve years as the founding president of Stanford, David Starr Jordan professed that public higher education was the key to America's evolving social and moral experiment for two reasons. First, private colleges and the small number of private research-oriented universities remained, on the whole, tied to the relatively small, sectarian communities that created and sustained them. These institutions had no inherent need or desire to expand access or to meet the regional educational and economic needs of a rapidly expanding and increasingly diverse population. Second, these institutions could not garner the fiscal resources necessary to keep pace with the need for a better-educated society. Only public coffers could subsidize such a massive and consistent commitment of resources and institution building. In the final analysis, concluded Jordan, private higher education could not fulfill the needs of a democratic society; conversely, it was the obligation of the state to furnish education to the large mass of Americans and ultimately to empower the average citizen. While reserving an important role for institutions such as Stanford, Jordan pronounced that the growth of public higher education was the "coming glory of democracy," the "most wonderful thing in educational development since Alfred found Oxford and Charlemagne Paris."[6]

In an iterative process that reacted to and shaped this new market demand, policymakers in government and within the nation's growing education community redefined the purpose of higher education. Public institutions, responsible more directly to the wants and economic desires of Americans and chartered and funded by lawmakers, became the primary vehicles for redefining the purpose of American higher education. It did not happen overnight. The ever-expanding role of public higher education in society has a long and complicated history, with significant differences between regions. Along the eastern seaboard, for example, the infrastructure of private institutions essentially delayed the growth of public higher education. In the more recently settled American West, the lack of an existing network of private institutions created a vacuum which lawmakers rushed to fill by creating new public institutions. Among southern states, a strong antistate political culture and a society rooted in an agrarian economy and racial segregation resulted in the slow development of higher education institutions, both private and public.

World War II provides an important transition point in this long process of institution building. Before the war, more students attended private than public colleges and universities. Particularly in states along the eastern seaboard, private institutions dominated. However, the college-going rate was relatively low. Five years before America's entry into the war, only 12.5 percent of high school graduates continued their education in postsecondary institutions. The age of the robber baron and the image of the entrepreneur with moderate or no formal education driving economic innovation, though faded, still remained. Access to postsecondary training was related largely to economic and social class, often to the exclusion of the middle class, women, and ethnic groups. Higher education was a luxury to the mass of Americans—particularly under the demands of the Great Depression.

The post–World War II years ushered in the era of mass public higher education. By 1960, the national college-going rate of high school graduates was 45 percent. In 1975, it was 51 percent. In 1990, that figure had grown to nearly 60 percent. Equally important, the number of students over twenty-four years of age increased dramatically, reflecting the broadening of both academic programs and the demand for "lifelong learning." As a result, enrollment growth since the war has been staggering. In 1945 the nation's colleges and universities enrolled 1.5 million students; by 1990 that number had increased to nearly 15 million.

Public institutions are the bulwark of this movement toward mass higher education. Nearly three-quarters of all students participating in higher education now attend public institutions. The surge in the number and size of public universities also supported a dramatic increase in graduate and professional degree programs. In 1900, a total of only 382 doctoral degrees were granted; by 1960, and shortly after the scientific and political spectacle of Sputnik, the number of doctoral degrees had grown to nearly 10,000; and by 1990 the number of doctoral degrees conferred in the United States was approximately 35,000.[7]

Access to higher education has become both a real and imagined determinant for success in American society. As David O. Levine explained, "Not only must lawyers and doctors attend college before beginning professional training, but would-be entrepreneurs and social workers also must acquire several years of postsecondary schooling before Americans deem them qualified to practice their chosen vocations."[8] American popular culture also embraced education as a panacea, a new American religion with moral, applied, and intrinsic values. In the nineteenth century, the focus was on building the common school. In the twentieth century, higher education became the new mantra. Americans, explained Martin Trow in 1970, are increasingly sending "their children to college to share in the high culture, for its own sake as well as for its instrumental value in gaining entrance to the old and emerging elite occupations." Higher education, concluded Trow, "is assuming an increasingly important role in placing people in the occupational structure and, thus, in determining their adult class positions and life chances."[9]

Another important yet largely unstudied stimulus for the expansion of public higher education—one examined in this book—is the perceived role of colleges and universities in regional economic development. As states assumed the burden of financing and expanding higher education, communities increasingly saw the establishment of public colleges as vital components for training and educating the local labor market, for infusing state funding into their economies, and for attracting businesses. The aphorism that all politics is local has special relevance to the development of state systems of higher education. The political repercussions of the rising demand by communities for state-funded institutions were profound: Representatives in local and state governments, particularly after World War II, engaged in heated races to gain new campuses and to expand academic programs and enrollment at existing colleges and universities. To be without a public college or university was, and continues to be, a decided market disadvantage.

In the initial rush to build new and primarily public institutions that began in the early part of this century, most states failed to coordinate their network of institutions. As described by Lyman Glenny in a 1959 study of state systems of higher education, American higher education represented "a happy anarchy" of colleges and universities. The wave of new and primarily public institutions was the result of the entrepreneurial drive of local interests, often businessmen and their representatives in state legislatures. Public colleges and universities usually had their own governing boards. They independently created their own academic programs and sought students for admission with little, if any, regard for the mission or programs of other colleges and universities, public or private.[10] Not until after World War II did most states attempt to restructure and give coherence to their evolving public systems of colleges and universities. To expand access and to control costs, state governments attempted to impose order on what were often politically powerful and competing institutions.[11]

The California Idea

California departed significantly from this national trend. Around the turn of the century and in the midst of a powerful political reform movement intended to reshape California society, three interrelated goals emerged that would redefine the notion of educational opportunity. First, advocates for expanding higher education argued that all high school graduates should have the opportunity for postsecondary training. It was a compelling interest of the state, they claimed, to expand access and empower the individual to participate in the economic life of the state and in its social reform movement. Second, these advocates also argued that California government should aggressively expand the number of public higher education institutions throughout the state, especially near growing population centers. Finally, in the course of this expansion, new types of institutions and academic programs should be established to cater to the social and economic needs of a rapidly changing California.[12]

A higher education system to match the ambitions of Californians—this was the call of California Progressives engaged in one of the nation's most potent reform movements between 1900 and the end of World War I. The translation of these goals into concrete and meaningful institution building created a powerful and influential model that exuded the values of America's emerging middle and professional classes. By 1920, California government had established a formal and coherent hierarchy of public institutions that could be found in no other state. California boasted the nation's first and largest network of public junior colleges. The University of California was America's largest postsecondary institution in enrollment and was also the nation's first multicampus university, with campuses in Berkeley and Los Angeles and with research stations along the coast and in agricultural centers of the state. It was also the first public university to receive direct budget allocations for research from state government. Completing the creation of a tripartite system, the state began the transformation of a set of teacher's colleges into regional and liberal arts colleges. This was a transition that came slowly and was accompanied by heated debate.

These many accomplishments came within the framework of two important values that shaped policymaking and further distinguish the California Idea. The first relates to balancing the three goals of broad access, affordability, and quality—what has proven to be one of the major challenges for American higher education and for other national systems of public higher education. Most states did not fully understand the difficulty of creating this balance within their evolving public systems, and they often gave the most weight to access and affordability. Particularly in the Midwest, states often responded to populist demands for greater access by attempting to make their land grant universities all things to all people, incorporating not only the goals of a research university, but also the educational responsibilities and admissions standards of a junior college, including vocational training. These accommodations often led to a decline in the quality of these institutions. California explicitly rejected this path. Each segment of the tripartite system was assigned a specific and rather rigid mission. The objective was to decrease redundancy among the state's network of colleges and university campuses and to encourage public institutions to excel in their own sphere of responsibility.

The second value that distinguishes California within the landscape of American higher education is the concept that the state's public colleges and a multicampus university are part of a logical and interconnected system. As noted, many states attempted to tie together their collection of public institutions by centralizing them under a single board, particularly in the post–World War II era. Creating a coherent system of higher education was, essentially, a top-down process, imposing change on the culture and function of existing institutions.

In California, integration was created not at the governance level but within the operational aspects of each institution and at the earliest developmental stages of the tripartite system. As early as 1910, matriculation agreements linked the tripartite structure: A student at a junior college who completed a two-year degree program accredited by University of California faculty would have guaranteed admission to the Berkeley campus. A similar guarantee existed by the 1920s for undergraduates attending California's teachers colleges. Within the rubric of California's "educational ladder," the university played a central role in management. Its faculty helped to develop the idea of the junior college, formulated the concept of the associate of arts degree, set standards, and accredited junior colleges and high schools. For a time, public funding of high schools was directly tied to university accreditation. Articulation agreements and accreditation provided formal ties within the state's public higher education system, in effect making it greater than the sum of its individual parts.

Some eighty years after the invention of the state's tripartite system, its conceptual framework remains largely intact. Today, California's massive effort to invest in human capital and research includes the University of California, the California State University, and the California Community College systems, each with a mission that reflects the vision of California's Progressives and each with its own governing board. Nearly 2 million students are now enrolled in more than 140 campuses. Combined with a relatively small number of traditional private institutions, such as Stanford and

Caltech, California stands as an internationally renowned center for higher learning.

In retrospect, the tripartite structure has proven a remarkably durable and flexible system for expanding educational opportunity and for meeting the growing and evolving training and research needs of California. During the 1920s, due primarily to the proliferation of junior colleges and the immense size of the multicampus University of California, more Californians went on to a higher education than did residents of any other state. In the midst of the Great Depression, public colleges and universities absorbed a portion of California's labor pool and trained students for emerging sectors of the state's economy. During World War II, the size and academic quality of the University of California attracted federal funding for science that helped drive new technologies, created the national lab system, and helped support the tremendous wartime growth in the aeronautics and electronics industries. In the cold war era, the state's tripartite system grew dramatically in enrollment and academic programs, playing a key role in California's rise as a major economic force in high technology. The location of Silicon Valley, the concentration of biotechnical firms, and the growth of communications industries all relate directly to the productivity of California's mix of public and private higher education.

For the California taxpayer, the tripartite structure has also proven extremely cost-effective (a topic discussed in the epilogue). The reasons are numerous. The early development of the junior college, in particular, offered a relatively efficient mechanism for expanding educational opportunity under the idea that not all students were prepared or able to enter the university. The monetary focus on the University of California system as the primary state-funded source for research also controlled costs. As a result, the state's investment per student in public higher education has historically been rather low in comparison with other large state educational systems. In 1960, for example, California ranked twenty-fifth in the cost per student funded by state taxpayers—just below Alabama and South Carolina. Since that time, the cost per student has remained at or just below the national average.[13]

It would be a mistake, however, for the reader to begin this story thinking it chronicles a slow and rational march of policymaking. California's path toward a vast network of public college and university campuses is intertwined with sharp political battles, power politics, racism, sexism, sometimes slow adaptation to economic change, miscalculations, and poor decisions with unforeseen consequences. The twists and turns are many. As this narrative describes, the development of California's higher education system is intricately tied to the often turbulent and certainly spectacular history of California.

Population Growth, Political Culture, and Higher Education

In explaining why Californians developed their pioneering system of higher education, two important themes are discussed in this study. The first relates to the state's unparalleled population and economic growth and the subsequent emergence of a political culture that profoundly shaped institution building in the state. The second relates to the process of policymaking and the powerful role of the University of California in creating the tripartite structure.

The terrific energy of a state rushing to redefine the American Dream has its roots in California's argonaut beginnings. Yet, after the initial rush for gold, California soon gained worldwide attention for other attractions: cheap land, a moderate climate, employment in agriculture and industry, a sense of a new beginning without the difficulties of the frontier, and the ideals, if not the reality, of a classless society. As a result, the initial population surge was followed by successive and massive waves of new Californians. Unlike most of the American West, California not only quickly rivaled the dense population of most eastern seaboard states, but its gold rush beginnings and subsequent economic development concentrated a high proportion of its population in urban areas. By the turn of the century, California had 1.5 million people, making it the fifteenth largest state in the country. It also had a population evenly divided between rural and urban areas—a transition point not reached in the United States as a whole until 1920. Depression and war only further catapulted California toward its destiny as an economic powerhouse. "California has not grown or evolved so much as it has been hurtled forward, rocket-fashion, by a series of chain-reaction explosions," stated Carey McWilliams in 1949 and in the midst of yet another surge in immigration to the state. "In California the lights went on all at once, in a blaze, and they have never been dimmed."[14]

Nineteen years after World War II, California celebrated its new status as the nation's most populous state when it surpassed New York. Governor Pat Brown designated a day for his fellow Californians to honk their horns and help announce to the world the state's new status and its unique place in American history: the ultimate land of opportunity, only distantly rivaled by other states in the Union. This was more than self-proclamation. California was the focus of a national press that looked for affirmation of America's greatness in the cold war era. No state paralleled California in its population and economic growth. No other state had media coverage to reinforce its self-image—California had Hollywood. "California is a window into the future," remarked *Look* magazine in the wake of California's new status as the nation's most populated state." [It has] the most fertile soil for new ideas in the U.S. The migrating millions who vote with their wheels for California are responding not only to the lure of sunny skies, but the lure of opportunity."[15] Though the image would be tarnished by the upheavals of the 1960s and by a renewed recognition of the complications of such a huge and diverse society along the Pacific, California's allure remains strong.

Today, California has over 31 million people and an economy that, if it were a country, would rank among the top seven in the world. Thus far, every generation has seen the state's population nearly double. Throughout much of this expansion, Californians have espoused what might be termed the "politics of optimism": a sense of destiny and confidence in their ability to shape the future. The caveats to this positive self-image are many, constrained by the realities of economic recessions, the consternation of race riots, and the pervasiveness of poverty. However, this sense of fate and glory, what Peter Schrag has called the "re-rendering of the old myth of El Dorado," is a powerful part of California's history, affecting not only the average citizen, but government itself.[16] California sought to both nurture and anticipate population and economic growth, making large public investments in the state's infrastructure and public institutions, including higher education. The innovation of the tripartite system is, in no small measure, a reaction to this constant desire to serve the expanding needs of a burgeoning population and economy—the efforts of an activist state government to shape the future.

California's first decades of statehood brought a mix of new blood and ideas with reliance on existing models of civic institutions found in the home regions of immigrants. A strong contingent of Yankees espousing the fervor of Whig-Republican ideals was particularly important in this early period of policymaking. As in other states, establishing a public university was viewed as an avenue for social and economic mobility and as a primary source of training and research for agriculture.

In California, it was also seen as an institution that could provide social and economic stability within a new society created by fortune seekers. A public university, it was hoped, would induce civility and culture, and attest to California's aspiration to be a new experiment in American democracy, despite frontier roots and geographic isolation from the nation's perceived cultural center on the East Coast. In California, pride mixed with status-anxiety, creating a strong desire for a public university and a general expansion of educational opportunity.

By the early part of the twentieth century, higher education gained further relevance. The University of California was a breeding ground for Progressives and a major source for the conceptual ideals of Scientism. It was a public institution that would release California from the rogue clutches of monopoly and rampant corruption. "The university was their Progressive dream come true," remarked Kevin Starr in his study of the Progressive Era. "[T]heir vision of elite high-mindedness in the public interest translated into buildings, libraries, faculty, students, research and teaching programs."[17]

Other states, Wisconsin in particular, linked their political reform movements to the expansion of their state universities. Yet the saliency of higher education to California's reformers transcended the public university in ways that were unique and influential. California Progressives translated higher education into a public good that needed to be allocated in a rational, cost-effective, and egalitarian way. University leaders such as Benjamin Ide Wheeler (president of the University of California between 1899 and 1919) and Alexis Lange (dean of the School of Education at Berkeley) provided ways to accomplish this, while protecting their vision for the University of California. They argued and lobbied for the establishment of the nation's first network of public junior colleges and an expansion in the number of state normal schools.

Lange, known among his contemporaries as the father of the junior college movement, argued that each of these institutions would serve the growing appetite of Californians for access to postsecondary training. Each would also deflect demand from the University of California and would allow Wheeler and his successors to pursue the relatively new model of the American research university: a selective institution in admissions, focused on advanced training, research, and public service. In no small part, the tripartite structure that emerged was built not only to serve a Taylorite vision of specialized institutions but also to support the aspirations of the University of California.

In successive years, the political power of the University of California acted as an important conservative force for maintaining the tripartite structure, strengthened politically by its elevation in 1879 to a public trust under the state constitution. Few public universities have enjoyed the level of autonomy granted to the governing board of the University of California. Attained during a turbulent period of constitutional reform in the late 1870s, the university's Board of Regents assumed a level of independence that buffered it from sometimes rancorous state politics. More importantly, this autonomy gave the board, the university president, and faculty the ability to develop academic programs and make internal management decisions—including developing new campuses and setting selective admissions standards—enjoyed by few other public universities.

University officials and key legislators constructed the legal foundations of the tripartite system in an era of consensus policymaking. However, consensus would soon dissolve into conflict. The emergence in the 1920s of the regional college movement in California created a new rival for the university, fighting for state funds, academic programs, influence in the economy, and the loyalty of lawmakers and the public. The University of California, its alumni, and its political friends argued that state colleges should focus on educating teachers, which was their historical mission. Increasingly, supporters of the state colleges argued for the maturation of their institutions. Proposals emerged for new campuses, for four-year degrees in a number of fields beyond teacher education, and for master's and professional programs in areas such as engineering. The state colleges found support in local communities, in part because of frustration with the University of California. Although a campus of the university was established in Los Angeles in 1919 and another in Santa Barbara in 1944, such geographic expansion was reluctantly undertaken by university officials. The university's unusual status as a public trust meant that lawmakers could not create new campuses by statute. They needed the agreement of the Board of Regents, who sought to focus funds and energy largely on their campuses at Berkeley and Los Angeles. Hence, the only route for lawmakers to expand educational opportunity was to create new state-funded regional colleges and encourage the growth of junior colleges.

From the 1920s up to 1960, the regional college movement gathered up steam, despite the political opposition of university officials. Particularly in the post–World War II era, the battle over the future of the tripartite structure intensified, and the university's political influence to defeat legislative bills and to restrict the growth of state college campuses and programs waned. By the late 1950s, three interrelated factors raised the real possibility of a major reorganization of the state's public higher education system under a single "superboard": one, the infighting between the university and the state colleges; two, the sometimes frantic attempts of lawmakers to capture the political prize of a new campus; and three, the spiraling costs of expanding a higher education system increasingly subject to ad hoc policy-making and entrepreneurial efforts of local communities. Despite significant state budget deficits, local representatives scrambled to pass legislation to get a new campus in their districts.

As the following narrative details, California's 1960 Master Plan for Higher Education provided resolution to this debate and a path for ordered growth in the state's higher education system. The Master Plan was the result of a negotiation process between the higher education community and lawmakers that, in the end, preserved and codified the best aspects of the California Idea in public law and numerous agreements. Conversely and perhaps more importantly, the plan ended the threat of lawmakers to reorganize California higher education under a central governing board. The Master Plan renewed and redefined a social contract with the people of California to expand access to higher education. It also stands as one of the most profound and influential efforts at socioeconomic engineering in post–World War II America—one that remains the focus of interest nationally and internationally as a model for planning systems of higher education. Yet, as this history explains, it did not invent or even reinvent California's system of higher education.

A New World?

In his seminal 1963 study of the modern university, Clark Kerr stated that higher education was the "prime instrument of national purpose," the essential element for developing the "knowledge industry."[18] Since then, American higher education has become a $140 billion sector of the national economy, with the vast majority of resources going to public institutions. No other nation has a similar array of public and private colleges and universities that feed the technical and professional labor pool and research needs of a postindustrial economy while also providing broad access and the promise of socioeconomic mobility. America's multifaceted higher education institutions, despite their many failings and redundancies, have proven to be a major market advantage in the new global economy.

California, in particular, is a source of inspiration and study for nations caught in the complexities of transforming an elite and relatively small network of institutions into high-access, populist vehicles for social change and research.[19] A similar transition was undertaken long ago in California.

Like the transatlantic influence of the German research university during the nineteenth century, the movement toward mass higher education in America is a model aspired to, in one form or another, by other nations. "Higher education," noted a 1993 report by the RAND Corporation, using the lexicon of the late twentieth century, "is increasingly perceived as America's principal point of comparative advantage against international competition. Human capital is clearly becoming the central engine for economic growth, and human capital is the main product of higher education."[20] Of all states in the Union, California's higher education system provides the greatest success story of a broadly accessible and high-quality network of colleges and universities.

Yet, California's tripartite system and, more generally, American higher education have entered a new era of transition. There are a number of factors that will alter the structure and delivery of postsecondary education in the new millennium. For one, operational costs have been rising. Since World War II, these costs have far outstripped other major sectors of America's economy. Traditional institutions, one might argue, appear to be inherently inefficient, much like the nation's health care profession, which is now undergoing a major restructuring process. One result of these soaring costs has been a rise in tuition that has outpaced the cost of living. It has also resulted in rising student-to-faculty ratios—an important gauge of the quality of the traditional college and university with its dependence on human contact and mentoring. Add to this conundrum limited public resources and a political era that embraces small government, and you have a corresponding erosion in public funding for public higher education. All of these circumstances pose challenges for California's higher education system—a system that is under increasing strain from the pressures of growing enrollment demand, battles over affirmative action, and a shift in political culture that, thus far, is extremely reluctant to invest in its infrastructure of public institutions.[21]

Perhaps more importantly, a relatively new dichotomy has emerged that will test the resilience of California's and other states' systems of public and private colleges and universities. While the consensus that formed in the post–World War II period to fund and expand higher education has dissipated, the market for new forms of education and training continues to expand. The arrival of "virtual universities" and other technologically induced innovations, intended to expand access to train and to retrain the nation's labor force, provides an important and relatively new catalyst for change. The combination of expanding demand and technology-driven forms of education and training may substantially alter what Virginia Smith, the former president of Vassar College, has called the monopoly of traditional colleges and universities in the postsecondary market. The ability of these institutions to "protect their almost exclusive share of the market of certain students who seek higher education," she predicts, "cannot be sustained."[22] Indeed, the monopoly of what have become the "traditional" colleges and universities is already eroding. However, this does not necessarily imply their demise. The market for higher education is growing, creating an environment for a greater array of institutions and providers of training and research.

Peter Drucker and others have warned that big universities will be relics of the past within the communications environment of the new century. Despite the proliferation of electronic communication, however, the physical cohabitation of a community of students, scholars, and researchers remains salient. This explains, in part, why the vast majority of biotechnology businesses are located within a mile of a research university—linked physically and not just electronically to the research and training productivity of the academic community. Universities provide "a critical mass of intellectual collegiality," notes Denis Cioffi, "which, although supplemented by modern high-technology toys, will not soon be replaced electronically."[23] The collegiate experience also fulfills a logical and productive transition for Americans moving not only from school to work but also from the parental household to independent living.

The growing demand for higher education and for university-based research and training suggests a greater diversity of choices and institutions, not a paradigm shift to a singular model of virtual universities and on-line education. However, the savvy of existing institutions to strategically and aggressively adopt new technologies will likely be a key variable in determining which will be the leading institutions of tomorrow. As the world slides increasingly toward a postindustrial and technology-driven economy, the shape of existing institutions will change, and new modes of developing human capital will emerge. What will American higher education look like in twenty years? This question is beyond the scope of this book. Suffice it to say that forces of change and the possible magnitude of organizational restructuring appear to be similar in scope to those of the last major period of transformation in American higher education in the early part of the twentieth century. With the largest system of public universities in the nation, within the most demographically diverse state in the Union, which also contains the highest concentration of high technology businesses in the world, one cannot help but think that California will continue to be on center stage. As outlined in the epilogue of this book, innovative change on the scale first imagined by California Progressives will require significant reflection on the purpose of the academy and a greater recognition of the pivotal role of higher education in the economy and society of tomorrow.

CHAPTER 1

Statehood and the Idea of a University

Westward the course of empire takes its way;
The four first Acts already past,
A fifth shall close the drama with the day;
Time's noblest offspring is the last.

—BISHOP BERKELEY, 1795

California's venture to build what would become the nation's largest public higher education system has humble beginnings. With the discovery of gold ore in 1849, the first interest of the argonauts clearly was not to build communities but to seek fortunes.[1] Establishing a set of common schools, let alone a university, was hardly the concern of prospectors. Most hoped to strike it rich and return home. These new Californians led transient lives, working frantically in the hills during the summer and congregating in the few valley cities and along the San Francisco Bay in the winter. "It is rare to meet with a man or woman who seems at all stirred by any but the money phase of this country," wrote adventurer Eliza Fernham to her family back east. In most mining towns, she complained, there are, generally, "no churches, and religious meetings are held, if at all, once or twice a month by appointment."[2] Lamented a young Josiah Royce, "The first business of a new placer community [is] not to save itself socially, since only fortune could detain for even a week its roving members, but to get gold in the most peaceful and rapid way possible."[3]

A growing minority with vested interests in land and business, however, saw things differently. A rising class of merchants, lawyers, bankers, ranchers, and other beneficiaries of the explosive growth in population and wealth sought the means to bring stability to a chaotic California. It was largely this contingent that gathered in Monterey at California's first constitutional convention in September 1849 to develop a proposal for statehood. When the delegates met in Colton Hall, creating an institution of higher education appeared to be a mandatory goal for any self-respecting new state. The constitutions of existing states provided for one or more state-supported institutions of higher learning as a means to further social and economic progress and as a legal mechanism for securing federal land grants for education under the Northwest Ordinances of 1785 and 1787. Creating a system of education and a university was only one of the many difficult tasks that the California delegates faced. Indeed, the very legitimacy of their meeting was unclear.

At that time, California was not officially recognized as a territory, normally a prerequisite for statehood. The convention delegates had no authority from Congress to deliberate.[4] Though Alta California had become a part of the United States just one year earlier under the 1848 Treaty of Guadalupe Hidalgo, the United States Senate and House of Representatives remained embroiled in a divisive debate over the future of slavery and a proposal by Representative David Wilmot that all territory acquired from Mexico remain free-soil areas. In late May 1849, word arrived that Congress had adjourned without an agreement on the organization of California's civil government. In the perspective of the newly appointed civil governor of California, General Bennett Riley, there was an urgent need for a more ordered government. In the midst of the rush for gold, federally enforced military law was in shambles. With the tacit approval of President Zachary Taylor, a southern Unionist, Riley issued a call for the convention.

California's First Constitution and Education

The task of the delegates was to form a new government acceptable to Congress and to chart the future of Alta California. This meant defining its boundaries, deciding on the volatile issue of slavery, determining the rights of its Mexican and American citizens, forming an elected and representative legislative body, defining the state government's powers of taxation and debt, and, finally, inaugurating a system of public education. Once completed, the new constitution would be placed before Congress and President Taylor. Acceptance as a state, proclaimed the delegates, would allow California, "the bright star of the west, to claim a place in the diadem of that glorious Republic, formed by the union of the thirty-one sovereign states."[5]

Of the forty-eight delegates to the convention, most were relatively new arrivals in California. The push for California statehood had, in fact, not come from the more established, pre-1840s expatriate Americans who had adapted to life under the laws of the rancheros. Rather, it came from younger, more recent immigrants, most of whom lived in northern California and had little understanding of the culture and life that had developed under Spanish and then Mexican rule. Only eight delegates were Californios, notably Mariano Guadalupe Vallejo of Sonoma and Jose Antonio Carrillo of Los Angeles. Most of the delegates were adventurers who, similar to the majority of those toiling in the foothills of the Sierras, had left the East Coast with few belongings to start life anew.

The excitement of the era bred a sense of optimism and self-importance. "I think you must be quite lonely in the states," quipped one argonaut to family back east. "[I]t seems that they will soon be depopulated there is so many coming here."[6] As the final destination of the westward movement, there was a collective understanding among the delegates that California's emergence marked a new age in American and, perhaps, world history. In the spirit of Jacksonian Democracy, the delegates hoped California would personify what they viewed as the true meaning of the American Dream: social and economic opportunity relatively free of the constrictions of class and social status. That this ideal might not apply to all races, or to women, was not a central concern of the delegates. They ignored such caveats.

While there was much rhetoric about California's pending emergence as a new society along the Pacific, the majority of delegates sought the structure and representative aspects of Yankee institutions to support their entrepreneurial and social interests. They looked to their home states—many with mature common school systems and colleges—as models for the proper relationship of state government to education.[7] Delegate H. W. Halleck opened the convention, arguing that California's constitution might simply borrow from "the constitution of every state in the Union."[8] While it appears that the delegates attempted to do just that, the constitutions of Michigan, Wisconsin, and, more importantly, of Iowa and New York influenced them most. A total of sixty-six of the 137 sections in the first constitution appear to have been taken from Iowa's constitution (passed in 1846), while nineteen can be identified as coming from that of New York, the home state of many of the delegates.[9]

In discussing the structure for California's future system of education, the delegates were decidedly shaped by a growing and powerful common school movement. Public education was considered a basic building block for creating not only a democratic society but also an ordered world vital to American capitalism. This was the ethos of the best-known common school and compulsory education advocates of the time, men such as Henry Bernard from Connecticut, radical Republican leader Thaddeus Stevens, and, most famously, Horace Mann, Massachusetts's superintendent of instruction. According to Mann, public schools were essential for promoting an egalitarian society, for the "Americanization" of immigrant populations, and for developing adequately educated workers. Yet, in much of the country, particularly in the Midwest and South, opposition to the common school movement remained substantial. The harshest criticism came primarily from three different groups: those who based their agrarian economies on apprenticeship, those who resented any form of taxation for social purposes, and those concerned with public education's intrusion on local religious and cultural traditions.[10]

Common school advocates in California and throughout the nation recognized these obstacles to their campaign for state-sanctioned and publicly funded education. Mann and other leaders of the movement (Whig-Republicans, as were many of the delegates to the California Constitutional Convention) were bent on developing state systems of taxation that would fund and expand the common school and develop new institutions of higher learning. An egalitarian system of education was likely to gain the support of the general public, but Mann knew that success depended upon convincing the upper classes, both merchants and landowners, of the need for the common school.

If the common school was a vehicle for egalitarian ideals, it also was an institution advanced by Whigs who believed that large and powerful institutions should shape American society. In speeches given at social clubs for the economic and political elite, Mann aimed his rhetoric accordingly: "Does any possessor of wealth, or leisure, or learning, ask 'What interest have I in education of the multitude?' I reply, you have at least this interest, that, unless their minds are enlightened by knowledge and controlled by virtuous principle, there is not, between their appetites and all you hold dear upon earth, so much as the defense of a spider's web." Mann went on to remind all that "[e]ven a guilty few can destroy the peace of the virtuous many."[11]

Most Whig and some Democratic delegates to California's 1849 Constitutional Convention embraced Mann's persuasive arguments, but no legal or moral mandate dictated that a public system of education be established in California. A minority of delegates, mostly Democrats who hailed from America's southern states, argued that state government should avoid such an obligation. Indeed, in much of the South, education remained largely under local authority. Yet the Yankee and Protestant predilections of most of the delegates made such an arrangement in California unthinkable. These American emigrants to California "believed that the church and the school were the bulwarks of our civilization," remarked William Warren Ferrier in 1937. Many came with a great devotion to education, "to that furnished by the common school and academy, and also to that by the college and the university."[12] While sectarian institutions should have ample room to develop, thought the delegates, public-sanctioned and public-supported education was vital for a new and geographically large state.

Most of these delegates were self-made men who found their fortunes in the business generated by the gold rush. They sought mechanisms, such as public education, to ensure similar opportunities for future California citizens. Moved by this notion of egalitarianism and idealism, many of the delegates professed a hope that the new state could avoid the harsh class distinctions they themselves had escaped.

Idealism, however, was severely tempered by the reality that California had virtually no infrastructure of existing schools on which to build a system of education and had no institutions of higher learning. During California's brief rule by Mexico, the liberal federal government had promised funds for education, but it had never delivered. The lack of money, the opposition of the friars within the missions to anything but religious instruction and vocational training, and the apparent apathy of the Californios effectively arrested the development of education. California's forced annexation to the United States and the tremendous influx of population, largely to the Bay Area, that followed brought new interest in establishing schools. Editorial pressure from transplanted New Yorker Samuel Brannan, exerted in his San Francisco paper, the *California Star*, helped articulate the need for public education, leading to the establishment in 1848 of the state's first publicly funded school and its first local school board in San Francisco. But the transient nature of life in California soon brought an end to the experiment. Only a year later, the school was temporarily closed, and Thomas Douglass, the school's teacher and a graduate of Yale, fled to the foothills of the Sierras searching for gold. Few other schools existed at the time of the convention in Monterey.[13]

In considering the state government's potential role in education, the convention president, Dr. Robert Semple, urged enlightened and aggressive action. A native of Kentucky, Semple had published California's first newspaper, the *Californian,* and came to Monterey as a delegate from Sonoma. Semple argued that any school funding, whether derived from federal land grants or local taxation, needed to be equitably distributed throughout California. The vast wealth generated by California's numerous mines presented a unique opportunity. "I think that here, above all places in the Union, we should have, and we possess the resources to have, a well-regulated system of education," Semple stated.

> It is the duty of the members of this House to unite together and secure the reputation, character, and ability in our public teachers which can only be obtained by a liberal and permanent fund that shall be uniform throughout the State; that any surplus fund collected in one district shall not be appropriated to that district, but that the aggregate fund from all the districts shall be appropriated strictly to school purposes, and distributed equally through the State. Education, sir[s], is the foundation of republican institutions; the school system suits the genius and spirit of our form of government.[14]

Influenced by Semple's leadership, the delegates agreed to four major constitutional provisions related to education and intended to "encourage, by all suitable means, the promotion of intellectual, scientific, moral and agricultural improvement."[15] A letter to "the People of California" from the delegates explained that "a free people in the enjoyment of an elective government, capable of securing their civil, religious and political rights, may rest assured these inestimable privileges can never be wrested from them, so long as they keep a watchful eye on the operations of their government, and hold to strict accountability, those to whom power is delegated."[16]

Contending with the realities of a rapidly growing and often rancorous society, the delegates stated that education, along with law enforcement, was the key component for creating a civil society. The delegates spoke of "[t]he peculiar circumstances in which California [became] a state with an unexampled increase of population coming from every part of the world, speaking various languages, and imbued with different feelings and prejudices." California required institutions that would help bond the people, develop trust, and foster economic prosperity. "No people were ever yet enslaved who knew and dared maintain the co-relative rights and obligations of free and independent citizens," continued the delegates. "A knowledge of laws—their moral force and efficacy—thus becomes an essential element of freedom, and makes public education of primary importance."[17]

Fear of political and social disorder was compounded by the influx of largely young, male, and sometimes aggressive fortune seekers. It was a season of "heaven-defying crime, violence, and blood," explained Henry Dana.[18]

Building a strong, publicly funded system of schools, remarked delegate M. M. McCarver, a farmer from Sacramento, would mitigate these tendencies; it would induce families to come to California. "Nothing will have a greater tendency to secure prosperity to the State, stability to our institutions," he insisted, "and an enlightened state of society, than by providing for the education of our posterity."[19]

In an open letter to the people of California, the delegates explained that the new constitution guaranteed "in the most ample manner, the establishment of Common Schools, Seminaries, and Colleges, so as to extend the blessing of education throughout the land, and secure its advantages to the present and future generations."[20] One provision, based largely on the constitutions of Iowa and New York, created an elected position of state superintendent of public instruction. The superintendent would help organize school districts, establish policies for school trustees, and assist the trustees in building schools and securing teachers. Only five other states had thus far established a similar constitutionally elected position.

The second and third provisions outlined California's financial commitment to build a system of schools and to encourage "by all suitable means, the promotion of intellectual, scientific, moral and agricultural improvement." Under the Northwest Ordinance of 1787 and the Oregon Plan passed by Congress in 1841, California could anticipate managing and profiting from a grant of 500,000 acres of federal land for the establishment of public and democratic institutions, including common schools.[21] It was assumed that much of this land would be in the gold-rich areas of the state and, hence, would be of exceptional value. The generous profits anticipated were thought sufficient to obviate the need, at least during the first years of statehood, for the creation of a property tax to support schools. During the convention, Sacramento lawyer and delegate Winfield Sherwood even presented a motion that would allow the new legislature to spend a portion of the profits from federal land grants on purposes other than education.

Both Semple and McCarver, however, argued against Sherwood's proposal, urging as large a school fund as possible. "There cannot be too large a fund for educational purposes," Semple stated at the convention. "Why should we send our sons to Europe to finish their education? If we have the means here we can procure the necessary talent; we can bring the President of Oxford University here by offering a sufficient salary."[22] Sherwood's proposal was voted down by a slim margin of one vote. The delegates agreed that revenue from federal land grants should be "inviolably appropriated to the support of common schools throughout the state."[23]

Finally, a fourth provision was concerned with establishing a university. Article IX, Section 4, of the new constitution provided that the state, if given federal land or private funds for such a purpose, would create California's first public institution of higher education. The Northwest Ordinance provided a specific grant of land to each new state for the establishment of a "seminary of learning." Delegates assumed an exceptionally high profit margin from sale of the federally donated land. Based almost word-for-word on Iowa's constitution, California's provision for a state university read:

> Funds accruing from the rents or sale of such lands, or from any other source for the purpose of aforesaid, shall be and remain a permanent fund, the interest of which shall be applied to the support of said University, with such branches as the public convenience may demand, for the promotion of literature, the arts and sciences, as may be authorized by the terms of such grant.[24]

The Idea of a University

When California entered the Union under the Compromise of 1850, many of California's legislators assumed that the state constitution required the establishment of a state college or university. Almost immediately, proposals surfaced to create a secular state university or to support several new and struggling sectarian institutions, including the Methodist-oriented College of the Pacific in San Jose (est. 1852) and the Congregationalist-leaning College of California in Oakland (est. 1853). The latter proposal would have been the most expeditious course. Yet, Californians, like residents of most states, had formidable philosophical objections to the concept of Western government funds supporting sectarian institutions. These objections and the development of a common pattern of governance and funding for public universities in the United States would have a profound effect on California's plans for a university.

Throughout the colonial period and the early 1800s, religiously affiliated private institutions were the predominant form of higher education in the nation. Yet, their existence depended on approval, or chartering, by the colonial and later state governments, and most embraced a form of institutional governance built around a board partly consisting of laymen. This corporate-public model of governance represents one of the most important American modifications to the European notion of a college or university.[25] There was also the predilection of these boards to anoint relatively strong presidents and a push toward meeting the market demands of a largely pluralistic society. But this catering to markets would come later. With the exception of small amounts of state aid for many private institutions and the development of a handful of public universities, chartering remained the primary source of control of higher learning for state governments in the period of early nationhood. This seemed to be the extent of government responsibility, and with good reason: State legislatures had neither the money nor the interest to take on the burden of funding and managing institutions of higher education.[26]

Instead, states continued to rely on philanthropic and sectarian organizations to help create and sustain colleges. Even with federal land grants for "seminaries of learning," available by 1800 under the Northwest Ordinance, most state governments looked to the individual boards of institutions of higher education to directly obtain and manage their own finances. Both philanthropic and sectarian activities were presumed protected from state jurisdiction. These factors help to explain the substantial, if undefined, distance between state authorities and the institutions of higher education chartered in the immediate period following the Revolutionary War.

In the early 1800s, however, an increasing number of legislatures attempted to gain greater control over the colleges and universities in their states. An important legal ruling came in 1819 in the U.S. Supreme Court's decision *Dartmouth College v. Woodward*. The Dartmouth case had implications for public higher education and for the evolving system of corporate capitalism.[27] Three years earlier, citing its charter of Dartmouth College, the New Hampshire Legislature had intervened directly in the administrative affairs of the college, which had been founded by members of the Congregational church. Dartmouth President John Wheelock came under attack by both the college trustees and faculty. Wheelock, a Jeffersonian Republican and the son of past Dartmouth President Eleazar Wheelock, was more a military man than he was a scholar, and his administration was seen as inept and partisan. His involvement in a sectarian quarrel within the local Congregational church further angered the trustees. Shortly thereafter, the trustees dismissed Wheelock. His political allies in the state legislature, however, attempted to reorganize the college to reinstate him, setting in motion a series of court battles pitting the right of the board to govern the college against the power of the state government to intervene. The trustees' case was argued by famed Dartmouth graduate Daniel Webster. Under Chief Justice John Marshall, the Supreme Court finally settled the issue, stating "that any act of a legislature which takes away any powers or franchises vested by its charter in a private corporation . . . is a violation of the obligations of the charter."[28]

The Dartmouth case established the autonomy of a private institution, whether it received financial support from the state. The case also contributed to a general withdrawal of state subsidies to private institutions. Providing funding for colleges without gaining a say in their operation seemed unfitting of the democratic process. As a result, state legislators became more interested in establishing and expanding public institutions.[29] Influenced by the University of Virginia as the first great experiment in public higher education, legislators wanted to create institutions that would be secular, provide greater educational opportunity, and offer curricula that included practical and applied courses. The scientific and industrial revolution was transforming American society but was making slow inroads into the curricula of the nation's private, elite colleges with their ecclesiastical origins.

In state legislatures, representatives of farmers and the emerging class of merchants and manufacturers, impatient for reform, wanted new, public institutions to embody their interests. This led to the establishment of the University of Michigan (1817), Indiana University (1820), the University of Iowa (1847), the University of Wisconsin (1849), and the University of Minnesota (1851), and it launched a major movement toward public institutions of higher education.

From the start, public institutions were at odds with the majority of private colleges, with their classical curricula aimed at training the wealthy for professional careers as lawyers, ministers, diplomats, and physicians. America's own landed gentry were the first to embrace higher learning in a quest to replicate European institutions. The tide of Jacksonian Democracy attacked the colonial colleges as vestiges of an old order, "preoccupied with character to the exclusion of substance," in the words of historians Christopher Jencks and David Riesman, "idealizing a character-type best suited to an Eastern drawing room or parish house."[30]

By the time of California's 1849 Constitutional Convention, the delegates assumed that the state would create one or more public institutions of higher education. They would be purveyors of moral and practical learning, Christian in orientation but strictly secular in purpose. The delegates saw public institutions without religious affiliations as more accountable to the people and more focused on the greater good.[31] In announcing the results of their deliberations, the delegates wrote in their letter to the people of California that the new constitution "guarantees in the most ample manner" the establishment of a public state university, "so as to extend the blessing of education throughout the land, and secure its advantages to the present and future generations."[32]

The idealistic rhetoric of Semple and the other delegates, however, met the harsh reality of a disorganized and violent frontier society and a financially poor state government. The desire for a social and economic experiment along the Pacific Coast quickly dissipated into a struggle to simply cope with waves of migration, vigilantism, sectionalism, political corruption, and the difficulties of creating private enterprises and public institutions within the vast stretches of the state.[33]

According to Theodore H. Hittell in his 1898 history of California, one-tenth of the state's forty-niners were politicians displaced by elections and changes in administrations back east. Many of these migrants were former Democratic appointees who found themselves unemployed after the election of Whig war hero Zachary Taylor in 1848. Many came from a culture of political corruption, ventured to California for economic gain, and gravitated toward politics as a familiar way to achieve wealth. This contingent included Thomas Jefferson Green, formerly of Texas, who first came to California to put his slave laborers to work on a mining claim on the Yuba River. Green became a state senator and chairman of the Senate Finance Committee in the first legislature. Along with several other ambitious politicians, Green operated a bar in which he encouraged his fellow legislators to indulge in free whiskey as part of his lobbying to become a militia commander. Green's generosity prompted newspapers to satirically call the first session of the state's new government the "Legislature of a Thousand Drinks."

Green's behavior was not an anomaly. The self-interest and greed of lawmakers thrived during the Democratic Party's domination of California state politics in the 1850s. Nearly every major state election was won by a Democrat during that decade, with the exception of the gubernatorial election of 1855, when the Broderick-Gwin rivalry gave the Know-Nothing candidate, J. Neely Johnson, the governorship. The death of the national Whig Party and the slow rise of the Republican Party in its place hindered effective opposition to the Democrats.[34]

Democratic domination had a powerful impact on the willingness of California state government to fund and develop public education. Democrats, both the honest and the corrupt, tended to see local government as the proper place for developing public services. In the Jacksonian tradition, the Democrats believed the less government the better, even if it meant preventing the development of a more egalitarian society. At the local level in California, the Democratic opposition to state-funded education found support. The sparse communities that dotted the expansive new state (with the exception of cities such as San Francisco) remained largely populated by transient fortune seekers, miners with no interest in starting families in California and providing for the education of children.[35]

Lawmakers, including California's first governor, Democrat Peter Burnett, largely ignored the call of the 1849 Constitution for the rapid development of a system of public education. Born in 1807 in Nashville, Tennessee, and raised in Missouri, Burnett received little schooling. He professed no great interest in education as a policy issue during his administration. In his first address to California's new legislature, Burnett made no mention of education. Instead, he focused on the adoption of a civil and criminal code as the most important duty of government, followed closely by a requirement "to confine [California's] expenditures within bounds, to keep the young state out of debt."[36] The legislature's standing Committee on Education justified inaction, based on the difficulties of establishing a school fund. According to the committee, it would take three or more years to organize the sale of federal lands for such a purpose, and they refused to burden Californians with additional taxes until then.[37]

In his report to the legislature in January of 1852, California's first superintendent of public instruction, John G. Marvin, complained bitterly about the confusion of state government. Nearly three years had elapsed since the framers of the state constitution provided for the establishment of common schools and a state university, he stated, yet no adequate provision had been made for their funding, and no legislation had been passed for the chartering of a university. Was the constitution "a dead letter?" he asked. "For want of the means of public instruction, the permanent settlement and consequent prosperity of our state is retarded: and those families here have cause of complaint that some tangible and effective provisions have not been made." Further, he stated, "[I]n a republic, at least, knowledge is the great leveler; it is the true democracy; it levels up, it does not level down."[38]

Another California advocate for public education supported Marvin and, in particular, the call for a state university. "There is a very great importance to California in the establishment of a University in the sense of stability and settlement it will produce, and the greater permanence it will give to her population." It would invite immigration, he noted, and persuade immigrants to make California their home, start families, and create the semblance of a civilized society. "How many families, and precisely those which you most want to establish society, are never brought to California, just because there is no fit means of education here; and how many return after a short time, for the same reason, carrying back with them the fortunes they have made . . . impoverishing the country." How many California families, he wondered, would need to send their offspring to the East Coast for a college education, lost perhaps forever to the affluence of more established states. "And what is worse," he concluded, "every such case of sending away for education is a confession that California is only an outpost of the nation, where some of the principal endowments of enlightened society have not yet arrived. This reflects more and more depressingly, the longer it is continued, on the public respect and confidence."[39]

In part at the urging of Marvin, in 1852 state senator Frank Soule, a representative from San Francisco elected on the Whig ticket, sponsored successful legislation allowing for state and local taxation for the financing of common schools. The law also created a State Board of Education and authorized the sale of federal land at $2 per acre for the benefit of the common schools. All profits would be placed in state bonds, creating a "permanent fund" that would yield interest of about 7 percent for teachers' salaries. Yet the school fund envisioned by the convention delegates never materialized. The new state tax of five cents on each $100 of assessed property value was revoked in 1853, although local taxation was retained. Thereafter, state funding for schools was limited to interest from the sale of federal lands and a new state poll tax. Purchases of the federal land scrip were disappointingly slow. In California, no free schools existed, only "rate bill" schools that charged a fee for enrollment.[40]

Management of the state's federal land grant for higher education also yielded a paltry sum. In 1853, over 46,000 acres were granted to California for a "seminary of learning" under the provisions of the Northwest Ordinance. In Michigan and several other states, similar grants had been sufficient to start their state universities. At first, lawmakers were optimistic that in California the land could be sold for $15 per acre. This would have yielded a total of $691,200 for higher education alone, which was possibly enough, according to Governor Bigler, for two institutions, one north and the other south of San Francisco. However, the granted land was not placed on the market until 1858 and then at the low price of $1.25 per acre, which was charged for other lands in the public domain. Land speculators bought up the entire grant, generating only $57,000 for the university fund.[41]

Failure to create an adequate fund for common schools caused Paul K. Hubbs, the state's second superintendent of public instruction, to complain in 1855 that "the effect of the legislative sleep of the past session will be evident soon in the immoral tendencies of trained ignorance in our land." Three-fourths of California's school-age population, he noted, were "growing up devoid of learning to read or write." To those who objected to public financing of the common school, Hubbs argued: "[I]t is purely ridiculous and mean in the individual to say 'I will not pay for the education of the children of others.' You pay for roads over which you never travel, and you pay for prisons which you never inhabit."[42] At the time, California state government was in fact spending twice as much on prisons as schools. Despite Hubbs' plea, not much had changed by the end of the decade.

A shift in political priorities occurred by the early 1860s. Clarence King, a Yale-educated geologist who was part of the first geological survey team of the Sierra Nevada, likened California's social and cultural changes to the region's geological history. Like the cataclysm of the glaciers overrunning the Sierras, the violence, lawlessness, and squalor of the gold rush era, he surmised, would give way to a "new, nobler" California. "By 1860," he later wrote, "California had made the vast inspiring stride from barbarism to regularity. . . . [S]omething like social equilibrium had asserted itself."[43]

Leland Stanford's election as governor in 1862 influenced King's opinion. Stanford's victory marked the beginning of Whig-Republican power in California and the emergence of a business class that would come to dominate the politics and economy of the state. This contingent proved much more interested in education as a state policy issue than the Democratic administrations, largely because of substantial differences in their view of the role of government in American society.

The Republicans advocated government activism in both the social and economic development of the state. In strong contrast to the Democrats, the

Whig sensibilities of Republicans viewed the rise of centralized power, whether corporate or government, as an opportunity to foster economic growth and to create an ordered and prosperous society. It was no coincidence that these California Republicans were often from northeastern states, the stronghold of Whig thought. Nationally, a new class of capitalists dominated the Republican Party, quickly building their fortunes and looking to state and federal governments to serve their economic interests. Leland Stanford was of this ilk. The son of an innkeeper from rural New York, he studied law while working in Albany. He then ventured west to Wisconsin to practice law before moving to Sacramento in 1851 to join a partnership with his brothers in an extremely successful grocery and dry goods business. After failing in his bids for state treasurer in 1857 and for governor in 1859, he finally became governor in 1862.

In the midst of Stanford's first year in office, he and his partners in the newly formed Central Pacific Railroad were soliciting the federal government for funds and land to build the proposed transcontinental railroad. Stanford was also the first governor to advocate the establishment of a state university, but the California Legislature rebuffed him. As with earlier proposals for such an institution, a select committee of the assembly stated that adequate funds for such an enterprise had not yet accrued from the sale of land scrip. The exigencies of the Civil War also preoccupied state lawmakers: Stanford's plea for a public university seemed to be a distraction during wartime.[44]

It was not the rise of Whig-Republican power in California, however, that finally compelled state legislators to establish a public university. Rather, the impetus came from their counterparts in the federal government. Beginning in 1857, Congressman Justin S. Morrill of Massachusetts offered a series of bills to encourage states to create colleges that would train young men for the farm, factories, and professions. As with the Northwest Ordinance and other federal efforts to encourage the development of education, Morrill proposed that federal lands be granted to the states to create educational institutions focused on agricultural and mechanical arts and to promote applied research. His legislation also required the inclusion of military science as part of any land grant institution, and he specifically stated that other science and classical studies need not be excluded. The federal government could promote all of this with the one resource it had plenty of: land, largely in the West.

But steadfast opposition, primarily from Southern Democrats, blocked Congressman Morrill's efforts. One congressman complained that Morrill's proposal, with its applied orientation and interventionist intent, was one of "the most monstrous, iniquitous and dangerous measures which had ever been submitted to Congress." The election of Lincoln, the onset of the Civil War, and the subsequent control of Congress by the Republicans rooted out Morrill's opponents. Radical Republican rule of Washington during the war finally resulted in passage of the Agricultural College Land Act. Lincoln signed what is more commonly known as the Morrill Act into law in July 1862. Within a year, nine states had established land grant institutions.[45]

California was not so quick to take advantage of the federal land grants. The Morrill Act, however, eventually forced California government to create a public state university. As a condition for accepting federal scrip, by 1866 each state would need to charter either existing or new institutions to fulfill the purpose of the act: namely, to provide agricultural, mining, and mechanical education in support of the state's economy. The total federal allocation was based on a grant of 30,000 acres for each member of Congress in a particular state. Under this rubric, California stood to gain 150,000 acres of land.[46] In 1864, the California Legislature passed a bill accepting the federal land grant. California government was now dominated by Republicans who were anxious to expand public education. John Swett, the new superintendent of public instruction, exclaimed that the new legislature was a marked departure from the past, "devoted to patriotism, marked ability, and abiding faith in public schools."[47]

However, while the California Legislature accepted the federal scrip, there remained the more difficult task of creating a charter for a new state university in time to meet the 1866 deadline set by Congress. The intent was to compel state governments to quickly establish institutions and programs that Morrill felt met a national need. What immediately emerged in California were competing visions regarding the primary purpose of a new state university.

A University or a Polytechnic?

The same year that California accepted the federal land grant, the state legislature appointed a special commission composed of Superintendent Swett, State Geologist Josiah Dwight Whitney, and Surveyor General J. F. Houghton to recommend how the new university might be organized. Though endowment funds could be used to create applied programs in areas such as engineering and agriculture in existing institutions or to create several new colleges or universities, California lawmakers assumed that it would go toward creating a single institution as outlined in the 1849 California Constitution.

The commission returned to the legislature with the recommendation to create a polytechnic college in San Francisco with professional programs in the sciences and agriculture. They also suggested that the new state university complement and not compete directly with the handful of existing private and traditional colleges in and around the Bay Area. These small and financially struggling institutions included the College of California in Oakland, established, as noted previously, in 1853. Most provided a classical curriculum intended for the sons of California's emerging elite class. In form and emphasis, they were essentially college preparatory schools. California's new land grant institution, argued Swett, Whitney, and Houghton, should teach "some other portion of the great field of Science and Art not yet cultivated here, rather than trespass on regions already occupied," essentially offering the next logical tier of educational training. "The Colleges would be feeders to the State University," they explained, "and thus one institution would aid in developing the other."[48] Perhaps more importantly, although not openly stated, they advocated that all land grant funds be funneled to publicly controlled institutions and not to the existing private colleges.

The proposal reflected the prior thinking of both Swett and Whitney. With his election to state office in 1862, Swett had embarked on an ambitious campaign to build a system of public education, one that would in the most idealistic sense afford all classes and races an opportunity for training entirely at public expense. While the vast majority of California's common schools still charged tuition to help subsidize operational costs, Swett was determined to enact legislation that would create a statewide tax on property that would make all common schools free. Swett argued: "If one state in the Union needs a system of free schools, that state is California. . . . The next generation will be a composite one, made up of the heterogeneous atoms of all nationalities." Viewing California's demographic mix of Irish, Italian, Chinese, Mexican, and numerous others, he reiterated the mantra of the common school, advocating that nothing could "Americanize these chaotic elements and breathe into them the spirit of our institutions but the Public Schools."[49] Swett's Yankee and abolitionist background also caused him to insist that if all classes paid taxes, there was no reason why "the children of all classes, whether white, black, tawny, or copper-colored, should not be educated." It was a matter of "common humanity," he insisted.[50] In Swett's view and those of the other commission members, the establishment of a state university should not distract the state from building these schools or from Swett's personal campaign to develop a state-chartered school for training teachers.

A native of New Hampshire, Swett arrived in California in 1853 after a 135-day trip from Boston Harbor to San Francisco on the schooner *Revere*. He intended to try his hand at mining, but he soon turned to his previous profession of teaching and became the principal of one of the state's first public schools in San Francisco. The serious lack of teachers in 1857 San Francisco caused Swett to help establish a city-operated normal school, Minns' Evening Normal School, and to eventually call for a state-supported institution to train teachers. In 1861, State Superintendent of Public Instruction Andrew J. Moulder, on the advice of Swett, appointed a committee to propose just such an institution.[51] Swett became the state superintendent a year later and proceeded to draft a bill to transform the local school into the California State Normal School. Governor Stanford signed it in early 1862, along with a bill establishing a board of trustees.[52]

In pushing the development of a new polytechnic with federal land grant funds rather than a university, Swett thought it simply a matter of priorities. The idea of the American university was in its infancy, without the formal commitment to research and public service that would soon emerge. For Swett, a call for a university conjured images of the classical college found in New England, strongly class-oriented and largely devoid of the practical and applied curriculum that he thought vital to California. "The higher good for the greatest number is the foundation principle of our educational system as well as our government," he told legislators. "When the State has provided for every child the means of a common education, then let the high schools and state universities be established, and until then let private institutions and colleges already established furnish the means of a higher education." Swett also suggested dividing the Morrill funds between the proposed polytechnic and the new state normal school, "which in the next fifty years may grow into a solid institution of learning."[53]

Any new state university, the 1864 commission agreed, should initially be limited in scope, providing primarily applied instruction to meet the urgent needs of the state for training in mining, agriculture, manufacturing, and other professions. Reflecting Whitney's strong opinions, another major purpose of the proposed "California Polytechnic School" was to create a state library and museum that would house the California Geological Survey—which Whitney directed.[54] Many California legislators were interested in developing a public institution in the mold of an emerging group of private technical schools, which included the Sheffield Scientific School at Yale, Rensselaer Polytechnic in New York, and the Chandler School of Science at Dartmouth.[55]

While legislators did not formally adopt the detailed approach of the commission, they did agree to the general idea of a polytechnic, but not at the exclusion of liberal arts instruction. Lawmakers finally passed a statute known as the Organic Act of 1866 only two months before the federal deadline—sixteen years after the California Constitution called for the creation of a state university. "To carry out in good faith the provisions of an Act of Congress . . . for maintaining an Agricultural and Mechanical Arts College," stated California's legislation, instruction would "embrace the English language and literature, mathematics, civil, military, and mining engineering, agricultural chemistry, mineralogy, metallurgy, animal and vegetable anatomy and physiology, the veterinary art, etymology, geology, technology, political, rural and household economy, horticulture, moral and natural philosophy, history, bookkeeping, and especially the application of science and mechanical arts to practical agriculture in the field and mining."[56]

In passing the 1866 Organic Act, California sanctioned the formation of a single and secular new institution. At the urging of Swett, Whitney, and Houghton, the Organic Act stated that the university should "not be united to or connected with any other institution of learning in this State."[57] California, however, appeared to be one of only a handful of states that decided not to allocate land grant proceeds among existing institutions. Connecticut, Massachusetts, Michigan, New Hampshire, New Jersey, New York, Rhode Island, Vermont, and Wisconsin had already taken action to secure agricultural land grants and divided the proceeds among existing colleges. In New Hampshire, Dartmouth College divided the money among existing departments and established a college of agriculture and mechanical arts. Rhode Island funneled the funds to Brown University. Massachusetts divided its grant between the Boston School of Technology (what would become MIT) and the agricultural college in Amherst. In Connecticut, Yale University received funding for its scientific school. In 1866, New York appropriated the funds to Cornell University, which had been established a year earlier. Rutgers University created Rutgers Scientific School in New Jersey. Michigan, Pennsylvania, and Wisconsin allocated funds to their existing state universities.

By 1866, only Iowa and Minnesota had used the funds to create new institutions, and several states, including Indiana, had not yet acted. In subsequent years, particularly in the South and West, many of the relatively new states with sparsely settled populations sought ways to establish several institutions.[58]

In California, the provision in the 1866 Organic Act to not share the federal land grant funds with existing institutions proved a great source of frustration to the small number of private academies and colleges. All were struggling to survive financially. "Mind before mines," protested H. W. Bellows in an attempt to gain public support for the College of California in Oakland. Bellows and the college's president, Reverend Henry Durant, attempted for nearly ten years to put the College of California on a solid financial basis. Durant, a major figure in California history, was a Congregationalist clergyman, a former Yale faculty member, and a professor of philosophy. Originally from Massachusetts, he had made the arduous trek to California in 1853, the same year as Swett's journey. Unlike most of those who traveled the long route to the Pacific Coast by sail or by wagon, Durant was not a young man when he came West. He made the trip at the age of fifty-one, obsessed with the idea of providing education to a rapidly developing society and prompted by the death of his only daughter, an event that caused him to find solace in starting life anew.

The promise and spectacle of California, a seeming anomaly on the western frontier with its great wealth, growing population, and rapid urbanization, was well known within the halls of Yale University. Durant was one of many individuals from this prestigious eastern institution who would come to California with a missionary-like zeal to build a new society and to instill the Republican and Yankee values they so admired. The very year of his arrival in San Francisco, Durant established the Contra Costa Academy. In 1855, the academy became the College of California, chartered by the state and operated by a nondenominational board of trustees that included leading citizens of the state. "I came here with college on the brain," reflected Durant, "and opened a college school the next month."[59] Reverend Horace Bushnell and Sherman Day, the president of the San Francisco Board of Education and the son of Jeremiah Day, president of Yale, joined Durant in this venture, attempting to serve a rapidly growing Bay Area population by offering preparatory and college-level courses. In the absence of a state university, it was a void that others also attempted to fill, notably in the ambitiously named University of the Pacific chartered in 1852 in San Jose, later moving to Stockton, and the Catholic College of Santa Clara established in 1853. Yet none of these fledgling institutions had a leader as politically adept as Durant.

Though nondenominational in orientation, the College of California was designed to "furnish the means of a thorough and comprehensive education under the pervading spirit and influence of the Christian religion."[60] The mission of the school was to unite and find support among all Californians in "the common interest in securing the highest educational privileges for youth, the common sympathy of educated and scientific men, and a common interest in the promotion of the highest welfare of the State, as fostered and secured by the diffusion of sound and liberal learning."[61] Reverend Andrew L. Stone, the pastor of the First Congregational Church of San Francisco, stated that the new college would be an integral component in the future glory of San Francisco, a city, he confidently announced, that would soon rival any on the American continent. The college would serve the city and the entire state, Stone continued, by teaching the "security and honor of republican principles," and by "correcting the materialism against which all new communities contend."[62]

Durant and his colleagues were ambitious. They quickly made plans for their college to eventually become a university modeled after Yale, melding a classical curriculum with advanced, professional training. Durant led a crusade to gain the political and financial support of the Bay Area's rising class of capitalists, lawyers, and politicians to support the venture, knocking on the doors of all who would hear his plea.

By 1858, Durant secured sufficient funds to purchase land in the area of Strawberry Creek, some four miles north of Oakland, as the future site of his imagined university. An editorial in the newspaper *The Pacific* claimed that there was not a better site in all of America, indeed in the world, for an institution of higher learning. Overlooking the bay, and with a view of the Golden Gate and Pacific, the prospect of a university in the hills of what would become Berkeley appeared a preordained symbol of California's promise. The editorial continued: "Many nations a few years hence, as their fleets with the wealth of commerce seek those golden shores, will see the University before they see the metropolis, and their first thought of our greatness and strength will be impressed upon them."[63]

On the occasion of the College of California's graduating ceremonies in 1864, state senator and future governor Newton Booth, ignoring California's failure to create a state university, praised the good work of Reverend Durant and the new college:

> Let the day be marked with white in our intellectual calends. All honor to the College of California! How many thousands of encorporation's have

> been formed here [in California] to develop the material resources of our coast, to enrich the fortunes of their stocks. How they have strewn the shores of our history with wrecked hopes and expectations! But, [the college has been] formed to develop the immaterial, the imperishable wealth of the soul, keeping her eye fixed upon her star, her course true to her mission, her garments free of taint. Today she sends into the world her first disciples, duly accredited and bearing her commission, to take their places in the warfare of life. Advance-guard of the California division of learning, pioneer corps of the battalions of her scholars that shall follow them from these gates, may they fight a good fight, loyal to country, to freedom, to truth![64]

In spite of such enthusiasm for the College of California, Durant found his dream of gaining private sector financial support and of making the transition from college to university elusive. In 1866, eight years after purchasing the land in and around Strawberry Creek, money remained a problem. The college was steeped in debt and dogged by bill collectors.[65] Durant's only encouragement was the passage of the Morrill Act and a hope that the California Legislature might entertain the idea of absorbing the College of California in the proposed state university. The language of the state's 1866 Organic Act appeared to preclude gaining proceeds from the federal land grant. Yet there still existed no well-defined plan for how California might locate and organize its new College of Agricultural, Mining and Mechanical Arts and how this institution would embody the idea of a state university that had been first articulated in the 1849 California Constitution. The legislature had created a Board of Directors to accomplish this task and appointed Governor Frederick Low, a former congressmen and friend of Durant, to be its chair. Meeting for the first time in June 1866, the board solicited offers for the sale or donation of a potential site. Seven proposals were received, including one from Henry Durant.

The College of California and the Second Organic Act

It was not long before Governor Low realized that the original recommendation to form a new secular state university posed financial and political difficulties. It appeared that monies derived from the sale of land grant properties alone would not be sufficient to purchase land in the San Francisco area, to build facilities, and to fund the operation of the university. Moreover, Durant and other representatives of California's private colleges continued to voice their opposition to the 1866 Organic Act. The presence of a new, government-subsidized competitor for students, they argued, could result in unhealthy competition for both students and faculty.

Durant presented an alternative plan to Governor Low and his Democratic successor, Yale graduate and lawyer Henry H. Haight.[66] He called for the merger of the College of California with the land grant college to create a new, secular University of California. Durant argued that forming a technical school as outlined in the 1866 act would not fulfill California's need for a center of general education and a symbol of its cultural development. The advantages were twofold. First, the new state university would gain the college's faculty and the ability to instantly provide instruction in liberal arts fields—areas that would need to be offered as part of a general education program. Second, the new state university could occupy the college's building in Oakland and then move to the Strawberry Canyon property.

To help persuade Low, Haight, and the legislature, Durant drew on his Yale heritage. In the midst of his campaign, he invited Dr. Benjamin Silliman Jr. to speak at the College of California's 1867 commencement ceremony. A noted chemistry professor at Yale, Silliman was the first of a new breed of academic scientists concerned with soil chemistry, crops, and scientific agriculture. He gained fame for his role in establishing Yale's Sheffield Scientific School in 1861 and for his financial exploits in mining and oil exploration on both the East and West Coasts. Silliman represented a growing contingent of academic leaders who advocated a mix of traditional and practical curricula. Yale had become the center of innovation in higher education, embracing not only new professional and scientific programs but also the German university model of research. The same year that Silliman helped to create the Sheffield School, Yale awarded the first Ph.D. in the United States. Silliman believed strongly that the role of America's emerging universities was to create new leaders and to place the nation at the forefront of the scientific revolution.[67]

Durant was not loath to exploit his ties to Yale, asking Silliman to lobby state lawmakers for the creation of a "complete university." Silliman obliged, explaining to Low and others that the California Legislature's 1866 charter "is far too special and restricted." Reiterating the sentiments of Durant, Silliman noted that the act appeared to be "drawn up somewhat hastily . . . called forth specially to meet the exigency of securing to the State the benefits arising from the appropriations of [federal] public lands." A comprehensive curriculum was needed, he concluded, with the institution organized in a manner that would avoid "the fluctuation of party politics. . . . No merely polytechnic or trade school—no simply professional school—is a University."[68]

Durant's efforts proved fruitful. With the support of Low and the concurrence of Governor Haight, in 1868 Assemblyman John Dwinelle of Alameda County carried a new university bill, co-written by Durant, which would supersede the 1866 legislation. Another forty-niner with Yankee roots, Dwinelle was a New Yorker who had graduated from Hamilton College with a law degree and had been an editor of the *New York Daily Gazette* in the 1830s before becoming the city attorney in Rochester. Shortly after his arrival in California, Dwinelle started a law practice in San Francisco. Several years later, he moved across the bay and was elected mayor of Oakland. The ever-astute Durant urged Dwinelle to run for the assembly for the specific purpose of sponsoring his proposal to merge the College of California with the new state university.[69]

Dwinelle's bill passed in the assembly on March 5, 1868, and was signed by Governor Haight seventeen days later.[70] The only alternative bill had come from state senator Charles Maclay of Santa Clara County, who wanted half the land grant proceeds to go to a new School of Science and the rest to existing private institutions, including the University of the Pacific in his district. The 1868 Organic Act called for the creation of a state university to be governed by a twenty-two-member Board of Regents. Six regents would be ex officio members: the governor, the presidents of the State Agriculture Society and the Mechanics' Institute, the lieutenant governor, the speaker of the assembly, and the superintendent of public instruction. Another eight members would be appointed by the governor and the remaining eight by joint approval of the entire board. While the University of California would have a president, he was to serve at the discretion of the board, and, for all practical purposes in this early period, the board was involved in virtually all matters of university management, with one exception. Following the recruitment of a core faculty group, responsibility for the teaching and administration of the university and for faculty professional advancement was vested in an Academic Senate, composed entirely of faculty and including the university president.[71]

In autumn of 1869, the new University of California began operation in Oakland. Eleven students were inherited from the College of California. Another twenty-nine entered the freshman class.[72] Under the direction of Acting President John LeConte, four colleges were formed under the rubric of the Colleges of Arts: a college of agriculture, mechanical arts, mines, and civil engineering. A fifth College of Letters adopted the curriculum of the College of California and proceeded to serve the great majority of the students in these early years. In total, the university consisted of ten faculty members.

When the regents met for the first time in early 1869, it was apparent that California's new state university was not going to be free of partisan politics. The sixteen appointed members of the board, including former governor Low and former assemblyman Dwinelle, were equally divided between Republicans and Democrats. However, four of the six ex officio positions were held by Democrats. After reviewing a number of potential candidates for president, several regents demanded the recruitment of Democrat and Civil War General George B. McClellan. The general had been fired as the head of the Union Army by Lincoln, then in 1864 he ran an unsuccessful presidential campaign, advocating capitulation to Confederate demands on slavery.

McClellan's candidacy was strongly opposed by Regents Low and Dwinelle and shocked many of the state's most ardent university supporters.[73] A San Francisco newspaper protested: "[T]he university cannot afford to encounter political prejudice at the threshold of its career. . . . If the university is to be made a political machine or that in any respect it is to be partisan in its character, only a short time will elapse before its support will come only from those who are of the same party."[74] The Democratic majority among the regents, however, demanded and got a formal offer of the position to McClellan. To the relief of many, the general turned it down.

The regents then offered the presidency to Daniel Coit Gilman, head of the Sheffield Scientific School at Yale. Gilman was a rising star, who, along with Silliman, had formed a faction attempting to push Yale toward the forefront of university reform. But Gilman also declined the position. He was preoccupied with the prospect of becoming the president of Yale and with the difficulties of raising two daughters, following the death of his wife. The attempt to draw a figure of national prominence to California gave way to the more practical need for an immediate leader for the university. The regents returned to Henry Durant, at that time in his late sixties, who accepted the position. Only two years later, upon Durant's retirement, Gilman was again offered the position. This time he accepted, confident that the University of California would one day emerge as a vibrant rival to Yale.

With the benefit of a prominent president, an established group of faculty, and a secure source of funding, the new university appeared to have a bright future. The regents and lawmakers believed that the university was now in good financial shape for future expansion. It was assumed—falsely, as it turned out—that the management and proceeds from the federal land grants could create a large enough endowment to fund the vast majority of the university's operational costs for decades. Exuberance over the prospective federal windfall and the ideal of democratic access led lawmakers to proclaim the new state university as tuition-free. The 1868 Organic Act required that "admission and tuition shall be free to all residents of the State" and that economic class should not be a basis for enrollment. This egalitarian spirit also led lawmakers, after substantial debate, to ensure the right of women to enroll in the university; it was one of the first institutions of higher education in the nation to have such a policy. The right of women to enroll was reinforced by a resolution of the regents stating "that young ladies be admitted into the university on equal terms with young men."[75] In the university's second academic year 1870–71, forty men and eight women were enrolled. Some thirty years later, women represented 46 percent of the university's total enrollment, in an era when most co-ed colleges and universities had quotas and separate classes.[76]

The Reverend Horatio Stebbins, an early supporter of the College of California, proclaimed the new state university as pivotal to "free Republican government." "[T]he state is bound to furnish the citizens the means to discharging the duties imposed on him. If the state imposes duties that require intelligence, it is the office of the state to furnish the means of intelligence. . . . [I]t is for the dignity of the commonwealth." The Morrill Act, he concluded, would enable California to create a "complete system" of public education. "The University, then, is the last term in the ascending series of public schools."[77]

The name chosen for the university's new site in Strawberry Canyon connoted a link with the other great experiments in American higher education and at the same time the colloquial sense that California's state university, like the state itself, marked the beginning of a new era. The new site of the university was named in honor of Bishop Berkeley, the eighteenth-century Irish philosopher and poet. Berkeley's verse, "Prospect of Planting Arts and Learning in America," had inspired the founders of Yale. His name was now used as a method to capture the spirit of university supporters and their hopes for California.

There shall be sung another golden age,
The rise of empire and of arts,
The good and great inspire epic rage,
The wisest heads and noblest hearts.

No such as Europe breeds in decay;
Such as she bred when fresh and young,
When heavenly flame did animate her clay,
By future poets shall be sung.

Westward the course of empire takes its way;
The four first Acts already past,
A fifth shall close the drama with the day;
Time's noblest offspring is the last.

In 1871, a year before the new university was to move to its two new buildings in Berkeley, Governor Henry H. Haight pronounced confidently that "with patient zeal [the University of California] will soon become a great light-house of education and learning on this Coast, and a pride and glory of California, long after those who assisted in its birth and watched over its infancy have passed away and been forgotten."[78] Reverend Stebbins proclaimed that the site of the new university was an awe-inspiring promise for the future. "This fair southern slope," he stated at the dedication of the Berkeley campus, "where a delicious climate broods with gentle heat like that which hatched the world; yonder young city, its limbs not yet matured to beauty and grace, but destined to be a disposing power on the earth where the lines of industry, commerce and art shall connect the electric brain; in front the gate of the sea, arched with golden splendor, whose portals open to the Orient of the ancient time, the Occident of the modern time; and behind, these hills that keep watch and ward at the morning and evening sun."[79] Haight and Stebbins did not anticipate the rancorous debate that would soon follow over the purpose and future of California's young university.

CHAPTER 2

A Fourth Branch of Government

However well we may build up the University of California, its foundations are unstable, because it is dependent on legislative control and popular clamor.

— DANIEL COIT GILMAN

The Morrill Act of 1862 launched a revolution in American higher education. The stimulus of federal land grants caused states to establish new colleges and shaped the activities of many existing private and public universities. More importantly, American higher education was given a major new incentive to meet the more applied and scientific needs of society. Historian Walter Metzger explained: "To serve the whole community in its vast variety of needs became a creditable aspiration, an important innovation for a system that had served mainly the limited needs of the learned professions." But every revolution is born in an old regime.[1]

While it promised to be part of this new order, the University of California was created on the foundations of a traditional college. The new state university simply absorbed the faculty and classical curriculum of the College of California. It also included the governance structure common to institutions of higher learning in America, consisting of a lay board with its legal and virtually exclusive power to make decisions, from the hiring and firing of faculty to establishing curriculum and degrees. One purpose of this board was to tie the local community, including benefactors, to the college.

Unlike the medieval seminaries at Oxford and Cambridge, which were built around a self-governing body of faculty, American higher education was created by the resolve of community leaders who shaped the organization of colleges in the mold of a corporate entity.

In its organization and governance, the new university in Berkeley appeared to be a vestige of the old regime to many Californians. This perception led to a battle over the purpose of the new university that would have a significant, if unintended, influence on the subsequent emergence of the state's entire higher education system.

The Price of Disillusionment

The establishment of the University of California in the Berkeley hills brought high hopes. Governor Haight stated that the institution announced the arrival of California as a enlightened and significant new member of the Union. The San Francisco *Evening Bulletin* proclaimed that the new state university had "not come a day too early. . . . It will be a good day for California when the University shall open its doors and freely invite the youth of the state to enter without price. What the Michigan University is now doing for the West we hope to see the University of California do for the Pacific Coast."[2] Another editorial mused that only twenty-three years had passed since "the Golden Gate was thronged with ships from all parts of the world, bringing thousands of gold-hunters who laid the foundations of the state. . . . Today the walls of the first free University in the world confront the Golden Gate from the opposite shore of the Bay, where soon will stand the perfect structure, a magazine of new thoughts and new motives, ready for the new and bright day of the future."[3] One proponent predicted that California's new university would quickly become "a mighty anchor in the stream of time," with the "present uncertainties and disorders hurrying by and leaving it unmoved."[4]

Yet in 1872, after only three years of full operation, the purpose and management of the university was already under attack. A growing class of farmers and laborers viewed the university and its Board of Regents as conspirators engaged in a plot to further a new and primarily urban caste of wealthy Californians. Gustavus Schulte, a prominent educator in California, noted the mixed feelings of many Californians when he both praised and chastised the new state university. "Of all the high institutions of learning, both in the new and old world," proclaimed Schulte, "the State University of

California is the only one which, responsive to the call of the people, through the liberality of its Board of Regents, has been created free—absolutely free."[5] Schulte viewed the university as perhaps the foremost agent to promote the culture and economy of a new state.[6] But this "august, crowning fabric [and] edifice of public education in California" was, according to Schulte, thus far a failure. He claimed that low enrollment and the seemingly elitist nature of the institution placed it in peril. How could California's venture into higher learning be so errant?

Schulte placed the blame on the composition of the regents: "The first and chief error, the error which originated minor errors, was the injudicious and defective organization of the Board of Directors, known and styled in the organic law of the university as the Regents." He claimed that all its members were "merchants, lawyers, physicians and devines [sic]," devoid of "one practical and experienced educator" or a representative from California's farming and working class. The regents also appeared highly partisan, a bastion of a new moneyed and privileged class in California. They seemed determined to establish a traditional seminary of learning that would fail to serve the "industrial classes" targeted by the Morrill Act of 1862. Schulte complained that this organization "has brought forth already bitter fruit," specifically the seeds of a conflict over the management, organization, and curriculum of a very young public institution.[7]

Schulte's comments reflected a general feeling among members of California's State Grange, a growing and significant political force in California's emerging economy. The Grangers charged that the regents and President Gilman had colluded to ignore the requirements of the university's land grant charge. The new state institution, stated the Grange, was manipulated and used by the same bankers, railroad owners, and other businessmen who restricted credit and victimized the yeoman farmer and the individual laborer.

The Grange Movement began in 1867 as a social and educational organization for farmers, and it quickly gave voice to their political interests in an age of increasing hardship. After the Panic of 1873 and during a national depression that lasted until 1877, several state Granges gained control of Midwestern legislatures. In California, discontented farmer's rose in anger not only against the owners of the state's banks and the railroads but also against the new university and its allegedly classical curriculum, one suited more for the training of gentlemen than for farmers.[8] Indeed, the required courses for all students at the university looked much like those at the great eastern citadels of knowledge. Federal land grant proceeds, contended the Grange, should be directed exclusively toward training students in agriculture and mechanical arts. The Morrill Land Grant Act stated that its "main objective" was "to teach such branches of learning as are related to agriculture and the mechanic arts, in such a manner as the Legislatures of the States may respectively prescribe, in order to promote the liberal and practical education in the industrial classes in their several pursuits."[9]

The Grange was soon joined by labor groups, and together they attacked the university. The state's 1868 Organic Act required "the development of a College of Agriculture, and that of a [college of] Mechanic Arts" before all other programs. Yet, a formal proclamation of the Grange stated: "[W]e find that of the monthly appropriations (six thousand dollars) for the regular expenses, only one twentieth is now devoted to the Agricultural Department, and that one Professor is discharging all the duties of instruction on the subjects specially related to it. No technical instruction in the mechanic arts has thus been given." Moreover, the regents, according to these detractors, were a bastion of "corruption and rascality," mismanaging California's federal land grants, possibly for their own gain. The leadership of the Grange asserted that land was being sold below market value to friends of the regents. It also charged that the management of all federal land grants in California, some 8 million acres with 6 million earmarked for education, was riddled with fraud.[10]

Fueling the protest, Henry George's *Daily Evening Post* publicized the protests of the Grange and the San Francisco–based Mechanics Deliberative Assembly. Distrust of the new institution by this politically powerful coalition, with the support of two of the university's fourteen faculty, created a furor.[11] William Swinton, professor of literature, and Ezra Carr, director of the university's College of Agriculture, joined the protests of the Grange, charging that Gilman's Yale heritage, autocratic approach toward the faculty, and lack of "knowledge, interest or sympathy for industrial education" were altering the true purpose of the institution. Perhaps in an effort to survive this mutiny, Swinton and Carr did not initially attack the regents. Their allegations were focused on Gilman, who, according to Swinton, influenced the board toward "a tacit attitude of antagonism to the wishes of the people of the State in regard to certain phases of practical education."[12]

Carr, in particular, thought that the university's curriculum and enrollment, as well as corresponding resources, should be dedicated primarily to agricultural and mechanical arts programs, perhaps in proportion to the total number of farmers within the state's population.[13] The lack of funds hindered the development of a university farm on the Berkeley site, Carr charged. In his opinion, the money was being siphoned off to build the more traditional elements of the new College of Letters and Sciences. Along with an intense personal animosity, Carr and Gilman differed pedagogically. Carr favored an agricultural curriculum, with hands-on experience to teach young farmers the technical and vocational aspects of operating a farm. Gilman advocated study within the classroom and laboratory, where students would be exposed to a liberal arts curriculum in the tradition of the great universities and participate in the process of research.

In a 1930 history of the University of California, William Ferrier called the university detractors a "contingent incited by journalistic exaggerations." His and other histories of the university dismiss the complaints of the Grange and the Mechanics Deliberative as misguided and reckless. Yet those protests and concerns were hardly frivolous; they related to the fundamental issues of the appropriate purpose, curriculum, and operation of California's land grant institution under the law. It was the height of hypocrisy that an institution funded and, in large part, brought into existence by the Agricultural College Act of 1862 should allocate the vast majority of its resources to a more classical than practical liberal arts program. Similar struggles over the role and purpose of land grant institutions raged in other states, attesting to the importance of this issue within the context of 1870s America and the opening period of the industrial age.

A 1874 joint resolution by the Grange and the Mechanics Deliberative stated: "[I]t is not our object to undervalue what has been well done in erection of buildings; . . . in opening the doors of the university to both sexes; in making its instruction in all departments free; . . . and in securing a Faculty of zealous and able men." However, "believing that the first and highest employment of men is to feed, shelter and clothe the world," the joint statement urged the hiring of teachers skilled in the practical fields, who might then introduce a curriculum in which "useless and impracticable theories may not be introduced."[14]

Bolstered by Carr's support and that of the Mechanics Deliberative Assembly, in early 1874 Grange members proposed a number of solutions for the legislature to consider. Most included reinforcing and enlarging the role of agriculture and mechanical arts programs, for example, by constructing new buildings and increasing funding. Another proposed solution was the reorganization of the university's governance system and, as a consequence, the reorganization of the governance of all other emerging public segments of education.[15]

To reorient the university toward its primary function as a college of agricultural and mechanical arts and to influence the general development of public education in line with their interests, the Grange proposed legislation that would abolish the Board of Regents. In its place would be a newly constituted State Board of Education with fifteen members and with authority over the university, the state normal school, public elementary schools, and a handful of new secondary schools. Six of the members would be the same ex officio representatives on the former Board of Regents: the governor, lieutenant governor, speaker of the assembly, superintendent of public instruction, and the presidents of the Mechanics Institute of San Francisco and the State Agricultural Society. Additionally, the board would include the head of the State Grange as an ex officio member and eight new members who would be elected to four-year terms from each of California's congressional districts.[16]

Gilman and a Legislative Investigation

The charges of mismanagement and corruption against the regents prompted a legislative investigation in 1874. Both Carr and Swinton stated their support for the Grange Bill before a legislative hearing. Carr moderated his charges, apparently concerned for his future at the university, but Swinton had resigned several days before and suggested, as a matter of economy, the "abolition of the office of President."[17] In later testimony, Swinton countered a statement by Gilman to legislators that independent agricultural and mechanical arts colleges were failures.

> Is it to be supposed that in the exploitation of the productive forces of nature there is no room for the practical applications of science, taught in schools in which theory is brought in contact with practice and experiment? If, between science and these divine creative functions of humanity [e.g., farming and industry], there is no connecting link, and lawyers, doctors, and priests alone are privileged to draw from the upper reservoirs, then, indeed, may thoughtful men well begin to inquire if science is out of joint. . . . The conviction had long prevailed that our higher institutions of learning not confer upon these pursuits equal advantages with the old "professions," and the idea of training young men in the direction of these pursuits, of putting brains into these industries, gained ground, and [was] embodied in the [federal] Act of 1862. And everybody, but President Gilman, believes that the experiment, wherever fairly and honestly tried, has been a most gratifying success.[18]

President Gilman was angered by Carr's apparent attempt to increase funding for university agricultural programs by exploiting the wrath of the Grange. He was also outraged by Carr's and Swinton's personal attacks and by the Grange's charges of mismanagement and inattentiveness to agricultural needs. He and members of the regents campaigned to thwart the Grange Bill.

At the 1874 hearing, President Gilman explained that agricultural programs were in place and were awaiting student demand. Gilman stated that the regents were adept managers of federal land grants, following the spirit of the Morrill Act. The 1862 federal grant was only one of six funding sources for the university. Others included previous federal grants and gifts from private donors. Gilman also presented a detailed listing of revenues and debts for the university. This data compared the management and sale of federal scrip in other states.

According to Gilman, the profits in California from the sale of regent-managed land were higher on a per-acre basis than in all but one other state. The University of California either used these proceeds for purchasing land and existing buildings from the College of California or invested them in the Bank of California. Interest from this account, the only income that could be used for operating costs under the Morrill Act, went primarily to the agricultural program, most of which paid Carr's salary. To demonstrate the good intentions of the university, Gilman presented plans to improve "practical training" in agriculture and to offer a series of lectures to the public on agricultural topics. Gilman also submitted a list of agricultural facilities needed by the university, which he hoped the legislature might fund. Reflecting the earlier sentiments of Benjamin Silliman Jr. and Governor Low regarding the university's founding principles, Gilman concluded that his trusteeship was for "a university, and not a high school, nor a college, nor an academy of sciences, nor an industrial school. . . . Some of these features may indeed be included in or developed with the university, but the university means more than any or all of them."[19]

An 1852 graduate of Yale, Gilman looked to his university experience in New Haven for ideas and inspiration. Gilman was devoted to a curriculum that balanced the arts and sciences, while providing studies in the emerging professions. Though Yale was helping to redefine the American university, in Gilman's eyes, it had not gone far enough: It still segregated and marginalized the sciences and saw limited value in purely practical training. California offered Gilman the chance to be more experimental. The irony was that his notion of how to build a young state university was not radical enough for a significant portion of farmer and labor interests.

Perhaps unaware of the brewing conflict between the university and the Grange and labor interests, Gilman delivered his inaugural address in 1872, only ten days after arriving in California, articulating the need for a balanced seminary of learning on the Pacific. He took it for granted "that in the State of California there is no occasion to make a plea for the study of modern sciences. . . . Science, though yet you have built no shrine for her worship, [is] the mother of California." He assumed that the new university might build on the experiments of Yale and MIT and be that shrine. "With all of this experience before us, intelligent men will be likely to admit that among the first wants of California are distinct, complete and well-organized schools of science and technology, such as your organic laws contemplate."[20] However, Gilman pleaded, California needed a university that would provide advanced training in history and the languages. Gilman knew that creating a public university that focused on both the sciences and humanities would take time, and he openly worried "whether the people of this coast are yet ready to pay for the luxury and the advantage of such [a] serviceable institution."[21]

Looking back on his fight with the Grange, in 1906 Gilman noted that California's university "was a state institution, benefited by the so-called agricultural grant, where it was necessary to emphasize the importance of the liberal arts, in a community where the practical arts were sure to take care of themselves."[22] Working with a sympathetic board of regents, Gilman sought to nurture the varied fields of a university, one that would look and operate much like the private institution he had left.

Although Gilman was among the first to articulate the concept of academic freedom and to define the role of the modern university, by 1874 he felt he was fighting for the life of his institution and specifically for the ability of its president and board to govern university affairs. Gilman's detailed defense of the university, combined with the radical nature of the Grange's "solution," resulted in a sound victory for Gilman in the legislature. The Joint Committee gave its "most hearty approval of the management of the land grant. The Regents, in our judgment, have made the most of it, and their administration of it has been about the best possible." Regarding both agricultural and mechanical arts programs, it appeared that progress was at hand. "The university is in its infancy. We cannot, therefore, reasonably expect, at this date, any great results. . . . The Regents and faculty have done well, considering their means and surroundings; . . . they deserve the sympathy and support of the people at large in the management of the university."[23]

John Dwinelle, author of the 1868 Organic Act, then secretly approached the chair of the Assembly Committee on Education, A. Higbie. Carr had become popular with farmers and labor interests in San Francisco. Dwinelle, now a regent, pledged that Carr would be retained in his faculty position if Higbie could manage to defeat the Grange Bill. The lobbying efforts of Gilman and the regents paid off. The Grange Bill was defeated in late 1874. Five months later, Carr was nonetheless dismissed by the regents.[24]

Gilman, however, saw his victory as temporal. Frustrated with the highly charged political environment that cast doubt on virtually every action by the university, Gilman left to become the founding president of Johns Hopkins University in 1875. In Baltimore and with the largess of benefactor and banker Hopkins, Gilman would successfully build his ideal university, devoted to research and graduate training under the German university model.

Gilman's departure was a statement of frustration, a blow to the university, and a warning to Californians. Gilman wrote in his letter of resignation: "[F]or university fighting I have no training; in university work I delight. I therefore beg of you to release me from the post I hold, at the earliest day you can consistently do so."[25] Gilman's resignation was also a victory of sorts for the Grange, but it was not enough to dispel the opinion of many farmers and urban social activists that the university remained an extension of a corrupt upper class of urbanites. Ezra Carr's dismissal from the university after the defeat of the Grange Bill angered farmers and labor and fueled the fire of capitalist conspiracy theories. Due to his popularity among farmers, Carr ironically proceeded to win the office of California's superintendent of public instruction. His election made him an ex officio regent, as stipulated by the 1868 Organic Act.

Carr's new position and the persistence of the Grange kept alive the political movement to reform the university. In 1876 and at the next legislative session following the defeat of the Grange Bill, legislation introduced by assembly speaker and ex officio regent Gideon J. Carpenter, and supported by Superintendent Carr, proposed to disband the regents and reform the institution's curriculum in the vein of a polytechnic. This time, the strategy of university reform proponents was legalistic. Carpenter claimed that the fifteen-year terms of the regents contradicted a provision of California's 1849 Constitution that stipulated four-year terms for all state officials. Under this rubric, Carpenter's bill would reconstitute the Board of Regents as an elected body with purview over all public education. In addition, land grant proceeds would be reserved for "practical instruction," and the superintendent of public instruction, who at the time just happened to be Carr, would become the chair of the board.[26]

The regents issued a statement warning of the "disastrous effects" if the Carpenter Bill was passed. John LeConte, returning to the post of president following Gilman's departure, claimed that the bill was unconstitutional. First, the four-year term limit was for elected officials, and second, the constitution intended the state university "to be an independent institution, having a complete unity in itself, and distinct from the general system of common schools."[27] The assembly passed the bill, but the state senate postponed consideration. A subsequent report of a senate subcommittee did not necessarily concur with the university's contention that the bill was unconstitutional, but it did disclaim Carpenter's insistence that term limits applied to the regents. Interpretation of Article XI "is not free from difficulty," explained the subcommittee, "but from the examination we have been able to make, and the light before us, we believe it does not" apply to the regents.[28]

The Carpenter Bill was defeated. Two years later, at the next session of the legislature, Senator N. Greene Curtis revived it, offering a bill that also advocated the establishment of regional institutions using land grant funds and, hence, establishing rivals to the Berkeley campus. The Curtis Bill, after additional university protests, was eventually withdrawn. The economic and political environment was changing. Like the rest of the nation, California had fallen into a deep economic depression. Bank failures, a severe drought that destroyed crops, and social unrest preoccupied lawmakers. The battle had been fought. At least for the time being, the effort to reorganize the university in the form of a polytechnic was over.[29]

The failed Grange, Carpenter, and Curtis bills, however, had another, if unintended, result. For the first time, Californians had discussed a method to coordinate and unify all public higher education under a single board. This would be an issue that would gain greater relevance in later decades as California's population grew and as the need for a comprehensive system of public education emerged as a political priority. Reflecting the disparate efforts to build a system of public education in California, and typical of similar efforts in other states, by 1878 there existed three entirely separate segments of public education in California. (See Figure 1.)

The first segment was California's public school system, funded with both local and state monies and managed by local boards that reported to the state superintendent of public instruction, a constitutionally elected officer. The

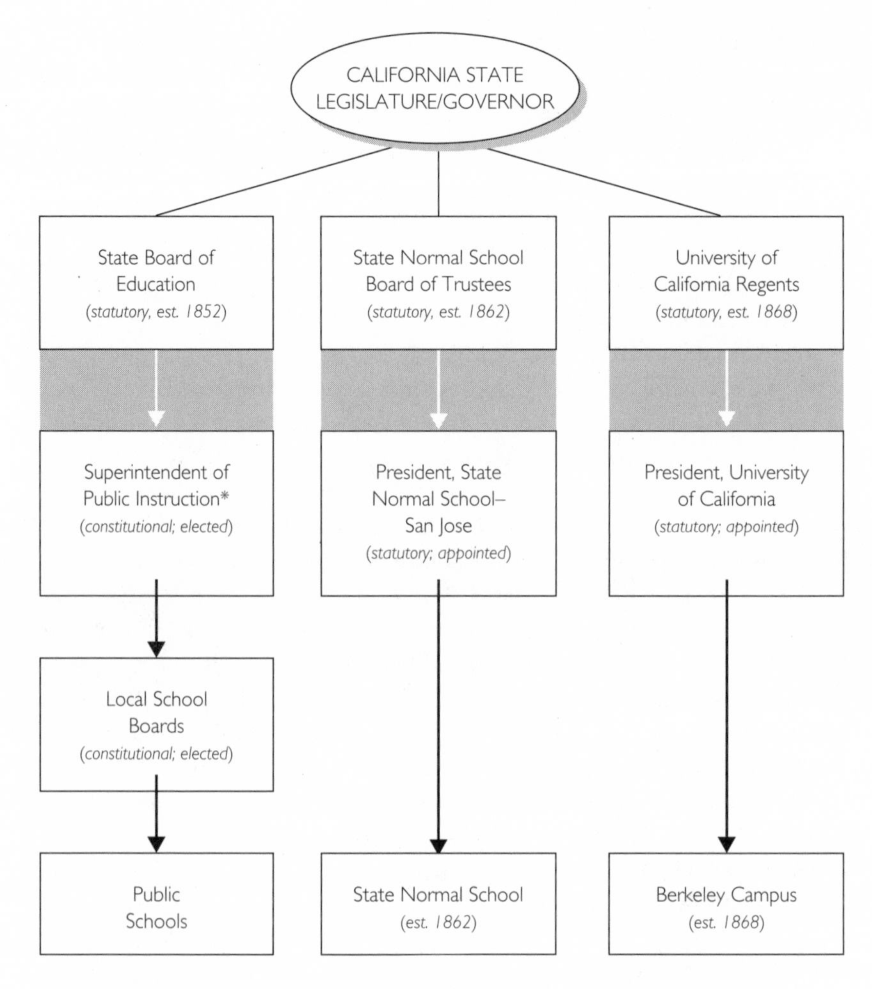

Figure 1. Governance of California's Public Education System, 1878

*The relationship of the constitutionally elected Superintendent and the State Board of Education (incorporated as a provision of the California State Constitution in 1884) has been the source of significant controversy over the past century.

SOURCE: California statutes

superintendent then reported to the State Board of Education, which had been established in 1852. The second segment of California's emerging system was the state normal school, which was established in 1862 in San Francisco and relocated to San Jose in 1871. This was the first of what would become a growing number of regional colleges by the early part of the 1900s. In the early 1860s, State Superintendent John Swett envisioned the maturation of California's public normal school into a land grant institution focusing beyond teacher training. However, the establishment of the University of California temporarily halted any further discussion of such a path.

In 1878, the State Normal School was a specialized institution with an enrollment of over 400 students—approximately the enrollment of the university. It received all its funding from state government. Charles H. Allen, the Normal School's fifth president, reported to the State Normal School Board of Trustees. While the trustees had members from the State Board of Education, in particular, the governor and the state superintendent, it was a separate governing board that also included professional educators: the superintendent of schools from San Francisco, the counties of Sacramento, Santa Clara, and San Joaquin, and two teachers.

The third segment of public education was the University of California in Berkeley, supported largely by income from regent-managed, federally granted lands. The university's Board of Regents managed the affairs of the university under the 1868 Organic Act.

This three-part governance structure would remain largely intact for another forty-five years. The major exception was a significant change in the status of the University of California.

The Call for a New Constitutional Convention

While university reform remained on the political agenda of the State Grange and other critics of the University of California, it was, as noted previously, a fading concern for most Californians. By the mid-1870s, political fervor focused on the regional effects of a severe drought, a nationwide economic depression, the proliferation of corporate corruption and swindles linked to the railroad industry, and racist anger over the increased use of Chinese labor. While financial institutions such as the Bank of California slipped into bankruptcy, the Central Pacific Railroad (what would become the Southern Pacific) increased its political and economic power. The railroad and its subsidiaries conspired to control government, increase land holdings, and expand their near monopoly of transportation. Federal land charters gave the Central Pacific 10 million acres of California land. This and subsequent grants made the company the largest landowner in both California and Nevada.[30]

High unemployment, depressed prices, and social upheaval in cities such as San Francisco caused many Californians to seek political solutions that would, it was hoped, cleanse the state of its multiple ills. In rural California, the State Grange increased its political strength, focusing its efforts on the water rights of farmers and unregulated railroad rates. In 1877, unemployed workers rioted in San Francisco. An angry crowd fought police, burned businesses, and murdered individuals in the local Chinese community. Only a massive military force, aided by local vigilantes, eventually brought order (a throwback to San Francisco twenty years earlier), inaugurating a period of restrictions on public gatherings and a semblance of martial law. A year later, California's Workingmen's Party was formed, headed by San Francisco laborite Dennis Kearney, a demagogue who talked of both class revolution and deporting the Chinese.

Henry George, a moderate member of the party, later reflected that Kearney was "the true spring and foundation of arbitrary power, the connection between Caesar and the proletariat" and that his followers were "men utterly ignorant and inexperienced."[31] Kearney alienated George and other possible rivals within the new party by his rhetoric of violence, including his call for "a little judicious hanging." With Kearney's base of power secured, the Workingmen's Party declared: "The rich have ruled us until they have ruined us. We will now take our affairs into our own hands. . . . We propose to destroy the great money power of the rich by a system of taxation that will make great wealth impossible in the future." If violence was necessary against either the Chinese "or those who employ [them] . . . let those who raise the storm by their selfishness suppress it themselves."[32] Feeding on economic instability, the Grange and "Kearneyism" formed an alliance on certain key issues, creating a potent political force.[33]

There was also widespread dissatisfaction with California's state constitution. The membership of the assembly was limited to forty representatives, irrespective of California's population. As a result, numerous farming counties had no representation.[34] California's population had expanded from an estimated 50,000 in 1850 to around 870,000 by 1870. By that time, the state economy was no longer dependent solely on the mining of precious metals. As the state's agricultural economy increased in size and importance, farmers demanded additional representation.[35]

The idea of drafting a second constitution presented an opportunity for reform-minded Californians to reorganize state government, restrict monopoly, and pull California out of its political and economic woes. The 1849 California Constitution, seeking flexibility and professing trust in the honesty and integrity of future officials, provided ample powers to the legislature to levy taxes, make appropriations, grant franchises, and allocate public land for economic development. Yet, according to the members of the Workingmen's Party and other reformers, it now provided a vehicle for plundering the state and serving the economic interests of the railroads. "The Workingmen, I may say the whole people," remarked William White, a future and influential representative of the party, "conscientiously believe that a majority of the members of (the) Legislature that has just adjourned, were bought and sold like things in the market by the powerful corporations and the thieving rings of the state."[36]

In the face of economic collapse and under pressure from urban and rural reform factions, there was growing support for a new constitutional convention. In 1876 and in the depths of California's economic depression, the California Legislature passed an act calling for, with the approval of the general electorate, a second constitutional convention to be held in Sacramento. This was, in fact, the fourth time voters were presented with such a proposal. Each proposal had been defeated, the first in 1859, the second and third in 1860 and 1873. This time, however, the voters approved a new convention, launching a fervent race to elect delegates.[37]

Democrats and Republicans had long been rivals with different visions of the role of government and the preferred dynamics of economic and political life. California Democrats advocated a limited role for state government, sought innovation from the yeoman farmer, and were wary of centralized power, corporate or public. California Republicans believed in entrepreneurial risk-taking and were convinced that an alliance of business and government was necessary to shape the national culture and economy. "[T]he Democrats saw a threatened as well as a real force for social exploitation in the rise of manufacturing, new technology, and an employing class," explained historian Robert Kelley in his review of California's political culture. The state's growing faction of "Whigs saw progress in all of this and applauded it."[38] The Republicans also formed the essential core of entrepreneurs and professionals, largely in San Francisco, that not only supported the development of the common schools, but also envisioned the university as a possible replication of the great eastern institutions of learning. Here was an influential contingent that served on the university's Board of Regents and provided political support for Gilman and his successors.

Fearing the radicalism and growing strength of the Workingmen's Party and its coalition with disenchanted farmers, however, Democrat and Republican Party leaders found their mutual differences less important. Economic hardships, racial fears, and outrage at corporate control over state government could allow radicals within the Grange and the Workingmen's Party to dominate the upcoming constitutional convention in Sacramento. To combat this possibility, Democrats and Republicans agreed to join forces to promote "nonpartisan" candidates in a vast majority of the district elections. This strategy was a significant step in limiting representation of the Workingmen's Party. It also marked the formation of an alliance of moderate factions that would determine the fate of the University of California during the convention.

Following elections, 152 delegates arrived in Sacramento in September 1878. The delegates included 51 Workingmen's Party members, 78 nonpartisans who were mostly farmers and lawyers, 11 Republicans, 10 Democrats, and 2 independents. Henry George explained: "The convention itself was vaguely divided into three groups: first, the lawyers, who largely represented corporate interests; second, the Grangers, who represented the ideas and prejudices of the farmers and the landholders; third, the Workingmen, bent on making capital for the new party, and desirous of doing something for the working classes, without the slightest idea of how to do it."[39] Most of the Workingmen's delegates represented moderate elements of the party. In part, this was due to a disproportionately low representation from the San Francisco area, where the more radical members of the party were based.

A Republican and vehemently anti–Workingmen's Party newspaper, the Sacramento *Record-Union*, assessed the strength of the different convention contingents, noting that the union of Republicans and Democrats as nonpartisans made the "the conservative wing . . . strong." Party distinctions "will be lost sight of when the real business of the convention begins." The real fight, explained the paper, would be between Socialists and Capitalists.[40]

Once in Sacramento, the delegates engaged in a struggle to control the organization of the convention. The first task was to select the convention's president and the membership of the various committees. While members of the Grange and Workingmen's Party met in a bid to control the convention, nonpartisans also formed caucuses for the same purpose.[41] After several internal splits, the nonpartisan caucus managed to elect their candidate, Joseph P. Hoge, as the convention president. It was a major victory for the more conservative elements of the convention. Hoge was a San Francisco corporate lawyer, chairman of the Democratic State Committee since 1868, and "noted for his legal ability, his vigor, and his profanity." Hoge proceeded to appoint nonpartisan representatives as the chairs for thirty-one special committees. Each committee was to focus on important policy area, including education.[42]

A Chance for University Reform

For six months, convention delegates engaged in debate over conflicting visions of California's future. Many of the delegates had come to Sacramento bent on expelling the Chinese, taxing the wealthy and regulating industry. The reform impulse also raised the question of the management and future role of the University of California.[43] Supporters of the university had approached the convention with apprehension, knowing that the university was still a target for reform among a large class of farmers and urban workers. The structure and control of the university were viewed as part of California's vast and complex problems. "Every settled institution, the university included, trembled with fear of menaced calamities," reflected William Carey Jones some years later.[44] Throughout the 1870s, the university had escaped the populist demands to convert the institution to a polytechnic and to wrest its management from the regents. The university was revisiting that crossroads, only this time the result would be conclusive.

In only the second week of the convention, with the committee structure just beginning to take form, William F. White, a Workingmen's delegate and farmer from Pajaro Valley, proposed strict language for consideration by all delegates. "The Legislature shall enact laws for the modification and management of the State university, so that hereafter all instruction shall be of a practical character, and confined to such teaching as shall properly belong to all mechanical arts and sciences, and to all sciences properly relating to agriculture, and no other."[45] Like the 1874 Grange Bill, White's resolution called for significant changes in the composition of the Board of Regents and also insisted that, until the University of California was reorganized to serve the desired purpose, no appropriations or proceeds from land grants should be used for the university's operation.

With the support of Grange and Workingmen's Party delegates, White even suggested that the constitution mandate that "every student shall spend at least two hours every day in manual labor, at some mechanical art or in cultivating the ground" to reinforce the apprenticeship system and draw students closer to the life of laborers and farmers.[46] This demand was, in fact, a reflection of a larger manual labor movement adopted by other innovative universities. At Rensselaer and Cornell, students were required to perform manual work to "provide illustration and verification of the principles learned in the classroom." Such requirements were, however, relatively minor components of a curricular reform movement centered around the elective system and practiced by only a handful of institutions.[47] White's demand for manual labor was, perhaps, more an indicator of his general frustration with what he viewed as the classical bent of the university's curriculum.

White's proposal instantly pitted the Grange members and Workingmen's Party delegates against supporters of the university.[48] Farmer Jonathan Webster from Alameda supported White's proposal to limit land grant resources to "practical purposes," but in his mind the proposal did not go far enough. Webster demanded that all regents be elected and their membership expanded. He proposed an amendment requiring the election of two regents from each congressional district.[49]

Though White's resolution and Webster's amendment were quickly embraced by most delegates, procedurally no action could be taken until the Committee on Education reported its recommendations. Here the university had substantial support for maintaining the existing board and increasing its autonomy. Joseph Winans, a nonpartisan lawyer from San Francisco, was appointed chair of the committee. Winans was a forty-niner who had graduated from Columbia and then practiced law for six years in New York before venturing West and establishing a firm in Sacramento. In 1852, he became the city attorney for Sacramento. Nine years later, he opened the extremely successful firm of Winans and Belknap in San Francisco. Shortly after, he was elected president of the San Francisco Board of Education and was appointed a regent of the University of California.[50]

Winans would become a ceaseless defender of the university at the convention, with the aid of a largely sympathetic committee. The committee included eight nonpartisan and five Workingmen delegates, including Jacob Freud, a recent graduate of Berkeley and the only university alumnus at the convention. The other twelve members included lawyers and farmers of largely moderate persuasion and another regent, J. West Martin, a banker from Alameda County and president of the Oakland Gaslight Company.

While Freud was a Workingmen's Party delegate, he was not a follower of Kearney or other radical members of the party. The young delegate sided with the committee majority in seeking to protect the existing university governance system. In lively debate on the convention floor, Freud gave a passionate speech for his alma mater. "I rise to speak in defense of the university. Objection has been raised to the appointment of a portion of the Board of Regents. It is urged that they be elected directly by the people. . . . But, sirs, experience has invariably shown that the election of Regents involves the destruction and ruin of the university." Freud protested that elections would allow political "prejudices [to] creep into the institution and poison its best blood, and vitiate its highest energies. It sets the university adrift upon the boisterous sea of politics, sure to wreck to pieces on the rocks of partisan life and party contention."[51]

Freud also combated the attacks of mismanagement, stating that "many rumors, nearly all utterly unfounded, prevail as regards to the agricultural department of the university." These included the charge that only one student was enrolled in the department, while there were actually "some twenty students." "To be sure, the students are not exercised in plowing, and hoeing, and reaping, and threshing, for these are mere mechanical operations of agriculture, and are best acquired on the farm at home," concluded Freud, "but they are taught why to plow, when to plow, and how deep."[52]

To clear the university from charges of mismanagement, Martin asked university president LeConte to submit a statement to the convention explaining the institution's finances and plans for its agricultural program. In similar detail to the report furnished by Gilman in 1874, LeConte provided cash receipts, disbursements, and investments between 1868 and 1878. Despite the contention of some, the president noted that the university was not operating with a deficit and had significant holdings in land and buildings. "What have the Regents of the university to show for their expenditure?" asked LeConte rhetorically, answering, the "establishment of a curriculum of studies which, for its range and variety, bears comparison to the oldest and best endowed institutions in the Eastern States . . . [and instruction] in all branches of culture and useful knowledge, free to all residents of California, both male and female." Such an investment, concluded the university president, had been wisely managed and would "bear its fruit in time, in the form of wise statesmen and legislators, accomplished scholars, original thinkers and investigators, able jurists, public benefactors, and virtuous citizens."[53]

Accompanying LeConte's statement was a report by Professor Eugene W. Hilgard, the director of agricultural programs at Berkeley since 1875 and Ezra Carr's successor. Trained in the geological and soil sciences at the University of Heidelberg, Hilgard held positions at the University of Mississippi and the University of Michigan in agriculture and agricultural chemistry before coming to California in 1874 at the age of forty-four. During his first year at Berkeley, Hilgard initiated the first exhaustive study of California soils—indeed, the most thorough analysis undertaken by any state—in which he investigated the relations between soils and vegetation. As later described by E. J. Wickson, a professor of horticulture at the university, Hilgard's pioneering work gained "world-wide significance." He studied "soils formed under humid and arid and semi-arid conditions and [demonstrated] the natural superiority of the latter" under a carefully regulated system of tillage and irrigation. His findings, along with those of other researchers such as Wickson, had tremendous implications for California's growing agricultural economy.[54]

In his statement to the convention delegates, Hilgard explained the need for university agricultural research to meet the needs of farmers, specifically to prevent cyclical crop failures. The role of the university, he insisted, was to aid farmers and further the science of agriculture, not to provide an apprenticeship system and trade school, as advocated by former director Ezra Carr and implied in delegate White's demand for forced student labor. Enrollment was growing, curriculum was more diversified, and "a garden of economic botany" was being laid out in Berkeley to conduct scientific experiments on key California crops. The university must provide a "professional education" to the sons of farmers, insisted Hilgard. "For mere drill in farm operations no sensible man will send his son to college, and business management of a farm will never be learned under the artificial conditions of a College farm. I am unable to see why, of all professional schools, the Agricultural College should be saddled with the task of converting young men to farming, by keeping them surrounded with what some are pleased to term an 'agricultural atmosphere.'"[55]

In his deliberations with the Education Committee, Chairman Winans conceded a need for the university to expand its service and training mission in agriculture and industry, but again he noted the complexity of that task and the need for patience. As Gilman argued in 1874, Winans noted that courses were in place, but students who were interested in farming and the like were slow in coming. Enthralled with Michigan's 1849 definition of its university as a "coordinate branch of state government" and seeking an end to the legislative forays of the Grange and other university critics, Winans advocated a similar level of autonomy for the University of California.

On January 21, 1879, some five months after the opening day of the convention, Winans presented the recommendations of the Education Committee. "The University of California shall constitute a public trust, and its organization and government shall be perpetually continued in their existing form and character, subject only to such legislative control as may be necessary to insure compliance with the terms of its endowments, and of the Legislature of this State, and of the Congress of the United States, donating lands and money for its support." Designation of the university as a public trust insured that future regents would avoid the electoral process. To further distance the university from the apparent evils of legislative politics, the Education Committee proposed that the university be "entirely independent from all political and or sectarian influences, and kept free therefrom in the appointment of its Regents, and in the administration of its affairs."[56]

In support of the elevation of the university to a public trust, Winans told the convention delegates that public education "constitutes the very cornerstone of republican institutions" and that "ignorance is the parent of vice, and vice soon hardens into crime."[57] Though the Education Committee was late in submitting its report, Winans urged the adoption of all nine sections of the proposed Article IX of the new constitution on education, which dealt with the university and all public education.

The proposal immediately spurred debate among convention delegates regarding the purpose of a public system of education and whether it should include high schools or a university. Summarizing the seemingly endless arguments and amendments, delegate C. W. Cross saw two sides. "The one says that no funds shall be taken from the public treasury to educate a boy or girl beyond the common English branches; the other says that it is better to educate beyond that limit."[58] It was as if the entire idea of publicly supported education was once again being debated, much to the frustration of Winans and other members of the Education Committee. Another delegate complained that the often-contradictory series of proposed amendments "shows that if the multiplication table was introduced here, there would be several amendments to it."[59]

Slowly the convention moved through the sections of the education committee's report, adopting most of its recommendations. However, the sentiment of the majority of delegates was decidedly against the university becoming a public trust. Jonathan Webster introduced a version of his earlier resolution, insisting that the university remain in the purview of lawmakers, that the regents be elected, and requiring that all funds generated by the Morrill Act be used exclusively for a new "College of Agriculture and Mechanical Arts."

As in 1874, Grange and sympathetic Workingmen's Party members believed that agriculture and mechanical arts programs remained "swallowed" within the university's College of Letters. How anyone could "claim that the best education for the lawyer is the best education for the future farmer," concluded one delegate, "is one of those dark and bloody mysteries which defy logic as well as common sense."[60] In support of Webster, delegate and Granger W. W. Moreland contended that land grant proceeds were being mixed with other university monies. Moreland and others worried that this might mean forfeiture of the federal grant and an obligation for the state to reimburse Washington. Despite this abuse of the Morrill Act, Moreland complained before the delegates, "we are not only asked to continue this institution in its present form, but in its present character" and with the status of a public trust that could not be revoked "no matter what naughty things it may do hereafter."[61]

On the floor of the convention, Moreland explained that news of the bold move by university supporters had reached even Kansas. He proceeded to read an article from a Kansan Grange newspaper, which protested that "the Congressional endowment for industrial education has been boldly and bodily gobbled up by the professional Universities in the several States; and, after consummating the fraud, the several Boards of Trustees of the Universities have patted themselves on the back for their arduous labor." There was no more "glaring" instance of this phenomenon than in California, noted the paper. The University of California "now seeks, by a clause in the new Constitution of that State, to forever secure to itself the million or more it gobbled several years since, despite the protest of farmers and mechanics."[62]

Thomas H. Laine, a nonpartisan delegate from Santa Clara, saw the need for the university to avoid the political pitfalls predicted by Winans, but he also wanted accountability. Thus he ventured a convoluted compromise. His amendment would make the university a public trust, but the composition and charge of the regents would remain under the control of state government. Gone was the insistence on the election of the Board of Regents, but also missing was the level of autonomy sought by Winans. The university, insisted Laine, "should be forever under the control of the State."[63] This position found great support among the majority of delegates. Despite the protests of the ever-vigilant Winans, Laine's resolution was adopted by the convention by a vote of 68 to 49.[64]

The Laine amendment was the official position of the delegates for over a month. As the convention came to a close, however, Winans managed to persuade Jonathan Webster of the error of his ways. Coming to the convention an ardent opponent of the regents, the Alameda farmer had since undergone a conversion and was now convinced by Winans of the merit of a university free from the political meddling of legislators. Webster now valued the idea of a highly autonomous university. He presented yet another amendment, drafted with the help of Winans, devoid of specific language requiring a direct link of land grant funds to a College of Agriculture and Mechanical Arts. Instead, Webster embraced the vague language of the Morrill Act, which essentially allowed states to use the land grant proceeds for a wide array of academic courses. The federal land grant, stated Webster's amendment, "shall be invested as provided by Congress; and the interest of said moneys shall be inviolably appropriated to the endowment, support, and maintenance of at least one college of agriculture, where the leading subjects shall be (without excluding other scientific and classical studies, and including military tactics) to teach such branches of learning as are related to scientific and practical agriculture and mechanical arts." Webster also added that any college moneys "diminished or lost" through "neglect, misappropriation, or any other contingency" would be replaced by the state.[65]

Most important, Webster's amendment stated that both the university and the regents should constitute a public trust. Laine angrily asked the convention delegates to reject the new amendment. "It is practically the same one that we disposed of after long debate. . . ."[66] The amendment was voted down by the delegates who were now rushing to bring the convention to a close.

Creating a Public Trust

There remained a final reading by the convention delegates of each section of the proposed constitution, including Article IX. Here was one last opportunity for university supporters to reverse the fortunes of the Berkeley campus. In late February, six days before the end of the convention, the delegates voted on Article IX. Delegate Laine was no longer in Sacramento, apparently making his way back to his ranch in Santa Clara. It was his assumption that the main constitutional issues were settled. The gathering in Sacramento had, in fact, exceeded its mandated 100 days, and many weary delegates, exhausted by the months of debate, were no longer receiving compensation for their efforts and were heading back to their long-neglected farms and businesses.

Perhaps encouraged by Laine's absence and at the urging of Winans, Webster once again offered his substitute for Section IX. "It is at the earnest request of the friends of the university that I offer it now," stated Webster to the some 130 delegates remaining in Sacramento. Winans protested that the existing language in Article IX would "not only throw the university into the hands of the Legislature, but make it the plaything of politics . . . as long as it is made subject to legislative caprice; so long as it can be made subject to the beck of politicians; so long as it can be made to subserve sectarian or political designs, it will never flourish." Winans went on to note the success of the university of Michigan under an autonomous board, which had resulted in "a magical effect," producing the "noblest college existing on the continent." For California's university to flourish, he insisted, it "must be beyond all power of assault and subversion." Winans urged adoption of the Webster amendment: "This amendment now pending meets the wishes of the Regents and of that class of agriculturists who take an interest in this institution."[67]

Joseph Brown, a farmer, noted his surprise that "this would come up again, after all that was said in opposition to it . . . we carefully avoided the words 'public trust.'" Yet, with the convention quickly coming to an end, discussion among the delegates remained limited. The Webster Amendment was brought to a vote, passing by a final tally of 70 to 59. Immediately after, the entire article on education was passed, sealing the autonomous position of the university.

Rather than significantly changing and restricting the governance of the university, the twisting events of the convention promised to transform the university into a unique entity of the state. The debate had lasted the length of the convention. The swift and calculating actions of the university's supporters, specifically Winans, helped to shift the sentiments of the convention.[68] The Webster amendment appeased agricultural interests by formally establishing the College of Agriculture and Mechanical Arts. The emergence of Professor Hilgard, Carr's replacement, also added to the farmers' faith in the university.[69] By the time of the convention, Hilgard had established clear goals and an experimental farm, which promised significant advances in agriculture, and won many converts among the more conservative and moderate Grange members.

However, the success of university supporters is perhaps best understood within the context of a deep distrust of the legislature. While delegates were divided on numerous issues pitting labor versus capital, including agricultural interests still angry over the university's administration, enough of the delegates were convinced of the need to protect the university from the seemingly inexhaustible corruption and politicking of lawmakers. Winans and Webster's amendment asked whether the regents or the legislature would provide the best management of the state university. In the end, the delegates to California's Second Constitutional Convention chose the regents.[70]

Among the majority of Californians who could vote, the new constitution was regarded as either too conservative or too radical. In San Francisco, the stronghold of the Kearnyites, the new constitution was rejected by 1,500 votes. Henry George, who at the time was engaged in writing *Progress and Poverty*, opposed the ratification largely because of its failure to incorporate his single tax concept on private land, which had been introduced in his 1871 pamphlet *Our Land and Land Policy*.[71] In the end, however, the agricultural districts with significant Grange representation provided the margin of victory for the new constitution. A verbose document reflecting the split among the delegates, the constitution passed in May 1879 with 53 percent of the popular vote.[72]

Besides making the university a public trust, the institution would now be "subject only to such legislative control as may be necessary to insure compliance with the terms of its endowment and the proper investment of and security of its funds."[73] The regents suddenly possessed exclusive power to operate, control, and administer the University of California.[74] It became virtually a fourth branch of state government, a "constitutional corporation . . . equal and coordinate with the legislature, the judiciary and the executive," according to the state attorney general.[75]

In future years, this unusual level of autonomy would be shared by only five other existing public universities: the state universities in Colorado, Idaho, Michigan, Minnesota, and Oklahoma. Unlike the university's Board of Regents, however, most state universities require the general election of their board members with shorter terms or other structural differences, which has profoundly affected the autonomy of their public colleges and universities.

The 1879 California constitution gave the regents tremendous freedom to manage the Berkeley campus, but with what? A year after the convention, the university received only a $10,000 appropriation from the state—approximately 8 percent of its total operating expenses. Nor was there a promise of any substantial increase in state funding. The university's elevation to the status of a public trust would be a profoundly important designation in later years. It would allow for the development of an internal organization of the university that would help create one of the world's premier research universities. It would also create a politically powerful institution that would successfully fight efforts to create any state-funded rival in higher education. As will be explained in later chapters, the structure of California's contemporary higher education system was largely constructed not only to increase access to postsecondary institutions, but also to complement and protect the university's place at the top of the state's public education ladder.

Throughout the late 1800s, the unusual autonomy of the regents caused most legislators to ignore the substantial financial problems of the university. While other states, such as Illinois, Michigan, Minnesota, and Wisconsin, built America's new class of public research universities, California's state university languished.

Other provisions of the new constitution hindered the development of California's emerging school system and, in turn, the university. The new constitution placed an emphasis on the state funding of common schools at the expense of the high schools. At the convention, Howard Volney, a Democrat from Los Angeles County, voiced the sentiments of the convention majority, insisting that levying a tax for high schools on Californians would be "a species of legalized robbery." It would not benefit the children of the working class or the farmer who, at the end of his or her common school education, would need to go to work. Public funding, stated Volney, needed to focus on common schools over all other forms of education, including the high school and the university. To argue otherwise, he charged, was "an utter fallacy."[76]

Another delegate agreed with Volney and reflected the sentiments first voiced by John Swett and most school administrators: "I say we must go forward and begin at the bottom, and keep the schools open eight months a year. If the people of the State wish to go farther, it is time enough to talk about it when they express themselves."[77] Throughout the nation, public high schools were just beginning to be seen as the appropriate bridge between common schools and higher education. In 1850, only fifty-five such schools existed in all of the United States. Ten years later, there were one hundred and eight. Out of that number, only two existed in California. San Francisco and Sacramento had established the first public tuition-based high schools in the state in 1856. By 1879, only nineteen public high schools were operating in California.

The new constitution denied state funds for the funding of high schools. At a time when most property taxes went into state coffers, returning to local schools via the State School Fund, only a few cities could then afford to levy a special local tax to support this relatively new American institution.

Rural areas had no means to establish local high schools. The new constitution also failed to include any mention of the State Board of Education, keeping it a statutory provision and relegating it to a rather minor role in coordinating the development of California's school system.[78]

Local communities proceeded to close a number of high schools that had previously used state funds. High school enrollment declined from nearly 4,900 in 1879 to 3,650 in 1881—a 25 percent drop. The effect on university enrollment was immediate. "How shall the young men and the young women, especially those in the smaller towns and the country, get proper preparation for the university?" asked newly appointed university president William T. Reid. In his first report to the Board of Regents in 1882, Reid noted that the new constitution made it virtually impossible to have a "well-rounded system of public education." It was "divided in its most vital part" Reid protested. "The higher education is freely offered, but the means of obtaining suitable preparation for it are denied." At the time, only seven public high schools offered preparatory college courses. "In other words, our boasted free university is free to those who can afford to pay for preparatory education, but is practically cut off from those who are not able to incur the preliminary expense—the very persons whose education it is of special interest to the State to secure."[79]

Superintendent of Public Instruction Fred M. Campbell concurred, noting that "a very important rung in our educational ladder is wanting, a ladder which, as some one has said, should reach from the gutter to the university." Campbell begged the incoming Governor and Democrat George Stoneman to remedy the "defect." In his 1882 report to the legislature, the superintendent claimed that California was on the verge of being the "most complete and the grandest system of public education" in the Union if and only if it sought the development and geographical dispersion of the high school.[80] But no substantial reform came.

The first five decades of California statehood brought only a slow development of public institutions. "Individuality is carried to an extreme in California," Henry Durant complained in the late 1860s. The foibles of California's evolving culture, he thought, hindered his efforts to secure the financial support of a young state university. "Our fast living may almost all of it be referred to intense selfishness," mused Durant. "Indeed, sentimentality and idealism seem lost from the mass of the people. They are sensualists and materialists, or nearer that than anything else—the very condition on account of which the Spirit of God forsook the antediluvian world."[81]

By the turn of the century, not much had changed in California's political culture. Writing in the *Atlantic Monthly* in 1898, Stanford University's new president, David Starr Jordan, complained that, despite breaking its dependence on mining, California remained a disjointed culture, mired in a get-rich-quick ethos and addicted to "the possibility of the unearned increment."[82] Reform and discipline were needed to develop what Jordan viewed as California's often neglected and abused political and social institutions. The result would be the creation of a more ordered and enlightened society.

A more expansive understanding and interest in the state's evolving system of education would have to await the rise in political power of the California Progressives. The ideal of mass higher education would become a topic of national interest, but its arrival in America would come through California.

John Swett, 1855. John Swett was one of many Yankees who ventured West not for gold but to participate in building a new American experiment along the Pacific Coast and to help establish public institutions. In 1855 he was the principal of the Rincon Grammar School in San Francisco, shown here with "a group of leading pupils." Three years earlier, he helped write legislation establishing the state's first public institution for training teachers. In 1861 after being elected state superintendent of public instruction, Swett toured California to assess the conditions of its public school system and initiated legislation for a state public school fund in 1866. *California History Room, California State Library, Sacramento, California.*

University of the Pacific in San Jose, 1870. The University of the Pacific in San Jose and the University of Santa Clara were the first two private colleges in California. Both were established in 1851 and predated the College of California in Oakland by four years. In the early 1870s, the University of the Pacific moved to Stockton. *California History Room, California State Library, Sacramento, California.*

Daniel Coit Gilman, 1875. In 1870 and while at the Sheffield Scientific School at Yale, Daniel Coit Gilman refused the offer of the regents of the University of California to become the insitution's first president. Two years later, he accepted the position. Gilman attempted to mold the institution into the new model of the American research university, balancing classical studies with emerging scientific and applied fields. By 1875 when this portrait was taken, Gilman had withstood the public's significant criticism of the university. Weary of the battle and the state legislature's numerous inquiries regarding the management of the university, Gilman left California for Baltimore to become the president of a new institution devoted to graduate training and research, Johns Hopkins University. *University of California Archives, Bancroft Library, University of California–Berkeley.*

Girls' High School and the California State Normal School, 1870. In 1857 California's first teacher education institution was established by the city of San Francisco. In 1862 John Swett and others persuaded the state legislature to convert the school into the California State Normal School (pictured here in 1870 from a print used in the annual report of the state superintendent of public instruction). A year later, the normal school was moved to San Jose, where city officials provided twenty-six acres of land for the institution to grow and prosper. *California History Room, California State Library, Sacramento, California.*

San Jose State Normal School, 1880. In 1880 the State Normal School in San Jose remained the only state-funded school for teacher training with approximately 400 students and twelve faculty. Teacher training was at the secondary school level until the Progressive Era when it became a postsecondary program. The school was governed by a board with membership from the State Board of Education, the state superintendent of public instruction, and leading citizens. *California History Room, California State Library, Sacramento, California.*

Inauguration of Governor Hiram Johnson, 1911. California's Progressive movement peaked in 1911 when Hiram Johnson took the oath of office as governor. As had many other leaders in the reform movement, Johnson attended Berkeley and saw in the state university a vital tool for economic expansion and social reform. But this faith in education as an agent of change extended beyond the University of California to the support of high schools and the development of the nation's first network of public junior colleges. *California History Room, California State Library, Sacramento, California.*

Los Angeles State Normal School, 1885. In 1881 California's second public normal school was established in Los Angeles. As with its counterpart in San Jose, the new campus in Los Angeles was governed by its own board with members from the local community and from the State Board of Education. Not until 1921, after the absorption of the Los Angeles campus by the University of California and with the addition of teacher training institutions in Chico (1887), San Diego (1897), Santa Barbara (1909), Fresno (1911), Humboldt (1913), and a Cal Poly campus in San Luis Obispo, did the state board become the governing body for what were renamed the California State Teachers Colleges. *California History Room, California State Library, Sacramento, California.*

David Starr Jordan, 1915. On the recommendation of Andrew White, president of Cornell, Leland and Jane Stanford recruited David Starr Jordan from the presidency at the University of Indiana to lead Leland Stanford Junior University. Jordan was attracted by the huge endowment for the university and the challenge and appeal of creating a private university with a public charge similar to that of Cornell—no tuition and a commitment to admit students from all social classes. Jordan was president of Stanford University from 1901, when it opened, until 1913. *California History Room, California State Library, Sacramento, California.*

CHAPTER 3

Progressives and the California Idea

Only by the slow but sure means of general education of the masses in character and in fundamental bases of liberty under law can governments that are safe and intelligent be created. In a far larger sense than anything we have yet witnessed, education must become the constructive tool of national progress.

—ELLWOOD P. CUBBERLEY

Between 1900 and 1920, California Progressives pursued a reform movement that promised to, among other things, purge government of corruption and political partisanship.[1] Within the cavalcade of reform legislation, and shaped by Taylorite visions, building a "modern" and "efficient" system of education offered a key mechanism for reforming California society.

The immediate concern of California Progressives was to destroy the political stranglehold of the Southern Pacific Railroad—what journalist Frank Norris derisively called "The Octopus," a railroad monopoly that controlled vast stretches of California land and capital. No other state suffered under the yoke of a single corporation with such economic and political power. Self-proclaimed reformers, representing a new and growing upper middle class, attempted to overthrow California's history of rampant political corruption and disorganization. They wished to replace the established structure with new institutions and a public morality that would reinvent the state. Direct elections, the initiative and the recall, cross-filing, and civil service reform were part of the elixir intended to do just that. These reforms would induce a participatory democracy and end the power of the Southern

Pacific. Expanding higher education opportunity was the long-term investment that would give such reforms meaning. It would provide a caste of trained labor and professionals, a source of culture and research that would build a more learned, competent, and productive society capable of wisely using these new democratic powers.

In advocating a greater role for higher education in California society, Progressives reiterated the ideals of common school leaders of the mid-1800s. There were, however, several new wrinkles to California's education boosterism, influenced by scientism, new theories of social reform, and industrialism. The result is what I have called the California Idea: the rise of a cohesive and popular vision of public higher education as an ameliorative and pro-active agent of state and local government, which would set the stage for a modern and scientifically advanced society. More specifically, the California Idea is the manifestation of this vision into a system of public colleges and university campuses.

Progressives built this system in reaction to several contextual changes in California. A rapidly advancing industrial economy required better-trained labor, a new class of professionals, and greater access to education. The social and economic fabric of California and of the nation was undergoing a substantial transformation. New forms of education, both pedagogically and administratively different from those advocated by Horace Mann and John Swett, were needed.

The large influx of population and the vast geographic size of California also posed serious difficulties in building this ideal of a broadly accessible and, in the lexicon of the era, rational and efficient network of educational institutions. The implications of emigration, both foreign and domestic, not only brought a sense of social upheaval in urban areas but also added mightily to California's total population. Between 1900 and 1920, the state grew by nearly 2 million people—an increase of nearly 130 percent. Approximately 87 percent of those 2 million came from outside the state, in turn changing the physical and political landscape of California.[2] The ever-present factor of large increases in the number of people—an irrepressible constant in California policymaking—and a corresponding expansion in the school- and college-age cohort pushed lawmakers and California's higher education community to assess the future of the public education system.

California Progressives placed particular faith in the social and economic advantages of higher education. A broadly accessible postsecondary education was the "crown" of the emerging system. It would act as a breeding ground for new leaders in business and government and as a source of research beneficial to industry and society, organizing "the energies of our scientists, of our physicists, chemists, mechanists, into armies of research."[3] In education and in the University of California, in particular, Progressives found perhaps the most powerful and enduring symbol for their ideals.

In these pursuits, Californians found inspiration in other progressive states. Much as Yale and the University of Michigan had provided a catalyst for the creation of the University of California in the 1860s, innovations at Cornell and the University of Wisconsin influenced a new generation of Californians. Wisconsin Progressives linked the campus in Madison to the daily social and economic life of the state. Governor Robert La Follette, a graduate of the University of Wisconsin, greatly encouraged this interplay. The state university, he proclaimed, should become the "minister in a direct and practical way to the material interests of the state."[4] It would become the state's primary agent of social and economic change.

Under the leadership of President Charles Van Hise, the University of Wisconsin pursued agricultural research and an extension service that fostered a prosperous and progressive rural economy. Faculty in engineering helped plan public works projects, and social scientists served on public commissions and drafted legislation. As historians John Brubacher and Willis Rudy observed, "[T]he university had become the 'brain of the Commonwealth,' making possible the progressive legislation in which Wisconsin pioneered."[5] This was the essence of what Charles McCarthy and Frederic C. Howe called in 1912 the "Wisconsin Idea." The state university, wrote Howe, was "an experiment station in politics, in social and industrial legislation, in the democratization of science and higher education."[6]

These manifestations of a national reform movement in education were mirrored in California. The University of California emerged as a symbol of progressive ambitions by expanding extension programs into rural areas and engaging in the political and social life of Californians. Yet, added to this potion was a significant commitment to expand access to higher education and the creation of new types of public institutions. For the first time, Californians articulated how the state's network of a state university, normal schools, and innovative junior colleges would interrelate to create a logical system of higher education.

In conceiving and adopting these reforms, University of California faculty and officials such as President Benjamin Ide Wheeler played a major role. In no small part, the development of the public junior college and other elements of the reform effort were intended to divert enrollment demand from the state university. This would allow Wheeler to build the Berkeley campus into one of the nation's premiere research universities. The tripartite structure that emerged was, essentially, built around a land grant institution that was both innovative and politically powerful.

Educating the Progressive

California Progressives were part of a relatively new, rising class of professionals, composed mainly of lawyers and small business entrepreneurs. Participation in public affairs, they believed with often religious fervor, offered a way to end the waste and blatant corruption of the era and improve the economic conditions of Californians. As recounted by historians such as George Mowry, participation in politics was also a method of promoting personal economic interests. Reducing the power of the railroad monopoly would create a more favorable climate for small businesses.[7]

While the Southern Pacific provided a motivating symbol for California Progressives, their reform desires were based on a larger world view than pure economic gain. They sought to bring order to an increasingly complex society and believed that rational policymaking could not only be achieved, but that it would solve California's problems. In themselves they saw a new generation of leaders, the new standard bearers of republican social values, the only ones who could benevolently alter the course of history. To do so, however, they would need the approval of the electorate. These solutions were within reach if pursued under the rubric of both scientific analysis and the consent of the larger population.[8]

The transition to reform politics would come slowly. In San Francisco, Mayor James Duval Phelan, a young millionaire and reform Democrat, led an effort to clean up municipal government in the late 1890s. Phelan's greatest achievement was the creation of a new city charter in 1898 and the semblance of a civil service system. His term as mayor, however, ended in 1902, with the city boss Abraham Ruef hand-picking his successor. For six years, San Francisco fell under the cloud of Ruef's corrupt rule, in part funded and supported by the Southern Pacific. With the reform movement temporarily stymied in northern California, Progressives found their first big victory in the 1906 municipal elections in Los Angeles. Shortly after, the Lincoln-Roosevelt Republican League was formed through the efforts of two future regents of the University of California: Edward A. Dickson, a journalist for the *Los Angeles Express*, and Chester Rowell, editor of the *Fresno Morning Republican*. The League banded together self-proclaimed nonpartisans and resulted in a dramatic electoral victory in 1910. Progressives gained control of both houses of the state legislature, and their candidate for governor, Hiram Johnson, defeated machine politician John N. Gillett. The Southern Pacific's power had been broken. "The hope of governmental accomplishment for progress and purity politically is with us in this new era," pronounced Johnson on his inaugural address. "Ours is a glorious destiny."[9]

The historic 1911 session of the California legislature promptly passed bills providing for direct voter participation (the initiative, referendum, and recall), cross-filing as a means to promote the election of "nonpartisans" to state and local offices, women's suffrage, banking reform, public utility regulation, civil service reform, tax reform, local and state government reorganization, and last, but not least, building a comprehensive system of public education.[10] California was on the crest of a powerful wave rushing to redefine state government and the rights of its citizens.

Yet there was a dark side to the movement beyond the specter of economic self-interest. Despite the call of Progressives for democratic reforms, in the area of educational policy many leaders of the Progressive Movement, but certainly not all, were notorious for reactionary and thoroughly undemocratic goals. Reformers such as Hiram Johnson and Chester Rowell shared the racism of earlier California reform movements, advocating segregation in local schools and calling for a halt to immigration from China and Japan. In most areas of the state, Chinese children were excluded from public schools until a court ruling forbade the practice in 1885. Separate schools remained a reality in many urban areas, such as San Francisco, and portions of rural California. By 1906, when the "Chinese" school in San Francisco burned down and was replaced by an "Oriental School," the city's board of education required the growing Japanese community to also send their children there. Anti-Japanese fervor held that they were another inassimilable population, a source of crime, and a dangerous influence on public schools. The actions of the San Francisco School Board brought protests from the Japanese government and an attempt at mediation by the Roosevelt administration. A year later, influenced largely by California's anti-Japanese movement and the events in San Francisco, the federal government excluded Japanese immigration to the United States.[11]

The support of Johnson and Rowell in anti-alien legislation illustrates a glaring contradiction within their rhetorical concern for "the rights of men." Recalling the inherent contradiction of the Colonial Era (for example,

Thomas Jefferson writing the Bill of Rights while living in a slave-owning society), the Progressive vision of a participatory democracy produced a theoretical framework that ignored the social realities of rampant racism and sexism.

The use of education to fulfill racist sentiments, while extremely important, stands in contrast to the larger emphasis that California Progressives placed on education as a tool of reform. Progressives represented a generation substantially different in social and economic background than earlier Californians. Most were upper middle-class, university-trained professionals and independent businessmen. Of those who joined the Lincoln-Roosevelt League, approximately three out of four were college educated and most were highly literate and fascinated by reform movements in other states. In their eyes, education was a great equalizer. It provided social and economic mobility for the individual. These reform-minded activists saw in their own financial and political successes a self-confirming model that needed to be broadened until, inevitably, it overtook and controlled both commerce and government. As Kevin Starr noted, they were, "abhorrent of both the corporate oligarchy and labor unions, forward-looking and reform minded, yet at the same time slightly nostalgic for a lost myth of American self-reliance and individualism that was, at bottom, the indispensable myth for their own professional success."[12]

Most Progressives came to California early in their lives and attended public schools. Los Angeles High School produced much of the movement's political leadership. After graduating in Los Angeles, like their counterparts in other parts of the state, most Progressives traveled to attend Stanford or the University of California. Edward Dickson was one such individual, traveling the 500 miles to Berkeley. Though southern California had no counterpart to these university campuses, the influx of Midwestern Protestants had created a large number of good elementary and secondary schools and had established a variety of academies: the ambitiously named University of Southern California founded in 1880, Pomona College and Occidental College both established in 1887, Throop Polytechnic, later renamed Caltech, in 1891, Whittier College in 1901, Redlands and Biola Colleges founded in 1907 and 1908, respectively, and Loyola Marymount in 1911. None of these schools fulfilled the aspirations of a large contingent of future reformers and their parents. Indeed, the lack of a "true university campus" in southern California would cause Dickson, a regent by 1912, to argue forcefully for a University of California campus in Los Angeles—what would eventually become UCLA.

Once at Berkeley or Stanford, the future reformers' affinity and faith in public education, and their ideals for reform in general, gained definition. Many found inspiration in Joseph LeConte, a professor of biology at Berkeley, who saw the American university as a laboratory of social thought and research and who influenced a generation of Californians. Born in Liberty County, Georgia, LeConte graduated from the University of Georgia in 1841, bent on becoming a physician. In the midst of study at the College of Physicians and Surgeons in New York City, he decided to travel to the headwaters of the Mississippi and to the Great Lakes. Though he finished his medical degree in 1845, this trip stimulated an intense interest in the relationship of the environment to the development of plant and animal life. Shortly after he began his lifelong study of geology and natural history under the famed Swiss biologist Louis Agassiz at Harvard, he made his way to California in 1869 to teach at the new state university with his brother, John LeConte.[13] John, a professor of physics, would become the president of the university.

A social Lamarckian, Joseph LeConte also represented a generation of scientists striving to adapt the ideas of Darwin in a manner that would be socially acceptable within the largely conservative academy. Although he conducted several important experiments on sight and physiology, LeConte's main emphasis was philosophical. In the classroom, he linked ethics with the new theories of organic evolution—the idea that environmental changes cause structural changes in animals and plants. The marriage of science with the social values of the era could, in his view, lead to a more progressive American culture. At Berkeley, he was known for "a singularly sunny disposition, a lucid literary style, and a deep feeling for nature," notes one observer. He was a close friend to John Muir, and along with several of his colleagues played an important role in the founding of the Sierra Club in 1891.[14]

As a young professor at Berkeley, Alexis Lange saw the elderly LeConte crossing the path of a young boy and his mother on the campus. LeConte proceeded to pat the boy on the head, proclaiming him merely an animal for now, but explaining that with education, he would "become a man." The mother was horrified by the encounter, and specifically at LeConte's seemingly atheistic equation of humans as animals. In reality, LeConte was a moderate, rationalizing evolution to make it palatable to students, clergymen, and scientists. Lange, who eventually became dean of the College of Education, recalled that the encounter said much about LeConte. The naturalist professed a tremendous belief in the effect of the environment, created largely by human activity, on the development of the individual.[15] LeConte also believed that the emerging American university offered the culminating transition in which the animal became civilized and ready to take a leadership role in society.

Just as the individual matured, thought LeConte, so would his social institutions, including the university. The university, he proclaimed, "has become now an institution in which the professor is no longer a teacher merely, but also a maker of science and philosophy." He felt that the relation of professor to student was "no longer one of teacher and learner, but also of coworker in the field of thought."[16] Not all of his colleagues at Berkeley shared such views. There remained, as in most American universities, a division between emerging scientism and the adherents of classical and religious conservatism. The champions of the old college order had dominated Berkeley at its inception—specifically the Yale and congregational influence found in so many of the West's young colleges and state universities. But a transformation was in the making.[17]

At Berkeley, Professor Eugene Hilgard was part of that change, elevating research in practical fields such as agriculture as nearly coequal to the more traditional academic fields. LeConte contributed a philosophical vision, which influenced reformers and his students, such as future governor Hiram Johnson, muckraker Frank Norris, and progressive San Francisco City Attorney Franklin K. Lane. LeConte's students were taught that "in nature, in human beings, and in human society . . . the higher builds itself upon the lower."[18] As LeConte argued, this lesson could be applied to theories of social progress.

Cubberley and the Cult of Efficiency

The University of California would become an important source of progressive thought by the turn of the century. But an equal participant in this social and economic reform movement was across the bay. Stanford University came into being in 1891 when the first class entered the new campus in Palo Alto.

Two major figures provided an intellectual basis for America's turn of the century reform movement in education: John Dewey and Ellwood Cubberley, a professor of education at Stanford. Working at the University of Michigan and later at Columbia, Dewey led the "revolt against formalism" in pedagogy employed by American schools—the reliance on rote methods of teaching. According to Dewey, the existing and rigid nature of the school curriculum was, in part, the result of the quest of common school advocates to standardize education in subject matter, books, grades, and teacher training. Pedagogical reform, claimed Dewey, Cubberley, and others, needed to incorporate the new science of the age. Influenced by Herbert Spencer, William James, G. Stanley Hall (the psychologist and founding president of Clark University), and a new breed of Pestalozian "behavioral scientists," progressive education sought to reshape teaching around the needs of the child.

Where Dewey led the pedagogical reform movement, Cubberley was the nation's leading advocate of administrative reform and an important historian of American education. Cubberley was a former city school superintendent in San Diego, an articulate speaker, and a prolific author. A onetime student of Edward Lee Thorndike at Columbia, Cubberley completed his graduate studies in New York by conducting the first nationwide study on how states funded local schools. At the time, most states had no standard for allocating funding (a pattern also found in public financing of higher education), resulting in huge inequities between schools and school districts. Cubberley persuasively argued for the adoption of a formulaic budgeting system based on the average daily attendance of students as the initial step toward establishing a more equitable network of schools within states, and to adequately fund their enrollment growth.[19] From this pioneering study and as a professor of education at Stanford University, Cubberley went on to write nearly a book each year, including *Changing Conceptions of Education* (1909), *The Improvement of Rural Schools* (1912), *Public School Administration* (1916), and *The History of Education* (1920), many of which would become compulsory reading for a whole new generation of professional school administrators and teachers.[20]

Cubberley's intellectual development and career were heavily influenced by the teachings and writings of David Starr Jordan. Born and raised in Antioch, Indiana, in 1886 as an eighteen-year-old, Cubberley attended a lecture by Jordan, then the president of Indiana University, on "The Value of Higher Education." Jordan's admonishment was "go to college." Jordan also noted: "[Y]ou cannot fasten a $2,000 education to a fifty-cent boy. The fool, the dude, and the shirk, come out of college pretty much as they go in. . . . Whatever you are, you must make of yourself, but a well spent college life is one of the greatest helps to all these good things." Cubberley would subsequently alter his plans to attend Purdue University, enrolling at Indiana as a physics major and seeking Jordan as a teacher and advisor. At Indiana, he took a course from Jordan on a relatively new concept of biological evolution and of social change. "That this course provided food for young Ellwood's thought is evident [in] that he later made that course a requirement for students of education at Stanford," later noted Cubberley's colleague and sometimes collaborator, Jesse B. Sears.[21] Jordan would eventually hire Cubberley as the first chair of the School of Education at Stanford.

Cubberley became one of the nation's most profound influences on American education, traveling throughout the country providing advice and lecturing on the history of education and the need for continued reforms in school administration. His prolific writing also brought him a small fortune. The popularity of his books generated a steady income that he used to help develop Stanford's School of Education, including fully funding the construction of a new building for the school in 1938. He also became a significant voice in Sacramento, helping to coauthor several bills related to higher education. As with other reformers of that era, he often looked to the skills of American business to transform education under the creed of scientific management. Administrative reform, he argued, could rid municipalities of multiple school boards steeped in ward politics. They could be replaced by elected citywide boards to alter the political control of schools. In conjunction with the expansion of graduate training in American universities, this and similar reforms would create a professional class of administrators and teachers. Efficiency and quality would replace anarchy and the vestiges of the one-room schoolhouse. Formulas for state funding of schools would create stability and provide equity, helping to reinvent American education.

These types of organizational reforms were also the natural progressions of an emerging civilization, Cubberley argued.

> The history of the gradual expansion of our educational system and the gradual transference of powers from district to township, township to county, and county to State, in the interest of better organization and efficient administration, forms an interesting part of the story of our nation's growth. To trace it would be to trace much of the story of our national development. From a collection of isolated villages and rural communities we have expanded to a large nation, each part bound to all other parts by close social, commercial, and political ties. New world relationships have been developed. . . . New methods of transacting both public and private business have been introduced, and the need for larger units for administration of the public's business has been made evident to practically all.[22]

Cubberley relied on historical analysis to describe the world as it ought to be. In part thanks to Cubberley's advocacy, business leaders and the new, rising class of professionals found in California and other states became infatuated with education policymaking. Education as a panacea was such popular clamor among American business interests that historians have since been engaged in a long debate over who actually led the reform movement: business leaders or professional educators with Taylorite leanings such as Cubberley.[23]

Some reformers, including Dewey and Jacob Riis, viewed aspects of Taylorism as another ideology developed to further exploit the laborer, a creed similar to social Darwinism. In their view, the intention was to over-specialize the tasks of the industrial worker, demeaning their livelihoods by equating them to machinery for the sake of increased profits. This skeptical view extended from the factory to the schoolroom. Particularly in the area of curriculum, Dewey opposed specialization and the narrow confines of vocational subjects. "Those who believe in the continued separate existence of [those] they are pleased to call the 'lower classes' or the 'laboring classes' would naturally rejoice to have schools in which these 'classes' would be segregated." Further, Dewey protested that "some employers of labor would doubtless rejoice to have schools supported by public taxation supply them with additional food for their mills."[24]

For Dewey, the purpose of educating the masses might include vocational aspects but not at the expense of nurturing "the appreciation and liberation of thought." As he explained, "both culture and utilitarian subjects [should] exist in an organic composite where the former are not by dominant purpose socially serviceable and the latter not liberative of imagination and thinking power."[25]

Most liberal reformers heartily embraced the ideal of efficient management and a "practical curriculum." According to Cubberley, it was both good and inevitable. Rather than reject Dewey's notion of liberal education, he embraced it. However, he claimed the necessity to accompany pedagogical progress and the expansion of educational opportunity with major innovations in the structure of the public education system, from the kindergarten to the university. Progressive Era reformers saw scientific management as a way to actually increase the value of the worker, bring better wages and working conditions, and open new possibilities for socioeconomic mobility. There was an obsessive sense that America's greatness came from its industrial innovations and business acumen. The schools needed to be transformed to meet the evolutionary needs of a new industrial age. "The condition of our schools before about 1890," Cubberley reflected, "was that of a manufacturing establishment running at a low grade of efficiency." Continuing his analogy of the school as a factory,

> [the] waste of material was great and the output small and costly—in part because the workmen in the establishment were not supplied with enough of the right kind of tools; in part because the supervision emphasized wrong points in manufacturer; but largely because the establishment was not equipped with enough pieces of special-type plant, to enable it to work up the waste material and meet modern manufacturing conditions.[26]

Cubberley greatly influenced California's school and university reform movement. He urged the creation of "specialized education" as a way to tap a major labor source. Such "principles of specialized production and manufacturing efficiency," he explained, were already in place "in other parts of the manufacturing world."[27] Industrial competition from Germany reinforced the view that public education provided the key element for developing an efficient and prosperous economy. Germany's industrial and military might were attributed almost solely to its proud education system.

In talks before the California Club and other civic organizations and meetings of educators, Cubberley frequently discussed the attributes of Germany's educational model. The most intriguing elements, noted Cubberley, were twofold: one, its inclusion of an additional two years of general education within its secondary schools (in essence a model that was the precursor to the American junior college), and two, the Humboltian model of the research university.

Jordan and the Rise of a Stanford

For California Progressives, the anointed battle to fight the evils of corruption and inefficient administration was a natural progression of human activity. A path lay before them that would lead to social and political evolution, which was, to no small degree, a moral imperative.

The same higher education institutions that helped shape the vision of the California Progressives and that sought to disenfranchise the political power of robber barons, ironically, were also the benefactors of the state's oligarchy. The great wealth accumulated by the Stanfords, the Hearsts, and others provided California with an opportunity to rapidly build two great universities. This level of wealth simply existed nowhere else in the vast stretches of the American West. Both institutions would recruit and attract innovative scientists and philosophers of social reform, including Cubberley. As a model of the American research university, Stanford University, not Berkeley, emerged first. Stanford's spectacular arrival would raise Californians' interest in higher education and eventually in supporting the state's land grant university.

Leland Stanford's fortune provided the opportunity for an innovative private university in California. As its first president, David Starr Jordan brought an unusual level of acumen for turning opportunity into reality. Jordan arrived on the West Coast in 1891 to open the new campus in Palo Alto and promptly built a private institution that mirrored the innovations of Cornell. He proceeded to recruit a distinguished faculty, largely from East Coast and Midwestern universities, quickly placing Stanford on the vanguard of the American university movement.

Born and raised on a farm in upstate New York, in a family of modest means, as a youth Jordan thought himself bound for Yale. However a scholarship offer from newly opened Cornell University and its promise of practical training in the sciences kept him in New York. As part of the 1868 pioneering first class at Cornell, Jordan studied medicine and natural history, setting the stage for a scholarly career that would make him a leading naturalist, a mighty protagonist for the theory of evolution, and a world-renowned ichthyologist.

Like LeConte, Jordan briefly studied with famed biologist Louis Agassiz. After graduating from Cornell, Jordan secured a series of high school teaching posts in Indiana. By the autumn of 1879, he became a professor of natural history at Indiana University. That same year, the U.S. Fish Commission appointed him to conduct a study of marine life along the Pacific Coast. On his first trip to California, he met members of the newly formed California Academy of Sciences (of which he would later become president), including Joseph LeConte and John Muir. It was "one of the most important events in my scientific career," he wrote in his memoirs. Four years later, with the endorsement of Andrew White at Cornell and Daniel Coit Gilman at Johns Hopkins, Jordan became the president of Indiana University.

Whereas Agassiz grounded Jordan in the merit of the scientific method, Cornell's president, Andrew White, influenced his ideas on history and specifically on the link between evolution and social progress. Yet another Yale graduate, White taught history and English literature for seven years at the University of Michigan. At the age of thirty-six, White imagined and helped create "the experiment at Cornell." It was to be an unusual hybrid of a land grant and privately funded institution, embracing the elective system two years before Harvard. At Cornell, White called for the "democratization of university education." Cornell broke from the earlier model of humanistic and denominationally controlled colleges in favor of a new age of science and industry.

A youthful President White, with the financial support of Ezra Cornell and federal land grants, provided an influential model for the modern state university: Cornell would serve the public interest, cater to regional economic needs in ways that were innovative, and empower the individual regardless of social background. In 1883, Senator Justin Morrill proclaimed that Cornell more nearly approached "my cherished ideal of what our country most needs than any other hitherto known."[28]

As Jordan later reflected, White combined exceptional intellectual powers with an ability to inspire. "I doubt if any other American university executive has been his equal in these regards," wrote Jordan. "Even President Eliot [at Harvard], with his great intellectual power, keen, analytical discrimination, and accurate scholarship, seemed to lack somewhat in personal sympathy."[29] White also provided a theoretical framework that made sense of world history. Though White and most of his intellectual contemporaries saw progress as inevitable, White reconciled this notion with the all too apparent economic and social ills of his day: civil war, demoralizing speculation, financial crisis, congested cities in the throes of industrialization, and what he called "philistine wealth in the midst of growing squalor." Everywhere there appeared the signs that Thomas Jefferson was right: The yeoman society still romanticized by intellectuals in the late 1800s had nearly vanished, replaced by robber barons and growing urban poverty. Material progress, explained White, seemed to come at the "cost of the happiness and lives of millions [and] grinds tender-hearted women and children to powder."[30]

Yet in White's Hegelian view of history, these ills were still the natural components of social progress, part of a compelling vision of a march from the lower to the higher. "More and more it becomes clear that the same law of evolution extends even through national catastrophes," reflected White in a commencement address in Ann Arbor in 1890. "The old doctrine of ever recurring closed cycles of national birth, growth, and death; the doctrine of national catastrophes without any effect save possibly to point a moral or adorn a tale, has virtually disappeared." White proposed that progress was achieved through a slow and thoughtful process or through catastrophe (what he called "revolutionary events").[31]

This integration of the historical record with theories of social change led Jordan to advocate for an activist society, one that could mitigate the number and magnitude of the revolutions in favor of a more-ordered process of progress. An activist university, as also preached by White, was part of that approach. It could introduce students to the merits of scientific thought, breed agents of social and economic progress, and, through its research, improve industry and agriculture, decipher trends, and propose solutions to the social problems facing America. Reflecting White's influence, Jordan advocated what he called "bionomics": the mixing of the lessons of science, in particular, the theory of evolution, with the analysis of social problems.

The Stanfords' quest for a president of their new university led them to Jordan, who came highly recommended by White. The Stanfords saw in Jordan a man "at the height of his powers" with "vigorous temperament." Jordan also shared with them their desire for new institutions of higher education that focused on "the practical," the scientific, as well as the classical. In Cornell, Leland Stanford found a model. He thought his own university, however, should integrate an even more vigorous goal of providing social and economic mobility.

Inspired by the idea of creating a memorial to his sixteen-year-old son and only child, Leland Jr., after his tragic death in 1884, Stanford wanted the new university to "be open to the poor as well as the rich," for it to teach "every useful calling," with "instruction to deal particularly with the welfare of the masses." He also professed a desire "that females shall have equal advantage with males, and to have open to them every employment suitable to their sex"—a reiteration of the policies at both the University of California and Cornell.[32]

Stanford's interest in creating a new university, however, represented more than an effort to memorialize his son. Stanford's decision to invest the vast majority of his fortune in higher education reflected a not so uncommon attempt to provide a cleansing legacy for his own accumulation of wealth. It also reflected his adherence to the Whig-Republican vision of the role of education in building a civilized society. Like Jordan, Stanford's views of the benefits of education were shaped by his humble background and by the Yankee culture of his native New York.

As noted previously, Stanford attended public schools near Albany before venturing West to become a frontier lawyer in Wisconsin in the 1840s. A decade later he became a highly successful dry goods merchant en route to his rise as a railroad industrialist and California politician. His often ruthless rise to power was facilitated by a partnership with the government that financed railroad construction and granted vast amounts of federal land to what became the Southern Pacific.

As California's first Republican governor, Stanford had been an important supporter of the University of California. As governor, he sat on the Board of Regents in the early 1860s and proved a valuable defender of President Gilman during the tumultuous attacks on his leadership in the 1870s. He was a regent for another brief period in 1883 when he was appointed to finish the incomplete term of Benjamin Redding.

However, Stanford's board membership came to a quick and frustrating end. He had been nominated to complete a new, sixteen-year appointment by Republican Governor George C. Perkins, pending confirmation by the California Senate. Newly elected Governor George Stoneman, a Democrat, successfully argued that the senate not confirm him. Stanford had considered naming the university as a major benefactor of his fortune, but this partisan experience altered his thinking. The subsequent death of his son and the idea of establishing a memorial to his life ended any thought on Stanford's part of becoming a benefactor to the University of California. The establishment of a rival university with the largest endowment of any university or college in the nation caused great dismay among the regents and faculty at the University of California. Leland Stanford envisioned a private university with a public mission that might simply overshadow the struggling campus at Berkeley.[33]

The chartering of Leland Stanford Junior University in 1885 by the California Legislature allowed Leland Stanford and his wife, Jane, to have personal control over a new university. Stanford stipulated in the charter that he and Mrs. Stanford would retain all the powers and functions of a board of trustees until their deaths. Further, he stipulated that the 8,800 acres in Palo Alto, "the farm," which he and Jane bequeathed to the university, could never be sold.

In choosing Jordan as president of his new university, Stanford noted, "I might have found a more famous educator, but I desired a comparatively young man who would grow up with the university."[34] Jordan came so highly recommended and the Stanfords were so desperate for a president in early 1891 after failing to secure the aging Andrew White, they offered Jordan the job after only a ten-minute interview in Bloomington.

As Jordan later reflected, he decided to continue his westward migration, on to Palo Alto, despite two apparent risks. He worried that "California was the most individualistic of the States, and still rife with discordant elements." He also saw risks in the new university's close association with Stanford. The new institution was to be "personally conducted" by Stanford as its sole trustee, "a business man who [is], moreover, active in political life."[35] The baggage of Stanford's political power and tie to the Southern Pacific worried Jordan. Would he have the independence to build Stanford University? Would Leland Stanford's enemies become his enemies?

In the years that followed, Jordan's worry over the source of the Stanfords' wealth came to roost after the death of Leland in 1893. Stanford and his lawyer had personally written the legislation chartering the university, but there were legal questions that had not been addressed adequately. Whereas his will granted a substantial sum to the new university from his personal fortune, several legislators insisted that it should be subject to taxation as corporate profits. This was a salient issue to the longtime political adversaries of Leland Stanford and the Southern Pacific. The money, it was claimed, was the fruit of years of extortion and monopoly. Stanford's fortune became mired in a tangle of obligations, including a demand by the federal government that his estate pay $15 million—his share of the original government loan to the Southern Pacific that remained unpaid.

In the midst of the 1890s depression, many thought the idea of a new university in California wasteful, the egomaniacal dream of a dead industrialist. A New York paper compared the establishment of Stanford University to the "building of a great summer hotel in central Africa, or an institution for the relief of destitute ship captains in the mountains of Switzerland."[36] The full largess of the Stanford fortune, free of all obligations, was made available to Jordan only after Stanford's numerous debts were settled and revision was made in the state charter for the university in 1899. Helped by the intense lobbying of Jordan and the strong support of a group of young and politically astute alumni, Stanford University achieved tax-free status as a public trust and gained Leland's money.

During the six-year effort to amend the state charter, Jane Stanford afforded Jordan the opportunity to rapidly build Stanford into a significant center of professional training and research. She delved into every resource available to her, including her share of the Southern Pacific that was not tied up in legal proceedings, and against the repeated opposition of Collis Huntington. Huntington despairingly entitled the efforts of Jane as "Stanford's folly." "Every dollar I can rightfully call mine," she wrote to Jordan, "is sacredly laid on the Altar of my love for the university, and thus it ever shall be."[37] Her tenacity allowed for the university's building program to continue, although Jordan and some faculty worried about her apparent concern with buildings over faculty salaries and struggled with the difficulties of her eccentricities.[38]

Jordan skillfully used the available moneys to recruit faculty with talents in both teaching and research. Many were from Midwestern universities, often personal friends of Jordan. The emphasis on research, Jordan explained, would not only expand the public service aspect of the American university. It would improve the quality of instruction. "Where the teachers are themselves original investigators," insisted Jordan, "devoted to truth and skillful in the search for it—men that cannot be frightened, fatigued, or discouraged—they will have students like themselves."[39]

By 1900, Stanford, not the University of California, emerged as a symbol of California's cultural aspirations, graced with the Richardsonian architectural designs of Charles A. Coolidge and Frederick Law Olmstead. Stanford also claimed a highly respected faculty for such a young institution so isolated from the cultural meccas of the East Coast. When the university opened in 1891, it enrolled 559 students, slightly more than its anointed rival across the bay. Nine years later, Stanford University enrolled over 1,200 students—nearly half the size of Berkeley's rapidly growing enrollment, yet enough to rank it among the ten largest universities in the nation. The ridicule of East Coast newspapers faded. Further, Stanford was the best-endowed university in the nation with a total of $30 million. At the time, Columbia had an endowment of only $6 million, and Harvard had less than $5 million.

Jordan molded Stanford University into an anomaly among private institutions, pursuing a broad social and scientific academic program more closely associated with the rising class of new public universities. Former state superintendent John Swett observed in 1911: "Though not under direct state control, [Stanford] fulfills many of the functions of a state university. It is open to both men and women; it has no tuition fees; it has a pedagogical department for the training of teachers; it has the elective system in studies." As if this were not enough, Swett exclaimed, it also "had from its beginning David Starr Jordan for its president."[40]

While Stanford might produce the new captains of industry and the professions, Jordan professed a greater interest in developing the individual student's philosophical ideals. Reflecting his experience at Cornell, he insisted that the university needed to be more democratic. The individual student needed sufficient freedom to make choices and prosper—a reaction to the didactic and lockstep curriculum that still dominated most institutions of higher education. Stanford's adoption of the elective system, explained Jordan, was a "recognition of the democracy of the intellect." The student should "not be driven over a prearranged curriculum, or a little race course, which should entitle him at the finish line to a time-honored badge of culture." Rather, the student should have the ability to choose the training that would most strengthen and enrich his or her life. "All students and all studies, therefore, were to be placed on an academic equality," he reflected in his memoirs, "for what will nourish one may not serve for another."[41] Yet there were certain universal truths. For instance, according to Jordan, bionomics could be taught in any course, in any discipline.

The experiment at Stanford, at least at the beginning, also included the enrollment of students from a broad spectrum of social and economic classes. Indeed, by 1899 Jordan professed the novel ideal that all could benefit from some form of education beyond high school—from the opportunity to reap the "rewards of investigation, the pleasures of high thinking, the charms of harmony." However, Jordan noted, this should not mean universal access to a university education. The broadening access to postsecondary education could, and should, be accomplished by the further development of new and primarily public institutions, including the relatively new concept of the junior college. It was financially impractical for private institutions of higher education to fulfill this role. More importantly, he decided, the narrowness of most private institutions prevented their evolution into the stalwarts of a new system of education: They were made for the few and were controlled by the privileged.[42] Stanford University was the exception. Jordan the evolutionist and Unitarian also believed that private institutions carried the baggage of sectarian ties.[43] They were influenced by antiscientism and religious dogma inappropriate for the modern university.

Jordan proclaimed that public education, from the elementary school to the university, was the key to America's evolving social and moral experiment. Private education was, in the final analysis, incompatible with democracy. Conversely, it was the obligation of the state to furnish education to the large mass of Americans and, ultimately, to empower the individual. Public higher education and the state university, in particular, were the "coming glory of democracy." Writing in *Popular Science Monthly* in 1903, Jordan argued that the state university now formed the culmination of a maturing, natural, and symbiotic system of education. Extending this metaphor, Jordan likened higher education to the topmost branches of a tree: Cut these highest branches, he explained, and the sap will cease to rise in its trunk and the social ills of an evolving and changing culture will be magnified.[44]

A Culture of Philanthropy

Jordan quickly became an influential advocate of social and economic reform, gaining the attention of the California public as a savant of the modern age. Jordan's influence and the impressive rise of Stanford University eventually encouraged support for the university in Berkeley.

Stanford University's endowment was part of a national philanthropic frenzy for higher education, inspired by the philosophical treatise of such figures as Jordan, Gilman, and White and by the industrial-speak of educationists such as Cubberley. The heady idealism of the era led industrialist Andrew Carnegie to exclaim, "wherever we peer into the first tiny springs of the national life, how this true panacea for all the ills of the body politic bubbles forth—education, education, education."[45] Such faith caused Carnegie to channel much of his wealth to the cause of education and the building of libraries. The most wealthy Americans held great faith and interest in education, as a tool for social change and for industrial and scientific research, as a control agent against social upheaval, and perhaps foremost as essential to the creation of new and enlightened leaders. This wealth and interest resulted in a cavalcade of philanthropic contributions to existing and new colleges, particularly to new universities. Clark University, Cornell University, MIT, and the University of Chicago all trace their beginnings to money that poured in from the Carnegies, Rockefellers, and Fords—a new caste of industrial giants, who sometimes, but certainly not always, emerged from middle- and lower-class backgrounds.[46]

In the early 1890s, Phoebe Apperson Hearst, the widow of senator and millionaire George Hearst, saw Stanford prosper under its huge endowment and charismatic leadership. Not only did Stanford University glorify the role of higher education but also the Stanford name. Hearst decided to make the University of California her cause célèbre. Yet Hearst's patronage was also tied to her interest in promoting education for women and for developing the kindergarten, which was a particular focus of a growing number of upper-class and socially enlightened women. Hearst argued that women should receive an education comparable to that available to men. Her first investment in the University of California came in 1891, shortly after the death of her husband. That year she established five scholarships for "worthy young women" as part of a long-term effort to build what was characterized by one East Coast paper as a "weak institution with plenty of land, a collection of broken down buildings, beggarly endowments and few students."[47] The campus was a series of seven permanent buildings and numerous temporary structures strewn among pine, eucalyptus, and cypress groves, with an orchard, vineyard, and experimental garden connected by dirt footpaths. The campus had no student union, theater, or residence halls and lacked a restaurant where faculty and students could eat and socialize.

Regent George T. Marye, still feeling the sting of Leland Stanford's lost patronage and seeing few other possibilities for private support, expressed his appreciation and hope for Hearst's continued contributions. "It seems peculiarly fit and pleasing in this instance that, as the University of California was one of the first to throw open its doors to women, a woman is the first to give the university a benefaction for the encouragement of undergraduates."[48] The scholarships were soon accompanied by Hearst's contribution of $2,700 to light the campus walkways and library and to construct residential and social clubs where women could live and study.

In 1896, Hearst agreed to sponsor a national design competition for a new physical master plan for the Berkeley campus. Stanford's cohesive match of buildings and landscape by well-known architects offered a sharp contrast to the architecturally sporadic and jumbled physical plant at Berkeley. At the suggestion of Bernard Maybeck, a young Berkeley instructor in architecture, Hearst agreed to finance an international competition to produce a comprehensive development plan for the university, thereby providing a lasting imprint of her family's philanthropy. Hearst wrote to a regent: "My son and I have desired to give some suitable memorial, which shall testify to Mr. Hearst's love for and the interest in this State. . . . [W]e feel that the best memorial would be one which would promote the higher education of its people."[49] Her generosity led to a conservative beaux arts design for the Berkeley campus by Frenchman Emile Bernard, which was adopted by the regents in 1900. Under the direction of campus architect John Galen Howard, a substantial portion of the plan came to fruition.

Hearst poured money into a series of capital projects under the plan, including Hearst Hall, the Hearst Memorial Mining Building, and a gymnasium for women. Other philanthropists followed suit. In his will, San Francisco businessman Charles Franklin Doe left 25 percent of his estate for the building of a new library at the Berkeley campus. Elizabeth Joselyn Boalt, the widow of a successful San Francisco lawyer, donated funds for the creation of a law school and a building. Mrs. Peder Sather, the widow of a California banker, provided funds for Sather Gate and the landmark Campanile. In all, some twenty buildings were completed under Howard's direction between 1903 and 1924, creating the core of the Berkeley campus.[50]

The "Hearst Plan" had another important benefit: It garnered national and international attention that elevated the status of California's state university. "There has never been anything in the history of education or architecture quite like the competition which the University of California owes to the munificence of Mrs. Hearst," stated a national weekly. Editors of *The Spectator*, a London periodical, wrote somewhat caustically: "On the face of it this is a grand scheme, reminding one of those famous competitions in Italy in which Brunelleschi and Michael Angelo took part." The editors further noted the competition as part of a worthy effort "to identify California in the thought of the world with something else than mines, ranches, and newly enriched millionaires."[51]

Hearst's philanthropic interest in the university led to her appointment as a regent in 1897 by Governor James Herbert Budd—the first in a long line of Berkeley alumni who served in statewide offices, including Governors Hiram Johnson and Earl Warren. At the age of fifty-five, Hearst became the first woman on the board, filling the vacant seat of Charles F. Crocker.

When it came time for her reappointment in 1899, the new governor, Henry T. Gage, at first refused. It was not the proper place for women, he insisted. A substantial protest ensued, the main sentiment of which was voiced in an editorial by the *San Francisco Argus*, noting the need for women on the board in light of the substantial enrollment of women and Mrs. Hearst's invaluable support. "To the world at large it must seem the rankest ingratitude to endeavor to humiliate a lady of such generosity, liberal mind and public spirit."[52] The regents and university officials feared that Phoebe Hearst, like Leland Stanford, might take her money elsewhere. Gage capitulated, and Hearst remained on the board until her death in 1919.

Hearst's appointment gave hope to a growing number of female students and university alumni, who urged the hiring of female faculty and staff and the integration of women into a broader spectrum of scholarly fields. The university had proven exceedingly liberal in the admission of women, who by 1900 represented 46 percent of the student population. In contrast, most colleges and universities in the East remained all male, and even such progressive universities as the University of Michigan and Stanford maintained quotas to keep female students at a magical 25 percent of the student body.

Once at Berkeley, women faced other obstacles. "For twenty-five years," complained Katherine C. Felton, an 1895 graduate, "the University of California has graduated women, many of whom have shown themselves eager and able to pursue the academic life" as faculty. Yet, because Berkeley faculty and the Board of Regents restricted the classes women might take—if not officially, by social mores of male faculty and students—and limited women's professional training largely to the field of elementary school teaching, nursing, and home economics, Felton argued that the promise of the state university was tainted. Further, no women had ever been appointed to the faculty. "There is nothing more so galling to a woman," stated Felton, "so paralyzing to her effort, as that she is shut out from the intellectual field, merely because she is a woman."[53]

Though Hearst's presence on the Board of Regents changed the status of women and the quality of their educational experiences at Berkeley, there was no revolution in the male-dominated culture of the university. Recognizing that change would come slowly, Hearst was primarily interested in improving the quality and financial support for women. As observed by historian Lynn Gordon, at Berkeley, women students and advocates, such as Hearst and Milicent W. Shinn (the longtime editor of the *Overland Monthly* and in 1898 the first woman to earn a doctorate from the university), "used separatism creatively to make a place for themselves at the university but found that men . . . [often still] objected to their very presence. Ultimately, women turned to the rhetoric of equality, asking why they should not have the same campus privileges as men."[54]

Wheeler and a New State University

The reappointment of Hearst to the regents corresponded with the choice of Benjamin Ide Wheeler as the new university president in 1899. Since its founding thirty-one years earlier, the development of the Berkeley campus had, as reflected by Orrin L. Elliott, Jordan's assistant, "proceeded under many handicaps." Support from the legislature had been minimal and often "not cordial." Internal conflicts between faculty and between regents had been common—highlighted by the attack of Professors Carr and Swinton on President Gilman in the 1870s. By the late 1890s, California's state university had already had eight presidents, explained Elliott, and "except for the four years of President Gilman's incumbency no really strong hand had been in control."[55] Gilman's presidency, in fact, had been one of turmoil, caught between the populist notion of a utilitarian polytechnic and a classicist and traditionalist vision of the New England college.

Wheeler's arrival initiated a new era that would transform the Berkeley campus from a relatively weak and poorly funded state university to one of the nation's premier research universities. In the relatively short period of two decades, California, at the end of the Western frontier, would boast two pillars of American higher education, Stanford and Berkeley.

Wheeler was born in Randolph, Massachusetts, in 1854 and attended the Colby Academy in New London, Connecticut. In 1875 he graduated from Brown University. Ten years later, he received a Ph.D. in classical philology from the University of Heidelberg. He then taught at Brown and Harvard before serving as a professor at Cornell for thirteen years. In Ithaca, Wheeler became an activist in both local and statewide politics and, as had David Starr Jordan, developed a close relationship with President Andrew White. An accomplished scholar, he published widely in both America and Germany, including *Introduction to the Study of the History of Language* (1891), *Organization of Higher Education in the United States* (1896), and *Dionysus and Immortality* (1899). In 1896 he held a visiting position as the chair of Greek literature at the American School for Classical Studies in Athens. In Greece, his field research at Corinth led him to participate in the international movement to revive the Olympic Games. Wheeler had the endorsement and admiration of both the academic and political world of New York and Washington, and he could count among his good friends both Grover Cleveland and Theodore Roosevelt.[56]

Influenced by both the German penchant for authority and efficiency and the model of the research university in which he was trained, Wheeler appealed to the regents as a new-age leader with the ability to match the stature and vibrancy of Jordan. Jordan cultivated a national reputation as a philosopher on education, in league with William Rainey Harper, his mentor Andrew D. White, and Charles Eliot at Harvard. Wheeler's greatest success came with securing an unprecedented level of state financial support, expanding the academic, research, and public service mission of his institution and influencing the development of California's public tripartite system.

Under Wheeler, the Berkeley campus retained its role as a center of classical study, but the University of California also gained a clearer definition as a utilitarian and democratic institution and the center of specialized research. These often competing missions had torn at the university and other land grant institutions. Wheeler found the means, as observed by Edwin E. Slosson in 1910, to mitigate such inherent conflict. "The combination of qualities that are quite diverse and even antagonistic give the institution a unique attractiveness. I know of no other university, which cultivates both mechanics and metaphysics with such equal success or which looks so far into space, and, at the same time, comes so close to the lives of the people; or which excavates the tombs of the Pharaohs and Incas while it is inventing new plants for the agriculture of the future."[57]

The result of the efforts of Wheeler, the regents, and the faculty was a new vision of the University of California as a great engine of equality and prosperity for the state. This vision, which can be traced both to Wheeler and his colleagues and to the socioeconomic ethos of the era, gave rise to a tremendous wave of political support for public higher education.[58]

Before coming to California in 1899, Wheeler shrewdly demanded and received significant powers from the regents. He acquired sole authority to hire and fire faculty and set salaries as a condition of his presidency. Wheeler saw a great opportunity to expand the role of the university in California society. A rapidly expanding population, improved schools, and the need for skilled labor and professionals in the state's growing economy caused more and more high school students to seek entrance to the Berkeley campus. Initially, Wheeler sought to fulfill this demand. Not only would it meet a need in society, but enrollment growth would help the expansion and improvement of academic programs and would ultimately elevate the reputation of the Berkeley campus.

But in 1899 Wheeler's ambitions, much like Gilman's, met the reality of a sparse budget. Indeed, most of the federal land scrip had been sold, and only new sources of funding could allow the university to grow and mature. Wheeler found his first success in garnering the interest of California's rising class of wealthy citizens, including Hearst, to fund a large-scale physical expansion of the Berkeley campus and to create scholarships and endowments for faculty positions. In Hearst, Wheeler gained a close personal friend. "Wheeler had a guardian angel in Phoebe Hearst," explains Hearst family biographer Judith Robinson. Much like that of Jordan and Jane Stanford, "Phoebe's relationship with Wheeler was close, personal, and complicated. He consulted her on minute details, including seating arrangements and programs for special ceremonies, courted her with deference and respect, treated her as an equal irrespective of sex."[59]

In turn, Hearst gave moneys for projects large and small: for dozens of new academic buildings, additional scholarships for women, lounges and dinner parties for students, scientific research equipment at Berkeley and at the Lick Observatory, subsidies for scholarly publications by the university press, faculty positions in anthropology, and for archeological expeditions to Egypt, South America, and elsewhere. By 1914, it was reported to the regents that Hearst had spent twice as much on buildings at the Berkeley campus as the state had since the university's inception.

Because of Wheeler's ability to nurture a culture of philanthropy and because of the rise of Stanford University, wrote the editor of *Harper's Weekly*, "the multi-millionaires of California have attested their interest in education on a scale which has excited the wonder of mankind."[60]

Bolstered by the support of Hearst and others, Wheeler also wanted to restructure the university so that it might better reflect the German research university and the applied and scientific bent of Cornell. Under Wheeler, research and public service for the first time joined teaching as coequal missions of the university faculty and as criteria for promotion. Yet, most of the gifts offered to Wheeler and the regents were for buildings and not for the operational costs of an expanding university. For these moneys, Wheeler turned to California's taxpayers.

With the passage of the 1868 Organic Act, California lawmakers initially assumed that federal scrip would provide a large enough endowment to require only occasional state funds and then mostly for capital construction. In many years, including the late 1870s, the university received no state funds. Not until the late 1880s would the state reconsider its role in the financial support of what remained a small and struggling institution. At that time, the university faced a major financial crisis. University officials realized that proceeds from the federal land grant would eventually decline. Lawmakers, mostly Republicans, professed their belief that the university needed a steady source of state support to expand enrollment and keep pace with the state's growing population.[61]

In 1887, the legislature passed the Vrooman Act to support enrollment growth at the university. For the first time, the state created a mechanism for granting the university funds on an annual basis: The regents would receive one cent per $100 of taxable property—the so-called mill tax. "It gave an impulse to the institution such as it had never felt before," stated William Carey Jones in 1899. "It opened up the possibilities of expansion" that, combined with its status as a public trust, "gave the officers and friends of the university a consciousness and power and freedom of action."[62] As a result of this act, the state's share of the university's operating budget increased steadily, moving from 10 percent to an average of approximately 40 percent until a depression in the mid-1890s.

The overall financial health of the university was still tenuous and stood in sharp contrast to Stanford University with its magnificent endowment. Coming from the relative wealth of Cornell, Wheeler considered Berkeley an under-funded and poorly equipped university. He complained that inadequate buildings and increasing enrollments meant that "[w]e are crowded out of house and home." In one of his first communiqués to the governor, Wheeler explained that there were 400 additional students over the previous year's enrollment. Wheeler was appalled at the large classes and the heavy workload faced by faculty.

> The situation here at present is, I sometimes think, pathetic, and sometimes ludicrous. There is nothing comparable to it in the United States today. The students have come down like an avalanche. We have no elasticity in our budget by which to provide for them. We are doing our best, but it is only by a miracle that the multitude can be fed with the seven loaves.[63]

Wheeler and the university benefited by the land boom in California and the subsequent increase in property tax revenues. They had also gained a modest 1 percent increase in the mill tax and occasional onetime state funding from the legislation. By 1909, Wheeler was lobbying for another 1 percent increase in the mill tax. With Progressives a majority in the legislature for the first time, Wheeler found many friends, often university alumni, in Sacramento. The legislature approved the proposal. However, Wheeler and Ralph P. Merritt, the university's first comptroller and lobbyist in Sacramento, soon recognized that there needed to be a fundamental change in the allocation of state funds to the university.

Reform came in the wake of a general overhaul of California's tax system during the 1910 session of the legislature. It was not, it appears, the result of deliberate policymaking. For sixty years, property tax was the financial mainstay of both state and local governments. In 1910, a constitutional amendment passed, giving cities and counties exclusive authority to impose and collect real estate and property taxes, except in the event of a deficit. Governor Hiram Johnson's tax reform package gave greater authority to local representatives as part of a larger effort to "place government in the hands of the people." The package also attempted to bring order to a loose system of state and local taxation, which, since the 1870s, had often fallen to the political maneuverings of the Southern Pacific and other special interests. The idea was to establish mutually exclusive sources of revenue for both state and local governments. Local government would no longer tax utility property. State revenues would come primarily from a new tax on the gross incomes of these same utilities and transportation sectors of the economy.

The impact of the tax reform bills on the university, however, was uncertain. The mill tax had vanished, and no substitute had been proposed.[64] "The unfortunate situation created by a change in our system of taxation," explained President Wheeler to faculty, "deprives the university of its greatest bounty, its connection with the prosperity of the state" with no device for its substitution.[65]

The lack of any identified method for state funding of the university was a source of great distress for Wheeler, but it also afforded an opportunity to make a revolutionary change. As a result of this temporary crisis in university funding, California was the first state to shift from a block allocation for higher education by state government to an enrollment-based budget. Shortly after the signing of the new tax bill, Wheeler and Merritt went to Governor Johnson to propose a new "state university fund." They argued that future state support should be tied to enrollment increases and the actual workload of the university. With Governor Johnson's endorsement, the California Legislature proceeded to approve the new fund. The university would no longer be dependent on property values for its state appropriation; instead, the university would draw from the state's general fund, based on a yearly increase of 7 percent. The 7 percent figure was chosen because it reflected the average annual increases in enrollment over the previous three years at the Berkeley campus. The bill also promised that the legislature would continue to include a 7 percent increase for each fiscal year until 1915.[66]

The innovation of enrollment-based budgeting was a major reform that not only promised to infuse a steady stream of state funding but also provided the first fiscal inducement for the university to expand enrollment. A similar change was occurring at the elementary through high school levels in California and other progressive states. State and local governments adapted workload-based budgeting, using average daily attendance formulas. However, in its original and crude form, state budgeting for the University of California was based on an assumed enrollment increase and not on actual workload.

Only two years after the deal was struck, enrollment growth at the university was nearly 14 percent per year. Wheeler's aggressive effort to hire new faculty and expand programs also brought higher costs. As a result, the university faced substantial debt. Before going back to the legislature for another request for additional funds in the midst of a recession, however,

Wheeler considered establishing tuition. As a public trust, the regents could simply invoke tuition, with no approval from the lawmakers. Beginning in 1895, the university started to charge a minimal "lab fee" for incidental costs, such as chemicals used in courses. No fees had ever been collected from students and their families for the salaries of faculty and the like. Early in the development of most other land grant institutions, tuition had become a mainstay. California prided itself on its deliberate attempt to reduce economic barriers to public education. Though desperate for money, Wheeler and the regents finally rejected the idea of establishing tuition.[67]

Merritt returned to Sacramento and offered lawmakers and officials in the Johnson administration a detailed account of the university's financial operations. State funding had dramatically increased, he noted, but it had not kept pace with enrollment growth. He then proposed a new budget based on the increase in enrollment, the hiring of new faculty, and the expansion of the agricultural extension program. The budget was approved by the Board of Regents and the newly formed State Board of Control.[68] Merritt argued for and gained the university's first million dollar state budget. The presentation of the university's budget requests would, from then on, be based on a detailed presentation of current and projected enrollment, faculty positions, and costs related to the university's research and public service activities.[69] The state of California, henceforth, funded 60 to 70 percent of the university's operation expenditures. Figure 2 demonstrates the tremendous increase in state investment in the university during the Progressive Era.

Wheeler's success in garnering benefactors and increasing state funding created tremendous opportunities for the state university. During his presidency, Wheeler helped to create some twenty new academic departments, largely in the social and hard sciences, reorganized the various colleges, and raised admission standards. The university now placed greater emphasis on graduate education by establishing a graduate division. Perhaps most important, Wheeler substantially elevated the role of research through a variety of innovative mechanisms, reflecting his experiences at Heidelberg and Cornell. He created a Research Board to allocate support moneys, and he led a campaign to build new library facilities and expand the university's meager collection. If the university was to take its place among the vanguard of America's universities, Wheeler insisted, it would need an extensive and well-organized library.

With Wheeler's help, in 1905 the Berkeley campus significantly expanded its library by acquiring the Bancroft collection. Six years later, the new Charles Franklin Doe Library housed approximately 400,000 volumes. The

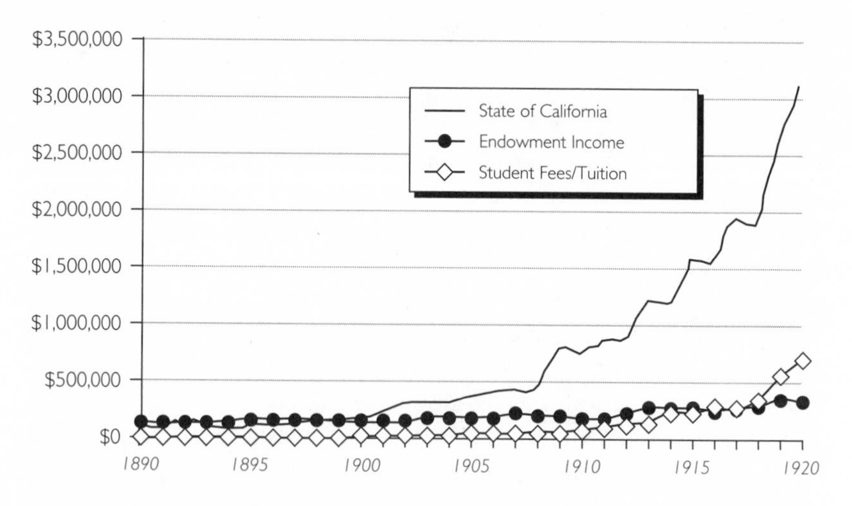

Figure 2. Three Major Sources of Funding for the University of California, 1890–1920

SOURCE: *Centennial Record of the University of California, 1967*

size of the university's collection had more than quadrupled since Wheeler's arrival in California.[70] Wheeler and university faculty also recognized the importance of disseminating their research. The University of California Press had been organized in 1886 but had published few manuscripts. Wheeler sought to substantially increase the output of the Press. The University of California was soon producing scholarly publications in addition to massive numbers of bulletins and instructional pamphlets on topics such crop diseases and viticulture.[71]

The newfound centrality of research and public service led to the establishment of a series of research stations that directly benefited key constituents in California's economy. The University of California grew beyond the confines of its Berkeley campus. In some instances, this expansion was a direct result of Wheeler's leadership. In others, the university was simply reacting, sometimes reluctantly, to public demands. The progressive vision of Wheeler and others in the higher education community was not instantaneous, and it was not their idea alone; much of it evolved from growing public demand for services, particularly from members of California's burgeoning agricultural sector.

The same year that the Doe Library opened, the university's first permanent agricultural research station was created in Davis. Professor of Agriculture E. W. Major and former State Agricultural Society president and ex officio Regent Peter J. Shields cowrote legislation that gave state funding for farm-related research. Shields had long clamored for such a facility in the heartland of the Central Valley to assist with the state's dairy industry. It was not until Wheeler's arrival that the idea was seriously considered by university officials. Repeatedly, the regents and faculty had been wary of any attempt to "divert" university resources out of the Bay Area. At first, Wheeler shared this view, but he changed his mind in light of the growing demand for university services. There were clearly great opportunities to expand the scope of the university and to garner political and financial support.

The success of the university's new Davis facility and the demand by farmers for additional services led shortly to its conversion into a University Farm School, which included secondary-level courses in a wide variety of agricultural subjects. Satellite farms, under the direction of faculty from Berkeley and Davis, were also created in Eldorado County and in Petaluma, focusing on developing the range cattle industry and investigating poultry diseases. Fifteen years after its establishment, the Davis Farm School employed forty-seven faculty and staff and conducted instruction and research on herd breeding, orchards, and vineyards. It also operated a commercial creamery. Among its enrollment were eighty-seven students from the College of Agriculture in Berkeley and 727 students taking high-school-level courses. In 1920, the Berkeley and Davis faculty directed over 5,600 students in correspondence courses and circulated some 850,000 copies of bulletins and circulars.[72]

Wheeler also coordinated the university's first expansion into southern California. When the Davis research station opened in 1905, faculty had already established a small laboratory at Alligator Head in La Jolla for "applied" research in marine ecology. By 1912 a philanthropic contribution by Ellen Browning Scripps and E. W. Scripps, the newspaper publisher, was used to build a larger facility, creating the Scripps Institute for Biological Research, which would eventually become the Scripps Institution of Oceanography.

In 1907 the university established a counterpart to the Davis school in Riverside. A new Citrus Experiment Station was created on twenty-three acres of land on Mount Rubidoux, which would eventually become the university campus at Riverside. Focusing on both research and training in horticultural management, fertilization, irrigation, and fruit handling, the Riverside station would grow to include two other experimental farms at

Porterville and Whittier: the latter to study the growth of citrus fruit on hillsides, and the former for studying plant diseases. The Riverside facility proved a tremendously important influence on the rise of California's citrus industry.[73]

Wheeler also oversaw the creation of the Hooper Foundation for Medical Research, a university hospital and training center for nurses in San Francisco, which was part of a consortium of university medical programs based in the Bay Area. In addition, he was an integral part of the significant expansion of the university's extension program and the inauguration of summer sessions at the Berkeley campus.[74]

Extension courses had been taught on an ad hoc basis since 1891 by university faculty. Not until 1902, however, was the program reorganized as a self-governing body within the university. An overly ambitious effort led to the creation of nineteen extension centers with over 200 courses in history, philosophy, mathematics, English, and vocational subjects. The difficulties of staffing these centers soon brought their number down to only four (Bakersfield, Sacramento, Sonoma, and Watsonville). By 1917, extension and summer session courses were offered in Los Angeles after repeated requests from Regent Dickson and others. Dickson helped lead a powerful political movement for the creation of a southern branch. The result would be a transformation in the organizational structure of the university.

Wheeler, along with the regents, Berkeley faculty, and students, proved extremely reluctant to "divide" the university into two potentially major campuses. However, in 1919, the last year of his presidency, Wheeler assisted in the establishment of the university's Los Angeles campus—a story that we will return to in the next chapter.

The university was evolving into a multicampus system, still dominated by Berkeley, but with teaching and major research programs in seven other locations. In San Francisco, the university operated programs in medicine, law, and art; agriculture was taught at Davis and Riverside; marine biology at San Diego; teacher training and liberal arts at Los Angeles; and astronomy at the Lick Observatory on Mount Hamilton. Various extension centers expanded the geographic reach of the University of California. By the early 1920s, the University of California had emerged as the largest higher education institution in the nation. Over a twenty-year period, the university's enrollment had climbed from 2,500 students to just over 12,000. The number of faculty also grew tremendously. When Wheeler arrived in Berkeley, the university employed 202 faculty. The infusion of state funds and a hiring spree brought the total number of faculty to 699 by 1920. Salaries also increased to help recruit young and established talent largely from Eastern and Midwestern universities—the same pool that Stanford competed for.

Regent John A. Britton remarked on Wheeler's retirement at the age of sixty-five: "He has seen rise from a mere shell a living and moving thing of his own creation, expanding day by day till it had become the peer of any educational institution in the United States." A Stanford loyalist admitted that under Wheeler, "California rather than Stanford became the educational pacemaker of the West."[75] Indeed, in a short two decades, the university was transformed into one of the major universities in the nation.

In 1911 and at the height of Wheeler's reign, Theodore Roosevelt gave a speech on Charter Day—an annual event to commemorate the university's founding. The rapid rise of Berkeley, along with Stanford University in Palo Alto, he stated, marked a new era in America. It was a major step in the evolutionary march to a new and dominant culture in the world. Now the nation "had on the Pacific Coast of America great universities looking across the last of the great oceans, looking across to the ancient civilizations of Asia. When this was accomplished, it was evident that the work of the mere spreading of civilization was through, and that what remained to do was to build deep and high a finer civilization than anything the world had yet seen."[76]

The arrival of the University of California as a major research university occurred in an era of increased demand for access to a higher education. At first, Californians looked to the Berkeley campus as the primary source for public postsecondary education. The aspiration of Wheeler and his faculty, however, was to build an institution focused on advanced training and research, not in supplying wholesale education to the masses—the fate of so many land grant institutions.

CHAPTER 4

The Promise of Mass Higher Education and the Junior College

> The school system is an organ of the body politic, bone of its bone, flesh of its flesh, an organ devised for each and all, from generation to generation. Its structure must therefore be shaped so that, as time goes on, more and more adequate recognition may be given to the educational rights of both the minority and the majority of child-citizens—that, in other words, provision may be made, not only for the length and continuity, but also for the breadth and completeness, of educational opportunities.
>
> —ALEXIS F. LANGE

> In every community where a junior college has been started the work in its inception has had a primary aim: the duplication as nearly as possible of certain courses at the University of California. This has been done with the avowed intention of making it possible for those who, through some series of misfortunes or through the desire of their parents to keep them at home longer, cannot go away to college, to do a part of their college or university education nearer to home.
>
> —A. L. GOULD, PRINCIPAL, SAN DIEGO JUNIOR COLLEGE, 1916

The idea of creating the nation's first network of public junior colleges in California grew from a national discourse over the future role of the American university. The concept of a junior college as a bridge between the high school and higher education emerged when several universities attempted to reform their curricula and build graduate and research programs. In 1883, the University of Michigan was the first to propose a partition of freshmen and sophomores and thus the creation of a "lower division," based on the German plan of the gymnasium.[1] It was an optional program that lasted for less than a decade. Alexis Lange, one of the few students to graduate under the plan, reflected: "[Students] were to select a major subject and two collateral subjects, to pursue with or without the assistance of courses, and to stand on examination covering the whole of our effort." Lange explained that he "survived the examination" and "profited greatly."[2] A similar proposal was made at the University of Minnesota and was tried briefly.

Shortly after becoming the first president of the University of Chicago in 1892, William Rainey Harper offered the most compelling argument for the junior college idea. Concerned with the proper role of the American university, Harper saw the growth in number and quality of the secondary schools as an opportunity to restructure postsecondary education in a manner that would best serve the labor and intellectual needs of the nation. Harper engaged in a debate with other university leaders as to where the line should be drawn between secondary training and a university education. He argued that the first two years of college were more akin to secondary training. The universities might simply admit students at the beginning of their junior year.

Charles Eliot at Harvard thought such a division of collegiate experience, while a legitimate theoretical concept, an impractical one. There were indeed two stages in the development of the student after high school, claimed Eliot: "[T]here is the stage of what we like to call general culture, which is sampling of the different kinds of knowledge." This was termed college-level work. "When [the student] has sampled knowledge," continued Eliot, and when "he has found out what he wants to do in the intellectual career and begins to work in his line, he becomes a university student." However, he insisted that this evolution was not bound by the first two years of training; it varied according to the individual. The university, Eliot noted, had the responsibility to fill the space between the high school and higher learning. "I am a hopeless heretic on this question of a division between college and university."[3]

Harper, however, insisted that there were pedagogical reasons for the division, as well as other advantages that would mark an important evolution in the nation's hectic collage of postsecondary institutions. The nation's numerous, small, financially struggling four-year private colleges, often with poor admissions standards, could be converted into two-year junior colleges. In the midst of the 1890s depression, Harper saw two-year institutions as more economically viable. They would result in a revitalization of America's colleges, he thought, and in the creation of new feeders for the nation's major universities. Speaking before the National Education Association, Harper noted: "The laws of institutional life are very similar to those of individual life, and in the development of institutions we may confidently believe in 'the survival of the fittest.'" Those that changed and were created to meet contemporary needs would survive and prosper.[4]

The transformation of small colleges into two-year junior colleges captured the imaginations of leaders in America's leading research universities but found few other enthusiasts. By 1896, an undaunted Harper divided instruction at the University of Chicago into a "junior college" and a "senior college." He also sought the cooperation of local schools to provide postsecondary courses under the direction of university faculty. This led to the establishment of the nation's first junior college. In 1902, high school officials in nearby Joliet agreed to the formation of a junior college department under a written agreement with the University of Chicago. Graduates at Joliet soon gained advanced standing not only at the University of Chicago but also at other Midwest universities, including the University of Michigan.

In the first years of his presidency at Stanford, David Starr Jordan joined Charles Eliot in his opposition to Harper's effort to "divide" the university. While Harper ventured to create the junior college program in Joliet, Jordan wrote in the *Popular Science Monthly* that "there is no real difference between the American college and the university, and there never will be any." In 1904, before a meeting of the Association of American Universities held in New Haven, Jordan stated: "The university and its schools should stand in the same grounds with the college. Going from the college to the university [should] be as simple as going from the lecture to the library or laboratory. I do not sympathize with those who would isolate the university from the college. The university furnishes the college its inspiration; the college furnishes the university its life."[5]

Two years later, Jordan reassessed his position. He now was enthralled with the idea of the junior college in part because it promised to reduce enrollments and control costs at Stanford. The 1906 earthquake damaged many of the fine buildings at Stanford. The financial cost of rebuilding was tremendous, even for an institution with the largest endowment of any American university. By completely dropping freshman and sophomore instruction, calculated Jordan, Stanford might release less ambitious and productive faculty, saving some $60,000 in annual operating costs.[6]

Jordan's conversion also reflected the influence of Ellwood Cubberley and discussions by Berkeley faculty to establish public junior colleges. Like Harper, Jordan turned to the German model of the gymnasium for inspiration. In direct conflict with his earlier pronouncements, Jordan now wrote:

"[T]he college can never be reorganized and made effective as long as it is all mixed up with the university. The two are telescoped together; the university methods dominate over the college methods, to the injury of the lower students [and the] discipline of the college is entirely destroyed." College teachers, he concluded, "who ought to be devoting themselves to making men out of boys, are striving pitifully to be recognized as investigators." The future of the American university lay in the greater selectivity of students, Jordan stated, and the "devotion exclusively to professional and technical training and research."[7]

According to Jordan, this proposed separation was as necessary for the college as the university. The two, it now appeared to him, were incompatible. The university remained severely hindered by sophomoric interests and activities, the "plug-ugly, senior circus wunder feeds," as one observer at Stanford put it, "the unnatural emphasis upon intercollegiate athletics." The rampant abuse of alcohol, offered liberally by saloon-keepers in Stanford's surrounding community (in contrast to Berkeley, where it was prohibited by state law) added much to Jordan's consternation.[8]

Writing to his mentor Andrew White at Cornell, Jordan conjectured that "the future of the American university is to deal with exceptional students, giving exceptional opportunities to students of superior ability and with industry and earnest purpose."[9] Jane Stanford agreed with Jordan: "I am fully impressed that our future aim must be to exceed other universities in quality, not in numbers."[10]

Though he found opposition among his faculty and his board, in 1907 Jordan proposed the creation of a Stanford-affiliated junior college. In turn, Stanford would raise its admission standards to admit only juniors. To Stanford's trustees, Jordan stated his belief "that the successful university in America must, as in Germany, part company with the college and devote itself exclusively to the three fields of technical, professional, and research instruction." He estimated that under his plan, by 1913 graduation from affiliated junior colleges or other colleges could be required for all students wishing to attend Stanford.

The trustees were perplexed by Jordan's ambitious plan. They were unsure of the financial advantages or if the new junior college would be successful. The university might suddenly become dependent on students from normal schools and smaller, private or denominational colleges. A drop in enrollment might follow. The trustees rejected the proposal. A faculty advisory group did the same. "I may say frankly," Jordan later wrote to the faculty, "that I am disappointed. . . . While a majority of professors are unfavorable or lukewarm, I think it is because they are looking at present conditions only."[11] Jordan would continue to offer versions of his plan for the next several years but to no avail. Though Stanford was not willing to assume the burden of creating its own junior college, Jordan found comfort in the efforts of others in California to create the nation's first network of public junior colleges.

The University Ideal and the Junior College

Professor Alexis Lange shared Jordan's enthusiasm for the junior college. In California, observed Lange, "Dr. Jordan has given general currency to the name junior college."[12] Unlike Jordan, Lange did not look to his own university to create a junior college. The junior college, he argued, should become an extension of the public high school. In this way, access to postsecondary education could be quickly and affordably accomplished.

Like President Wheeler, Lange had traveled to Germany for graduate training. In 1890, he came to the University of California as an assistant professor of English and eight years later became the dean of the College of Letters. In 1905, Lange became the head of the Department of Education at Berkeley and, as such, gained a position on the State Board of Education.

Much like the symmetry between Wheeler and Jordan, Lange was a leader of vigor and influence comparable to Ellwood Cubberley. Lange argued that America's state systems of education needed greater definition and a more-focused understanding of the purposes of the college and the university. In an 1887 speech, he pointed to the interchangeable names Americans gave to their higher education institutions. In Europe, he noted, the term *university* meant something. "How very different in our country," Lange asserted. "[H]ere the name applies to all sorts of things." Of the more than 130 so-called universities, he noted, perhaps only twenty-five deserved the name. What was worse, "there are over 400 institutions that go by the name *college* and this term is often used interchangeably with the term university."[13]

Lange was convinced that California could make sense out of its higher education and elementary and secondary school systems and in so doing lead a national reform movement. The powerful, if colloquial, image of California as a unique social experiment, braced to redefine the American Dream, fed into Lange's insistence that the public junior college was the next, and perhaps final, rational cog in the social engineering machine of education. It was in California, he claimed, that "our civilization will receive its characteristic stamp; it is here that our grave industrial and administrative problems will have to be worked out. And these problems can be solved only by highly trained and efficient intelligence."[14]

In Lange's view and that of Wheeler, the state university needed to articulate the need for the junior college and become its leading advocate. What would benefit the university would also benefit larger society, he surmised. "The difference between the first two years of college and the high school is one of degree only and has never been anything else," stated Lange in one of numerous speeches given before businessmen, teachers, and civic leaders. This fact implied a solution. The University of California faced unprecedented enrollment demand and the difficulty of finding appropriately educated high school graduates for admission. In support of the junior college concept, and in the interest of reducing the "swollen fortune of freshmen and sophomores" within the university, Lange advocated distributing lower division programs into normal schools and what would become six-year high schools. With such a development, he explained, the university's "most vexing problems would pass out of existence."[15]

Such an evolution would do more than free Stanford and the University of California of the first two years of collegiate training. Lange gave equal weight to the value of significantly expanding educational opportunities: The junior college would "popularize" college training. "In the interest of the public welfare," he wrote, "the junior college must do something far more vitally significant than to improve the care and culture of the privileged few and to ameliorate the sad lot of universities."[16]

Before a convention of California high school principals, he explained that the creation of junior colleges must be viewed as an integral part of a general reorganization of California's public education system. "The rise and progress of the junior college," pronounced Lange, would be "a constituent phase of a country-wide movement toward a more adequate educational system, a system that shall bear the institutional image of its American creators and that shall progressively function so as to seduce for the nation the greatest efficiency for the greatest number." The junior college could offer liberal arts programs of sufficient quality so that some, but not all, students might matriculate to Berkeley. The public colleges could provide a substantial expansion of vocational training. The junior college would be a new institution, shaped by the economic needs of modern society, a "normal development within a state school system in the making, which, in turn, is itself being shaped largely by factors and forces that are national and even world-wide in their scope."[17]

Under Lange's leadership and with the support of Wheeler, the University of California proceeded to develop the structural mechanisms that would make the junior college viable and attractive to Californians. Beginning in 1905, the university sought agreement with the state's collection of normal schools and private colleges to admit students to Berkeley in their junior year.[18] Two years later, the university offered a defined lower-division curriculum program that would lead to the nation's first junior college certificate—what would become the Associate of Arts degree. Any student completing the requirements laid out by the university at one of the state's normal schools or at any other institution in California could be admitted to Berkeley at their junior year.

However, to make the junior college a viable part of California's school system, Lange knew that he had to convince lawmakers in Sacramento of its urgent need. Lange gained the support of the State Board of Education for the idea of public junior colleges as extensions of local high schools, at least initially. He also found significant support in the state senate's Committee on Education, of which he was again an ex officio member because of his position at the university. There he found a powerful ally in the committee chair, Anthony Caminetti.

State senator Caminetti saw in the junior college an answer to his own frustrations with California's seemingly incomplete system of public education. A lawyer by training and a Progressive in political persuasion, Caminetti had long advocated increasing educational opportunities in California's rural communities, specifically in Amador County and the small mining town of Jackson, where he was born and raised. Like James Phelan, the reform mayor of San Francisco, Caminetti was a Democrat who, unlike many of his party's faithful, saw government as a tool to shape the economy of his district and obstruct the will of the common enemy, the Southern Pacific.[19] Caminetti was a persevering man whose political career had already undergone several reincarnations.[20]

At the age of twenty-eight, Caminetti entered public service as an assemblyman representing Amador County. Soon after, he became the district's state senator. In 1891 he was elected to Congress, but four years later he experienced his first electoral defeat and lost his bid for re-election. He blamed this bitter loss on the Southern Pacific's support of his opponent. Several years later, he won back his old assembly seat only to then announce his retirement from politics in 1900. After a five-year period out of office, life as a lawyer in the upland town of Jackson no longer suited him. Caminetti once again successfully ran for state senate and served from 1906 to 1914. During his long political career, he battled for the revival of the mining industry in his district (at times in direct conflict with the Sierra Club), worked for local farmers to gain state and federal funding for water reclamation, attempted to pass legislation for state funding for high schools, and finally became the major advocate in the legislature for the junior college.

Caminetti's appointment in 1906 to chair of the Senate Education Committee brought him into direct contact with Lange. The senator supported the apparent need for the university to focus on advanced training and research, but he was most interested in how the junior college might improve educational opportunity in rural districts. Creating high schools, let alone junior colleges, he observed, could not be done through local and county taxation in poor areas of the state. As a boy, Caminetti experienced firsthand the difficulties of gaining an education beyond the common school. The lack of a grammar school in Caminetti's district caused his parents to send him to distant San Francisco for schooling—much to the economic hardship of his family, who ran a small store. Returning to Jackson, he worked for three years in various jobs before gaining employment in a San Francisco law office and enrolling in the University of California. Two years later, he cut short his university education. The costs of living away from his parents' home and the difficulty of holding a job while attending Berkeley proved too great. Caminetti returned to Jackson and joined a local law office. Several years later, he successfully ran for the assembly.[21]

In his first year in Sacramento, Caminetti sponsored legislation to create and fund college preparatory courses in grammar schools. For a short few years before the law was repealed as a violation of the 1879 Constitution, state funds went to some schools for this purpose, creating what were commonly called "Caminetti Schools"—in essence, hybrid grammar and high schools. He also sponsored numerous bills to provide state funding for California's public high schools. In 1898 he offered an amendment to the state constitution for this purpose and in 1899 a proposal for an *ad valorem* tax. Both were defeated. By 1906, when he returned to the state senate, Amador County still had no high school. The senator and his wife, a graduate of one of the state normal schools, sent their daughter to San Francisco for secondary schooling. "It must be remembered," stated Caminetti to a *Sacramento Bee* reporter in defense of one of his bills, "that only a few of our people can send their children to distant places for High School or University instruction, hence the necessity to meet the wants of the majority of people at their home."[22]

George McLane, superintendent of schools in Fresno, noted that California's vast area required creative policymaking. "The element of distance is a most important factor to the individual in planning his educational career. Even though the financial consideration of railroad fare [can] be overcome, a parent will often hesitate to send his child so far from home. . . . Geographical-educational conditions in California are such as to demand that the public school system, in many sections of the state, shall meet the requirements for advanced training above the four-year high school course." To illustrate the problem, McLane explained that if a map of California were placed on the Eastern seaboard, it would cover the whole of Delaware, Maryland, Massachusetts, New Hampshire, New Jersey, Rhode Island, Vermont, and about two-thirds of New York, North Carolina, Pennsylvania, and Virginia. To provide citizens of such a vast state with an opportunity for higher education required the expansion of the high school curriculum and specifically the creation of the California junior college.[23]

During the 1907 session of the legislature and with the support of Professor Lange who aggressively campaigned for it, Caminetti successfully authored Senate Bill 528, which allowed for the establishment of state-supported junior colleges in California.[24] This was the first such legislation in the nation. Kansas and Michigan would follow, but not until 1917. The California bill authorized the "board of trustees of any city, district, union, joint union, or county high school [to] prescribe postgraduate courses of study for the graduates of such high school, or other high schools." Courses of study, continued the bill, "shall approximate the studies prescribed in the first two years of university courses."[25]

The first public junior college in California began operating in Fresno in 1910, under the direction of superintendent McLane, who, in his proposal to the local school board, justified it by the lack of collegiate institutions in the Central Valley. His plan also called for the establishment of a Fresno State Normal School, a proposal that had been repeatedly rejected by Governor Gillett but was finally approved in 1911 by Governor Johnson. Opening with twenty students, the junior college eventually became part of the new normal school. Local school authorities in Fresno proceeded to give a broad interpretation of the junior college mission, embracing vocational curriculum as an equal goal with university preparation. Not only would the institution provide university-equivalent courses for those "young people who cannot

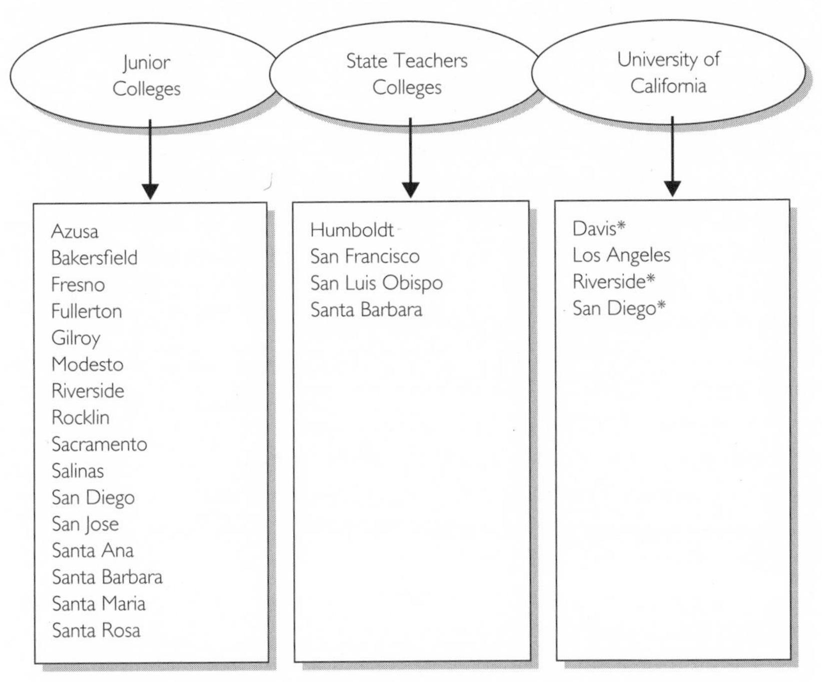

*Research stations at Davis (1905), Riverside (1907), and San Diego (1912) provided applied research and extension courses.

Figure 3. New Campuses and Extension Programs Established Between 1900 and 1920

SOURCES: California statutes; California Postsecondary Education Commission; D. N. Lockard, "Watershed Years: Transformations in the Community Colleges of California, 1945–60"

afford the time and expense of actual university attendance," explained the *California Weekly*, but it would also "provide practical courses in Agriculture, Manual and Domestic Arts, and other technical work."[26] The vocational and technical aspect of the new junior college at Fresno was incorporated into subsequent institutions established in both Santa Barbara and Hollywood in 1911 and in Los Angeles in 1912.[27] (See Figure 3.)

The vocational or "semi-professional" curriculum of the junior colleges helped to fulfill a seemingly insatiable demand in California's economy.[28] Leland Stanford's original vision of his university was, in part, to fill this void. Increasingly, the University of California sought ways to assist industry and agriculture with practical training. As part of the effort to expand the public service elements of the university, President Wheeler appointed Robert J. Leonard as professor of vocational education, and he established a division under his direction to study and foster "practical education" in California's schools. The advent of California's junior colleges, thought Leonard, opened a new and mass-based method to expand access to vocational training.

Leonard and Lange encouraged the State Board of Education to expand vocational programs in the public schools and the junior colleges. As a result, in 1914 the board hired Edwin R. Snyder as California's first commissioner of vocational education. A graduate of Columbia University and former superintendent of schools in Santa Barbara, Snyder felt that the "most distinctive movement in education not only in California but throughout the U.S. is along the line of practical, direct life education." The "revolution," as Snyder described it, was well developed in California by the 1910s, with nearly every high school and junior college providing courses in commercial and domestic arts, manual training and mechanical arts, agriculture, and gardening. However, this instruction in high schools, argued Snyder, "is purely pre-vocational, and while of higher value than much strictly academic instruction to the student who is to become an artisan upon completing his high school course, still falls short of providing the youth with the mental and manual equipment for immediately entering a trade."[29] In his opinion, the appropriate place for vocational training was in the junior college. Alexis Lange agreed.

In the 1916 meeting of the California Teachers Association, Lange stated that "the great mass of high school graduates cannot, will not, should not become University students." Through the two-year program of the junior college, the "[s]tate should provide for a reasonably complete education, whether general or specifically vocational."[30]

The Creation of the Tripartite System

The public junior college provided additional educational opportunities for a new age of economic and population growth in California. Here was an institution that could cater to the varying educational needs of a rapidly expanding society. The junior college was seemingly two institutions wrapped in one: a college that served as a stepping stone to the university and a technical school that trained the laborer for California's emerging industries—a source of schizophrenia that still characterizes the modern day "community college."

But the development of the junior college also opened a controversy that reflected the concerns of John Dewey and others. The invention of the junior college was, when combined with the expansion of the high school, the beginning of a systematic attempt to "track" the life of the student—a determination of ability that, in turn, stigmatized the student's role as laborer or professional. Tracking remains controversial. Samuel Bowles and Herbert Gintis wrote: "Social amelioration, open education, equalization of opportunity, and all the democratic forms could be pursued only insofar as they contributed to—or at least did not contradict—the role of the school in reproducing the class system and extending the capitalist mode of production." Such an innovation as the junior college, they argued, was a "rationalization of the process of reproducing the social classes of modern industrial life."[31]

Certainly, the reforms championed by Jordan, Ellwood Cubberley, and Louis Terman at Stanford and by Wheeler and Lange at Berkeley were intended to buttress economic development. However, the intent was not to sustain a stagnant class system based on social and economic status. Rather, the goal, which reflected their powerful, if at times romantic, sense that California could be a bold democratic experiment, was to reinvent and create a new, inclusive class structure based more fully on merit. In their paternal view, there were tremendous benefits for *all* in this emerging structure of higher education.[32]

The challenge was to expand access and the pool of talent—a difficult task considering California's geographic boundaries and the previous reluctance of Californians to spend tax dollars on anything beyond the elementary school, including the state university. Anthony Caminetti provided perhaps the most compelling argument for expanding educational opportunity. It was not elitist but democratic to use state funds to aid poor districts in supporting the high school and creating new public junior colleges. Formulas for the equalization of educational opportunity (including the introduction of average daily attendance as a budgetary unit for state and local funding), standardized curricula, and professionally trained administrators promised the "efficient" expansion of a system that needed to be built, as Cubberley later reflected, "piece by piece" and under trying circumstances. California was "a young state," in addition to being very large and varied in its physiography. "It began as a mining country and has only recently shifted to the emphasis on agriculture and industrial pursuits [with] a population that has grown rapidly and changed greatly in character." In 1900, California had nine and a half people per square mile. Two decades later, the state held nearly twenty-two people per square mile, with a total population of 3.4 million.

It is clear that the resulting system of education of this era—a system that boasted the promise of a unique mix of broad access with a meritocracy—was hampered by racism, by differential treatment, by the inadequacies of experiments with pedagogy and administration, and the limitations of "scientific management." What was offered, however, was the promise of opportunity at the postsecondary level, of an ability to matriculate through a system where once there was nothing. California's relatively young system of education was to grow and become more inclusive. Progressives offered the answer that, in the main, remains today: a tripartite set of postsecondary institutions with specific and largely separate missions, including a set of normal schools that would become regional liberal arts colleges.

In no other state was the vision of the junior college so vigorously pursued as in California. At the turn of the century, there were no public junior colleges. By 1915, the nation had nineteen, eight of which were in California at Azusa, Bakersfield, Fresno, Fullerton, Rocklin, San Diego, Santa Ana, and Santa Barbara—none of which was a bastion of capitalist power within the state. In the next five years, another six colleges were added under the Caminetti Bill: Gilroy, Riverside, Sacramento, Salinas, Santa Maria, and Santa Rosa.

A 1917 bill passed by the legislature provided for additional and direct state appropriations to junior college operations and allowed local government to form the nation's first junior college districts. The University of California also continued to set standards for the organization and curriculum of the junior colleges. By 1921, California Legislature passed a bill granting additional funds to junior college districts that maintained an affiliation with the state university, including allowing university faculty to review all collegiate courses and the qualifications of the faculty. Four years later, California had thirty-one public junior colleges, enrolling 6,300 students. Of these thirty-one, sixteen were organized as part of local high schools, six as departments within state normal schools, and nine operated as local junior college districts under the 1921 law. Most of these colleges remained small, enrolling as few as ten students in Eureka, for example. A few colleges, such as in Fresno, Sacramento, and Pasadena, enrolled more than 650 students. The surge in state funds for junior colleges resulted in the creation of an average of nearly two new colleges a year—a pace that would last until the 1960s.[33]

Growth in the number of junior colleges and in enrollment was accompanied by two other major changes in California's evolving higher education system. One was the expansion in the number of campuses and programs of the state's network of normal schools—renamed Teachers Colleges in 1921 under a bill developed by Stanford Professor Ellwood Cubberley. At the turn of the century, 1,800 students enrolled in California's five normal schools: Chico, Los Angeles, San Diego, San Francisco, and San Jose. Nearly two decades later, the campus in Los Angeles had been absorbed by the University of California, but three new campuses had been added: a polytechnic at San Luis Obispo and campuses in Fresno and Humboldt. During the Progressive Era, the total enrollment peaked at nearly 5,600 in 1917—the year the United States entered the Great War.

By 1919 enrollment tumbled to nearly 2,000 students. The reasons for the brief decline were multiple. Although the vast majority of students were women ineligible for military service, a significant number sought employment in war-related, high paying jobs. The second was the creation of the nation's first multicampus state university.[34] The acquisition of the State Normal School in Los Angeles by the university marked the beginning of a new framework for American higher education. Instead of simply establishing a new institution in an area of market demand for higher education, the University of California established a branch campus that would eventually rival the flagship campus at Berkeley. Other universities had created affiliated institutions, such as medical schools, but the idea of creating a branch campus, with liberal arts programs and the promise of graduate and research functions, was entirely new. The current organizational structure of the University of California and the high quality of its academic programs relate in large measure to a long history of being a multicampus system. The shift to a multicampus framework also created the beginning of a statewide political base of support for the university. As California's population grew and new metropolitan areas emerged, new campuses of the university could follow.

The geographic expansion of the university to Los Angeles, however, was not the result of a greater vision of the future of state research universities. As noted, the decision came reluctantly on the part of the Board of Regents, its president, and the faculty. They remained locked in the grip of northern California provincialism and were largely concerned with preserving the role of the Berkeley campus within the evolving hierarchy of public higher education. Alexis Lange's vision that the junior colleges would take the "swollen" numbers of freshmen and sophomores away from Berkeley never became a reality. Reflecting California's changing demographics, demand for entrance to the Berkeley campus had not only rapidly increased, but students were arriving from new parts of the state in greater and greater numbers. By the time of the first administration of Hiram Johnson, Los Angeles already sent more freshmen to Berkeley than did the San Francisco metropolitan area.

For all the rhetoric of expanding educational opportunities, university leaders were reluctant to entertain the idea of establishing a new campus in the south, despite growing political pressure. While proclaiming their obligations to all Californians, including the burgeoning metropolis some 500 miles south (which now exceeded San Francisco in population), Wheeler and the regents remained convinced that the university should remain "undivided." Funding was limited, argued ardent Progressive and Regent Chester Rowell. There was only enough to operate the campus at Berkeley. The fact that not one regent had come from southern California until 1913 added to the provincialism. That year, Governor Johnson appointed to the board Lincoln-Republican League cofounder, journalist, and Los Angeles booster Edward A. Dickson.[35]

Despite the opposition of the regents and university alumni, state senator Lee C. Gates of Los Angeles offered a bill in 1911 for a new state-funded "technical school" in or around his district. In a second reiteration of his bill, Gates suggested that the buildings at Pasadena's Throop Polytechnic Institute be acquired. In addition, he proposed that the new state institution should have its own Board of Trustees and use the name "California Institute of Technology," conjuring the image and substance of MIT.

The vagueness of the school's proposed charter raised immediate questions as to its eventual purpose: Was this to become a competing state-funded university? Wheeler thought so and sought the support of the regents and alumni, and from much of the nation's higher education leadership to successfully defeat Gates' bill. Wheeler was aided by strong northern California sympathies in the senate, which was still dominated by northern California farm districts. Former Berkeley professor Elmer Brown, nearing the end of his tenure as the U.S. commissioner of education, voiced his opposition to Gates' bill, noting that the efforts of other states to fund two public universities had failed. Columbia University President Nicholas Murray Butler derided the idea as irresponsible and catering to "local pride and zeal" at the expense of building a truly exceptional university. Jordan came to the aid of Wheeler and the Board of Regents, calling the bill "a blunder which would deepen into a crime."[36]

By 1915, though, the rise of Los Angeles's political power and the advocacy of Regent Dickson changed the position of Wheeler and the board. Aware of another petition to establish a southern branch of the university circulating

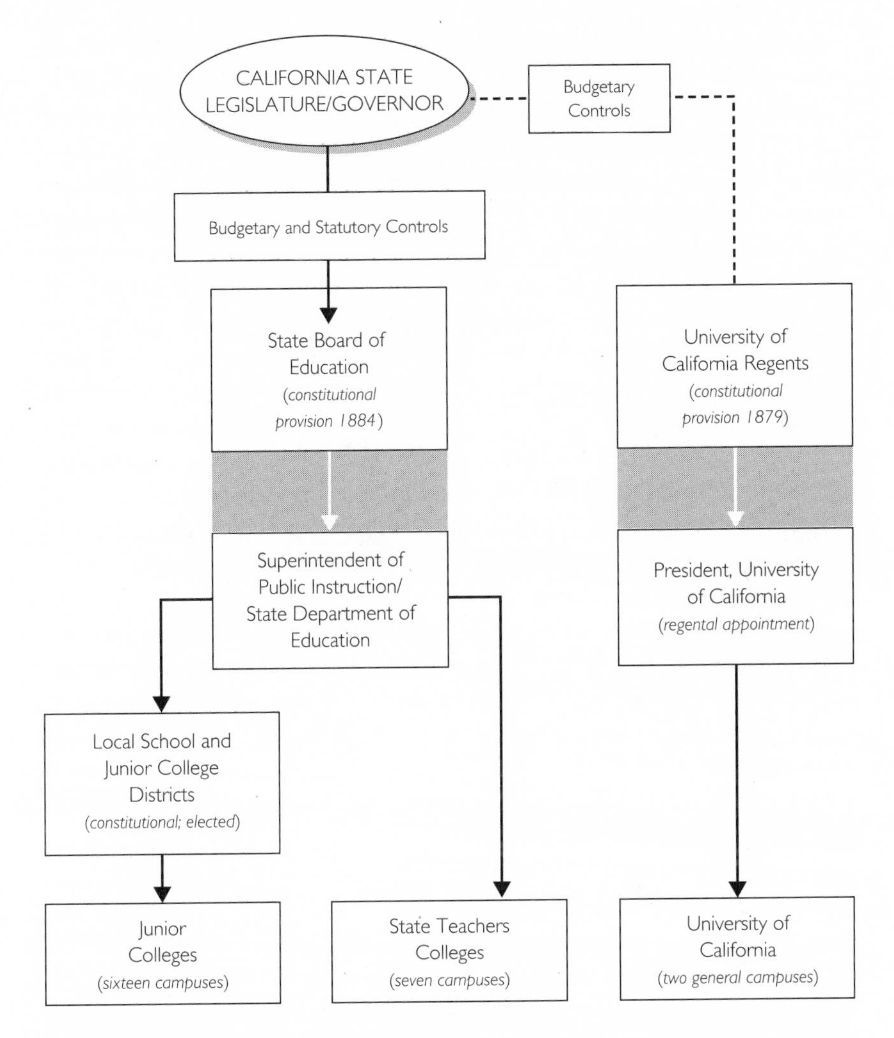

Figure 4. Governance of California's Newly Emerged Public Education System, 1921

SOURCES: California Constitution and statutes; 1921 legislation established the State Department of Education and reorganized the renamed State Teachers Colleges under the State Board of Education

in the legislature—the work of a consortium of local businessmen—the university first established an extension program that operated out of the Union League Building in downtown Los Angeles. This expanded into a yearly summer session that catered to the wartime interests of the local population. However, this was not enough for Dickson and other Los Angeles boosters. Ernest C. Moore, a former faculty member at Berkeley and Yale and president of the Los Angeles State Normal School beginning in 1917, proposed that the regents open a full-year campus. Formulated with the aid of Dickson and local school officials, the proposal suggested that the regents acquire the State Normal School to create a southern campus. The regents finally agreed, though reluctantly. Moore headed up the university's new campus until his retirement in 1936.

For the regents, the annexation of the state college in Los Angeles appeared the lesser of two evils. The threat by Los Angeles hopefuls—Moore, Gates, local Assemblyman Alexander Flemming, and a host of community power brokers—was that, barring just such a move, they would indeed seek state support for a new and competing state-funded university. Dickson bluntly told Wheeler that California should "keep the degree granting power of the State in the hands of a single corporation, provided that corporation is disposed to consider the real and pressing needs of the several parts of the State. If it is not, we intend to do our utmost to develop our work independently."[37]

Indicating their intention to preserve Berkeley as the flagship campus, at first the regents allowed for only a two-year collegiate-level program in Los Angeles. Despite the repeated opposition of Berkeley alumni, by 1922 Moore had succeeded in gaining approval for a four-year program to train teachers. Two years later, the southern branch inaugurated a four-year liberal arts program. By 1927, the southern branch was renamed the University of California at Los Angeles. Not until 1933, again under the stewardship of Moore and with the advocacy of Dickson, did the campus gain the power to grant graduate degrees.

The redefinition of the University of California into a multicampus system facilitated a significant jump in enrollment. In 1900 a total of 2,660 students attended the Berkeley campus and the medical school in San Francisco. By 1920, with the addition of the extension programs at Davis, Riverside, and San Diego and the southern branch in Los Angeles, enrollment climbed to nearly 14,000—a staggering 425 percent increase. The university had become the largest single higher education institution in the nation, enrolling nearly 14,000 students.[38]

The expansion of California's education system, in all it forms, had a powerful impact. California policymakers pushed the ratio of students to the state's total population from 15 percent in 1910 to nearly 22 percent a decade later—and this during a period in which the total population of California grew by over 1 million people. Accurate figures do not exist for the total expenditures for public education until 1912. However, between that year and 1922, and despite severe budget difficulties during the war years, which resulted in the closing of many rural schools, the public investment climbed from $28 million to over $101 million per year. A significant portion of these tax dollars went toward developing the high school. As a result of legislation in 1903, the ban placed on the use of state funds for high schools, a vestige of the 1879 California Constitution, was eliminated. The high school had languished and grew in numbers and in enrollment only in communities that could afford a special local tax to support them. After 1903, high school enrollment became the fastest-growing component in California's system of public education, growing from 17,473 students to a total of 227,270 by 1922. In turn, growth in the number of public high schools provided the avenue, and interest, of local communities to build junior colleges.[39]

As a result of Progressive Era policymaking, California embarked on a financial commitment that few, if any, could comprehend. The result was the beginning of mass higher education. A coherent set of public institutions had emerged, fashioned for a modern, vigorous, and perhaps most importantly, productive Pacific Coast society.

The End of an Era

The historic 1911 session of the California Legislature, Hiram Johnson's subsequent vice presidential run with Theodore Roosevelt on the Bull Moose ticket, and the 1913 legislative session marked the zenith of the Progressive Movement in California. The major goals of the Progressive platform had been achieved. Henceforth, the Progressive Party fell into decline, the victim of an economic downturn, labor strife, and internal disagreements. America's entry into World War I provided another major blow. Californians shifted their energies away from reform. In its place arose a conservative predilection that sought greater economic stability, retrenchment in government, and a focus on prohibition and anti-immigrant politics. The difficulties of a severe postwar recession added to the desire of voters for a less-ambitious state government. Campaigning on this platform, Republican Friend W. Richardson's gubernatorial election in 1923 marked the official end of a fractured and diluted Progressive Movement.

Corresponding shifts occurred in educational policymaking. Richardson's promise of "sweeping retrenchment" in state government initiated a brief but significant decline in state funding for education. There was also a newfound hostility toward the experimental ethos that Progressives had entrenched into the educational bureaucracy, particularly in the area of pedagogy.

Symbolic of the declining Progressive vitality were the retirements of Jordan and Wheeler. In late 1913 Jordan asked the Stanford Board of Trustees to relieve him of his duties as president so that he could devote his full time to the World Peace Foundation, of which he had been made director several years earlier. As articulated in his 1914 book *War's Aftermath,* Jordan extended his notion of bionomics to the tragedy of war: It reversed the process of natural selection, Jordan claimed, by killing the ablest men and leaving the weakest to propagate. The tragedy of war was thus the antithesis of developing a civilized and nurturing society in which education was a pivotal force.[40]

With the key support of alumnus and new trustee Herbert Hoover, a graduate of the class of 1895, the Stanford board acquiesced to Jordan's request, naming Professor John C. Brenner as his replacement. Jordan was named chancellor, though the responsibility of running the university was largely Brenner's. There was, in fact, a great sense of relief for the trustees, and for Hoover in particular, in easing Jordan out of the presidency. They had tired of his constant desire for innovation, and they sought a more traditional leader to build a more traditional private university. A year earlier, Jordan had once again returned to the board, arguing that Stanford should pursue a gradual plan to drop the first two years of "college training." "Sooner or later," he stated, "Stanford must choose whether it will be a college or a university, for it has not funds for both. As a university it can render its highest service to the state and to the nation."[41] The trustees, again, rejected Jordan's admonishments.

Jordan also grew weary of the increased conservatism of the trustees whose role in managing Stanford grew with the death of Jane Stanford in 1905. Even though he remained a tremendously productive scholar, by 1916 and at the age of sixty-five, Jordan had relinquished even the largely meaningless title of chancellor. He would devote his time to his interest in world peace, continue his research, and find other ways to exert his influence on American education. Divorced from the daily operations of Stanford, he remained a nationally renowned philosopher on education, serving for several years as the president of the National Education Association, a post previously held by Charles Eliot. Jordan remained an active voice in education and for the cause of world peace until his death in 1931.

With Jordan's departure, Stanford University came under the influence of a more conservative Ray Lyman Wilbur. Wilbur was a 1896 graduate and dean of Stanford's medical school. He replaced Brenner and would eventually become secretary of the interior under President Hoover. In 1917, despite Jordan's protest, military training was made compulsory. Soon afterward, Stanford's elective system was severely curtailed. By 1920 the trustees abandoned the free tuition policy, which had been a distinctive feature of Stanford. The Jordan era was over.

Wheeler's career followed a similar path. His commanding presence was no longer welcome at the end of his two decades at Berkeley. Wheeler's declining health, persistent pro-German sympathies, and clashes with the faculty resulted in his forced retirement in 1919. The difficulties of the wartime budgets and internal disagreements over creating the southern campus also took a toll on his popularity. A year before his retirement, the Board of Regents created a Council of Deans to take on most of Wheeler's duties. The once politically powerful president and his university became immersed in a period of internal readjustment and confusion.[42]

Berkeley's so-called faculty revolution profoundly reshaped the university's system of internal management. A sometimes fractious faculty united and sought Wheeler's retirement.[43] "The day was past," noted one observer, "when a president (such as Benjamin Ide Wheeler) could hold the reins so tightly that a professor was subject to censure if he appeared on campus without a hat."[44] Though some regents hoped to secure John Dewey as the new president, they settled on Berkeley political science Professor David P. Barrows. Yet the enigmatic and profoundly conservative Barrows did little to advance the two campuses in Berkeley and Los Angeles.

Barrows had difficulty managing the university's internal affairs and simultaneously alienated a significant portion of California's education community by his provincial opposition to a bill that gave greater state financial support to the junior colleges. The bill might prove a drain on university support, he argued, in sharp contrast to Wheeler and Lange's advocacy for the junior college. Barrows' replacement, internationally renowned professor of astronomy and director of the Lick Observatory William W. Campbell, proved a more effective leader. Campbell attempted to mitigate the antagonism between Berkeley and Los Angeles, facilitated the establishment of the

Westwood campus, and successfully courted philanthropic gifts. Not until 1930, however, with the appointment of Robert Gordon Sproul, did the state university gain a voice as effective as Wheeler's among the public and lawmakers of California.[45]

These changes in the political climate and in leadership resulted in a significant ebb in the flow of policymaking in higher education. California progressives had secured both a new framework of institutions and an intractable commitment of public funding to expand access to higher education—these were the seeds of a social and economic contract to the people of California. Major policy innovations would follow. However, in the Progressive Era the vision of a state system of education emerged, based on the ideal of a participatory democracy and intimately tied to a Whig-Republican faith in public institutions as a means to significantly shape California's socioeconomic future.

In the decades that would follow, both the University of California and the public junior college would essentially retain the mission and purpose articulated by California Progressives. The next major change in California's emerging tripartite system of higher education would be the transition of the state's collection of Teachers Colleges into regional liberal arts colleges. But this transition was bitterly opposed by University of California officials. The remarkable level of consensus developed by Progressives regarding the future development of public higher education in California gave way to often bitter debate.

CHAPTER 5

The Depression and a Regional College Movement

> If the history of public education in this country means anything, there must be but one state university, and by this I mean not only one institution which is called the State University, but only one state-supported institution in the field of higher education—there must not be so-called colleges or universities at every crossroads or even at every county seat.
>
> —ROBERT GORDON SPROUL, 1930

The Progressive Movement created new expectations for higher education among the people of California. Colleges and universities needed to be more accessible to the masses and more attuned to societal needs; they needed to supply training and research for regional economic development; and they needed to become a more important tool for social and economic mobility. What had been the ideal of a small Whig-Republican elite now resonated with much of California's growing middle class.

These new expectations heightened the public discourse over the role of postsecondary education. How might California's emerging public system of colleges and universities be equitably distributed over the vast stretches of the state? How should the promise of access to higher education be fulfilled? Clark Kerr observed that in the mind of the public and lawmakers, "the campus [was] no longer on the hill with the aristocracy but in the valley with the people."[1] However, new expectations did not mean that mass higher education, what can be defined as the transformation of postsecondary education from a privilege to a right, had arrived in California. The seeds of this ideal had been articulated, but the organizational and financial obstacles remained great, particularly in a state that nearly doubled in population every two decades.

The early 1920s were a transitional period for education in California, a relatively quiet decade of institution-building and few major policy innovations. The frenzy of Progressive ideas and legislation gave way to conservative politics. Not until the Great Depression did higher education again become the focal point of widespread discussion. The Great Depression shook the foundation of America's capitalist society, resulting in bread lines in California and reduced revenues for state and local governments. Because of this national economic decline, migrants from the dust bowl states and other areas of the country traveled to California. Within the context of Depression America, California fared relatively well. A national romanticism about California and exploitative promises of jobs in the state's agricultural fields attracted people to the West Coast. Between 1930 and 1940, California experienced a 22 percent growth in population. The result was an increased demand for public services in the midst of fiscal retrenchment.

At the outset of the Depression, California's newly elected and conservative governor, James Rolph Jr., a former mayor of San Francisco, looked for ways to drastically reduce state expenditures.[2] Despite dramatic cuts, in 1933 the state still faced what seemed to be a cataclysmic budget deficit of $42 million. By the end of the 1934–35 budget year, the deficit had shrunk to approximately $38 million, due in large part to a new round of budget cuts and new revenue generated by California's adoption of sales and income taxes. Even with an improved economy and the introduction of this new tax structure, however, the state deficit grew to $68 million by 1941.

California's evolving higher education system faced a conundrum that would accompany other periods of economic dislocation: the dichotomy of severe budget reductions and a surge in enrollment demand. The Depression elevated the importance of public institutions. In a crowded labor market, college provided both a refuge and a source of additional training. A new campus was also a source of jobs and a catalyst for local economies. Californians increasingly saw higher education as a source of social stability and eventual economic recovery.

At first, local politicians and business leaders looked to the University of California for new campuses. It quickly became evident that university officials had no intention to add additional campuses beyond Berkeley and Los Angeles. The university's transformation into a multicampus system remained a source of consternation within the academy. Berkeley and Los Angeles faculty and administrators engaged in their own internal and provincial battle for resources, academic programs, and prestige. The very innovation of a multicampus state university was a new experiment. At times, it would tear at the university but eventually would result in modes of management and operation, including greater faculty control of academic quality. This, in turn, would help to create one of the most productive and prestigious university systems in the world.

In 1930, however, the newly appointed university president, Robert Gordon Sproul, stated that the university should resist further geographic expansion. He argued that the state should focus its scarce resources on new junior colleges and expansion of the Berkeley and Los Angeles campuses, but no more.

The demand for access to higher education appeared insatiable. The search of Californians for "educational opportunities beyond the high school level," remarked Stanford Professor William M. Proctor, "is apparently a demand which will not be denied."[3] In spite of the steadfast opposition of the state university, local boosters and their representatives in Sacramento wanted to expand the scope and purpose of California's collection of State Teachers Colleges. The consensus built in earlier decades gave way to competing visions over the future of California higher education.

From Normal Schools to State Teachers Colleges

The slow evolution of California's teacher training institutions into liberal arts colleges followed a pattern found in a number of other states. As recounted previously, the first State Normal School was established in San Francisco in 1862. Nine years later, the campus was moved to San Jose. By the turn of the century, California had four additional schools operating in Chico, Los Angeles, San Diego, and San Francisco, with instructional programs at the secondary level that prepared teachers for careers in elementary schools. Each of these schools had their own governing board, which included professional educators, several members of the State Board of Education, and the state superintendent of schools. Twenty-one years later, the Los Angeles campus was part of the state university, but new campuses were added at Fresno, Humboldt, and San Luis Obispo.

Progressive reformers sought to expand the number of State Normal Schools to improve the quality and content of teacher training in California. In 1900, the first in a series of blue-ribbon committees was established to study the future development of public education. The Education Commission of 1900 brought together professional educators such as David Starr Jordan, Elwood Cubberley, Benjamin Ide Wheeler, Elmer E. Brown, and a retired but still vigorous John Swett with business and community leaders of the state. Harris Weinstock, a prosperous Sacramento merchant, chaired the commission, which also included newly appointed Regent Phoebe Hearst and San Francisco Mayor James Phelan. Among the commission's recommendations were the proposed creation of "unified school districts" and a proposal to provide much-needed direct funding for California's high schools. The commission also urged the establishment of a new polytechnic in San Luis Obispo to train teachers in vocational subjects, including agriculture and engineering.[4] By 1903, each of these proposals was enacted by the California Legislature.

The Education Commission was the result of a proposal by Berkeley Professor of Pedagogy Elmer Brown at a meeting of the California Teachers Association (CTA) the previous year. The CTA dated back to 1875 and had roots in a series of state-funded "teachers institutes." It was not a union, as it would later become, but it was an association intended to aid teachers, promote free public schools, and improve teacher training. Brown, and later his successor Alexis Lange, Cubberley, the state superintendent of public instruction, and the president of the University of California attended their yearly meetings.[5] In 1900, Brown was developing the new department of education at Berkeley and establishing teacher training programs for secondary schools. He had a formal role in both the CTA and as an appointed member of the State Board of Education—the result of CTA lobbying efforts which also created Brown's faculty position at Berkeley. Brown modeled his proposal for the Education Commission on the Good Government associations that were springing up throughout the nation in urban centers, creating a forum for business leaders and professionals to discuss major policy issues.

The commission inaugurated many of the Progressive Era reforms in California's schools and helped form a core community of influential leaders of the movement. Another important proposal of the commission was to elevate teacher training to a postsecondary experience. The slow development of the high school had earlier prevented such a step. After 1900, a more formal program for the teacher credential was established. Students could enter a four-year program to teach at the elementary school level after the completion of eight years of grammar school. High school graduates could attain a teaching credential after a two-year program. A number of the normal schools also operated local junior colleges, as noted previously, but their programs were viewed as separate from teacher training. By 1921, all students entering what were renamed the State Teachers Colleges would need a high school diploma, and by 1930 the teaching credential would become a four-year program oriented around a liberal arts curriculum.[6]

A significant proposal presented by the Education Commission of 1900, however, was not immediately embraced by lawmakers. The training of teachers remained decentralized within four separate institutions. The commission urged the consolidation of the State Normal Schools under the State Board of Education—a recommendation heavily influenced by Ellwood Cubberley. Placing these institutions under one board, argued the commission, would improve their management, help institute higher admissions standards, and promote uniform curricular reforms. This was accomplished in 1921 when a bill sponsored by State Senator Herbert Jones and coauthored by Cubberley placed the eight Normal School campuses under the board. Cubberley outlined this reorganization in a special report commissioned by Jones and Will C. Wood, superintendent of public instruction.[7] Under the bill, direct supervision then fell to the state superintendent of schools and a newly created State Department of Education.[8] The Jones bill renamed the Normal Schools the California State Teachers Colleges.

By the 1930s, many local communities wanted these institutions to grow and mature into regional institutions that could eventually offer graduate and professional degrees. Districts with no state teachers college looked to either convert their junior college into a four-year institution or to establish a new regional college that would have a function beyond teacher training.

Communities with the desire to expand educational opportunities realized that gaining a new public college was, theoretically, relatively simple: Their local representative could sponsor a bill. The juxtaposition of declining state and local revenues did not dissuade a number of lawmakers from offering legislation. The fiscal decline, in fact, increased the interest of communities in gaining the surge of state funds required to establish a regional college. Yet district-specific legislation failed to gain the support of the California Legislature, at least initially.

Within existing State Teachers Colleges, however, the demand for liberal arts and vocational programs led to an internal change, which in many ways was more profound. At Fresno, San Diego, and San Jose, college presidents and faculties proceeded to establish academic programs that had little to do with teacher training. They were responding to local labor needs and the desires of Californians for postsecondary education. Such programs had the tacit approval of the State Board of Education and the state superintendent. There was, however, no official approval of such programs by the board and no sanction under California law. Under statute, the State Teachers Colleges remained strictly teacher-training institutions. University of California officials protested loudly and mounted a significant campaign to halt the expansion of the curricula and academic programs of these regional colleges.

The Vested Interests of the State University

In the fall of 1930, President Sproul gave his inaugural address in Memorial Stadium on the Berkeley campus. The large crowd included the governor, regents, students, and faculty. In a booming voice signature of Sproul's decisive leadership style, the new president announced that the potential proliferation of these relatively new regional four-year colleges was an immediate threat to the mission and funding of the state's land grant university. While supporting the ideals of a mass-based system of higher education, Sproul thought such a system acceptable only if the university remained the preeminent state institution. This meant that it should be the sole public provider of liberal arts, professional, and graduate degrees. The university, he stated, needed protection from direct competition by other state-funded institutions. The establishment and growth of the junior colleges, argued Sproul, would provide the open door to all high school graduates and allow for the state university to focus on "higher learning" suitable for a select population. The junior colleges afforded California the opportunity to avoid the open-door approach of most other land grant institutions. It also avoided the need, thought Sproul, for regional four-year colleges.

In a direct appeal to lawmakers, Sproul forcefully exclaimed that "the counsel of experts is positive and unanimous against dividing the effort of the state." Citing a study directed by Henry Pritchett during his presidency of the Carnegie Foundation for the Advancement of Teaching, Sproul stated that where two competitive segments had been created, it was demoralizing alike to the institutions themselves: "Duplicate courses, low standards of admission, and log-rolling with the legislature are the natural outcome."[9]

Sproul's words demonstrate the sense of alarm within the university. The restrictive views of the president and the university regents were hardened by state budget cuts.[10] Between 1931 and 1939, state appropriations to the university declined by 26 percent. At the same time, enrollment grew by 25 percent. In response to the budget quandary facing the university, Sproul created a faculty Committee on Educational Policy specifically to develop recommendations. With the assistance of faculty, Vice President Monroe

Deutsch, and the regents, Sproul substantially reduced budgets and expenditures in the areas of general administration, maintenance, and plant operations. Capital projects were delayed unless, as with the Crocker Radiation Laboratory built in 1937, they were gifts or federally funded. Sproul also imposed a salary cut of around 12 percent, replicating a cut imposed on all state employees. Course sections were reduced, and a general hiring freeze was established.

University officials decided to expand enrollment during the Great Depression due in large part to public pressure for greater access to higher education. The university could hardly raise its admission standards, which were already restricted to approximately the top 15 percent of California high school graduates, to reduce future enrollment increases, simultaneously insisting that there was no need to open new regional institutions. In the midst of continued population growth, enrollment increased from around 21,000 students in 1932 to 29,000 in 1939. The cumulative impact was that the student-to-faculty ratio inflated from around 17 to 1, to 21 to 1.

To cope with these enrollment increases, Sproul sought the expansion of academic programs outside of Berkeley. Despite the protests of many influential Berkeley faculty and alumni, Sproul supported enrollment growth at Los Angeles. With a near-doubling of enrollment at the southern campus during the 1930s and charges of siphoning resources from Berkeley, the president of the Berkeley alumni in Fresno angrily proposed casting the Los Angeles campus out of the university system and revoking direct state financial support. "Our great state university is losing its entity," he wrote. Not only had the southern campus taken funds that belonged to Berkeley, he complained, but it had stolen Berkeley's name (i.e., the University of California), the campus' colors, tradition and reputation. "Now that [Los Angeles] has become a big college on its own, it should stand on its own feet."[11]

For different reasons, the thought of secession appealed to a number of influential southern Californians and faculty at Los Angeles, though not without public funding. The Berkeley campus hogged all the resources, so it was reasoned, and used its political power among the regents and the university hierarchy to squelch the growth of academic programs and even the hiring and promotion of faculty at Los Angeles. Indeed, at the time of the absorption of the Los Angeles Normal School into the southern branch, the campus acquired a status similar to the various research stations. There was no significant internal administrative structure, and the campus was subject to the rules and regulations set by the Berkeley faculty (who controlled the approval of academic programs) and the university president.

Fulfilling the need for greater higher educational opportunities among a growing metropolitan population and supported by a corresponding expansion of Los Angeles' political power, the southern branch was soon arguing for equal status with the Berkeley campus. The process was slow and irritating. In response, Assemblyman Charles W. Dempster proposed a bill that would incorporate the Los Angeles campus, the Scripps Institute, the Riverside experiment station, the Kellogg Institute of Animal Husbandry, and the State Teachers College in Santa Barbara as a new and independent public university system.[12]

Sproul effectively rebutted Dempster's proposal. "Let no small mind direct you along the paths of suspicion, distrust and jealousy," he insisted before a crowd of students in Los Angeles. As a symbol of his role as president of the entire university system, Sproul announced that he would take up residence for a year in Los Angeles.

In 1937, the president also called on the regents to make a formal proclamation of the multicampus "One University" concept. This university system, the first of its kind, was governed by the regents and centrally administered by the president, with shared processes in areas such as admissions and academic personnel and with shared values, including a commitment to serve the evolving research and public service needs of an expansive state. The difficulties of creating a multicampus state university, noted Sproul, were many and were uncharted territory in the world of higher education. Yet he promised that it would, in the long run, prove a great strength. Not only would it sustain the University of California as the largest single public university in the nation, but it would also prevent the emergence of a rival public university. The regents approved Sproul's "One University" statement, effectively ending any serious consideration of reorganizing the university.[13]

Sproul graduated from the University of California in 1913 with a bachelor's degree in civil engineering. The son of an accountant for the Southern Pacific, Sproul worked in various jobs to support himself through high school and his years at Berkeley. In the midst of his college career, he became a good friend of classmate and fellow Republican Earl Warren, who remained a lifelong friend. After graduation, Sproul worked as cashier for the city of Oakland before taking a series of positions within the university. In 1920 he became university comptroller—a job that required frequent interaction with lawmakers in state government. Five years later, he became one of two vice presidents under President William W. Campbell.

While not a trained academic, the thirty-nine-year-old Sproul appealed to the regents because of his expertise in the university's financial affairs and his experience as the university lobbyist in Sacramento. There was also a sense among the regents that recent and major concessions to the faculty in the academic management of the university justified the hiring of a proven manager. Remarked university historian Verne Stadtman: "Two of Sproul's most remarkable personal characteristics, a reverberating voice and a phenomenal memory, helped him win the awe of legislators." His quick recall of facts and statistics, continued Stadtman, "made him virtually unchallengeable in debate."[14]

The selection of Sproul also related to his strong community service record, giving him credibility with many important enclaves of California society. Throughout the 1920s, "Robert Sproul was on call for an endless variety of local civic enterprises," explained his longtime assistant, George A. Pettitt, "heading up community chest drives, Christmas Seal sales, American Legion funds; serving as the director and executive committee member of the Berkeley Chamber of Commerce, organizing and raising funds for Boy Scout troops, for natural resource conservation projects, etc."[15] Sproul was also an active member of the Republican Party, the dominant political party in California and the political affiliation of the majority of regents at the time.

In 1930, Sproul commenced a presidency that would last a remarkable twenty-eight years. In his view and that of the regents, the university faced a dire situation. It was confronted with Depression Era budget cuts and with a growing criticism that the university was elitist and hostile to the idea of regional colleges and a general expansion of educational access. This was, of course, not a new charge, but its fervency had grown. The attacks came from an increasingly broad cross section of Californians: from local community leaders, school teachers, legislators from areas outside San Francisco and Los Angeles, and farmers. All were concerned that the university was not doing enough to meet their needs. A blue-ribbon commission established by the legislature in 1930 to "investigate the educational, geographic, financial, and organizational problems of public education in the state" criticized the university over its control of high school curriculum.[16] Since the 1880s, the university had the authority to accredit the state's public high schools, creating a standard college preparatory curriculum at the secondary level. During the Progressive Era, high school accreditation was linked to state funding. This level of power over the public schools was increasingly a source of irritation for local communities. University officials and faculty, complained the Commission for the Study of Educational Problems, were neglectful of the role of the high school for non–college bound students. The accreditation process seemed to be geared almost entirely toward preparing students for university admissions. "It is unjust to handicap the many students who must prepare for their life work outside of the colleges," argued the commission.[17]

Though the university had proven a major contributor to California agriculture, there remained suspicion towards a university that was seemingly controlled by industrial and professional interests on the Board of Regents. This suspicion was compounded by the collapse of the economy. The university's apparent failings were given added publicity by the observations of other critics such as Upton Sinclair. California's most notable radical repeatedly attacked the university's affiliation with the "Republican Party machinery." According to Sinclair, the university was not the source of enlightenment and egalitarian ideals its supporters espoused. Rather, he called it the "University of the Black Hand." He claimed that the corrupt economic powers of the state, including heir to the Crocker fortune William H. Crocker (a member of the regents from 1908 to 1937), yellow journalism king William Randolph Hearst, and others, controlled the regents. Further, he claimed that this new aristocracy of capitalists used the institution to meet their narrow self-interests—to train professionals and create research for their oppressive and imperialist corporations. "Across the bay from San Francisco," wrote Sinclair in an exposé of American universities, "high up above the city of Berkeley, stands the University of California, a medieval fortress from which the intellectual life of the state is dominated; and here we also find one of the grand dukes of the plutocracy in charge—Mr. William H. Crocker."[18]

The past presidents of the university, charged Sinclair, were in general an evil lot. Benjamin Ide Wheeler had been an autocrat and personal friend of Kaiser Wilhelm. David P. Barrows hired students as scabs to break picket lines and was the "Dean of Imperialism . . . stumping the state of California proclaiming the destiny of the Stars and Stripes to float from the North Pole to the South." Sinclair's allegations of a capitalist conspiracy controlling the university would become one feature of his 1933 near-successful run for governor on the Democratic ticket.[19] California's establishment, including the university, shuddered at the thought of a Governor Sinclair.

In the eyes of university supporters, including a growing contingent of alumni who graced the halls of government and formed a major component of the business community, such attacks were simply the result of an era of economic collapse and political confusion. It was a time of New Deal experiments, of Sinclair's radicalism to end poverty in California, of the Townsend Plan, and of the weekly *The National Ham and Eggs*. According to university loyalist George Pettitt, "The atmosphere in the state was anything but intellectual." In the eyes of much of the public, he lamented, the university had become an obstruction for the popular panacea of education. "California's troubles of the moment, many thought, could be overcome only by breaking the alleged monopoly of the University of California." He further explained: "When the world is sick and wise men are unsure of the cure, self-appointed doctors spring up like mushrooms after the first rain, and the people are ready to listen to any proposal for change."[20]

In his commanding voice, Sproul gave the opening salvo in his defense of the university at his inaugural speech. To the university's critics in Sacramento and in communities that desired new state-funded institutions, he made no apologies. "The University of California occupies a proud but not altogether comfortable position. It suffers the inevitable penalty of leadership: envy, denial, and detraction. On the one hand it is criticized for being too aristocratic, on the other, for being too democratic." There were those who maintained that the university set its standards on an unreasonable plane, he continued: ". . . that it should admit every high school graduate. That, we believe, would be a fatal blow to the quality of education by the state and to the careers and happiness of great numbers of young men and women. Surely it is not aristocratic to insist that students who come to us should have such training as will make their success in the university probable."[21]

Sproul was convinced that the university should oppose any and all proposals coming from legislators, particularly in light of the decline in state revenues and cuts in funds to education. To capitulate on one proposal, thought the new president, opened the floodgates for other new campus proposals—if not now, then as soon as California's economy recovered. Sproul and the Board of Regents pursued a concerted lobbying effort.

Perhaps more than any president in the university's history, Sproul knew how to garner the support of the regents, faculty, students, and, more importantly, the growing number of alumni. Whether in opposition to bills for regional colleges or proposed cuts in the university's state budget, Sproul helped to develop a powerful network of alumni associations that he affectionately dubbed the "Old Blues." The dramatic expansion of the university during the Progressive Era and into the 1920s brought a corresponding increase of graduates who took leadership positions in California society. By 1930, the state's land grant institution had conferred more than 40,000 degrees, and its alumni included four governors of California, several U.S. senators and congressmen, and an expanding number of state legislators. During the budget battles in 1933 and following Sproul's plea for assistance in a radio broadcast, one legislator received over 200 telegrams in just two days denouncing a plan to include an additional cut to the university's budget.[22]

A Political Battle in Sacramento

During the legislative session in 1930, state senator J. M. Inman, representing Sacramento, offered the first of many bills to expand a junior college into a four-year program. His intent was to convert Sacramento Junior College into an entirely new state-funded institution with its own local board. Hence, it would be completely independent of the existing local school board, the State Board of Education, and the University of California. This new breed, argued the senator, would have a stronger link with the local community than a new state college campus. The proposal was largely the result of Inman's frustration with the State Board of Education and the university. Both were inattentive to the need for regional colleges. The board of education, argued Inman, appeared interested almost exclusively in the problems of local schools, while the university was clearly opposed to any effort to develop public four-year institutions. As the governing board of a constitutionally anointed public trust, the Board of Regents could seemingly do whatever they wanted, without regard to public needs; here was an increasing source of frustration for many lawmakers.

Inman's bill proposed allocating $300,000 of public money for the purpose of converting the junior college to a regional college serving the Sacramento area. Shortly after introducing his bill, legislators in Fresno, Redding, and San Diego authored similar bills to convert their local junior colleges. Sproul quickly stated the university's opposition. "[T]he American creed that every human being shall have the opportunity for his utmost development, and his chance to do the best he can, does not mean that everyone must be admitted to a college or university within a few blocks of his home and kept there, whatever his talents or his industry."[23] In a speech before alumni, he asked for their help. "Let us see that [the university] meets the cultural demands of all, or at any rate of all the important groups in the commonwealth. But let us not exchange it for a collection of little replicas, responding to purely local needs."[24] Playing politics with education, warned Sproul, would result in "the certainty of mediocrity and the possibility of bankruptcy."[25]

Sproul sought an alliance with the newly formed Federation of Junior Colleges (which became the California Junior College Association in 1947) to oppose regional college bills. The university and the junior colleges had shared interests. Both groups opposed the regional college movement because it would pose competition for limited public funds and because it threatened to erode their respective missions. Unrestrained growth in the regional college movement, explained Federation President Albert C. Olney, might erode support for the very notion of the public junior college. At the urging of Sproul, a resolution was passed by the federation stating "that under present conditions, this body does not favor the upward extension of two-year junior colleges to four-year institutions."[26]

Inman's bill for Sacramento and those for colleges in Fresno, Redding, and San Diego were subsequently defeated but were a harbinger of things to come. The unremitting position of Sproul and the Board of Regents against the regional college movement angered many Californians. Several lawmakers returned with new bills at the next legislative session and complained that the university was concerned with only its own welfare and specifically with its claim on state funds. Discouraged by the failure of Inman's bill, the editor of the *Sacramento Bee* charged: "[A]n increasing number of citizens are convinced the time has arrived to put a check on the omnivorous appetite of the Berkeley institution for more and more millions, as well as to curb its apparent determination to throttle any educational progress in the state outside the reach of its own domineering influence."[27]

University officials were also confronted with a deteriorating relationship with the State Board of Education and Superintendent of Public Instruction Vierling Kersey. The superintendent had attended the normal school in Los Angeles before gaining a graduate degree from the University of Southern California. Kersey had strong Republican credentials: he was a Mason, a member of the Optimist Club, and a vocal critic of Communism, a requirement for membership in the power elite.

Kersey was also one among many Californians who felt that the Great Depression required new approaches to social problems. Roosevelt's New Deal, he asserted, despite the protests of conservatives, was "not the end of our social order." He denounced "excessive profits" and articulated a vision in the tradition of Hiram Johnson and other California reformers. "We can accomplish by social reconstruction that recognition of social and economic equality for which many nations have found it necessary to undergo internal strife and revolution," he stated in *California Schools* in 1934. Reiterating the mantra of the educational community, he argued that public education was a key ingredient for creating equality and economic prosperity.[28] Kersey also occasionally taught courses at Berkeley and often noted his support for the state university's teaching, research, and public service missions.

However, Sproul's extensive campaign to oppose the development of regional colleges alienated Kersey, who saw a real need for the geographic expansion of higher education institutions. As an elected official, he also recognized that the surge in proposed legislation, such as Inman's bill, reflected a growing populist movement rooted in middle-class values.

Frustrated with the attacks being leveled at the university, Sproul searched for a method to reposition the university within the public debate and halt the growth of the State Teachers Colleges. In November 1930, Sproul met with Governor Rolph and offered a proposal. He suggested the state pursue a study on coordinating California's education system, to be conducted by an independent agency, specifically the Carnegie Foundation for the Advancement of Teaching. Such a study, he argued, would avoid the wrangling of California's internal politics and would take a hard look at the potential costs and difficulties of financing public higher education. "The problems of higher education in the State of California," explained university Vice President Monroe Deutsch, "should not be settled on a political basis—should not be decided by log-rolling and striving for votes—but should be settled on an educational basis." Sproul pointed to the policymaking successes of the 1926 Carnegie Foundation study on public education system in Texas and other states. These studies were completed under Foundation President Henry S. Pritchett, a former professor at Stanford and later president of MIT.[29]

Sproul was so confident that an independent review of California's postsecondary system would benefit the university that before his meeting with Rolph he sent Deutsch to New York to talk with the Carnegie Foundation's new president, Henry Suzzallo. Suzzallo was a highly respected expert on education, a native Californian, a compatriot of Ellwood Cubberley (they went to graduate school together at Teachers College), and the former president of the University of Washington. He also held an honorary degree from Berkeley.[30] Suzzallo was part of a relatively new breed of scholars, including Cubberley, who traveled throughout the nation, studying state governance and administration of public schools and universities and offering often-influential counsel. Sproul saw in the Carnegie Foundation and Suzzallo a friendly ally, with the prestige and independence to confirm the university's position on regional college expansion.

At Rolph's urging, in early 1931 the legislature subsequently passed a bill sanctioning the study. The state provided $25,000 for the governor "to engage the services of an educational research foundation of nation-wide scope [to] make a survey of the present system, plan of organization, and conduct of public education higher than high school grade in the State of California."[31] By October 1931, Suzzallo and members of his staff had held a series of conferences with representatives from the University of California, the State Teachers Colleges, the various junior college associations, the State Board of Education, and Superintendent Kersey. They also met with legislators and concerned citizens.

Well into this process, Suzzallo realized that he needed some mechanism for assimilating all the information surfacing in these fact-finding meetings. There were too few staff members for the task. There also was a desire to make the study more than just a Carnegie report, with its strong ties to the university. As a result, an independent "commission of seven [members] unconnected with the State of California" was established to make final recommendations to the Carnegie Foundation and, in turn, to the governor. Samuel P. Capen, chancellor at the University of Buffalo, was named chair.[32]

Sproul expressed high hopes for Capen's efforts. The commission, he explained, could provide a "calm study which alone is likely to lead to sound and purposeful planning. The legislative attack [has been] beaten off, chiefly by the reflective judgment of those representing districts with no self-interest in the contest." He assured a group of alumni that the university would "not go before the Commission with selfish motives . . . or with malice toward any other institution. . . . We are seeking honestly to interpret and intelligently serve the highest interests of education in the State of California."[33] However, the recommendations made in the final report and the subsequent reaction demonstrate the complexity of promoting a coordinated state system of higher education. The Suzzallo Report offered California the first attempt to assess the proper organization of California's post–Progressive Era system, but it also generated severe and broad political opposition.

The Suzzallo Report and Growing Distrust

In June of 1932, the report of the Commission of Seven, known to contemporaries as the Suzzallo Report despite Capen's central role, was delivered to the governor. "The present situation of education in California," noted the report, "involves problems of policy and organization, particularly with relation to the operations of higher education." Such problems, it was explained, were not particular to California. They were, however, more pronounced because of the "social aspirations and favorable economic conditions within the State [which] permitted certain experiments and developments not possible in equal measure in other commonwealths."[34]

With the arrival of the Depression and economic constraints, the commission noted a number of criticisms leveled by the general public at higher education. These included "the amount of money spent upon education, the distribution of educational expenditures, the cost of education in comparison with other State expenditures . . . an alleged restriction on educational opportunity through arbitrary standards, a lack of development of occupational education, and wide variations in the relation of cost to facilities available." According to the commission, three areas needed to be addressed to improve California's higher education system: a unification of control over all or major segments of the system, a more equitable distribution of the financial burden for operating the system, and a clear policy of articulation between secondary and postsecondary institutions. "The Commission is of the opinion," noted the 1932 report, "that much of the confusion in the educational situation . . . has arisen from a lack of necessary machinery to make effective the coordination of the several phases of higher education."[35] The proposed solution was a significant restructuring of governance.

Samuel P. Capen noted that they had considered the advantages of creating a single board for all higher education in California, including the junior colleges, but found that solution "impractical." The size and projected growth of the different segments of higher education made centralized control simply too complicated and cumbersome. In cooperation with the U.S. Office of Education, the Carnegie Foundation was in the midst of a survey of state systems of higher education that noted a general trend toward a single board for all higher education—what were termed "superboards." The survey described state governments as having "a tendency to develop institutions, public and private, with little regard to possible unneeded overlapping of their curricula. . . . Because no suitable state agency has been available to examine the educational questions involved in the chartering of new universities or colleges, institutions have multiplied largely as a result of persistence and interest of their founders, or the zeal of local communities, rather than because higher education in a state or region would be better served by their establishment."[36] Efforts at such unification of a state system, noted Capen, were usually ill conceived, often resorting to "legal or coercive measures [to] bring about formal rather than genuine unity of effort."[37]

In California, Capen insisted, the junior colleges should remain under the

State Board of Education. However, the Board of Regents, he noted, should be given the job of governing the State Teachers Colleges. This would allow the State Board of Education to focus on the public education system extending to the junior colleges, while granting the regents the authority to manage what they termed the state's new "university system."[38]

Finally, the commission argued for the creation of a State Council for Educational Planning and Coordination. The proposed council would be an agency for the coordination and planning of all aspects of the state's public education system. Recognizing the status of the university as a public trust, Capen explained that the council would need to be an advisory body, essentially a forum for key members of the education community to discuss issues and form a consensus. The council would then provide guidance to the legislature and the governor regarding new programs and new campuses. No action should be taken by the legislature, argued the Suzzallo Report, without the review of this new council. Figure 5 provides an illustration of the report's major recommendations related to governance.

The Suzzallo Report clearly favored the stand taken by Sproul and the regents. If adopted by the legislature, the State Teachers Colleges would be thrown under the yoke of university officials. The report also stated that California's regional college movement was more the result of the ambitions of individual legislators than of a rational need of the state's citizens. Any future attempt to create new four-year institutions, noted the report, should consider the net effect on "the State school system as a whole before it considers the political issues arising from the claims of certain localities or regions." The existing network of junior colleges offered "ample opportunities" for postsecondary education. Access beyond the sophomore level should be "open only to persons of unusual ability and interest." Those who complained about being denied access to the university simply did not meet the standards of admission. "State-provided facilities," concluded Capen, "for the fulfillment of [their] aspirations in reality end with the junior college. . . . The attempt to get the Legislature to establish such senior colleges apart from university management and under the control of separate State Boards, operating locally, is something to which the State ought never to consent."[39]

The Suzzallo Report represented California's most comprehensive review of public education since the Education Commission of 1900. Many of its recommendations were logical. Yet, the report failed to take into account the dynamics of California's political culture and the robust desire for expanded access to higher education. In no small part, it represented the viewpoint of the

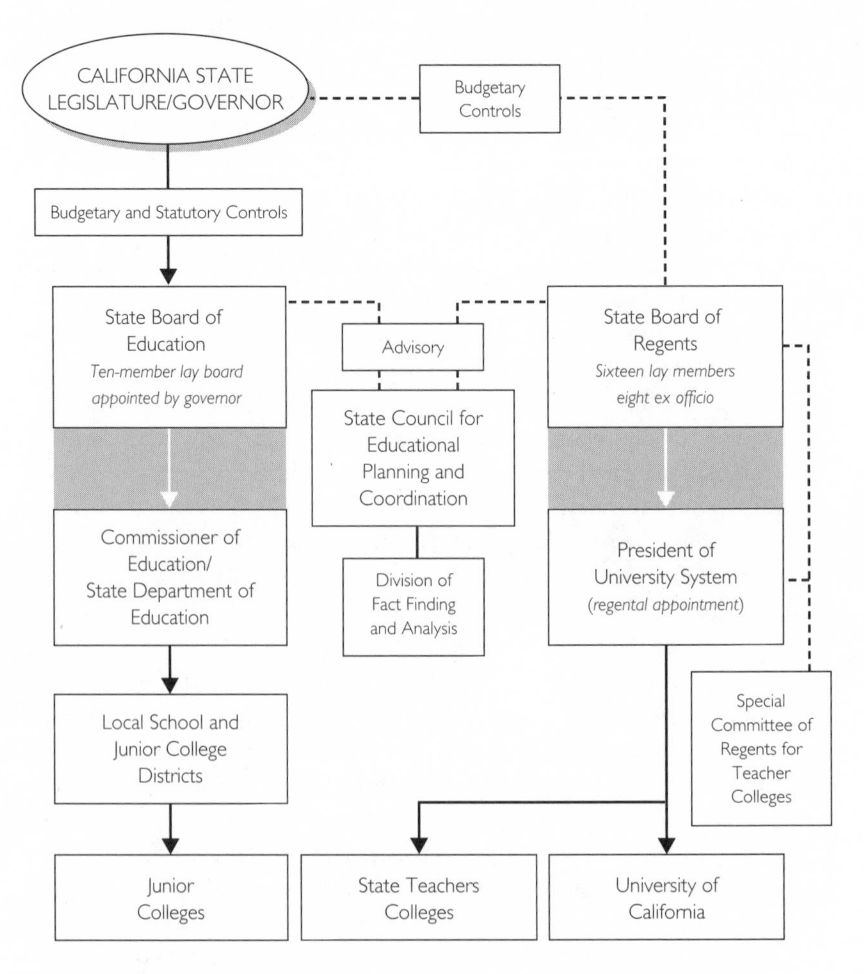

Figure 5. 1932 Suzzallo Report's Proposed Governance of California Public Higher Education

SOURCE: *State Higher Education in California*, report of the Carnegie Foundation for the Advancement of Teaching (known as the Suzzallo Report), June 24, 1932

elite members of America's research universities and private colleges. Consequently, it failed to attract the support of legislators and met the stiff opposition of most of California's educational community not associated with the university. Superintendent Kersey and State Board of Education members immediately criticized the report.[40] Not only did the report advocate a substantial reduction in the purview of the superintendent and the board of education, it also recommended the appointment of the State Superintendent of Instruction (since 1850, a constitutionally elected officer), the election of the State Board of Education, and the eradication of tenure for elementary and secondary school teachers. To cut costs, the report suggested the closing of the Polytechnic Institute at San Luis Obispo, which "might be properly utilized for junior college work." In the same spirit of fiscal restraint, the report called for the closing of the State Nautical School in Tiburon, which had been established only four years earlier.[41]

Many within California's education community were angry at what they considered the blatant attempt of university officials to control state educational policy. George C. Jensen, assistant superintendent of secondary schools in Sacramento, complained of both the lack of sufficient analysis of the operations of the university and the widespread feeling that the Suzzallo Report reeked of conspiracy between Sproul and the Carnegie Foundation. "Probably never before in the history of American public universities have such far reaching powers been recommended for any university" observed Jensen. In his view, the 1879 revision of the state constitution had created an autonomous state university, with virtually no public accountability, that consistently opposed the desires of the people of California. What good, Jensen asked, would then come from the proposed Council of Educational Planning and Coordination?[42] The constitutional status of the regents would allow the university to ignore the call of local communities and lawmakers for regional colleges.

Frank W. Thomas, president of Fresno State College, questioned the interest and ability of the regents to properly administer teacher education programs within the colleges. He also pointed to an "almost complete absence of any objective evaluation or scientific appraisal" regarding academic programs at the university and at the state colleges. "We had expected that such an evaluation would be made as to our relative costs, the character of our curricula, and the quality of our product." Jensen thought the lack of data, particularly for the university, was purposeful. It was an effort to thwart scrutiny of university programs and administration. "The educational problems of California will be solved not by advice but by information," Jensen complained. "This is what we have never been able to get about certain of our educational institutions."[43]

The California Teachers Association joined the vigorous opposition to the report and launched a campaign to prevent its objectionable recommendations from becoming law. Similarly, many legislators were unhappy with the report's opposition to establishing new regional colleges.

Although the report clearly had the interests of the university in mind, it did not represent a rubber stamp of Sproul's agenda. University of California officials saw problems with certain aspects of the report. Though initially attracted to the consolidation proposal, after further study Sproul and Deutsch were now wary of the proposed absorption of the State Teachers Colleges by the regents. A report by the faculty Committee on Educational Policy explained to Sproul that they were "convinced that there is necessity for some form of unified planning with respect to the development of higher education throughout the state. . . . Under divided control the teachers colleges are changing functions, and invading the university's sphere." Yet they also warned that any regents' association with the State Teachers Colleges would confuse the university's mission.[44] Most importantly, Sproul had questions concerning the political process that would be required for the Board of Regents to achieve a hostile takeover of the state colleges. It would entail changes in the state constitution. The provision for the State Board of Education would need to be amended to remove the State Teachers Colleges. Similarly, the provision for the Board of Regents would need to be amended to include these regional colleges. The amendment process, Sproul realized, was fraught with hazards. It might open the university to a Pandora's box of reforms. Legislators might add other changes intended to make the university more accountable to lawmakers and possibly end its status as a public trust.[45] This was a real threat in light of public criticism of the university and the heightened animosity caused by the Suzzallo Report. In Sproul's view, the disadvantages were too great. Yet he also professed that the "logic of this proposal is so great that I am convinced it will not be possible permanently to resist it."[46]

Sproul and the regents gave their public support for most of the recommendations of the report, in particular for the idea of a coordinating council.[47] In an effort to counter the vocal opposition of Kersey and the State Board of Education, Vice President Deutsch cautioned California's educational community not to "lightly dismiss the report as a whole or such recommendations as do not meet preconceived views. . . . Let us seek to use their report as the basis for agreement among the forces of higher education in California, to the end that we have an educational rather than a political program for higher education."[48]

In his lobbying effort in Sacramento, Sproul simply ignored the proposal that the regents absorb the State Teachers Colleges. Instead, he spent most of his time pushing for the proposed State Council of Educational Planning and Coordination (otherwise known as the Coordinating Council). Sproul hoped that this might become the mechanism to halt the legislative push for regional institutions. In late 1933, the legislature obliged Sproul and established the Coordinating Council. It would be the first in a series of efforts to create both formal and informal mechanisms to coordinate California's tripartite system of higher education.

The Coordinating Council's Failure

The first meeting of the Coordinating Council came in late 1933. The council was composed of nine members. With the exception of President Sproul and State Superintendent Kersey, all were laypeople serving for only one-year appointments. Members included longtime Regent Chester H. Rowell (the newspaper editor and Progressive Era political leader), board of education member Allen T. Archer, Annie Florence Brown (president of the Oakland Forum), and Mrs. William J. Hayes (president of the California Congress of Parents and Teachers). The three other members served as a link to California's business community and included Charles Albert Adams (an attorney from San Francisco), Will C. Wood (vice president of the Bank of America), and H. Gurney Newlin (an attorney from Los Angeles).

From the start, the council was an ineffective agency.[49] At the first meeting, the council agreed to launch a study on the proper functions of each segment of California's public education system—but it was a study that would never be completed. The promise of the council quickly dissipated, destroyed by the adversarial relationship between the university and the board of education.[50] "The State Council," lamented one observer, "was comparable to a League of Nations in the education field, holding insufficient authority to be effective, and weakened by lack of support from those who looked on it as a potential threat to their own sovereignty and private plans."[51]

At a minimum, Sproul hoped to use the council as a means to oppose the expansion of academic programs at the State Teachers Colleges. A year before the establishment of the council, despite the university's opposition, Superintendent Kersey and the State Board of Education approved new degrees in liberal arts fields at the state colleges in Fresno, San Diego, and San Jose. The pretext was the creation of new and specialized teacher training programs. The reality was a concerted effort to expand beyond this singular purpose. University officials complained bitterly that any such change required legislative action. Sproul gained formal agreement from the Coordinating Council to place a moratorium on any further changes in the programs of the State Teachers Colleges until the completion of their study. In clear defiance, the State Board of Education proceeded to sanction additional liberal arts degrees at Chico, San Francisco, and Santa Barbara.[52]

Two years later, again with university opposition and without any recommendations from the council, a bill sponsored by eleven assemblymen, including Earl Desmond of Sacramento and Alfred Robertson of Santa Barbara, changed the state charter of the State Teachers Colleges. "Under the new law," explained a State Department of Education official, "the primary function of the colleges remains as before, the training of teachers, but the courses previously offered may now be regrouped into liberal arts curricula which do not include professional courses in education."[53] A student was no longer required, as a condition of admission, to declare her intention to become a teacher. The 1935 act also changed the legal name of the colleges to reflect their new status as something more than teacher-training institutions—they were now the State Colleges of California.[54] By World War II, nearly half of all the students in the colleges were majoring in subjects other than education.[55]

The State College Act was a huge defeat for Sproul and the university. The state colleges, complained university officials, were taking an extremely liberal interpretation of the new legislation. New degree programs had nothing to do with teacher training, stated Sproul; they should be discontinued. Sproul lamented before the regents that "forty-seven public institutions are today at work in the field of higher education, of which the University of California was at one time the exclusive tenant, and each of these institutions is pursuing its own program with little or no regard for what others are doing!" The university, he continued, had "urged always, and we urge again, that there be educational planning rather than political log-rolling. The question before us is: what positive, constructive program of higher education can be launched that will discourage the dissipation of the state's resources for higher education, check the retardation of the work of existing institutions, and forestall mediocrity in advanced study and research."[56]

The 1935 bill encouraged legislators and community leaders to renew their efforts at establishing new state college campuses. Financial constraints aided the university's fight against such legislation. Despite numerous bills, between 1935 and 1947, only one additional college was created: a new campus of the State Polytechnic College located in San Dimas (later moved to Pomona). The establishment of San Dimas was actually prompted by a private donation for both land and buildings. Yet the political momentum clearly favored the development of regional colleges.

After 1935, university officials began to contemplate more radical methods for halting the regional college movement. The Coordinating Council was an obvious failure. Sproul revisited with the regents the idea of absorbing the state colleges.[57] They found support in a 1936 study of state government sanctioned by Governor Frank Merriam and completed with the assistance of the Chicago firm of Griffenhagen and Associates. It argued that the regents should acquire the state colleges, citing limited state revenues, efficiency of operation, and long-term planning as the reasons for "unifying" higher education.[58] Sproul began to seriously study how unification might be accomplished. There seemed to be two possibilities: merging all the state colleges under the regents in one swift and single action, or annexing campuses one or two at a time. Under this latter scenario, the university might avoid the potential widespread opposition of the public and the wrath of the State Board of Education and the colleges. More importantly it might mitigate the expected calls for revisiting the constitutional status of the university.

The eventual and arduous decision by Sproul and the regents to pursue this strategy, however, was reactive and not preemptive.[59]

A Plan to Absorb Santa Barbara

Shortly after the passage of the 1935 State College Act, Santa Barbara Assemblyman Alfred "Bobby" Robertson assisted the local county chamber of commerce in formulating a proposal for the transfer of Santa Barbara's state college to the university. Several years later, Robertson encouraged Santa Barbara *News-Press* Publisher Thomas Storke and Berkeley alumna Pearl Chase to build political support for such a transition. At the time, the university had only two other general campuses, Berkeley and Los Angeles, and an undergraduate program in agricultural sciences in the farming community of Davis. It also managed a number of research stations, notably in La Jolla and Riverside. The idea of converting a state college into a university campus was not a new idea. As noted previously, in 1919 the Los Angeles campus made the same transition, a move bitterly protested by Berkeley faculty, students, and alumni. The local Santa Barbara advocates knew that similar opposition would confront their proposal, but they argued that such a campus would help meet a growing demand for liberal arts and graduate training. Perhaps most important to community leaders such as Storke, it promised to buttress the long-term economic development of the region, infusing state funds into the community and enhancing the attractiveness of Santa Barbara as a place to live.

By 1939, Assemblyman Robertson coauthored a bill with local state senator Clarence Ward that would transfer both Santa Barbara and Fresno State Colleges to the university. The addition of Fresno was intended to gain wider support in the legislature. Robertson argued for both the central coast and valley locations to provide a geographic balance of university institutions, with Berkeley to the north and Los Angeles to the south. "We felt that the cultural background of Santa Barbara" in particular, explained Storke, "offered a real asset to the university family; that no community in the west had so much to give."[60] Shortly after the bill was introduced and under the advice of Sproul, wary regents told the Assembly Committee on Finance that they did not officially oppose the bill. In the privacy of their meetings, however, the majority of regents remained very much opposed to the absorption of any state college. Sproul suggested that they not flatly reject Ward and Robertson's bill. He worried about the political repercussions of yet another refusal by the university to a geographical expansion of its liberal arts programs. Still unsure whether the university should aggressively pursue unification, Sproul instead argued that the Santa Barbara bill might be a way to reinvigorate the Coordinating Council. The proposal could be given to the council, presumably to reject it. Sproul proposed that the council complete "a comprehensive survey of the entire higher educational system of the State, with particular reference to the need and possibility of the establishment of a branch of the University of California in Santa Barbara County or some central point in the San Joaquin Valley."[61] He personally asked legislators to await the results of the study before passing any legislation on higher education, including Robertson and Ward's bill. The legislature agreed.

Sproul's renewed interest in the Coordinating Council also related to the election of Walter Dexter as the new state superintendent of public instruction. Dexter desired a more amiable relationship with the university than his predecessor, Vierling Kersey. Sproul also knew that the board of education was opposed to the Santa Barbara bill. The board wanted to retain the state colleges under their aegis. For different reasons, there might be enough common ground to complete the proposed study.

Dexter was a Harvard graduate and former president of Whittier College. He had also served as the executive secretary to two Depression Era governors, Republicans James Rolph and Frank Merriam. Though he shared

Sproul's desire to make the Coordinating Council an effective body, he found little support among board of education members or state college presidents. And although he recognized the need for improved coordination, he would emerge as a strong advocate for expanding the colleges to the disappointment of Sproul.

A 1939 publication by the State Department of Education reflected Dexter's sympathies. It professed that "democratization" of higher education in California was, and should be, the primary objective of the state college system—not simply training teachers. "The state colleges more than any other group of institutions in California, face the task of interpreting democracy to society. They are young, they are vigorous, . . . they are closer to the people, they are more sensitive to social needs, they are less hampered by educational stereotypes." Clearly, with the university's elite air and apparent unwillingness to dramatically expand enrollment, a great need lay unfulfilled. "More than any other group of institutions," explained the report, the state colleges "are qualified to assume leadership in the development of the spirit of democracy on this west coast of America."[62]

Despite Dexter's plea for greater cooperation, the State Board of Education refused to participate in Sproul's study. In early 1941, the Coordinating Council could only produce a weak statement lamenting the lack of a "mutually agreed upon philosophy or joint program" for higher education between the regents and the board of education. The council would never meet again, although it remained in statute as the official body for coordination of higher education in California until 1960.[63]

The last gasp of the council caused Assemblyman Robertson and Senator Ward to return with another version of their bill in the spring of 1941. The exigencies of the war, however, preoccupied the legislature. The bill died in committee. It was assumed that Robertson and Ward would return with another bill at the 1943 session of the legislature. The failure of the council did not stop Sproul and Dexter from trying to develop an agreement on the future of higher education in California. Both wanted to halt the entrepreneurial efforts of individual lawmakers and their communities to create new state colleges or to convert junior colleges into four-year institutions. In anticipation of another Robertson and Ward bill, Sproul and Dexter agreed to create an ad hoc committee, drawn from California's higher education community, that would submit a report to both of them. This time, the goal was not to pass judgment on expansion or individual bills but to seek a logical and comprehensive form of governance over the public tripartite system. Sproul and Dexter would then make a recommendation to both the regents and the State Board of Education.

In August of 1941, Sproul and Dexter asked Ernest J. Jaqua, president of Scripps College, to chair the committee. Eight months later, the so-called Jaqua Report was issued.[64] Two alternative organizational structures of higher education were thought feasible. First was a proposed Board of Overseers, which would have the responsibility for all public education, from kindergarten to the University of California. This new, single board would essentially be an expanded Board of Regents. Hence, it would result in the abolishment of the State Board of Education. There would be two appointed executive officers, presumably Sproul and Dexter. One would be the chancellor of higher education and the other the superintendent in charge of all schools up to the junior colleges.

A second alternative was a reconstitution of the Board of Regents into a Board of Higher Education with authority over the state colleges and the university. Membership on the board would be slightly altered. The State Board of Education and the superintendent would then focus on governing the schools and the junior colleges.[65] This proposal captured the interest of both Sproul and Dexter and essentially reiterated the recommendations of the 1932 Suzzallo Report. Sproul and Dexter then attempted to gain support for the proposal among the faculty and administrators within the university and the state colleges. Eventually they planned to present the proposal, including a draft constitutional amendment, to their respective boards.[66]

While Sproul was a domineering and powerful leader, he was also acutely aware of the need to consult with faculty and garner the support of alumni. The proposal offered by Jaqua would require a significant lobbying campaign, as well as the united muscle of the university's contingent of Old Blues. Much to Sproul's frustration, both the Berkeley and Los Angeles alumni associations rejected the proposal. For the same reason that alumni had opposed the annexation of the Los Angeles campus in 1919, they wanted no change that might threaten the growth of their campuses.

A report by faculty opposed it for similar reasons but noted the need for some form of unification. The senate's recommendation was to revisit the concept of absorbing one or two state colleges at a time. To maintain the distinction of the Berkeley and Los Angeles campuses, these new campuses should remain "regional colleges." The senate leadership declared that they should not become "little Universities of California."[67] A subsequent academic senate report noted that if Santa Barbara was acquired, it might provide the university with the opportunity to "experiment with a genuine liberal arts college, a college where it might cultivate young minds not bent on specialization, and develop graduates with a capacity for sound and intelligent social judgment."[68]

A subcommittee of the regents considered the Jaqua Report and the comments of the alumni association and faculty. Sensing that the State Board of Education and the regents would likely reject the report's recommendation, the subcommittee chair, Chester Rowell, offered a variant on the Jaqua Report's proposals. The existing membership of the regents would remain. There would be no need for a constitutional amendment; the state colleges could simply be placed under the regents by statutory law, argued Rowell. The university's constitutional charge might simply remain unchanged. Statutory action would thus shelter the university from the dangers of the constitutional amendment process. Though there were still serious disadvantages to this merger and potentially severe opposition in the legislature, noted Rowell, the logic of it might bring success in Sacramento. While cognizant of the difficulties of this approach, Rowell concluded, the possibility of unrestrained growth of the state colleges without regent control constituted a "greater evil."[69]

With the support of Rowell, Sproul thought he was on the verge of an answer to the regional college movement. However, in early 1943, the regents rejected Rowell's proposal in a vote of 8 to 3. Only Sproul, Rowell, and Fred M. Jordan voted for it.[70] James K. Moffitt, the new chair of the Board of Regents, explained that the university should avoid major changes in its authority. Aware that a new bill was circulating in Sacramento to transfer Santa Barbara to the university, Moffitt stated that the regents must refuse any effort that would result in "the amalgamation of the state colleges as part of the university system." In a letter to Governor Earl Warren, citing their power as an autonomous member of California state government, the regents expressed their "opposition to making any of the State colleges a part of the University of California."[71] Shortly after, the State Board of Education also rejected the Jaqua committee's proposal.

Sproul and Rowell knew that the political pressure to accept Santa Barbara would be substantial. Despite the objections of the regents and the State Board of Education, the Santa Barbara bill passed through the assembly and the senate in May 1943. The act proposed the transfer of the college and all property to the regents. At the request of Clarence Phelps, the president at Santa Barbara State College, Robertson provided an amendment to protect the jobs of current college faculty. Most did not have Ph.D.'s, and Phelps worried that university officials might fire most of his faculty. In recognition of the university's constitutional autonomy, the regents had two years to reject or acquiesce to the offer.

Governor Warren, a university alumnus and a close friend of both Thomas Storke and Sproul, asked the university president for his advice on the bill: should he sign it? Considering the regents' reluctance, Sproul felt he could not take an overt and definitive position. Yet, he indicated to Warren that it could be the beginning of a long-term acquisition of the state colleges by the university. "If there is to be a unification of higher education in California," he explained to the governor, "it will apparently come, as in the case of the Los Angeles Normal School, by the transfer of single institutions to the university." This, he noted, had its advantages. "[T]he problems involved can be attacked one at a time and above all, the constitutional position of the university and the status of the Regents can be protected."[72]

Warren signed the bill in June 1943. The regents began a consultation process with university faculty to consider what their response should be.[73] Several regents as well as Sproul met with Assemblyman Robertson and President Phelps. As explained by Phelps, not everyone in Santa Barbara was keen on the idea of becoming a part of the University of California. Phelps was a protégé of Ellwood Cubberley. Since 1918 he had guided the Santa Barbara campus, building programs that met regional needs. In his view, the campus had the promise of maturing into a strong liberal arts institution as a state college—the hope of the majority of state college presidents for their institutions. Merging with the university would significantly hinder this ideal. It would suddenly regulate the college as a second-class citizen under the Berkeley-dominated university and seemingly disdainful regents.[74] Local community support for the merger among business leaders such as Storke, however, simply overshadowed the concerns of Phelps and most of the faculty.

Sproul now pleaded that the regents accept Santa Barbara. The new university campus, he explained, should remain primarily an undergraduate and liberal arts institution. Santa Barbara, Sproul announced, could become the "Williams College of the West." Under this scheme, the campus would retain most of its existing academic and vocational programs and faculty. Santa Barbara would not become a "little university." Sproul saw in Santa Barbara a model for future transfers. Limiting the campus to that of an undergraduate college might ease the fear of state college faculty of wholesale dismissals. It might also mollify the Berkeley and Los Angeles faculty and alumni concerned with the diversion of state funds. If the strategy of slowly acquiring state colleges was to prove successful, assurances of a peaceful transition were imperative.[75]

Sproul told the regents they should not acquire the campus "unless [you] regard it as the first step in a policy of unification of higher education." Four months after the passage of the bill, in October 1943, the regents voted 14 to 4 to accept Santa Barbara as a undergraduate college within the university system. On March 24, 1944, the regents adopted a plan to take over the Santa Barbara campus by July and in August took title to all land and facilities.

The university had embarked on an ambitious merger program.[76] However, there remained substantial opposition from the State Board of Education. The board's attorney claimed that the acquisition was unconstitutional. The state college presidents reiterated the charge that the university was attempting to limit access to higher education. Though the legislature pushed Santa Barbara into the fold, most state college faculty and their surrounding communities saw the university as the new-age "octopus." Sproul had stated again and again that there was no immediate need for additional full-service university campuses besides Berkeley and Los Angeles.

The State Board of Education sought a political remedy to Sproul's bid. Shortly after the regents took title to the land in August, the board's attorney filed a lawsuit demanding that they "return Santa Barbara to the possession, jurisdiction and control" of the board. The regents responded with a letter stating that they had no intention of returning the campus. Hindered by a lack of support within Warren's administration, nothing came of the board's threatened suit.[77] The State Board of Education, however, found another way to thwart the unification plan and possibly regain Santa Barbara. The board formulated an initiative-based constitutional amendment. Backed by the California Teachers Association, the State Board of Education and new State Superintendent of Public Instruction Roy Simpson coauthored Proposition 3. The amendment, among other things, forbade any future legislative transfer of a state college to the regents. In the November 1946 general election, the proposition passed easily.[78]

Proposition 3 promptly ended Sproul's takeover bid. Yet, it seems unlikely that Sproul's plan would have worked. The demand for regional college programs and campuses was rapidly building in California, buttressed by a postwar expansion in the state's population and economy. University officials and many others simply did not fully comprehend the growing demand for higher education.

Regent Phoebe Apperson Hearst and UC President Benjamin Ide Wheeler, 1918. Hearst and Wheeler worked closely together to build the University of California into one of the nation's premier research universities. Hearst provided a huge infusion of money for capital costs, scholarships for women, and support for research. This affiliation was matched perhaps only by the joint efforts of Jane Stanford and David Starr Jordan at Stanford. In 1918 and for the last time, Hearst and Wheeler led the Charter Day procession at the Greek Theater—one of many buildings constructed with funding from the Hearst Foundation. Wheeler was in ill health and coming to the end of his presidency. Hearst would die one year later. *University of California Archives, Bancroft Library, University of California–Berkeley.*

Berkeley campus, 1913 and 1916. In 1913, the University of California campus in Berkeley was in the midst of a major building boom. South and North Halls (the two original buildings on the Berkeley site) had been completed in 1872 (both facing a quad and overlooking the bay). Durant Hall (1911), California Hall (1905), University Library (1911), and Agricultural Hall (1912) had just been completed. Sather Gate was under construction, and university officials were about to break ground for the campus's signature, the Campanile, or Sather Tower. It was completed three years later (photograph below). *University of California Archives, Bancroft Library, University of California–Berkeley; California History Room, California State Library, Sacramento, California.*

Benjamin Wheeler and Theodore Roosevelt, 1911. In March 1911, President Roosevelt attended the University of California's Charter Day event on the Berkeley campus at the invitation of his longtime friend, university president Benjamin Ide Wheeler. The annual Charter Day ceremony marked an important political event and drew students, alumni, university regents, and influential politicians. *University of California Archives, Bancroft Library, University of California–Berkeley.*

Mission High School in San Francisco, 1914. Mission High School was one of a growing number of high schools with new buildings and expanding enrollment. Until the Progressive Era, California had lagged behind much of the nation in development of public high schools. In 1890 there were only thirty high schools (public and private) in the entire state. However, by 1902 a constitutional amendment was passed qualifying public high schools for state funding as part of a number of Progressive Era reform measures. Combined with substantial population growth in California, the result was a rapid expansion of public high schools with enrollment jumping from approximately 17,500 in 1903 to 227,000 in 1920. *California History Room, California State Library, Sacramento, California.*

Sacramento Junior College, 1927. Sacramento Junior College was housed in a wing of Sacramento High School when it opened in 1916, one of three such colleges established that year under the 1907 Caminetti Bill passed by the California State Legislature. This was the first legislation in the nation that provided for the establishment of public junior colleges. With rapidly growing enrollment, the college moved to a new site in 1927 (shown here). By the end of the 1930s, California would boast thirty-nine junior colleges. Sacramento Junior College would be the focus of a number of bills in the legislature intended to convert it into a four-year liberal arts institution, independent of the University of California and the state college system. *California History Room, California State Library, Sacramento, California.*

Boalt Law School class of 1922. The class of 1922 included five women out of approximately fifty students. The University of California was one of the most progressive universities, public or private, in the admission of women. In 1900, women constituted nearly half of all undergraduate enrollment at the university. Yet the academic majors women pursued were largely, although not exclusively, in fields such as English, teacher education, and home economics—reflecting social norms of a university dominated by male faculty. Graduate education was even more segregated. Women persistently made gains, though, and the University of California has been one of the nation's leading producers of graduate and professional degrees among women and minority populations. *University of California Archives, Bancroft Library, University of California–Berkeley.*

CHAPTER 6

Postwar Planning and Higher Education

> Anyone who has had the opportunity to travel and consult with Western business, finance, and industrial leaders during the past year has been heartened by the atmosphere of expectancy, faith and determination which is everywhere encountered. The efficient manner in which California government is marshaling resources, manpower and initiative in support of the war effort leads to the perfectly logical conclusion that we possess the essentials for tremendous peace time development.
>
> —GOVERNOR EARL WARREN, 1944

World War II initiated an economic boom of dramatic proportions in California and another wave of migration to the state.[1] Similar to the gold rush some ninety years earlier, war mobilization brought unprecedented economic activity to California and ushered in new types of postindustrial and technology-based industries. The fear of a Japanese invasion on the mainland and California's logistical advantages in supplying troops in the Pacific resulted in new military installations and a huge flow of federal dollars. Factories suddenly materialized in major cities, supplying military hardware for the war effort, creating jobs, and, in turn, attracting a new wave of migrants. Of all the moneys spent by the federal government during the war years, California secured the largest share—about one-tenth of all federal outlays.[2]

Reflecting on this surge of federal money and economic activity, Governor Earl Warren observed, "our Western pattern of employment has not only been changed in line with the National Conversion, but our change has been three or four times as drastic as the national average." For instance, noted Warren, while total civilian employment in the nation was up 14 percent since 1941, California's was up 40 percent; manufacturing employment rose 51 percent in the nation, while California's was up a spectacular 201 percent; and total civilian population had dropped 3 percent throughout the country, but in California it had risen 15 percent.[3] Largely due to the federal government's massive wartime investment, noted one legislative report, the state's "economic structure has been transformed from a raw material producing economy, where agriculture, mining, forestry, and fisheries were the predominate basic industries, to one in which the value added by manufacture far exceeds the combined total value of all the products of these extractive industries."[4]

Quite suddenly, the war made California a major economic power in the nation and, indeed, in the world. The traditional and resource-based sources of state income in agriculture, mining, and timber remained, but they were no longer dominant. Defense industries in particular brought staggering war and postwar economic growth, particularly in southern California. Previously a center for citrus and moviemaking, Los Angeles suddenly found itself with over $10 billion worth of war production grants in 1944.[5]

Earl Warren began his first term as governor in 1943 with a relatively sophisticated understanding of the complexities of California's wartime socioeconomic transition. His optimism for California's long-term economic future was tempered by the realization that the state's economic boom, nurtured by war-related industries and the projections of massive population increases, posed serious challenges to state government. California's economy might experience a significant decline in the demand for its products. Unless a portion of those affected industries shifted their production capabilities to consumer goods, the result would be either overproduction or dormant factories.

A letter from Mervyn Rathborne, the CIO secretary in California, to the governor outlined what Warren and his staff already knew. "The tremendous wartime industrial expansion of California," noted Rathborne, "has amounted to an industrial revolution." The impact of the war upon the economy, he explained, compressed fifty to sixty years of normal economic evolution into four hectic years. "Unless remedies are found soon, this wartime economic stimulation will lead to the biggest postwar hangover in the nation. That is, our wartime production of more than $11 billion [in manufacturing goods] a year can slide downhill to the prewar figure of only $3 billion." Unless aggressive steps were taken, concluded Rathborne, unemployment would skyrocket.[6]

Warren's own administration projected that the end of the war could mean 500,000 California workers being discharged in the shipbuilding and aircraft industries. Another 100,000 could be laid off in other defense-related industries. Many of the 700,000 men and women inducted into the armed services from California would soon be looking for jobs in California's crowded labor market as well. It was anticipated that many of the out-of-state members of the armed forces would plan to stay in California. As a result, California would claim the largest World War II veteran population, some 2 million according to one estimate. Under these assumptions, by 1946 California could experience unemployment of approximately 15 to 20 percent and as high as 30 percent among factory workers.[7]

Warren was also concerned that the problems of a capitalistic society exposed by the Depression remained. While the New Deal generated heated debate regarding the proper role of the federal government, there was no longer any doubt that government needed to create policy to ease economic downturns. Warren shed the moderate Republican demeanor that gained him the governorship in 1943 to argue for an activist government. Only this time, argued Warren and other governors, the primary agency for change would be the states. While fighting raged in Europe and the Pacific and the outcome remained very much in doubt, committees on postwar planning were formed by the National Planning Association, the Committee for Economic Development, the National Manufacturers Association, and the Council of State Governments. Warren was active in this last group, serving on its Interstate Committee on Postwar Reconstruction and Development and assisting in the writing of the council's influential report, *Wartime and Postwar Problems and Policies of the States*.[8]

Fearing high unemployment rates and a directionless postwar economy, in his 1943 inaugural address Warren warned that California would need "shock absorbers" to handle the anticipated influx of civilians, as well as mechanisms to guide the state's transition to a peacetime economy. California was forever changed, and "government has special responsibilities in these critical days," remarked Warren.[9] California had two choices, he stated: "to become a casualty of the War" or to prepare itself "for further advance" during the postwar period.[10] Planning, insisted Warren, needed to be incorporated into all facets of government activity. "Our production and employment problems have become so complex," he told the legislature, "that it seems nothing less than dangerous for us to drift along on optimism and guesswork, improvising from day to day, without any means of detecting the underlying signs of the times until disaster is actually upon us. . . . The time has come for us to be realistic—factual—and to equip ourselves and chart our future course."[11]

Warren's plea for state-level planning found substantial support within the California Legislature but not only because of the fear of a postwar recession. Mounting state surpluses brought intense interest among lawmakers, such as Charles W. Lyon, speaker of the assembly, regarding how this money would be spent equitably throughout the state. The surplus offered California a tremendous opportunity. The Depression Era deficits were gone. The scale of economic expansion and conservative budgets of the war years provided a huge fund for postwar reconversion and for imaginative state leaders, such as Warren, to redefine government services and build the state's neglected infrastructure. In 1943, the state controller anticipated state revenues of approximately $249 million and expenditures of around $170 million. This meant a surplus of over $90 million within California's general fund. Even with the administration's plan to reduce the state sales tax from 4 to 2 percent and the cutting of income taxes for primarily lower- and middle-income families, the state could anticipate a surplus of nearly $230 million in 1945.[12]

Higher Education and Warren's Strategy

Warren presented two major strategies for assisting California through the transition to a peacetime economy—two "shock absorbers" that would form the base for long-term economic growth. Both ideas relied on spending the state's massive wartime surplus, and both fit into a Keynesian view of public investment. First, Warren argued for the rebuilding and expansion of California's infrastructure, including roads, public buildings, aqueducts, and public parks. The result would be an improved environment for commerce and thousands of new jobs. "We must avoid the dole," Warren insisted. "We must set ourselves to the scientific preparation of a backlog of construction projects [to] coordinate . . . the physical improvement of our state and bolster morale through beneficial utilization of surplus manpower."[13]

The second strategy was to fund a massive expansion of public higher education. Vocational, professional, and liberal arts programs could retrain displaced workers while California industries converted to a peacetime economy—industries that would rely on skilled and professional labor. Increased support for higher education and for the University of California, in particular, noted Warren, would also bolster research to help California industries, both in the development of new products and in an improvement in productivity. Expanding higher education opportunity, explained Warren, was also necessary to uphold California's socioeconomic experiment. New campuses and new programs would need to be established to meet the changing needs of society. Such expansion would also help the state absorb the anticipated influx of veterans who would return to California at the end of the war.

In the postwar period, no other state would match the size of California's veteran population. "An estimated two million servicemen are expected to return to California," explained Julian A. McPhee, acting chief of the Division of Readjustment Education for the State Department of Education. McPhee, future president of the San Louis Obispo campus, also projected that more than 10 percent would seek some form of higher education.[14] This expected surge in enrollment demand would bring federal dollars to California, helping to subsidize the corresponding expansion of the state's colleges and universities. The Roosevelt administration had already laid plans for the G.I. Bill. McPhee estimated that California could anticipate getting a large portion of more than $1 billion that would be available to veterans.[15]

For the governor and legislators, meeting the needs of these returning veterans, many of whom would not be native Californians, was a moral obligation following their contribution to the war. As stated by Warren, "for those working here and at home who left their future in our hands while they serve in uniform, the best and the only lasting contribution we can make is the building of a sound economy."[16]

State government had special duties to make sure that economic growth continued and that veterans were fully integrated into California society. Their presence, later noted Warren, "was both a problem and a blessing. It was a blessing because it reduced our average age to a number considerably below that of most of the other states and it gave us a productive labor pool that was attractive to industry. On the other hand, the influx was so great and so sudden that we were put to our wits' ends to use these people adequately and locate them in jobs. . . . In keeping with the experience of the state with World War I veterans, we concentrated on helping the new civilians to find jobs, to complete their education, and to purchase a home or a farm." According to Warren, the combination of returning veterans and general migration to California meant that "we are getting the greatest population bargain in all time."[17]

Some argued differently. The vast majority of newcomers were no longer middle-aged and retired, as in earlier decades, but were young and without much money or job-related skills. Warren insisted, however, that he "would rather have the production of the best years of the young people now migrating to our state than the dollars the retired people earned elsewhere."[18]

Public higher education could partially absorb the huge number of veterans as it helped industry in California. Junior colleges could provide vocational and credential programs, while the state colleges could increase their role in training technical professionals, including engineers.

California Progressives had already provided the concept that all graduates of the state's high schools could enter any public junior college. Warren now advocated open access to anyone who could benefit from their programs. The University of California would expand its undergraduate enrollment and become an even more important source of research relevant to local communities. In agricultural research, the university had long proven a highly productive investment of state funds, providing numerous inventions and studies beneficial to farmers. California's urban character and relatively small rural population required mechanization on the farm and in the orchards to make up for the lack of labor. Agriculture had other characteristics that benefited from university research. Because of previous patterns of land ownership and the need for irrigation in what was often arid land, farming was a capital-intensive activity in California. Large farms and ranches dominated production. Orchards, vineyards, and the introduction of a large variety of new crops required new techniques to improve crop yields. The university was a valuable friend to farmers dependent on innovation.

During the war, the University of California proved its value as a source of defense-related research. With federal funds, the university created a series of defense laboratories and administered the Manhattan Project. It also supported existing industries and attracted new ones. The university, Warren later remarked, was "a great friend to the farmers of the state, and was the basic source of the scientific and technological skills that brought so much war and postwar industry to our economy—without which we would have experienced a calamitous unemployment situation in the postwar era."[19]

Warren also had a personal affinity for the university. The son of a railroad worker, he graduated from Bakersfield High School before going to Berkeley and then Boalt Hall for his law degree. While at Berkeley, he was a classmate and personal friend of Robert Gordon Sproul and played clarinet in the Berkeley marching band in which Sproul was the drum major. Sproul, a fellow Republican, proved a loyal friend. At the 1948 Republican Convention in San Francisco, Sproul nominated Warren for the presidency as California's favorite son. Warren would subsequently run on Thomas Dewey's ticket as the vice presidential candidate.

Warren's vision of postwar California reflected the ideas of several key lawmakers. In 1942, before Warren took office, the legislature created a committee to study "postwar planning." Consisting of powerful Speaker of the Assembly Charles Lyon, Democrat Thomas J. Doyle, and Stockton Republican Charles M. Weber as its chairman, the committee touted planning as the potential salvation for California.[20] Though planning had the connotation of socialism for many lawmakers, these mainstream assemblymen saw things differently. "There are already grave dislocations in the economic and social structure of the state," explained the subcommittee's report in December 1942. "[M]oreover, there are dark clouds appearing on the horizon which portend coming events, somber in aspect, which will require comprehensively planned policies in government."[21] In a report submitted to Warren during the first months of his administration, Weber's committee broadly defined state governmental responsibility as encompassing both the "physical requirements of the people" and "those relating to the economic and social requirements." It placed particular importance on coordinating the development of the state's pioneering higher education system.[22] Yet, Weber noted, there was no "organized procedure in government" to encourage planning in higher education or in other policy areas.[23]

Weber and Assembly Speaker Lyon requested that Warren convene a special session of the legislature in 1944 "to consider matters pertaining to planning."[24] With the end of the 1943 session, the legislature would not convene until 1945 under the California Constitution. Warren called the special session and created a Postwar Planning Commission to advise him and the legislature on how, among other issues, to expand higher education opportunity.

The Postwar Planning Commission

The Postwar Planning Commission consisted of both state officials and a series of subcommittees with lay representation. Colonel Alexander Heron, a former director of finance under Governor C. C. Young and a member of the Interstate Committee on Postwar Reconstruction and Development, was appointed director of the commission. The commission's board consisted of nine members, including Charles Henry Purcell as the chair (the designer of the San Francisco–Oakland Bay Bridge and an engineer in the California Division of Highways), Warren's Executive Secretary William T. Sweigert, university president Sproul, and Superintendent of Public Instruction Walter Dexter.

At the first meeting of the commission in March of 1944, Warren had high hopes for their work. "We have been changing at a speed with which nothing in our past can logically be compared. Neither the colorful gold rush nor any other dramatic period in our history brought quite so many new people or caused the same sweeping changes to our economy and social life. We find that the war has caused us to actually jump into our future."[25] Warren urged the newly formed commission to pursue a broad agenda. He hoped it would identify needed state, local, and private capital projects deserving state support, formulate policies that would promote the education and employment of veterans and displaced workers, direct the conversion of industry to peacetime pursuits, and attract new businesses to the state. In short, the commission would study the human, economic, and natural resources needed for California to successfully enter the 1950s.[26]

Within this agenda, public education was a major concern. The new commission launched two studies to assess the problems and challenges of California's entire public education system. The first focused on education from the elementary school to the junior college. Completed under the direction of Dr. George D. Strayer, professor emeritus of education at Teachers College, Columbia University, and with the assistance of faculty at Stanford and the University of California, the 1945 report focused on reforming state financing of local schools and the creation of unified school districts. It also proposed the reorganization of the State Department of Education and revived the proposal to appoint the state superintendent of public instruction and to elect the State Board of Education.[27]

"There is a direct relationship," explained Strayer in his study, "between economic well-being or prosperity and the amount and character of education supplied . . . California has led in providing support for public education on a state-wide basis. It still has ahead of it the necessity of equalizing educational opportunity throughout its borders and of equalizing the burden of supporting this program." In the coming years, he noted, the school population would increase significantly. Under the existing system of school financing, the result largely of the shift in funding from state coffers to local property taxes under a 1933 tax reform program, there would be substantial inequality between schools.[28]

Strayer argued for an improved distribution of state funds to at least partially equalize the amount of funding per student between rich and poor school districts.[29] The tax reform bills in the mid-1930s had altered the flow of funds to schools, shifting the burden from state government to local government. State aid continued but was no longer the major source of school financing. The decline in property values during the Great Depression and the surge of school-age children during the war magnified the differences in the quality of schools between communities. Strayer also noted job opportunities for people between eighteen and twenty years of age would be extremely limited in the immediate postwar period, and he urged a substantial increase in funding to California's developing junior college system. The quality and type of programs varied greatly, and there were many areas of the state without any junior college program. "In the postwar years," continued Strayer, "there must be established a state-wide program of offerings to meet all the needs that are developing." These needs included vocational and pre-professional programs "to provide a great variety of experiences suited to the needs and capacities of all boys and girls, and geared to the requirements of society as indicated by opportunities for work."[30]

As a result of Strayer's study, the Postwar Planning Commission proposed legislation to help equalize school financing that was then passed as a constitutional amendment by California voters. The Fair Equalization Law of 1945 increased state funding for local schools by providing three forms of state aid. "Basic aid" continued and provided approximately $125 per pupil. The bill offered two new forms of state financing. Those districts where property values fell below a prescribed amount received an additional state allocation called "equalization aid." Districts with high levels of poverty received yet another allocation per student. Nearly half of school financing now came from the state. Despite these reforms, substantial inequities remained between districts.[31]

The second report sponsored by the Postwar Planning Commission focused on the future development of California's higher education system. The economic and social consequences of World War II jolted the higher education community in California. The exigencies of the war effort first drained enrollments and further delayed capital construction already slowed by Depression Era budgets. Between 1940 and 1943, the number of full- and part-time students within public and private postsecondary institutions decreased by 52 percent, from 126,000 to 60,200 students.[32]

The postwar era promised a huge surge in the demand for higher education in California. In preparation for the postwar planning study, university president Sproul asked the regents and faculty to ponder "what the university is going to do after the War? Shall we be prepared for the hordes of students which some authorities predict will invade the campus? What shall we do if State appropriations for university support are drastically reduced, as they well may be in a [possible] period of economic crisis after the war?"[33]

In 1943, Stanford Professor Walter Crosby Eells pondered the future of the state's junior colleges. "Each generation of American parents has wanted and has secured for its children a higher level of educational opportunity than that which they themselves enjoyed." California's innovative tripartite public system, the pending passage of the G.I. Bill of Rights, and the general demand for increased access to higher education, Eells concluded, might make a college education "as common in the decade following this war as a high school education became after the last war."[34]

The subsequent report, "Postwar Objectives of Public Higher Education in California," was issued in February 1945 and stressed the need to coordinate the tripartite system. Unlike the report authored by Strayer, few recommendations were provided. The failure of the Coordinating Council for Higher Education, Sproul's not so secret plans for a hostile takeover of the state colleges, and assorted other differences continued to sharply divide the higher education community in California. As a result, the report simply noted two objectives: one, the need for another and more complete study, and two, the need for improved joint cooperation between the regents and the State Board of Education.[35] Clearly, the report did not meet the expectations of Governor Warren and legislators.

Creating a Liaison Committee

The lack of a unified voice among the higher education community on key issues of enrollment and program expansion, and Warren's demand for planning and coordination, offered the likelihood of legislatively imposed solutions. Several members of the State Board of Education met prior to the board's regular meeting on January 12, 1945, worried about the growing hostility between the state colleges and the university. Among them was Joseph P. Loeb, a 1905 Berkeley graduate and former editor of the campus paper the *Daily Californian*.

Loeb was an attorney in Los Angeles and a trustee at the Claremont Graduate School. He wanted to improve the relations between the two boards and create a forum for discourse. The lack of communication and debate between the two boards, he concluded, led not only to honest differences but also to misunderstandings. The original purpose of their meeting was to focus on agricultural education in the Fresno area, but Loeb's desires brought a more important result.[36] He urged that a joint group of the State Board of Education and university officials meet regularly to discuss bills before the legislature and to attempt, on a voluntary basis, to coordinate the efforts of the two boards.[37] With Warren's signing of the Santa Barbara bill fresh on the minds of the State Board of Education, Loeb was anxious to prevent similar ventures.

With the support of key members of the board, including chairman William L. Blair in early 1945, Loeb approached Sproul with the idea. Several days later, an informal meeting was held at Sproul's home in the Berkeley hills to discuss the proposal. Loeb attended as a representative of the State Board of Education. Also in attendance were university vice president Monroe E. Deutsch, professors Joel Hildebrand (former chair of the Academic Senate Committee on Educational Policy), George Adams, Frank Freeman, and George Louderback, and Ralph T. Fisher, president of the California Alumni Association. They agreed that Loeb's proposal might be the best way for the two boards to discuss their differences and to head off legislative forays and bills mutually opposed by the higher education community. The boards could then debate and negotiate major issues. Perhaps most importantly, they might avoid public displays of their differences.[38]

Four days later, Sproul offered a resolution to the regents for the establishment of a "Liaison Committee" to "perfect a plan of coordination . . . which will provide a permanent basis for the economical and adequate development of all education." The committee would be composed of the university president and the state superintendent of instruction, along with three members from the regents and three from the State Board of Education. The resolution recommended that "any major changes in the organization of the public educational system of the State of California, including changes in the status of institutions (for example: 1. the taking over of state colleges by the university, 2. the conversion of Junior Colleges into four-year colleges granting the bachelor's degree, and 3. the conversion of state colleges from undergraduate colleges to institutions of university grade giving graduate work) await the submission of the [Liaison Committee's] final report."[39]

The regents promptly passed the resolution, but nearly a year passed before the State Board of Education gave its approval. The board was in the midst of endorsing Proposition 3, which would successfully preclude any further annexations of a state college by the university. They sought the resolution of that issue before agreeing to participate in the Liaison Committee. Superintendent Dexter's unexpected death in late 1945 also delayed action by the board.[40] Governor Warren appointed Roy E. Simpson to replace Dexter. Even after approving the idea of the Liaison Committee, the State Board of Education and Simpson proceeded to focus on issues of school district reorganization and equity proposed by Strayer's report on school financing. Sproul's hope for yet another study on California higher education languished.

What prompted the first meeting of the Liaison Committee was a flood of bills related to higher education in late 1946. Warren had once again called a special legislation session that year to work on the pressing job of "reemployment and reconversion." The work of the legislature had turned into a full-time affair. Warren claimed that the Great Depression and the war placed the burden of policymaking on the federal government. In the postwar era, he noted, the onus was on state government. The problems of employment, housing, and education, he stated before the legislature in January 1946, "will not solve themselves. Inaction and inertia will only add to the difficulties and confound the confusion. Especially in California, we dare not be guilty of this. . . . Our university and State colleges are becoming so crowded that soon they may have to deny many of our young people, including war veterans, their legal right to a higher education."[41]

A month later, Warren again came before the legislature to speak, focusing his attention on legislation related to veterans. He projected that 100,000 veterans would return to school full-time under the G.I. Bill, placing the burden "largely on our university, state colleges and junior colleges." He concluded: "The great educational stimulus, coupled with the fact that our state population has increased by 2,000,000 during the last four years, will most certainly over-tax our university and college educational system to the breaking point."[42] There was an urgent need, he concluded, for a rapid expansion of the state's pioneering higher education system.

Many lawmakers took Warren's call for action to heart. Yet the governor's plea for a deliberate effort to plan and expand higher education opportunity was overshadowed by legislators attempting to create new colleges and programs in their local districts. Once again, bills emerged for new state colleges and for the conversion of junior colleges to four-year institutions. Similar to the 1930 Inman bill, state senator Earl Desmond of Sacramento offered two bills. The first proposed the conversion of Sacramento's junior college into a new state college. The second would allow the state colleges to grant, for the first time, master's degrees. Desmond explained that greater access to public higher education was a major issue for Californians and specifically for his constituents. It was time to do something about it.[43]

While the State Board of Education noted their support of graduate-level training in the state colleges, they were less sanguine about the conversion of a junior college into a state college. The regents stated their fierce opposition to both. Sproul gained the support of Loeb and other members of the board to make an appeal to lawmakers: No legislation should be passed, they argued, until the Liaison Committee could study the need for such institutions and programs. Here was a strategic approach used repeatedly by the higher education community. At Sproul's request, in October 1946, state senator Hugh Burns sponsored a bill requesting that the Liaison Committee "study the adequacy of existing facilities at Sacramento Junior College to serve as an institution for higher learning in the Sacramento Valley." Burns' bill also suggested converting the college "to a four-year college or branch of the State university."

Although the legislative mandate had limited scope, it represented an important first step towards a more comprehensive study of California's needs. It offered the two boards a chance to prove that they could cooperate in the aftermath of the feud over the Santa Barbara campus. The Liaison Committee proceeded to appoint a "survey team" that included representatives from both the university and the state department of education to review Desmond's proposal, along with a similar bill that proposed the conversion of Los Angeles Junior College into a state college. Aubrey A. Douglass was named chair of this team. Douglass earned his doctorate under G. Stanley Hall at Clark University. He was also a founding faculty member and director of studies at the Claremont Graduate School, a former assistant superintendent of public instruction in Sacramento, and now superintendent of Modesto City Schools.[44] In addition, the new chairman had valuable experience working with Warren and previous governors.

Creating State Colleges in Los Angeles and Sacramento

Desmond hoped for an affirmative response to his bill. Less than three months later, the Douglass subcommittee, via the Liaison Committee, submitted their report to the legislature. The proposals for Sacramento and Los Angeles provided a catalyst to elaborate on the larger question of how California's postsecondary system should expand. A favorable decision for Desmond's proposal, explained Douglass, would lead to a precedent that could seriously affect the future structure of California's entire system. The report advised against the transition of any junior college to a four-year, state-supported institution. Neither the administrative structure nor a properly trained staff to support a four-year program existed, and developing these resources would be costly and time consuming. "The junior college," explained Douglass, "should be preserved and protected." Bills for the conversion of junior colleges to four-year colleges must be defeated.[45] Further, Douglass stated that the junior college programs operated by three of the state colleges, Fresno, San Diego, and San Jose, should be discontinued, and separate and locally funded colleges should be created.[46]

Yet it was also recognized that there remained a great need in both Sacramento and Los Angeles for greater access to four-year institutions. Instead of simply endorsing legislation for new colleges, Douglass urged the legislature to sanction the Liaison Committee to complete a formal study on the need for new colleges and universities throughout the state. This was essentially the study for which Sproul had long argued.[47] Sproul and various regents, including Chair James Kennedy Moffitt, were already lobbying Sacramento lawmakers and the State Board of Education for just such a study, as well as for a moratorium on any new state colleges. Sproul had recently conducted the second systemwide meeting of University of California faculty where he found great support for the study and the moratorium. Faculty complained that the state colleges were deserting their primary and statutory responsibility to train teachers. "It is a startling fact," announced one professor, "that only a very small number of students graduating from the state colleges each June go into teaching. The state colleges are aiming rather to become liberal colleges, and eventually want to confer the M.A. degree."[48]

The suggestion that the legislature wait for the result of yet another study caused consternation among many lawmakers. State Senator Desmond was joined by Assemblyman Ernest E. Debs of Los Angeles in arguing against the moratorium. Debs had just proposed his own bill for a state college in Los Angeles. Yet the rationale for a proper "planning study" was powerful. Governor Warren noted his support, and other legislators argued for a deliberate expansion of California's entire higher education system. To that end, Assemblyman Francis Dunn Jr., chair of the Assembly Education Committee, sponsored legislation authorizing the study. Such a study, he noted, should assess the "present and future needs of the State for education above the high school, with particular needs of each area in the State." His bill also asked for a judgment on the appropriate organization of the system and how it might be financed.

At the insistence of Desmond and Debs, however, the bill did not preclude possible legislation for new campuses until the report was finished. At Desmond's urging, language was added, stating that there "exists an urgent need for a survey of the organization of publicly supported higher education in California" and that "this act is hereby declared an urgency measure necessary for the immediate preservation of the public peace, health and safety." In April of that year, Warren signed the bill.[49]

The ever-vigilant Desmond and Debs promptly offered new bills to create new state colleges. Desmond teamed with Los Angeles state senator Jack Tenney to offer legislation that would convert the site of the Sacramento State Fair into the location for Sacramento State College. Both Desmond and Debs got their bills approved in the frenzy of activity at the end the 1946 legislative session. In an attempt to placate Sproul's contention that any decision regarding new campuses should be delayed until after the state-sanctioned study, both measures stated that, for the time being, the new colleges should not "constitute a part of the public school system of the State, nor of the university."[50] The two new campuses were, in other words, to exist in statute but not in reality until the completion of the study. This was hardly a relief to Sproul and the regents. There remained, however, the governor's signature.

At a June 1947 meeting of the Liaison Committee, university lobbyist James Corley asked the members of the committee to "go to the Governor and request him to veto the bills, pending receipt of the survey report." Sproul then noted that "all members of the committee would agree that a better system of higher education would result if the planning were done by educators . . . rather than by legislators in the last hurried week of a controversial session." Superintendent Simpson noted his sympathy, but he also explained the inability of his department to "actively fight many of the bills before the legislature."[51] Most State Board of Education members, in fact, supported new campuses in both locations. The rift within California's higher education community remained substantial.

Despite the clear opposition of the university and in the midst of the Liaison Committee's effort to organize the planning study, Governor Warren signed the bills, creating Sacramento and Los Angeles State Colleges. Legislation was pending for the establishment of a Mount Shasta State College, a Stanislaus State College, and a Stanislaus Polytechnic School. Also proposed in the legislature were a School of Agriculture at Fresno and a motion to expand the function and change the names of the existing polytechnics in San Luis Obispo and Pomona from "schools" to colleges. President Sproul feared that "a dangerous expansion" had begun.[52]

The First Master Plan

Because of the political success of his 1945 report and the need to project an appearance of impartiality, the Liaison Committee asked George Strayer to direct the new study on California higher education. He would, in essence, continue the work he undertook under the Postwar Planning Commission.

Strayer remained a respected national figure on education policy. As a young professor at the Teachers College at Columbia University, he had worked with Ellwood Cubberley on a series of studies on city school administration. Following his retirement from Teachers College in the late 1930s, he pursued a lucrative career as a consultant, completing numerous studies on state systems of education. Prior to his new appointment by the Liaison Committee and shortly after his work for the Postwar Planning Commission, Strayer had directed a study of the state of Washington's public education system. He would later go on to conduct a review of university systems in Georgia and Iowa.[53]

The Liaison Committee asked two others to be members of what became known as the survey committee to work with Strayer: Aubrey Douglass and recently retired university vice president Monroe E. Deutsch. Each had been protégés of Progressive Era educational leaders. Douglass, as noted, had studied under G. Stanley Hall. Deutsch was a 1902 graduate of Berkeley who became a professor of Latin under President Benjamin Ide Wheeler before becoming the Dean of the College of Letters and Science at UCLA. When Sproul was appointed president of the university in 1930, he asked Deutsch to serve in the new position of vice president.

With a staff of eight and a legislative deadline only nine months away, Strayer, Douglass, and Deutsch began their work in late May 1947. By December of that year, both the regents and the State Board of Education were reviewing the report, "A Survey of the Needs of California in Higher Education," otherwise known as the Strayer Report.[54] The comprehensive nature of the study, with its focus on the functions of the three public segments, projecting enrollment growth, and the need for new academic programs and future campus sites, made it an innovative and tremendously influential planning effort, not only in California but also throughout the nation. No state in the Union had thus far attempted to plan the future of its public higher education system. Previous efforts had focused on surveys of existing programs and preferred modes of organization and governance. Most notable was the extensive survey of public and private education within the state of Illinois, which was conducted by the University of Chicago in 1939. The study detailed the academic programs and admissions practices of the state's numerous colleges and universities.

Under the influence of Warren's push for planning, the Strayer Report marked a clear departure from past state studies. It represented California's first attempt at a "master plan" for a state system of higher education.[55] The final report was also a well-balanced political document. It instantly gained wide support among legislators, and it forced the regents and the State Board of Education, at least for the time being, toward a common course. The political acceptance of the report was partly the result of the relatively minor influence wielded by the university—the segment with the most resistance to change. The aging Deutsch suffered a broken hipbone and other health maladies shortly after his appointment to the study. The burden for completing the study fell largely on Strayer and Douglass. Deutsch's minor role in the development of the final report presented an unexpected blow to Sproul and other University of California officials.

At a Los Angeles meeting of the Liaison Committee in February 1948, Strayer and Douglass presented the major elements of the study. Deutsch could not attend because of health reasons. Reflecting on the postwar growth in California, Strayer stated, "You can't increase population by three million people and not provide opportunities which have been characteristic of this state." Public higher education needed to be greatly expanded, particularly at the junior and state college levels. Through these institutions, the great majority of Californians could gain access to postsecondary training, they argued. "We have looked to California for many years," continued Strayer, as the leader in developing "the junior colleges and state colleges, and it has, among all the states, the most distinguished University." If California was "to hold this record," the changes recommended in their report needed to be adopted quickly. This meant expanding the system, particularly the four-year regional institutions, into more areas of the state—a conclusion of both state senator Desmond and Assemblyman Debs.

Reflecting the vision first articulated by California Progressives, Strayer and Douglass explained that educational opportunity was largely a matter of providing higher education institutions and programs throughout the vast state of California and at minimal cost to students and their families. Though California had made steady progress toward expanding the geographic location of public institutions, Douglass explained that about half of the state's high school graduates were denied the opportunity for higher education because of the lack of regional institutions. Reiterating the observations of Anthony Caminetti some forty years earlier, Douglass observed that many families could simply not afford to send their children to the university in far away Berkeley or to the state college in, say, San Jose. The further development of regional and tuition-free institutions was the key for increasing accessibility. In turn, the results would be improved socioeconomic mobility and an expansion of California's skilled and professional labor pools.[56] As the first step in a long-term planning process, the Strayer Report articulated the purpose and responsibilities of each segment of the tripartite education system that would, some twelve years later, form the basis for the 1960 Master Plan for Higher Education.

THE JUNIOR COLLEGES

The junior colleges, the report explained, represented California's commitment to a "democratic way of life." One function was to provide "terminal education," which was predominately vocational, for young Californians between the ages of eighteen and twenty-one. The report noted that the terminal program was a unique component in California's system, which was not always fully appreciated.

Another function of the junior college was to provide "general education" intended to prepare students so that they may "function effectively as a member of a family, a community, a state, a nation, and a world." The report also explained that the colleges provided "orientation and guidance," so that a student could find his particular aptitude, "choose a life work, and prepare for the successful pursuit of such work." Its "adult education" function, explained the report, provided all interested adults in a junior college with cultural and vocational education opportunities.

Finally, the junior colleges provided an "essential matriculation function" for students moving on to four-year institutions. In this last and important area, the local colleges provided a lower-division program that enabled talented students to then transfer to the university, a state college, or a private institution. From "the standpoint of community interest," noted the report, this was "perhaps its most important function. . . . The importance of the transfer function is destined to increase."[57]

THE STATE COLLEGES

The state colleges, stated the Strayer Report, should offer more than teacher education, including a "wide variety of curricula" leading to the bachelor's degree and the master's degree in selective fields.[58] Strayer and Douglass sought to provide an official recognition of the state colleges as regional institutions—a distinction that was not clearly mandated in statute. They also sought to end the debate over whether the colleges should offer the master's degree.

In early 1947, while they worked on their study, legislation sponsored by three assembly members from San Diego attempted to revive the bill offered by Senator Desmond in 1945 to sanction master's-level training at the state colleges.[59] At the request of San Diego State President Malcolm

Love, Assemblywoman Kathryn Niehouse, the main sponsor of the 1947 bill, argued for the addition of graduate-level programs in aerospace engineering and other applied fields to bolster the regional economy of her district. Such applied and postgraduate programs remained the purview of the University of California, yet the university showed no indication that it was willing to fulfill this growing need outside of the San Francisco Bay Area or Los Angeles.

Sproul and the regents opposed the bill but to no avail. "The primary function of the state colleges is the training of teachers," proclaimed the final legislation signed by Warren. However, the state colleges could also "offer courses appropriate for a general or liberal education and for responsible citizenship; offer vocational training in such fields as business, industry, public services, homemaking, and social service; and offer the pre-professional courses needed by students who plan to transfer to universities for advanced professional study."[60] The language was vague, but it cracked open the door for program expansion at the master's level.

Strayer and Douglass proceeded to offer strong support for master's level programs in the state colleges. In the final report, they noted that, "in a great majority of instances, the master's degree marks an important advance for a teacher." Salary increases and professional advancement had become dependent almost exclusively upon graduate course credit, they explained. There was also a great need for fifth-year training in a variety of fields, such as engineering, which they deemed appropriate for state colleges.[61]

At the same time, Strayer and Douglass acknowledged the legitimate worries of university officials regarding the entrepreneurial, unregulated growth of college programs. They insisted that the State Board of Education apply a rigorous process for approving new programs at both the bachelor's and master's levels. "Many courses and curricula have been organized, placed in the catalogues, and made available to students without the knowledge or approval" of the board. Such was the case with all existing undergraduate engineering programs within the state colleges. Strayer and Douglass insisted that this should not continue. Their report also demanded that both the State Board of Education and the regents, through the Liaison Committee, "continue the study of this matter and set up precise definitions of the distinct aims and programs in engineering."[62]

Another problem identified by their report was the varied admissions policies of the state colleges. The flood of veterans into the system forced many of the campuses to admit students of varying potential. According to the Strayer Report, tougher admission requirements were needed. The open-door approach of some state colleges wasted state money. A large proportion of admitted students, it was presumed, would fail.[63] Another significant concept for California public higher education was emerging: Admission of students to each of the public segments should be based on criteria that indicated their eventual graduation.

THE UNIVERSITY OF CALIFORNIA

In describing the function and service area of each segment, the Strayer Report stated that the university should have "exclusive responsibility . . . for training for the professions, for graduate work on the Doctor's level, and for research and scholarly endeavor of the highest type." Anticipating the desire of many state colleges for the doctorate in education, the report insisted that supervision of the state colleges should respect this policy to ensure that expenditures for advanced study would not be "dissipated among several institutions." The university should also be viewed as a statewide institution and, reflecting its pivotal role in the war effort, one that also served the needs of the nation.

Strayer and Douglass provided a direct appeal to legislators, who, frustrated with the university, were considering methods to bring it into more direct influence of lawmakers. They claimed that most state-funded universities were condemned to perpetual mediocrity because of the influence and controls of state government. This made "it impossible for them to devote themselves freely and continuously to the slow process of scholarship, research, and the extension of the frontiers of knowledge and those of the application of knowledge." California's university, however, was different largely because of provisions of the 1879 California Constitution, granting it considerable independence from "fluctuating and political influences of current legislative direction."[64]

The authors of the report made an observation on the historical reasons for the success of California's state university: The strength of the university was not purely intrinsic. Three factors had helped developed a great university: the advantages of self-management provided by the California Constitution; the state government's consistent and expanding financial support to the university, particularly following Progressive Era reforms and including the expansion into a multicampus institution; and California's investment in a system of junior and state colleges. Without the junior and state colleges, it was suggested, the university could not have attained its present status. It was a symbiotic system, where the health of one affected that of the others.

California's state university, concluded the Strayer Report, provided a marked contrast to other land grant institutions. "Usually, state universities are, either by popular sentiment or by actual legislative enactment, prevented from devoting themselves centrally and primarily to the extension of the knowledge and the development of high scholarship, by the requirement that all graduates of accredited high schools shall be admitted to the university." This meant that most of the energies of an institution would be turned "to the education of large numbers of young people" and would thus alter its focus. While the value and usefulness of this service "can not be questioned," it would not result in an institution like the University of California.[65]

ENROLLMENT PROJECTIONS TO 1965

Articulating the role of each segment provided a framework for the Strayer Report to project enrollments and outline segmental expansion. For the first time in California history, the authors attempted a systematized analysis of potential higher education enrollment demand within the state. They looked at age cohorts and made assessments of immigration and birth rates within ten areas of California, including Sacramento, the San Francisco-Oakland area, the Peninsula-San Jose area, and the Los Angeles-Orange County area. They also studied past attendance to assess the college-going rate. In the 1930s, they observed, approximately 20 per cent of the college-age groups were enrolled in institutions of higher education. This was up from a rate of approximately 8 percent in 1920 and reflected largely the expansion of both the junior college and state college segments. But what percentage of youth ought to be attending college or a university? This was a difficult question, and for guidance the committee turned to three national reports.

In 1943, as part of the Roosevelt administration's efforts at postwar planning, the National Resources Planning Board (NRPB) issued the report *Equal Access to Education*. The report argued that expanding higher education opportunity was critical not only to improve socioeconomic mobility and support economic growth but also as a matter of national defense. A better-educated workforce would help to create the brainpower and technology necessary to confront the spread and threat of communism. To this end, the NRPB argued that by the 1950s, higher education enrollments throughout the nation should double. This would mean that approximately 40 percent of all high school graduates should matriculate to a postsecondary institution. Reaching that goal would require a deliberate effort by state governments to both invest and coordinate their evolving systems of higher education, most of which were really a collection of public and private institutions with few of the formal links found in California.[66] The federal role would focus on financial aid to students (a program started by the National Youth Administration in 1935) and grants for research.

The surge of federal funds for defense-related research during the war marked a major transition for America's research universities. This flow of funds expanded under new federal programs, such as the National Science Foundation, established in 1950, and with a substantial impact on the activities of the University of California.[67] However, the movement toward mass higher education, one in which California was a major leader, would remain the purview of state and local government.

Another influential study followed the NRPB's report. In 1944, the Educational Policies Commission, a joint body of the National Education Association and the American Association of School Administrators, noted that "a large proportion of youth [need] free public education beyond the twelfth grade" and an "education appropriate to free men in American democracy."[68] Both reports gave added credence to the need for a dramatic expansion of both junior and regional colleges.

While Strayer's committee worked on enrollment projections, a third influential report from Washington was nearing completion. In 1946, President Harry Truman appointed George F. Zook, president of the American Council on Education, to head a twenty-eight member commission to "re-examine our system of higher education in terms of its objectives, methods, and facilities; and in light of the social role it has to play."[69] The president's commission produced a multivolume report, *Higher Education for American Democracy*. The commission concluded that "at least 49 percent of our population has the mental ability to complete 14 years of schooling," and that "32 percent . . . [had] the ability to complete an advanced liberal or specialized professional education." What prevented Americans from achieving these college-going rates? The reasons were several: economic hardship; racial, religious, and geographic barriers; and simply the lack of enrollment capacity in existing institutions. The report argued that every American should be "enabled and encouraged to carry his education, formal and informal, as far as his native capacities permit."[70]

Strayer and Douglass, referring to all three national studies, provided what they termed "a conservative assessment" of enrollment growth in California suitable for an industrial and technological age. If the state continued to expand its network of colleges and universities, more than 30 percent of California's eighteen- to twenty-one-year-old population should attend a postsecondary institution by 1950. The huge influx of veterans into California's public higher education system, many older than twenty-one, added another source of enrollment demand. In 1947, approximately 130,000 veterans attended both public and private postsecondary institutions in California—30,000 more than projected by the Warren administration in 1945. Half of all enrolled students within the university were veterans registered under the G.I. Bill, while 70 percent of state college and 36 percent of junior college students were veterans. Under the assumption that the surge in veteran enrollments would soon recede, the Strayer Report projected that more than 250,000 full-time students would be enrolled by 1960 and over 300,000 by 1965—up from an enrollment of 121,000 in the prewar year of 1940.

NEW CAMPUSES

The match between enrollment demand and enrollment capacity of each existing campus, explained Strayer and Douglass, provided a basis for recommending expansion. The fast-growing Los Angeles–Orange County area would account for nearly 45 percent of California's projected enrollment growth in the 1950s. The other areas with the largest enrollment projections were San Francisco–Oakland, Peninsula–San Jose, Sacramento, Riverside–San Bernardino, and San Diego. Depending on the area, private institutions could grow and new ones could be established to meet some of this demand. Most growth, however, would require the establishment of new state institutions. In 1947, approximately 29 percent of all enrollment was in the private segment of California's postsecondary system. The report's authors hoped that this percentage would be maintained; however, the financial burden of such expansion and the lack of any coordinating mechanism seemed to place in doubt the ability of this segment to maintain its market share.[71] This assumption proved correct. By 1980, enrollment in private institutions accounted for a little more than 10 percent of all postsecondary enrollment in California.

Although California had by far the most developed junior college system in the nation, there were numerous areas throughout the state with substantial populations and no junior college. In 1947, California had fifty-five junior colleges with two additional campuses under construction. Many more were required, stated the Strayer Report. New colleges were needed immediately in the East Bay, including Alameda and Contra Costa Counties, as well as in Merced, Kings, and Tehama/Shasta Counties.

The Strayer Report gave its strong endorsement of the bills already signed by Governor Warren for new state colleges in Sacramento and Los Angeles. The legitimacy of the study within the legislature, no doubt, hung on just such support. "The Los Angeles situation is striking," they noted. Over

10,000 students already overcrowded the city's junior college. There was a desperate need in "this great expanse of population" for both a new state college and an expansion of what would soon be known as UCLA. Indeed, the authors noted, the tremendous population growth in southern California required more state college and perhaps university campuses. They recommended new state colleges in the area of Compton, Long Beach, and Fullerton, and the expansion of the university's experiment station in Riverside and facilities in Davis into general campuses with a full liberal arts curriculum. These last two proposals were being pushed by local lawmakers but not by university officials.[72]

COORDINATION

Past efforts at coordination had clearly been failures. Strayer and Douglass again considered the idea of creating a single governing board to take control of the state's public four-year colleges and university campuses. Any such notion, though, was both impractical and ill conceived. California's public higher education segments had already grown to such a size, explained Strayer and Douglass, that a single board could not possibly provide the guidance necessary to maintain program quality and direct expansion. During the Progressive Era, the University of California emerged as the nation's largest higher education institution. In the midst of the post-World War II emphasis on expanding higher educational opportunity in the state, however, California's state colleges surpassed the university in total enrollment. This was a historic transition—one that university officials, and Sproul in particular, had long fought to prevent. There were numerous political implications to such a shift. University alumni who had gone on to elected office in Sacramento and in local communities would be replaced, in part, by state college alumni. The rapid growth in enrollment and the establishment of new campuses would expand the geographic presence, public support, and political power of the state colleges.

For the authors of the Strayer Report, there really was no other acceptable alternative to the existing system of governance. Strayer and Douglass wanted to preserve, as much as possible, the semiautonomous status of California's individual segments: they had different roles and often different constituents. Strayer and Douglass also wanted to present a report that all constituents, namely, the education community, the governor, legislators, and the public, would be willing to embrace. The authors' call for the master's degree in the state colleges and the list of suitable sites for new campuses and programs were radical enough; they were recommendations that might find opposition, although probably muted, within the University of California. For these reasons, the Strayer Report simply endorsed the voluntary model provided by the Liaison Committee—the very body that would need to endorse the report on its way to the legislature.[73]

As a document intended to immediately influence the legislature, the Strayer Report had substantial success. Most of its recommendations were not intended as legislative measures, but, rather, were a basis for planning. However, the report sanctified legislation that permanently established Sacramento and Los Angeles State Colleges. Bolstered by the report's recommendations, in 1949 Assemblyman John Babbage sponsored legislation successfully asking the regents to elevate Riverside to a general campus of the university with instruction to begin in 1954.[74] Legislators passed bills for the establishment of a new state college in Long Beach, and the regents approved new professional programs in medicine, law, and engineering at UCLA. The report also encouraged local initiatives to create new junior colleges. New state subsidies supported the establishment of fourteen junior colleges between 1945 and 1950.

The Strayer Report forced a truce between the University of California, the state colleges, and their respective supporters. For the first time since the Progressive Era, there appeared to be a consensus. The report gave the Liaison Committee credibility, at least for the time being, as a coordinating agency for the state's rapidly growing higher education system. The higher education community, it was shown, could produce effective leadership in setting policy and influencing the legislature.

The Postwar Experience

The postwar years represented a transitional period for California's economy, marked by high unemployment, a scarcity of raw materials for industry, and a lack of consumer goods. These trends reflected national norms, but California had particular difficulties. Employment in manufacturing industries fell from a wartime high of approximately 1.2 million jobs to a postwar low in 1947 of 735,000. This was the only major sector in California's economy to quickly decline with the end of the war. As Warren and others had feared, California's unemployment rate rose sharply. In 1943 and 1944, the state had less than 1 percent of the labor force unemployed. Shortly after the war, federal expenditures to defense-related industries declined, and a total of 583,000 veterans returned to civilian life, significantly expanding the state's labor pool. In total, veterans suddenly represented approximately 15 percent of California's work force.[75]

As a result, in early 1946 unemployment jumped to approximately 11 percent. However, as many veterans took advantage of the G.I. Bill and entered higher education institutions, unemployment declined to roughly 9 percent by the end of the year. The rate would then fluctuate before declining to 7.7 percent by 1950.[76] While even lower unemployment rates were certainly the goal of Warren, they stood in stark contrast to the 1944 projections of possibly 20 percent or higher. Compared to the nation as whole, however, California still had very high unemployment, reflecting the state's postwar dependency on federal expenditures. National rates were approximately 4 percent in 1946 and rose slightly to 5.3 percent in 1950.[77]

State government policies mitigated what could have been an even more devastating postwar decline. Perhaps more importantly, planning efforts positioned California for long-term economic growth. Warren's administration embarked on the public works projects and the expansion of public higher education, outlined in the various studies by the Postwar Planning Commission. These programs were subsidized by federal grants for housing, highway construction, and the G.I. Bill and were fueled by the state's sizable budget surplus. State government expenditures rose significantly. Between 1945 and 1950, expenditures increased from approximately 250 million dollars per year to California's first billion dollar budget in 1950, a 333 percent increase.[78]

By 1950, California state government was also spending more than it was generating in revenues. (See Figure 6.) California could balance its budget yearly by dipping into the state surplus generated during and after the war. In 1948, the state had a surplus of over 813,000 million dollars, a sum larger than the state's entire budget for that year. The size of the surplus and the recovery of the state's economy essentially delayed reform to a tax structure that dated back to the Great Depression.

The vast majority of the state budget went to capital construction, local assistance, and education. Expenditures increased from a paltry 13 million dollars for capital outlay in 1944 to 225 million per year in 1950. Funding for education received an even greater increase: it escalated from $92 million in 1944 to $352 million five years later.[79] Approximately one third of this increase went to public higher education and helped fund a nearly threefold increase in enrollment (from 26,400 to 79,500 students) in the University of California and the state colleges. The public junior colleges accommodated a

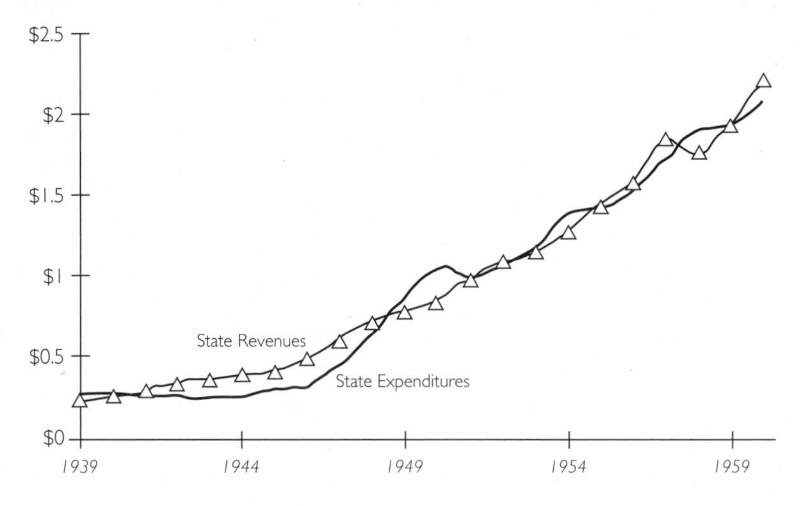

Figure 6. California State Government Operating Expenditures and Revenues, 1939–1960 (billions)
SOURCE: *California Statistical Abstract,* 1961

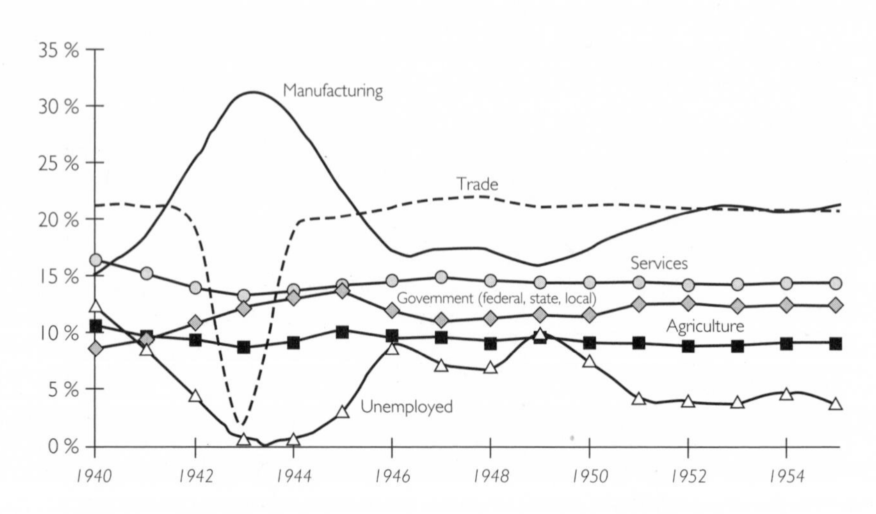

Figure 7. California Civilian Labor Force in Six Major Categories, 1940–1955
SOURCE: *California Statistical Abstract,* 1961

similar surge, growing from approximately 60,000 full- and part-time students to over 142,000 in 1950. Veterans supported by the G.I. Bill made up approximately 40 percent of all public higher education enrollment in the three years after the war.[80]

By the time these veterans were reentering the job market, California's postwar economy was recovering. The state's manufacturing sector was once again growing with the largest percentage of new jobs in aircraft, transportation, and electronics industries. Nonagricultural jobs had declined from a wartime peak of 3.1 million in 1944 to a postwar low of 2.9 million in 1946. By 1950, however, the nonagricultural jobs had rebounded, topping 3.2 million. Both in the total number of workers and in the value of goods and services, California's manufacturing sector became the state's primary source of economic growth for the next two decades.[81] (See Figure 7.)

California's relatively successful transition to a postwar economy was certainly due to other variables besides the expansion of higher education. For one, as in the rest of the nation, pent-up consumer demand during the war led to the building of substantial savings among Californians. The wartime surplus of funds and voter approval of bond acts also allowed state government to maintain low tax burdens for Californians. This helped create jobs in the private sector and allowed Californians to keep a larger portion of the incomes for the purchase of goods and services. Another significant factor was the ability of Californians to claim a substantial flow of funds from Washington during the postwar period, both for defense-related industries and for housing and highways. In part, the state's success at gaining these moneys was a result of the planning efforts launched by the Warren administration. When federal funds were allocated for housing and other needs, local planning agencies were in a position to argue for their fair share and often for more.

State and local officials and business interests also campaigned hard to retain key industries and military bases. As a result, while overall military spending declined after 1945, California managed to increase its share of the federal budget. By 1948, the cold war had renewed federal funding for the increasingly technology-dependent defense industries that had emerged in California during the war. There never was a full transition to a peacetime economy.[82]

CHAPTER 7

Rising Costs, the Red Scare, and the End of the Postwar Consensus

> Nearly every local chamber of commerce in the state was working to get a campus of the university or the state college system [with] the same significance as a new factory or business establishment. Here was no yearning for culture but for all the economic advantages of payrolls and purchases.
>
> —ARTHUR COONS, 1968

> While American youth is being conscribed to die fighting Communistic barbarism in Korea and elsewhere, it is proposed to accord to thirty-nine professors and assistant professors on the many campuses of the University of California the privilege of defying a simple regulation to protect the institution which is engaged in research vital to national defense.
>
> —*SAN FRANCISCO EXAMINER*, 1950

The postwar years brought major changes to American higher education. The G.I. Bill, the creation of the National Science Foundation, and the substantial increases in direct student aid under post-Sputnik federal legislation initiated a new era of federal involvement in higher education. Such injections of federal influence significantly shaped the research activities of the nation's leading universities, led to curricular reforms intended to bolster training in the sciences, and generally elevated the importance of higher education within American society.

Another postwar trend was equally important. Virtually all states were engaged in a political discourse on how to expand their respective systems of higher education. At stake was the development of a high-quality work force and a competitive environment to attract and retain industries, as well as the expansion of the research prowess of a nation immersed in the cold war. The ideal of a high-quality state system of higher education for the masses was a goal shared by a growing contingent of public leaders. How might this be achieved? The burden fell largely to the nation's public institutions and the coffers of state and local governments.

Despite the rancorous debate regarding the role of the state colleges within California's tripartite system, the state retained a relatively orderly network of public and private colleges and universities. As described by Lyman Glenny in the first comprehensive study of state higher education coordination and governance, American higher education throughout most of the century represented "a happy anarchy."[1] The diversity of institutions was staggering. The largely postwar idea of coordinating these institutions, in particular public colleges and universities, into a cohesive whole that would expand higher education opportunity posed a major challenge to policymakers. How might a state expand enrollment and programs within what were traditionally highly autonomous and often regionally oriented institutions, and at an affordable cost?

A National Movement Toward Centralization

In the midst of cold war fears and a new faith in science, numerous national studies continued to argue that the United States needed to significantly expand higher education opportunity. In 1954, the Commission on Human Resources and Advanced Training, one of several federal agencies studying America's future labor needs, explained that the nation was "not preparing enough men and women to meet the growing demands in teaching, engineering, the social sciences, the humanities, the natural sciences, and the health sciences." Not enough qualified high school students, it was stated, were going to college. States had not sufficiently expanded college and university programs and enrollment. Failure to develop the talents of America's youth, continued the report, "constitutes gross neglect of the country's most valuable resources."[2]

Leaders in state government increasingly saw the need to equalize educational opportunity, to essentially lower the economic and social barriers to attending a higher education institution, and to provide a greater geographic distribution of colleges and universities. State governments, it was believed, needed to guide and shoulder a significant new financial burden to expand higher education.

However, this was not the only concern of state governments. State coffers needed to fund a great variety of other services that were deemed essential to a growing population. These included the expansion of schools, highway construction, mental health services, new prisons, and social welfare programs. While the 1930s and the war had defined a new role for the federal government in the life of the nation, the postwar period fostered a significant expansion in the responsibilities of state government. With this new activist role, states sought new organizational structures to deal with a plethora of relatively new policy issues. Legislatures, including California's, expanded their staffing and moved toward year-round deliberations. Governors attempted to reorganize state government and gain greater authority to make budget decisions and direct state agencies.

Within this larger context of state building, lawmakers in California and in other states discussed methods to gain greater control of their respective networks of higher education institutions. "Not only is higher education in severe competition with other governmental services," observed John Lederle, a former a state budget officer in Michigan, "but individual colleges and universities are in competition with each other for that portion of total funds to be allocated to higher education. . . . In this highly competitive atmosphere, state budget officers, governors, and legislators are understandably asking more and more detailed questions about the management and programs of public colleges and universities."[3] By the 1950s, lawmakers in many states began to consolidate public higher education institutions under one or more boards to promote "efficiencies" and to develop regulatory controls in areas such as academic personnel—much to the consternation of the higher education community.

With the trend toward greater state control of higher education and the increased scrutiny of universities and colleges as alleged sanctuaries for communist and socialist ideologies, Richard Hofstadter and Walter Metzger called the growing assault on institutional autonomy and academic freedom "one of the central issues of our time."[4] Was autonomy, a major feature of American higher education and an ideal cherished by university and college presidents and faculty, to wither under the pressures of ideological shifts, unprecedented enrollment expansion, and budgetary constraints?

Marritt M. Chambers voiced his alarm at what he called the "meat cleaver" approach of legislators. "It is the responsibility of state legislatures to find the means for supporting a great and growing system of public higher education in an affluent society—not to design the system in the likeness of a chain of filling-stations." The impulse of lawmakers and bureaucrats, he caustically noted, is for centralization and a reduction in autonomy that tends "to cripple or destroy the fundamental nature and functions of a university." The politically induced path toward coordination and centralization was "self-defeating, resulting in mediocrity."[5]

Chambers's concerns were also those of a group of educational leaders meeting as the Committee on Government and Higher Education in 1959 and chaired by Milton S. Eisenhower, president of Johns Hopkins University. A report issued by Eisenhower's committee, *Efficiency of Freedom,* attempted to reconcile the goal of efficient state government and the need for autonomy: "Intellectual freedom may suffer seriously," they warned, "if public colleges and universities are subject to the same controls as other state activities."[6]

Rising Costs and the Regional Demand for New Campuses

In California, the logic of the tripartite system and the forming of the state's first plan for the expansion of higher education in 1948 stalled any serious discussion of reorganizing higher education. By the early 1950s, two factors broke the postwar consensus. First, California's economy and population grew at a much faster pace than anticipated in the Strayer Report. The results were an unanticipated level of demand for higher education by college-age Californians and an increasing interest of lawmakers to create new institutions in their own districts. Second, and in the midst of a national recession, the rising cost of funding higher education alarmed many lawmakers, who, in turn, began to demand a greater role in the management and expansion of the state's public colleges and universities.

In the eyes of lawmakers, and often for different reasons, the expansion of California's education system was too important to leave simply to the individual boards or to academic administrators and their school faculties. Improving social and economic mobility was at the heart of every lawmaker's demand for a new college or expanded programs in existing public institutions. It was also vital for regional economic development. While this was not a new theme, the change in the labor needs of the state made it a more salient part of the political discourse.

California business leaders constantly complained of skilled labor shortages in areas such as engineering and other "applied" and technical professions, which were often linked to California's booming cold war defense industries. While many companies expanded their own training programs, the business community increasingly looked toward public and private schooling to educate professionals. In turn, local community leaders demanded new state-supported institutions to maintain existing businesses and attract new ones. To be without a college or university campus, noted local government representatives and their legislators, was a form of discrimination, hindering economic growth and forcing local and promising students to other more prosperous regions.[7] "A higher education is now practically a must for our youth," explained a legislative committee during the legislative session. "[T]here are so many high positions available in the engineering field, [and] technical work . . . that are not supplied." In his effort to support a bill for a state college in Stanislaus County, Mayor E. S. Christofferson of Turlock stated:

> [T]he area surrounding the state colleges is favored with the students coming out of the college with the proper education and taking employment in that vicinity, leaving areas many miles away from the college with a greater percentage of their requirements unfilled for college trained personnel. . . . This shortage in our area is not giving us equal rights with the locations of the present state colleges. We are, therefore, retarded from proper growth of industrial expansion.[8]

The bid for a campus in Turlock came in the midst of yet another flood of migration to California from other states. "Since the last war there has been a heavy migration of footloose Americans," explained the *Saturday Evening Post*. In great droves, Americans were leaving the country for industrial centers or were shifting from cities into new suburban developments. The greatest shift was toward the West, with the largest migration to California.[9] "The vast influx of people to man the garrisons and defense plants of California," reflected a 1957 legislative report, brought 2.2 million people to the state during the war and 1.3 million between 1945 and 1950. But the greatest surge was yet to come. A second tidal wave of humanity, bigger than that of the war years, rolled over California with an increase of 2.99 million people from 1950 to 1956.[10] California's growing population brought a corresponding increase in demand for access to public higher education. In 1953, enrollment in institutions of public and private higher education exceeded the projections of the Strayer Report by 16 percent.

The crush of people and the desire to bolster regional economies led to a new onslaught of bills. Despite the call by the 1948 Strayer Report for a careful study of any new campus proposal by the Liaison Committee and the two higher education boards, many lawmakers announced that they were not willing to defer to the higher education community. In 1953, state senator Hugh P. Donnelly introduced a bill to create a state college in his home district of Modesto.[11] Powerful assemblyman Carlos Bee of Alameda did the same for his district, and Ben Hulse announced his plans to create a college in El Centro.[12] None of the bills were presented to the Board of Regents or the State Board of Education of Education for study. "Everybody wanted a campus in the worst way," explained Hubert Semans, an analyst for the State Department of Education.[13]

Despite the renewed entrepreneurial spirit of lawmakers to create new campuses and programs, there existed a significant barrier to their ambitions. The continued influx in population and the increased demand for access to higher education were accompanied by significant fiscal problems for the state. Since 1949, yearly state expenditures had outpaced revenues. Under the strain of a substantial postwar expansion of government services, the war-time surplus had rapidly dwindled. For the first time since the Great Depression, California government faced the prospect of substantial and prolonged budget deficits. In 1952, Governor Warren advocated increasing taxes, noting that the tax burden of Californians was among the lowest of the major industrial states. To rely on the state's "rainy day fund" or on raiding various pensions to balance the budget, stated the governor, was like the "improvident farmer who would eat up his seed corn, and then face a certain deficit."[14] However, Warren's pleas for a new sin tax on cigarettes and increasing levies on liquor and horse racing were vehemently opposed by most lawmakers and powerful lobbying groups.

California's vexing budget problems in 1953 corresponded with a national recession, as well as with Warren's resignation as governor in September. With his presidential ambitions thwarted by the election of Dwight Eisenhower, Warren accepted the president's invitation to become the chief justice of the U.S. Supreme Court. Lieutenant Governor Goodwin Knight, Warren's republican and conservative rival, subsequently became governor. Knight shared the opinion of a growing number of lawmakers: The way to solve California's budget problems was to cut services, not raise revenue. Knight argued that Warren had created a revenue-eating monstrosity in the postwar period, and he asked legislators to reduce state costs. In short, Warren had created in California his very own "New Deal" built around the foundation of an activist government.

Within this context, Assembly Ways and Means Committee members questioned why California should have three different public higher education segments. Was this not a waste of administrative costs? Was there indeed a large difference in the undergraduate training of the different institutions or in the capabilities of their graduates? In the midst of an economic recession, the seemingly endless series of conflicts between the regents and the State Board of Education, and the efforts of a number of legislators to establish new campuses in their districts, the Republican leadership in the assembly and the senate grew more frustrated with California's higher education system. Various legislative committees requested detailed information on program activities and the costs of operating the three and disparate public segments. For the first time, legislators expressed the fear that public money was being wasted on a large scale.

Before the Assembly Ways and Means Committee, A. Alan Post, the legislative auditor, complained that some junior college programs were providing upper division courses as part of a renewed effort to become four-year institutions. He also expressed the worry that California's public tripartite system fostered other instances of unnecessary duplication. There appeared to be no effective method of regulating new program growth. Concerned particularly with the rising costs of the junior college system, the Senate Finance Committee directed Post to "determine the amount of Junior college courses which are above the 14th grade level or comparable to upper division (15th and 16th grade) offerings of a college or University."[15] At the same time, the Assembly Ways and Means Subcommittee on Education requested Superintendent Simpson to present a study of the financial expenses and future needs of the junior colleges and state colleges and to explain the relationship between the three public segments.

Assemblyman Lloyd Bowers, a Yolo County Republican and the chair of the Ways and Means Committee, was upset with the prospect of substantial state debt. He proclaimed that the legislature should not pledge another dollar until the education community could tell the committee how much it costs to educate a teacher and how much it costs to build a new campus of either the state colleges or the university. How could the legislature make budgetary decisions, explained Bowers, without understanding the differential in "unit costs" between the segments and the institutions?[16]

Bowers' frustration was a result of a confusing and largely antiquated budgetary process. It was virtually impossible to understand the current and future costs of the disparate segments. There also was no comparative analysis of costs among the various public and private segments and their individual campuses. The legislature's methods for fund distribution to different public postsecondary institutions dated back to the Progressive Era. The University of California would approach the legislature and the governor with a single budgetary request that included both operating and capital budgets. However, when the state committed to construction or additional personnel for a new program on one of its campuses, there was no projection of what the state's future costs would be.[17]

The same questions of future costs could be asked of the state colleges, with much greater complexities. Reflecting the independent nature of these institutions and their historical developments as separate entities, each of the ten campuses submitted their own budgets to the legislature after a cursory stamp of approval by Simpson and the Department of Education. Combined with the persistent effort of different legislators to gain new campuses by statute, the budgetary picture for higher education was murky.

When asked detailed questions about their current and future budgets by Bowers and others in 1953, neither the university nor the state colleges could provide adequate answers. On the one hand, the university, with the benefit of a centralized system of governance and the acumen of their Sacramento lobbyist James Corley, could provide some data on the direction of their budget and its meaning. On the other hand, the State Department of Education did not know how to outline the current and future costs of the state colleges. Following the normal yearly cycle, state college presidents continued to visit Sacramento, pounding on the doors of lawmakers and lobbying for the budgets of their individual campuses. The State Department of Education, specifically Superintendent Simpson, came under increasing legislative criticism for not taking a stronger leadership role in managing the state colleges.

The demand for an analysis of unit costs within California's public higher education system was soon accompanied by a similar request by several legislators for comparable costs within private colleges and universities. Since its entrance into the Union, California scrupulously avoided any financial support to private institutions, in part because of their sectarian ties, but also to focus state funds on the development of a public and tuition-free education system. Indeed, since 1879, the state constitution specifically forbade any direct funding of private education. However, the growing costs of the public tripartite system and doubts about its efficiency brought a shift in the position of the legislature.

The 1948 Strayer Report had recommended the creation of a state scholarship fund that, like the G.I. Bill, students could use for enrolling in either public or private institutions. The State Board of Education had approved the idea; but the university officials opposed it. Fearing a further drain on their share of state resources, university officials claimed that the California government should not provide subsidization to private colleges and universities. Assemblyman Joseph Shell, whose district included the University of Southern California, and state senator Donald Doyle revived the idea. Shell and Doyle speculated that private colleges and universities could take on more students at less cost to the state than, say, the University of California. Further, Shell argued, it was in California's interest to maintain and encourage a vibrant private college and university segment.

The cavalcade of questions from lawmakers and the number of new bills to create new campuses alarmed university and state college officials. William Blair, the chair of the State Board of Education, and Edward Dickson, the new chair of the regents, met with President Sproul and Superintendent Simpson to explore how the higher education community might respond. The problems they confronted were numerous. Several legislators suggested that it was time to "restudy" the Strayer Report. Assembly Speaker James W. Silliman proposed that a new plan for California higher education should not be conducted by the higher education community, as in the Strayer Report, but under the auspices of the legislature. Silliman favored a survey group with people from "business, industry and the professions," who would report to a special joint committee of the assembly and senate.[18] In Silliman's opinion and those of lawmakers such as Shell and Doyle, there were other indicators that California's higher education community was perhaps incapable of devising a useful new plan.

The Complications of the Red Scare

The relatively newfound interest in the internal workings of the state's higher education system dovetailed with another and politically volatile issue: the arrival of McCarthyism. The growing antagonism between lawmakers and the higher education community was colored, in part, by charges of communist sympathizers within California's public colleges and universities. Particularly after 1947, California's political environment had turned decidedly conservative. Was the university an instrument serving the needs of the state and the nation or a hotbed of subversive activity?

The hysteria of the Red scare added considerably to the difficulties of legislative and public postsecondary relations. In part to mollify the concerns of the legislature, the regents struck a hard line intended to eliminate any appearance that the institution would harbor or tolerate communist sympathizers within the faculty or among the student body. The result was a conflict within the university that shook the institution and compromised its reputation as a bastion of free thought.[19]

As early as 1941, the legislature established its own "Little Dies Committee," a version of Congress' Committee on Un-American Activities, chaired for years by Senator Martin Dies. The fact-finding joint committee in California was chaired by Jack B. Tenney, a Republican state senator from Los Angeles, a member of the legislative subcommittee that worked with Strayer's survey team, and onetime protégé of famous and influential Sacramento lobbyist Arthur H. Samish. Tenney's fame lay in his unrelenting attacks on supposed Communist infiltration of California society. He also was one of several legislators who chaired investigative committees on subversion and sedition, as well as committees on education. Hugh Burns, Tenney's successor, and later Senator Nelson Dilworth also followed this path. Tenney's Committee on Un-American Activities "bullied witnesses and denied them the rights of due process, bracketing the innocent with the guilty," noted California historian and Berkeley Professor Walton Bean. Like McCarthy, Tenney convicted by accusation.[20]

Tenney and his committee repeatedly attacked the university. Precisely because campuses such as Berkeley were such an important source of basic science research and defense-related technologies, conservatives focused on higher education in their search for subversives. Indeed, the upheaval of the Great Depression and the destruction of the war caused many university scholars to express sympathy for alternative ideologies to capitalism. Throughout the 1930s, the regents had shown a level of tolerance toward alternative opinions. However, at the outset of the war, the regents stated that "no member of the Communist Party shall be employed by the university." The regents, with the support of President Sproul, began a concerted effort to keep the university free of communist sympathizers. While many in the university supported the regents and Sproul in this endeavor, a fervent minority of faculty and students saw this as a threat to academic freedom.

In early 1945, a small group of UCLA students chose to support the union movement in Hollywood. In October of that year, with the pending conversion of Russia from ally to foe, they joined a picket line at the entrance of Warner Brothers Studio. Some were members of a supposedly Communist organization, American Youth for Democracy, which had a chapter at the Los Angeles campus. In turn, a legislative committee investigated the strike, and the attention embarrassed the regents. Lieutenant Governor Frederick F. Houser commented at a meeting of the regents that student participation in the strike, and the apparent sympathy of some faculty, was doing "great harm to the University in the Legislature." The regents needed to take action or it was doubtful that the university would get "one-half of the funds requested for postwar buildings and perhaps would get nothing."[21] Houser then collaborated with the chair of the regents, Edward Dickson, a member of the Republican Central Committee of California and the "father of UCLA," in drafting a resolution. "The basis of education and instruction at the University of California shall be loyalty to American Institutions and to the American form of government. Any member of the faculty violating this principle shall be subject to dismissal." Further, the resolution stated, "no Student shall engage in any off-campus activity in which he shall do anything intended to or which does convey the impression that he represents the University of California" without university authority.[22]

Several days later, the regents adopted a slightly more subdued version of the resolution, but the gist of Houser and Dickson's approach remained. The regents were intolerant of any hint of subversive activity. While the regents were concerned that the charges of the Tenney Committee were true, their actions were intended to comfort the legislature. A year later, at the second All-University Faculty Conference, Sproul led a discussion of the postwar context that faced the university. Increasing public hostility toward the university, Sproul observed, was the result of both the university's opposition to new state college campuses and the fear of subversive activity. A special Academic Senate committee, chaired by Professor Harold Ellis, explained: "There are altogether too many who believe that there is a large and solid core of faculty members who not only are ultraliberal in their views, but are in fact subversive in their actions—that they use their positions to expound and promulgate the theories of government and society not tolerated in the thinking of the great majority of American citizens."[23] Another Academic Senate study group noted the paradox faced by the faculty: "To be silent is to incur the charge of secluding ourselves in the ivory tower; to speak out is to expose ourselves to attack as impractical meddlers." As a result, the report urged that the more vocal elements of the faculty might moderate their activities "by limiting our public statements to matters in which each of us is an expert. . . . " In this manner, "we can perhaps in time gain greater respect from the public for the scholar."[24]

In 1947 and 1948, while the Strayer Committee met, Senator Tenney's Committee on Un-American Activities produced two reports charging faculty and students with involvement with allegedly Communist organizations. The Communist Party, lamented a 1947 legislative report, had secured "a certain degree of collaboration from faculty members of the University of California in Berkeley and at Los Angeles."[25] Guilt by association extended to several faculty members, including Professor J. Robert Oppenheimer, former director of the Manhattan Project. The publicity generated by such charges did much to boost Tenney's fervor, and in the 1949 legislative session the senator proposed thirteen bills intended to cleanse state government and its institutions. One bill would require all state employees to attest to their patriotism—essentially a pledge of allegiance—and confirm that they had no affiliation with the Communist Party. Because of the semiautonomous position of the university under the state constitution, Tenney proposed a constitutional amendment that would require the same of university officers and employees.

President Sproul worried that the proposed amendment, by linking the university to other state agencies, might compromise the ability of the regents to govern its affairs. At the same time, controversy was brewing over student participation at UCLA in a pro-union paper, the *Hollywood Quarterly*, and a planned campus lecture by British Labour Party member Harold J. Laski.[26] Worried over the public perception of another instance of harboring subversives, the regents attempted to disassociate themselves from the paper and made it clear that such a lecture on university property was unwelcome.

These pressures caused Sproul and Corley to urge the regents to create their own loyalty oath. The proposal gained the fervent support of Regent Lawrence Mario Giannini, the president of Bank of America, and the regents agreed. University faculty and other employees would have to swear that they did not believe in, were not members of, and did not "support any party or organization that believes in, advocates, or teaches the overthrow of the United State government." Subsequently, Tenney dropped his amendment. While the strategic move of the regents brought a level of solace to legislators and perhaps the public, it launched a heated debate between the university's board and a contingent of faculty who claimed that the oath seriously compromised academic freedom. Many distinguished professors warned that they would not sign any oath.[27]

With the support of Governor Earl Warren in early 1950, Sproul reversed his support of the oath and asked the regents to reconsider. Shortly after implementation of the new university oath, Tenney was censured by the legislature and forced to resign. His McCarthy-like allegations had become so wild that he accused fellow legislators of being Communist sympathizers. Senator Hugh Burns, the conservative Democrat from Fresno and member of the legislative subcommittee that worked on the Strayer Report, became chair of Tenney's committee. Under his somewhat more moderate leadership, Sproul and Warren felt the university could back out of the loyalty oath.

Initially, Warren was quiet on the matter and, like past governors, he rarely attended meetings of the regents. Later, however, he declared the oath ineffective, one that "any communist would take—and laugh about it."[28] At a March 1950 meeting of the regents, Warren announced that he was an alumnus of the university with three children already attending the institution. "I would cut my right arm off before I would willingly submit my youngsters to the wiles or infamy of a Communist faculty. I don't believe that the faculty of the University of California is Communist; I don't believe that it is soft on Communism, and neither am I."[29]

Despite Warren's call for moderation, Giannini, along with Regent John Francis Neylan, a strong booster of UCLA and an admirer of Senator McCarthy, gained the support of a slim majority of regents to uphold the oath. Neylan's interest in the development of the Los Angeles campus intensified his desire to require the written allegiance of faculty. After several failed attempts between the regents and Academic Senate representatives to seriously modify the oath, in 1950 thirty-one faculty members were dismissed for not signing. The faculty truly pondered the meaning of academic freedom and the purpose of the Academic Senate. The senate had, in fact, proven to be a disjointed and poorly structured vehicle for presenting the collective opinion of the faculty. "Antagonism was in many ways less severe between the board and the senate than among members of the faculty holding positions of leadership and their nonsigning colleagues," stated David Gardner in his 1967 book, *The California Oath Controversy*.[30] What began with pronouncements of principle, notes Gardner, broke down into a "failure of educated, competent, and allegedly rational human beings bound together in a good cause—the service of truth and knowledge—to resolve their difference without injury to the University as a whole."[31]

"The whole sorry story of the oath is one of confusion and repudiations, acerbity and bitterness," explained Russell H. Fitzgibbon in his history of the university's academic senate, with "more concern at times with procedural than substantive aspects. . . . The scar tissue was hard and durable."[32]

While certainly not united in their opinion, a large majority of the faculty now felt a level of alienation from its board and from the administration. Even after the state supreme court invalidated the oath in 1952 and authorized the reinstatement of the thirty-one faculty members, the turbulence within the university continued.[33]

The oath controversy resulted in an internal reevaluation of the direction and purpose of the university. The academic senate began a process of reorganization, including the establishment of a Committee on Academic Freedom. Regent Neylan's fight with Sproul weakened the university president's ability to guide the will of the regents. Neylan, ever interested in the issues that would legitimize UCLA as a coequal of the Berkeley campus, successfully pushed for a more decentralized system of administration. Despite Sproul's opposition, in 1952 the regents established the position of chancellor at both Berkeley and Los Angeles with the respective appointments of Berkeley professor and labor economist Clark Kerr and Raymond B. Allen, former president of the University of Washington.[34] In his post in Washington, Allen had guided the institution through its own oath controversy, which had led to the dismissal of two professors.

The strong action of the regents to enforce the oath failed to mollify Senator Burns and other legislators' concern with Communist sympathizers. In the early 1950s, Burns managed to develop contacts at every campus, according to Kerr, to help screen or clear appointments "on the grounds that Burns' committee had the best files on subversives."[35] Several years later, Burns' Committee on Un-American Activities complained that "there is not the slightest doubt about Communist infiltration of higher learning. When this committee undertook to make some inquiries about subversive infiltration of the University of California in 1952, there was a storm of faculty protest."[36]

As a result of the university's oath controversy and the heightened sense that America was in a mortal battle against Communism, both in distant places such as Korea and at home, the California Legislature passed the Levering Act of 1952. The "Levering oath" was a constitutional amendment, endorsed by a large majority of Californians and a politically motivated Governor Warren. It was essentially an adoption of the 1949 proposal by Senator Tenney. Under the amendment, all public employees, including those of the university, would need to attest to their patriotism. Other groups required to sign the oath included "all taxpayers who claim an exemption . . . groups using public schools facilities for civic or recreational activities [and] members of county central committees of political parties."

A fear of conspiracies within Los Angeles' school system, allegedly supported by the activity of UCLA faculty and students, led to the 1953 Dilworth Act. Sponsored by Senator Nelson Dilworth, chair of the Senate Committee on Education, this act prohibited the "advocacy or teaching of Communism," required local school teachers to take the oath, and, under a 1955 amendment, provided "a method of questioning teachers about their membership in the Communist Party." Numerous legal challenges made it difficult to purge subversives. Under Dilworth's proposal, if a teacher, or a professor, did not adequately answer the questions of membership by a legislative investigating committee or of the governing board of the university or state colleges, he or she could be dismissed. Under this law, a San Diego State professor and several teachers were fired in 1955 by the State Board of Education.[37]

The Red scare had a far-reaching influence within all sectors of California's public education system. Dilworth's committee demonstrated the mixed feelings of many legislators towards higher education. The senator, a farmer from Hemet, was one of the most knowledgeable representatives in the legislature on school financing and administration. In 1949 he introduced the first large-scale sale of state bonds for local school construction.[38] Along with Governor Warren's director of finance, Jim Dean, and Alan Post, the legislative auditor, Dilworth developed a general method for capital planning (e.g., five-year building programs, state funding by project phase) that is still in place. Stanley Van Buren, Warren's director for the State Planning Agency, which took over the work of the Readjustment and Reemployment Commission in 1948, also worked with Dilworth and the Public Works Board (created in 1946) to provide state funds for expanding the university and state colleges.

However, as one observer noted, Dilworth, who had also been a member of Tenney's Committee, "saw communists behind a lot of bushes."[39] Dilworth's committee spent as much time worrying about subversive activity within the schools and the university as planning for enrollment growth. As a result, between 1949 and 1959 six of the approximately fourteen major reports of the Senate Committee on Education were on anti-Communist themes with such titles as "Communist Attack on the Schools" (1949), "Are Loyalty Oaths Effective?" (1952), "Opposition to Loyalty" (1953), and "Patriotism or Pacifism, Which?" (1956).

The Red scare took a particularly heavy toll on the University of California. It embroiled the institution in internal conflict and shattered the long-held perception within the legislature of the university as a politically powerful and united monolith. Discord connoted weakness, reflecting upon the university, as well as on the ability of the entire public higher education community to chart their collective future.

A "Restudy" of Higher Education

Adding to the sense of disarray within the higher education community in 1953 was a renewal of hostilities between University of California and state college officials revolving around a single policy issue: engineering education. The Strayer Report placed pressure on the higher education community to further develop the concept of differentiation of functions. For President Sproul and the regents, this meant limiting the expansion of state college programs in areas such as engineering. In the intransigent position of the university, this was the domain of the Berkeley and Los Angeles campuses. Yet, several state college presidents and their local assembly and senate representatives saw things differently.

California's economy increasingly needed people with professional skills. Several state colleges, including those in San Diego, San Francisco, San Jose, and the new campus in Los Angeles, sought to expand their programs in engineering. With the support of the State Board of Education, James Enochs of the Department of Education and Frederick E. Terman, the Dean of Engineering at Stanford, completed a study recommending further expansion of these programs. Enochs and Terman also urged the state colleges to seek accreditation by the Engineers' Council for Professional Development (ECPD). Graduation from an ECPD-accredited program was a requirement for gaining an engineering license in California. Sproul and other university officials bitterly opposed any such development: It was just one of many instances, argued Sproul, of irresponsible program growth in the state colleges that encroach on university programs.

The Liaison Committee, created to foster cooperation between the university and the state colleges, found itself at yet another impasse. Sproul, with the support of Edward Dickson, the chair of the regents, voiced his opposition to the accreditation of state college engineering programs. State Superintendent Simpson, along with State Board of Education Chair William Blair, argued that these programs were necessary, especially in light of the university's stated inability to offer similar programs in key areas of the state, including San Diego and San Jose. Only the Berkeley and Los Angeles campuses offered engineering programs, and enrollment was limited. Yet, business leaders throughout the state, particularly in defense-related industries, clamored for qualified engineers.

Sproul, Dickson, Simpson, and Blair, however, agreed that they needed to devise a way to update the Strayer Report, arbitrate their differences, answer the queries of lawmakers regarding budget matters, and halt the aggressive effort of a growing number of legislators to establish new colleges. As in 1947, they also sought a method to delay pending legislation in Sacramento until a study could be completed. Reflecting on the success of the Strayer Report, Sproul once again proposed that the Liaison Committee form a study team, sanctioned by the legislature and headed by an independent professional similar to George Strayer—someone without direct ties to either the university or the state colleges.[40] Sproul sought the support of Governor Warren for the study and for a moratorium on pending bills for new college campuses. Warren, only a few months away from his appointment as chief justice of the U.S. Supreme Court, vigorously endorsed the proposal.

In early 1953 and with the full support of both the regents and the State Board of Education, Sproul and Simpson asked the Assembly Ways and Means Committee to sanction a "restudy." In the "interests of efficiency and economy," they stated, the Liaison Committee should "be authorized and directed to make a survey of the objectives, future enrollments, curricula, and the costs of collegiate grade public education in California, with due attention to comparable curricula and costs in private institutions."[41] Because of the magnitude of this task, Sproul and Simpson requested a period of almost two years to complete the report, suggesting a submittal date of January 1, 1955. This deadline corresponded with the beginning of the next budget session of the legislature. Assemblyman Bowers was assured that a detailed analysis of costs among both public and private institutions of higher education would be included.[42]

In March 1953, the Ways and Means Committee approved the proposed study. They also provided a minor allocation of state funds for its completion and gained a general agreement by the legislative leadership to delay all bills for new campuses. The action of lawmakers was a major victory for the higher education community. Shortly after, Sproul and Simpson announced the appointment of Thomas R. McConnell, former chancellor at the University of Buffalo and a noted expert on educational policy, as the "chief consultant." McConnell was teamed with Hubert H. Semans and Thomas C. Holy, representing the State Department of Education and the University of

California, respectively, as the main authors of the pending report. Semans was a former dean at the Cal Poly campus in San Luis Obispo. Holy was a retired director of the Bureau of Educational Research at Ohio State and a participant in similar studies in Ohio, Oregon, and West Virginia. Both had been hired two years earlier to act as the main team support for the Liaison Committee. With the restudy team under T. R. McConnell's direction beginning their work in early 1954, President Sproul noted: "[S]peed is important. . . . Our budgets and our relations with the legislature and the public in general are involved."[43]

However, as a method to ameliorate the relations between the legislature and the higher education community, the Restudy Report would prove a disaster. The restudy failed to mollify the diverse interests of the legislature and the public segments, and it offered a controversial method to control costs: cease the construction of new public four-year campuses and enlarge only existing institutions.

At the outset, the restudy appeared compromised by political pressures. "I don't think anyone realized how conservative our enrollment projections were," explained coauthor Hubert Semans. Based on projections completed in consultation with the Department of Finance, the report estimated that approximately 234,000 students would be enrolled by 1965. Semans later noted that he, McConnell, and Holy thought the projections should be higher. The lower estimate reflected the political agenda of Governor Goodwin Knight, Warren's successor, to contain future state costs.[44] Nevertheless, the authors sought an economical way to expand the tripartite system. One important variable was the enrollment capacity for existing campuses.

The 1948 Strayer Report contended that large campuses were undesirable for pedagogical and financial reasons. Strayer stated that there were no real economies of scale when a campus grew past 5,000 students at a state college and around 10,000 students at a university campus. Once enrollments had exceeded these figures, a campus became unwieldy, impersonal, and mechanical in its treatment of students; below these magical numbers, "administrative organization can be efficiently maintained, small classes can be avoided, personnel, health and other services can be provided without unreasonable costs."[45] In an age when a university campus with more than 20,000 students was rare, force feeding students into only a few large-scale campuses would lead to bureaucratic inefficiency and degradation of the collegiate experience. Strayer and his coauthors also insisted that a key factor to expand higher education access was the creation of new institutions in areas with a growing population. Only in this way could the state provide a more equitable distribution of postsecondary education. Since there was no correlation of cost for operation of large and small campuses, it was in California's interest to expand the number of campuses in the near future. Anything less would reduce access.

Enrollment limits, explained the authors of the Restudy Report, had a profound impact on future planning and state costs. "The Restudy staff found no evidence that the quality of education at large institutions suffers in comparison with that at smaller ones,"[46] stated McConnell, Semans, and Holy. Further, there was clear evidence, based on their study of unit costs, that there were indeed economies of scale: smaller campuses, in general, cost more to operate. Further, new campuses required a substantial initial capital investment. The authors thus recommended that no new state college or university campuses be established before 1965. In light of the state's budget difficulties, they insisted that additional enrollment in four-year public institutions be simply absorbed by expanding existing campuses. To further reduce costs, the report requested that the university and state colleges reduce their lower-division student enrollment. The concept was to push more students toward the largely locally financed junior colleges with lower operating costs. To make this work and to further access to a postsecondary education, the team proposed the establishment of new junior colleges in several areas, including the counties of Alameda, San Diego, San Mateo, Santa Clara, Riverside, Colusa-Glenn-Butte, Santa Cruz, Merced-Madera, Siskiyou, Lake-Mendocino, and Los Angeles.[47]

The authors also anticipated a significant expansion of enrollment in California's private colleges and universities, and they again recommended the establishment of a state scholarship program that students could use to attend a private institution. This proposal was first introduced by the 1948 Strayer Report and was now supported by Assemblyman Shell and Senator Doyle.

Cognizant of anxious legislators clamoring for new state-supported campuses, McConnell in particular hoped that the ten-year moratorium would somehow appeal to the political interests of Governor Knight and other lawmakers concerned with containing state costs. The gamut might then halt what he viewed with alarm as the increasingly political process of establishing new campuses.[48] The proposed moratorium was a bold attempt to retain decision-making within the higher education community. But it was not the only daring proposal by McConnell and his coauthors. McConnell thought it important also to recommend the reorganization of California's tripartite system of higher education.

At the time, a number of states were engaged in review and restructuring of their education systems. In New York, where McConnell had spent most of his professional life, in 1948 the state legislature created the State University of New York to help the state expand higher education opportunity in the postwar environment. The reorganization placed twenty-seven existing postsecondary education institutions outside of New York City under a single board. This group of institutions consisted of ten teachers colleges, six agricultural and technical institutions, five institutes of applied arts and sciences, the State University Maritime College, and the five contracted colleges at Cornell and Alfred Universities. While each college and university was to be locally administered by a "council" of nine members appointed by the governor, the new State University Board of Trustees had the authority to coordinate their activities, including the expansion of academic programs and managing their budget. At the same time and reflecting the complexity of New York's system, the trustees were subject to the authority of the Board of Regents of the State of New York, which also had authority over the state's other major public conglomeration of higher education institutions: the City University of New York.[49]

North Carolina also sought methods to develop greater coordination of its public higher education system. As early as 1931, the state "consolidated and merged" its three existing, state land grant institutions into a single three-campus university called "The University of North Carolina," which was governed by a single board. There still remained nine other state-supported four-year colleges and some forty independent institutions. While the restudy team worked on their recommendations, the North Carolina Legislature created a Board of Higher Education to coordinate the activities of all higher education, public and private, in the state. As in New York, however, each institution retained its own local governing board. The statewide board was essentially a planning and coordinating authority, with a role in the annual state budget process. The power of the purse tended to be the major tool for controlling costs. Efforts to bring greater coordination of state systems of higher education were also being pursued in Indiana, Michigan, Minnesota, Ohio, and Oklahoma.

McConnell, Semans, and Holy recognized an urgent need to bring greater coordination to higher education in California. But they clearly did not favor any wholesale unification of the three components of California's system under a single board. McConnell was not sympathetic to the insistence of Sproul and the university that program growth at the state colleges should be severely restricted. He also recognized that the entrepreneurial efforts of college presidents, often without any supervision by the State Board of Education, were unacceptable. In light of significant budgetary problems for the state and a general sense of disarray within the higher education community, McConnell sought a way to improve the governance of the state colleges and modify their role in California society. He argued that "the most important task ahead is to bring [the state colleges] together into a clearly conceived, well coordinated system without weakening—rather, by actually strengthening—their regional responsibilities." To do this, the Restudy Report recommended that the state colleges no longer be governed by the State Board of Education: they should be placed under a new board devoted to their management. No other state, with the exception of New York's multilayered system, had a governing board with so many institutions to administer as California's Board of Education. Nor was Superintendent Simpson "with his heavy duties able to give day-by-day attention" that they deserved, explained McConnell.[50]

The Restudy Report proposed a nine-member state college lay board, with the superintendent of public instruction as an ex officio member. The other eight members would be appointed by the governor and confirmed by the state senate for four-year terms. A chief administrative officer would also be appointed for the development of policies and their implementation. Further, the report suggested that the board have a level of autonomy that would allow it to transfer funds from within its budget, as educational and administrative needs and operating efficiencies dictated. The growing restrictions imposed by the State Department of Education and other state agencies, it was observed, prevented such management and stifled creativity. Such restrictions were not faced by the University of California because of its status as a public trust.[51]

Much to the consternation of Sproul and other university officials, McConnell and his coauthors also advocated moderate changes in the mission of the state colleges. For one, they argued that the research efforts of state college faculty should be recognized. McConnell concluded that there should remain "a decided distinction between the University and the State College." The university should have the fundamental research function, he noted, but a "modest program of investigation or creative work should not be denied faculty members of all collegiate institutions . . . [and] certain special studies should be the particular province of the State Colleges." This included "service" research, which is "fact finding related to, and necessary for, the services of State Colleges to business, industry, public education, and civic agencies in their communities." University research, it was explained, should also be engaged in "applied," as well as "fundamental" or basic research, but most applied work should be statewide in character.[52]

Finally, McConnell, Semans, and Holy advocated the continued existence of the Liaison Committee as a voluntary coordinating agency.

A Major Political Mistake

In December 1954, the Liaison Committee had its first chance to review the recommendations of the restudy team. The report was due in approximately one month to the California legislature and Governor Goodwin Knight. It was quickly apparent that the lengthy study would not resolve the conflicting interests of the education community. University officials and faculty were wary of the proposal to create a new board for the state colleges. It would become a vehicle, it was believed, for the eventual expansion of state college programs into doctoral degrees and other areas thought to be the strict purview of the university. Sproul and key regents also were dead set against any statement that state college faculty should engage in research. While McConnell noted that the report did not advocate state appropriation for such activity, Sproul argued that any general statement that research was a legitimate activity of state college faculty was bound to result in claims for state funding. Before the Liaison Committee, for the first time President Sproul noted that "the University is now reconciled to the fact that there is a need for training in occupational fields beyond the baccalaureate degree, and that the State Colleges are the institutions to provide it."[53] He insisted, though, that such training should be only in certain master's programs and research should remain the sole domain of the university.[54]

On the other hand, Sproul found solace in the report's analysis of unit costs within the various public colleges and universities in California. Here was a potentially threatening element of the report for the university: If university costs appeared excessive in comparison to other California institutions, legislators might then favor state college funding requests and program expansion. However, because of the report's attempt to separate research from teaching costs, the instructional costs at the university were shown to be roughly equivalent and in some cases lower than those of the state colleges. The restudy analysis "should refute charges of excessive instructional costs in the University," explained McConnell, and "aid in explaining why the University will require proportionately greater appropriations as it becomes primarily an upper-division and graduate institution."[55]

The restudy data showed, however, a wide disparity between institutional costs depending on enrollment size. Great economies could be gained, McConnell argued, by expanding existing campuses.[56] For Sproul and other university officials, this was the most appealing element of the report. The "no new campus" recommendation held out the hope of ending the proliferation of new state college campuses. Yet Sproul recognized that the proposed moratorium would not be welcomed by many legislators.

The reaction among most members of the State Board of Education to both the proposed state college governing board and the moratorium was anger. The chair of the State Board of Education, William Blair, noted his great reluctance to give up the responsibility of the state colleges. Many board members were also dismayed with the statement that, in light of its other responsibilities, the board was not capable of managing the colleges.[57]

At the December meeting of the Liaison Committee, Simpson found little to support in the entire study. Sproul knew of Simpson's sentiments and stated to the committee that he was "not convinced that the resultant good . . . would offset the difficulties which would be created." Sproul understood that the Liaison Committee and both boards were on the verge of a major political disaster. Without the full support of both boards, few lawmakers would take the Restudy Report's recommendations seriously. Turning to McConnell, Sproul urged him to revise certain recommendations. Sproul asked McConnell to reassess the proposal for a new board for the state colleges and the moratorium. Failure to do so, he lamented, might "jeopardize the entire report."[58]

McConnell's response to Sproul's rejoinder was strong: he had never presented a report that was intended solely to make all parties happy. McConnell attempted to gain the support of the Liaison Committee for the new board by discussing the alternatives. Supported by the presence of Holy and Semans, as well as Lyman Glenny (a Sacramento State faculty member and a major contributor to the report), he noted that it was essential that California's three public segments "be looked upon as integrated systems." For this purpose, the idea of a superboard was considered but rejected by the restudy staff. Among other things, the size of the different segments and their different functions made one board unwieldy. Subsequently, it was important to improve the governance and administration of the segments, particularly of the state colleges. The "State Colleges are numerous and have been developing rapidly," noted McConnell. "The problem of governing ten institutions . . . is such a tremendous enterprise that a separate governing board is essential."[59]

For Simpson, however, the proposal for a separate board was viewed as both a political and personal attack, despite McConnell's assurances that it was not.[60] The superintendent did not want to lose the state colleges, particularly under the guise of his poor management. In part because he faced the rigors of reelection, Simpson was extremely sensitive to criticism of his leadership and management skills. Although the unseating of an incumbent superintendent of public instruction had not happened since the 1800s, Simpson remained concerned about his public image. He and Burton Vasche, since 1952 the associate superintendent responsible for managing the state colleges, also faced an increasing barrage of criticism from both the state college presidents and legislators. In Sacramento, many lawmakers viewed Simpson and Vasche as political appointees of Warren and not necessarily the best people for the job.[61]

Despite his displeasure and private protests, Simpson could not sway McConnell to modify the report's recommendations.[62] The superintendent's disposition on the matter found a futile path of protest. With only days left before the final report was due to the legislature, McConnell, Holy, and Semans frantically worked on the final revisions in Sacramento. Working late into the night, the coauthors finished their copyediting and called Simpson. As in previous studies sponsored by the Liaison Committee, the Restudy Report would be printed under the auspices of the Department of Education. McConnell phoned the superintendent asking that a staff member in his department deliver the final product to the state printing house. Simpson proceeded to again voice his opposition to the study and joked that he was "going to dump this [report] into the bottom of the Sacramento River." Soon afterward, Simpson's personal assistant and driver arrived to pick up the only completed version of the report. The copy never arrived at the state printing house. McConnell, Holy, and Semans found themselves laboring the following day to create another version of the report. McConnell then personally delivered it for printing.[63]

Simpson could not stop the eventual submission of the report to the assembly and senate, but he clearly understood that its recommendations were not a fait accompli. Neither the State Board of Education nor the regents endorsed the full report. In the formal cover letter to the legislature, Simpson and Sproul offered excuses for their respective boards' reluctance to back

McConnell's study. Neither board, they explained, had sufficient time to take formal action on the report's numerous recommendations.[64] In effect, both Simpson and Sproul absolved themselves, and their respective boards, from endorsing or rejecting the most controversial elements of the study: the moratorium and the proposed governing board for the state colleges.[65]

There were other problems with the Restudy Report. Unlike the 1948 Strayer Report, the new study failed to incorporate an advisory group of legislators. In negotiating the creation of a new study in 1953, the members of the Liaison Committee worried over the politicization of the study. Lawmakers might prove too influential and diminish the ability of the restudy staff to work independently. They forfeited the guidance of select legislators and the advantages of having informed representatives in the legislature explaining the final report's complexities. The result was that there were no key leaders in either the higher education community or in the legislature who were ready to openly endorse the efforts of McConnell and his coauthors.

CHAPTER 8

The Commodity of Education and the Race for New Campuses

> In the technological society, the system of higher education no longer plays a passive role: it becomes a determinant of economic development and hence stratification and other aspects of social structure.
>
> —A. H. HALSEY, 1960

The report coauthored by Tom McConnell, Hubert Semans, and Tom Holy was intended to increase the credibility of the public higher education community. University president Robert Gordon Sproul had hoped that it might persuade California legislators that the policy issues and the management of expansion should be deferred to the two governing boards, the Board of Regents and the State Board of Education. The result was the exact opposite.

The Restudy Report offered a logical scheme for expanding the tripartite system. It even offered support for private higher education in California by endorsing a state scholarship program—a proposal that would find support among key legislators in the Los Angeles area. In the end, major components of the report were politically naive. When the California Legislature convened in early 1955, they had before them the most comprehensive study on a state system of higher education ever undertaken. Yet no lawmaker would embrace it. Assemblyman Carlos Bee led a long list of legislators who complained bitterly about the study and its lack of political savvy. Bee had agreed to withdraw his bill for a new state college in his district until the study's completion.[1] Other legislators anxious for a new campus did the same. They had expected a report that would provide a clear analysis of unit costs among public and private segments and a priority listing of new campus locations.

When legislative hearings began, McConnell met with several committees to explain the merits of the report. Yet, McConnell, noted Lyman Glenny, "was just a cipher when it came to dealing with legislators. He just couldn't talk their language."[2] Hubert Semans later reflected that, among many admitted miscalculations, "we made a huge mistake by not at least approving Carlos Bee's proposed [state college] campus in Alameda County," in addition to two other campuses within the districts of select and powerful legislators.[3] The open rejection of the Restudy Report opened the floodgates for new bills.

Assemblyman and future speaker Ralph Brown submitted legislation for a college in his district, Stanislaus County, a sparsely populated area in the central valley. In the state senate, Hugh P. Donnelly also proposed a new campus in the town of Modesto; this proposal was similar to legislation he submitted in 1951 and 1953. Initially, Donnelly's bill would establish one four-year college in his home district. However, as the legislative session progressed, he sought wider appeal for his bill among his peers in Sacramento, many of whom were in the process of authoring their own legislation for a state college. By the time Donnelly's bill passed through committees on education and finance, it proposed the establishment of seven other new campuses besides Modesto: one each within the counties of Imperial, Santa Cruz, Alameda, Kern, Sonoma, Amador, and Napa/Solano.[4] Other bills to establish new institutions followed.

Key legislators, however, argued against the free-market approach of Donnelly and his compatriots. Democrat and State senator George Miller Jr. led the fight, arguing that state government could not afford an uncoordinated expansion in campuses and enrollment. To make his point, Miller caustically offered an amendment to establish a state college in his district. He then invited other lawmakers to do the same. New campuses in the counties of Glenn, Mendocino, Merced, Monterey, Placer, and Siskiyou were added to Donnelly's bill. Miller then proposed a new college in Calaveras County located in California's hinterlands. "Frog U.," announced Senator Miller, would be located in Angels Camp, the site of Mark Twain's famed short story about a frog-jumping contest. In all, Donnelly's bill now proposed the establishment of nineteen state colleges at an unknown but certainly spectacular price tag.[5]

Ironically, Miller also hoped for a state college in his own metropolitan district of Contra Costa County. However, he opposed the open-market race for new campuses. It was necessary, in his opinion, to carefully determine the need and possible costs for state government. In subsequent years, Miller proved an important leader in demanding a coordinated expansion of public higher education. With all of the amendments to Hugh Donnelly's bill, only fourteen senators voted for it.[6]

Only one major recommendation made by the Restudy team resulted in legislation. Assemblyman Joseph Shell managed the passage of his bill to establish a state scholarship fund, despite the continued opposition of President Sproul and the regents. For the first time in California history, state government was now engaged, indirectly, in the subsidization of private colleges and universities. Modeled on the G.I. Bill, the scholarship program (what would later be entitled Cal Grants) provided funds to deserving students. They could then use the scholarship to attend a higher education institution, whether private or public. As noted previously, one purpose was to offset the cost of attending a private institution and thereby make attending a private institution more desirable. The program might reduce the demand on the public higher education system.[7] However, it was clear to lawmakers that the new scholarship program would not significantly alter the general trend of students entering public institutions.

As a result of Miller's parliamentary maneuvers, no new state college campuses were established in the 1955 session. However, the open rejection of the Restudy Report led to numerous requests by lawmakers for new studies by legislative committees on the future of the state's higher education system.[8] Donnelly and other legislators were preparing a new round of bills for the next budget session of legislature in 1957. California government remained on a two-year cycle for budget sessions—a schedule that would soon give way to the official adoption of a full-time legislature.

An Attempt to Set Priorities

At a Liaison Committee meeting in January of 1956, the recommendations of the Restudy Report seemed like a distant memory. The "no new campus" proposal had been flatly rejected in Sacramento. Discussion between Sproul, Superintendent Simpson, and the eight members of the State Board of Education and the regents focused on how to react to an unmitigated political disaster. In an effort to reassert the role of the two boards in policymaking, the Liaison Committee's "joint staff," Hubert Semans and Tom Holy, recommended the quick formulation of a list of possible new college and university campus locations. Indeed, just such a list was what legislators had assumed would be part of McConnell's study. With the 1957 legislative session a little less than a year away, there would be little time for a thorough examination. Such an effort would also require a level of cooperation between the two boards that, thus far, had proven lacking.[9]

At that same Liaison Committee meeting in January, J. Paul Mohr, president of Sacramento Junior College, explained the motivation of lawmakers: In short, the desire for a four-year public college or university was driven by the market force of state subsidization. "Local taxpayers," he explained, "see no reason why they should pay district property taxes to support a junior college when the cost of support for state colleges and campuses of the university are spread over the whole state." State funds paid only 33 percent of junior college operating costs, while providing 72 and 68 percent, respectively, for state college and university campuses. No moneys came from state coffers for junior college capital improvements. In contrast, all state college capital costs and 78 percent of the university's were funded by the state. Expressing the view of his fellow junior college advocates, Mohr noted that if the state provided greater support for two-year colleges, "a lot of pressure for additional state colleges would be removed."[10]

The Liaison Committee agreed that encouraging the development of junior colleges was a key element in satisfying local community demands. Yet this alone could never appease the insatiable desire of Californians for new state college and university campuses. Sproul, Simpson, and other members of the Liaison Committee agreed that they should revise the Restudy Report's low enrollment projections and then develop a priority list of new campus sites. Only in this way might the two boards reassert their policy role.[11]

With approximately ten months until the beginning of the next legislative session in early 1957, Semans, Holy, and a staff of four began their work. McConnell had taken a post at Berkeley and was no longer associated with their efforts. In a joint agreement between the board of education and the regents, several planning principles were agreed upon. Semans and Holy were to avoid controversial issues related to governance and functions. New campus locations would be based on the "optimum use of the state's resources" and an assessment of the "greatest relative need both geographically and functionally."[12] Before any new state college or university campus could be established in an area, there would have to be at least two junior colleges in a region.

When Sproul and Simpson submitted the unsolicited report to the legislature two months before the beginning of the general session, they explained that the regents and the board of education were forced to reassess expansion plans. Enrollment growth had already exceeded the Restudy Report's projections by some 15 percent.[13] Holy and Semans stated in their new report: If California wished to offer its citizens a "measure of educational opportunity equal to that now offered," new campuses would need to be established quickly.[14] Mindful of the prerogative of legislators to create state college campuses by statute, their report offered a "guide" for lawmakers. "The chief advantage . . . is that each interested community can learn from a single report that other communities in the state have significant, unserved needs for public higher education, whether the needs are for new junior colleges, state colleges, or campuses of the University of California."[15]

The "Additional Centers Report" stated that new junior colleges, state colleges, and university campuses were needed in both rural and urban areas of the state. However, the shift in California's population centers, such as in the greater Los Angeles area, created a much larger demand for new institutions. According to their analysis, eighteen areas could justify the establishment of new junior colleges, including, in order of descending enrollment demand, Los Angeles County, Alameda County (two campuses), the city of San Diego, Santa Clara County, the city of San Mateo, a college serving Butte, Glenn, and Tehama Counties, Merced, Humboldt, Santa Cruz, Kings, Siskiyou, Mendocino, Lake, and Riverside Counties.[16]

While maintaining the dictum that new junior colleges should be provided by local initiative, Semans and Holy reiterated J. Paul Mohr's earlier argument for an infusion of state support. The reliance on local funding meant that some areas could not fund the expansion and establishment of new colleges. More importantly, they explained, financial incentives were needed to drive junior college expansion. By providing dollars for capital costs and increasing the level of operating support for junior colleges, state government could realize cost savings. Without increased support, "there will unquestionably be continuous and increasing demands for new state colleges, and meeting these demands could ultimately cost the state more than would increased assistance to junior colleges."[17]

Nine new state colleges could be justified, argued Semans and Holy, with priority to those areas with the highest projected enrollment demand. It was assumed that a junior college expansion plan would be pursued and that there was a minimum economical size for a new state college. "The Joint Staff believes . . . that it is safe to conclude that 2,000 full-time equivalents of regular students, after five years of full operation (freshman through graduate classes), is a minimum potential that would justify the establishment of a state college." Alameda County headed their list, followed by the San Bernardino–Riverside area and Contra Costa, Kern, and Stanislaus counties. The remaining possible areas included Monterey–Santa Cruz, Sonoma-Marin, Napa-Solano, and Tulare counties.[18]

It was now time, concluded Holy and Semans, to consider new and full-service University of California campuses. For decades, Sproul, with the support of the regents, resisted any major geographical expansion of the university, fearing that it might result in a general erosion in political support and financing for Berkeley and to a lesser extent the Los Angeles campus. The Santa Barbara campus, still an undergraduate college, had been forced on the regents. The "other campuses," including Davis and Riverside, had only recently expanded their programs beyond agricultural training and research. A College of Letters and Sciences was established at Davis in 1951 and at Riverside in 1954. Neither offered graduate programs, and each had relatively small enrollment. The proposal by Semans and Holy, made in consultation with Sproul and other university officials, marked a major transition.

University expansion, explained Semans and Holy, should include two new campuses, one in the Los Angeles area and the other in the San Francisco Bay Area. These new metropolitan campuses would be required to "relieve the enrollment pressures on the Berkeley and Westwood Campuses and to provide University-type public education closer to the homes of large numbers of future University students."[19] Otherwise, it was noted, both Berkeley and UCLA would need to double their enrollment. Even with such expansion, it was doubtful that the two existing university campuses could adequately service the regional enrollment demand at a reasonable cost. Additional land would be needed to expand facilities, and real estate costs would be substantial in both areas.

While the university was in essence a statewide institution, drawing students from all corners of California, the Additional Centers Report suggested that expansion should be based on an analysis of regional enrollment demand. As outlined by Holy and Semans and similar to the 1948 Strayer Report, one could envisage ten university service areas. In a clear attempt to broaden the political appeal of their study, they stated that after 1965 the university might need to add three new campuses, including a new campus in the San Joaquin Valley, possibly in Madera County, and one in the Redding area of northern California. With the expansion of the Santa Barbara, Davis, and Riverside campuses and with a proposal to expand the San Diego campus into graduate and professional training to help the booming aeronautics and defense industries in southern California, the university system

State Colleges

Priority	Projected Enrollment in 1970
1. Alameda Co.	13,600
2. San Bernardino–Riverside	11,500
3. Contra Costa Co.	6,800
4. Kern Co.	4,200
5. Stanislaus Co.	3,800
6. Monterey–Santa Cruz	3,800
7. Sonoma–Marin	3,800
8. Napa–Solano	3,100
9. Tulare Co.	2,100
10. Shasta Co.	1,400
11. Mendocino–Lake	1,300
12. Imperial Co.	800
13. Amador Co.	600

University of California

Priority	Projected Enrollment in 1970
1. Southern California Metropolitan District Center Section (LA/Orange Co.)	17,500
2. South Central California Coast Section (Santa Clara Valley)	11,900
3. South Cross Section (San Diego)	6,100
4. San Joaquin Valley Section (Madera Co.)	5,000
5. North Cross Section (Redding)	1,700

Figure 8. 1957 Additional Centers Report: Priority List for New State College and University of California Campuses

SOURCE: H. H. Semans and T. C. Holy, *A Study of the Need for Additional Centers of Public Higher Education in California,* 1957

might grow to a total of twelve general campuses (including the San Francisco medical campus).[20]

For now, the report contended, the need was most apparent in California's two large and growing urban centers.[21] Population growth in the areas of Madera and Redding were not yet sufficient to justify planning a new university campus. In total, it was projected that both would produce only 9 percent of all high school graduates in the state by 1970. The greater Los Angeles area alone would account for an estimated 46 percent of all graduates. The Bay Area and the growing Santa Clara Valley would have a projected 23 percent of that total. Combined, these two metropolitan areas would produce nearly 70 percent of all California high school graduates.[22]

The 1957 Session

The Additional Centers Report represented a major cooperative effort by the California higher education community, one that would guide most new campus expansion throughout the 1960s. Still, the report failed to halt the ambitions of legislators. Despite the mounting imbalance in the state budget, at the opening of the 1957 legislative session there was an even larger wave of bills for new campuses than in the previous budgetary session. For those lawmakers who found their district on the list of possible campus sites, irrespective of priority, the report gave license for legislation. Legislators were not deterred even if their district did not make the list. In total, twenty-two bills appeared proposing seventeen new state college campuses or the reorganization of California higher education, including a bill to create a separate board for the state colleges. Nelson Dilworth, chair of the newly created California Senate Investigating Committee on Education, alone offered legislation that would fund site acquisition for a total of nine new state colleges.[23]

Assemblyman Carlos Bee pointed to what he believed was a major flaw in the report. He was pleased to see that his district, Alameda, was given the highest priority for a new state college. However, the report insisted that a new college not be established until at least two junior colleges were operating. Bee thought such a stipulation ridiculous. There was an immediate need, he noted, for a four-year college in his district, and he was not going to wait for the establishment of a second junior college. Bee and nineteen other assembly members proceeded to cosponsor a successful bill to establish a state college campus in Hayward.

Encouraged by Bee's legislation, other lawmakers offered successful bills for new state colleges in Los Angeles and Orange counties in areas that were not on Semans and Holy's list: Northridge and Fullerton. Senator Donnelly's persistent effort for a state college in Stanislaus County also paid off. Stanislaus was only fifth on Semans and Holy's preferred campus sites. According to their report, a much higher need for a new campus existed in the San Bernardino–Riverside area, followed by Contra Costa County (George Miller's district), and then Kern County.[24] Legislation was offered that would have established new institutions in these areas, each sponsored by Democrats. Each was defeated. The passage of the bills for Fullerton and Stanislaus, favored by the Republican leadership still in control of the assembly and the senate, showed that a more important influence was the political affiliation of the sponsoring legislator.[25]

Resolutions also passed asking the Department of Education to study the need for an additional state college in Los Angeles County and a new campus in Imperial Valley. Parallel initiatives in the assembly and the senate asked the regents to "study the feasibility of a [new] UC campus in the Santa Clara Valley" or on the Monterey Peninsula. In all cases, the two boards deferred to the Liaison Committee and its staff to complete new studies.[26]

While legislators pushed for new campuses, many also renewed their concern over the increased shortfall in state revenues. Like the rest of the nation, California entered a recession in 1957, which would continue into the second quarter of the following year. In part because of the state's mounting debt, a bill to provide some $30 million in direct outlay for junior college construction was defeated. More importantly, lawmakers raised questions regarding the management of the three public higher education segments—much as state senator Bowers and others had in 1953.

At a hearing in Sacramento, Legislative Analyst A. Alan Post criticized the university's consumption of state funds. Despite the fact that enrollment in the state colleges exceeded that of the university, funding for the university was nearly double that of regional colleges. Why was the state placing so much money into the university, he asked, when the other two public segments would be taking the larger burden of future enrollment? In addition, university officials assumed that with each new student enrolled, they should receive the normal state allocations for facilities and faculty, stated Post. This budget allocation included funding for a generous allotment of faculty time to conduct research. The budget problems of the state, Post insisted, should bring a reevaluation of the state's funding formulas for the university.

Post also had harsh words for the state colleges. As shown in the Restudy Report, their admissions standards varied among the campuses and sometimes were surprisingly low. As he later noted at a Liaison Committee meeting, "admissions affects numbers, numbers affect location, location affects budget."[27] The slack admissions practices of some colleges required simply a B average during the last three years of high school, with no specific academic requirements. For those who failed to meet this standard, admissions could be gained by a score at or above the twentieth percentile of the national norm of a standard college aptitude test.[28] In February of 1958, Post convinced the subcommittee of the Assembly Ways and Means Committee to look into state college admissions standards. In turn, they asked Simpson and the Department of Education to report back to them on the possibility of establishing higher admissions criteria and requiring an aptitude test of all applicants. The committee never received a report from Simpson. What Post and university officials had originally suspected was later confirmed in a 1959 study of admissions practices. Nearly 50 percent of all high school graduates were eligible for entrance into the state colleges. Of those that enrolled, more than half failed to make a C grade their first year, and the majority of this group eventually would drop out—an indicator of how postsecondary students were not being matched to the appropriate segment.[29]

Post also claimed that California incurred tremendous costs due to lack of coordination in the curriculum of the different public segments. Other legislators, such as Miller and Assemblyman Bruce F. Allen, shared Post's concerns. A Republican from Santa Clara, Allen had a long history of battles with both the regents and the board of education over various issues, including engineering accreditation. He had little faith in either Sproul's or Simpson's interest to fulfill the needs of his constituents, including the faculty and students at San Jose State. Shortly after the submission of the Additional Centers Report, Assemblyman Allen offered a bill to establish a new state college board similar to that offered by the Restudy Report. Simpson worked with State Board of Education Chair Blair to defeat the measure, finding support from Sproul and the Liaison Committee. "There is no need for such a new and competing group," noted Simpson in a memo to the legislature.[30]

There were other, more grandiose efforts to reorganize California at the 1957 session, demonstrating the growing animosity of lawmakers toward Simpson, Sproul, and their respective boards. The most threatening was a bill that would establish a special lay commission to study "long range financing . . . and the nature and extent of public education desired and needed." Sproul and Simpson quickly garnered the support of the Liaison Committee in a successful effort to oppose the bill. The subject "is continually under review by the State Board of Education, the Regents, the Liaison

Committee and Joint Staff, and if such a survey is to be made it should be made by the Liaison Committee," read their statement. "Another commission or study group is not needed."[31]

Resourceful legislators such as Allen, Bee, Donald Doyle, and Dilworth, however, were undaunted by the opposition of the two boards to any legislatively directed planning study. They and other legislators wanted to impose their own solutions to higher education coordination and expansion. The political debacle of the Restudy Report fueled their desire to take action. Cold war fears, specifically the launching of Sputnik in late 1957, added to the increased hostility toward the higher education community.

Sputnik and California

Sputnik had several important implications for California education. To begin with, it raised substantial interest among lawmakers and the general public about the quality of the state's schools and postsecondary institutions. What was once a concern became alarm: The leaders within education, particularly at the secondary and postsecondary levels, lacked an understanding of the nation's need for science and technical training. California lawmakers and the public recognized the state's crucial role in the cold war. California's technological prowess was central to the development of ballistic missiles and related aeronautics and electronic research. Defense industries drove a major portion of the state's economy. A 1961 study by the Stanford Research Institution estimated that between 1947 and 1957, California's employment increased over 40 percent. Of that total, defense-related industries accounted for roughly half of the growth. By the time of the Sputnik launch, California led the nation in the value of military and space contracts.[32]

In no small part, the University of California helped to build these industries in California through research (including the weapons labs in Los Alamos and Livermore) and by supplying scientists and engineers. With the establishment of engineering programs in the state colleges after 1947, these colleges contributed to the state's fastest and most profitable industrial sector. Both Stanford and Cal Tech also created a critical base for California's rise as the nation's largest single source for technological innovation.[33] While California's education system fed these vibrant new industries, it did not satisfy them. California business leaders continued to complain of skilled labor shortages in areas such as engineering and other "applied" professions.

In the late 1950s, the shock of the Soviet success provided an important contextual factor for educational policymaking. Sputnik was a technological marvel. It was the first intercontinental missile, opened the space age, and marked the beginning of satellite communications. It was also a profound political event. American popular opinion credited the Soviet educational system with Sputnik's success. Here was the source for its scientists and research. Conversely, the reason for America's apparent second place position in both the arms and space races was its faltering schools and universities. Thomas N. Bonner explained in the *Journal of Higher Education*: "For several years independent observers have been warning us about what the Soviets were doing in education, especially in science education, but they were crying in the wilderness until October 4, 1957, when the Russians punctured our magnificent conceit by making it clear that in a number of related areas of basic research and applied technology they have already outdistanced us. . . . Science and education have now become the main battleground of the Cold War." Bonner was not alone when he pronounced his belief that "[i]t is upon education that the fate of our way of life depends."[34]

The Soviet success brought an unprecedented desire in American society to analyze the purpose and functions of education. The October launch of Sputnik was followed by another successful launch a month later of Sputnik II. Both "shocked our citizens and our government out of their complacent faith in our ability to maintain a scientific and military lead over the Russians and in the superiority of our educational program," explained another article in the *Journal of Higher Education*.[35] The impulse was to compare the competing Soviet educational system to our own. Sputnik had "imparted a sense of urgency and, indeed, at times almost an atmosphere of panic to a searching examination of the techniques, methods, and philosophy which have enabled the Soviet Union to achieve so dramatic a sequence of achievements and, at the same time, have aroused a widespread demand for an equally comprehensive reevaluation of American education."[36]

The quick conclusion of many was that America's system of education was disorganized, it failed to provide sufficient training in the sciences, and it catered to mediocrity at the expense of the promising student. Nicholas DeWitt's explanation of the Soviet success became popular fodder: reduced to its fundamentals, our enemy had concluded that the "advancement of science and technology is best promoted through central planning of education and research . . . that scientific and educational efforts are primarily a means for the advancement of the social, economic, political and military interests of the nation."[37]

California, with its economic dependency on the cold war, became deeply embroiled in this national debate. A legislative committee on public education in Sacramento observed that, following the launching of the "Russian 'Sputnik' into the skies of our universe, parents, educators, and legislators were suddenly made aware that perhaps there was something lacking in the system of education as we know it in the United States." The people of California were no less concerned than the people of other states. Legislators noted: The event sparked a flood of "letters to the editors of newspapers, talks at club meetings, articles in magazines, and thousands of letters to California legislators, all with the same theme: What is the matter with the education system of California, and is the Russian system superior?"[38]

In three short months after the Russian launch, the California State Senate and Assembly held a series of lengthy hearings on education, noting the "need for a re-evaluation of the primary purposes, tools and techniques of our public education program . . . since the advent of Sputniks."[39] In early 1958, the legislature created the Joint Interim Committee on Public Education with the responsibility of studying all phases of the education system. In turn, this committee established a Citizen's Advisory Commission with twenty-seven members. The legislative committee and the Citizen's Advisory Commission came to the same conclusion. There were numerous large problems with the state's education system. These included the vastness and independence of the Department of Education, the lack of a coordinated effort to expand enrollment and programs in higher education, and the noticeable lack of legislative influence and responsibility in guiding public education.

UC–Los Angeles, 1929. The conversion in 1919 of the Los Angeles State Normal School (located on Vermont Avenue) into the southern branch of the University of California came after threats by local community leaders to establish a new and independent state university. In the wake of this forced geographic expansion, the University of California became the nation's first multicampus university. In 1925, the regents purchased property in Westwood and began construction of four buildings for a new campus. In 1929, the new campus opened with an enrollment of a little more than 6,000 students. *University of California Archives, Bancroft Library, University of California–Berkeley.*

UC Agricultural Extension, 1927. The University of California's extension program was established in 1891 as a method to provide courses in academic and applied areas throughout the state. By the 1920s, when this photograph was taken, the university had the nation's largest extension program, with much of it focused on providing courses and programs related to improving the largest sector of California's economy, agriculture. *University of California Archives, Bancroft Library, University of California–Berkeley.*

Edward A. Dickson, Robert Gordon Sproul, and Ernest Carroll Moore, 1944, UCLA. In 1944, Robert Gordon Sproul had been president of the University of California for fourteen years, proving a commanding leader and a staunch defender of the university. In spite of the reluctance of faculty and alumni at the Berkeley campus, Sproul helped to embrace the Los Angeles campus as a full member of the university system, and he articulated the idea of one university with multiple campuses. Here he is shown with Regent Edward Dickson and the former provost of UCLA, Ernest Carroll Moore. *University of California Archives, Bancroft Library, University of California–Berkeley.*

Governor Earl Warren signing the bill for a new Sacramento State University site, May 1949. In 1947 the legislature passed a bill to establish a state college in Sacramento, pending a comprehensive review and plan for the state's system of public higher education. The subsequent Strayer Report noted the need for new state colleges in Long Beach and Los Angeles, in addition to one in Sacramento. In May 1949, Governor Warren signed a bill to develop the new campus on what was then a peach orchard along the American River. Witnessing the event are (starting third from left) Aubrey A. Douglass (coauthor of the Strayer Report and associate superintendent of public instruction), Guy West (first president of Sacramento State University), and Assemblyman Earl Desmond. *The* Sacramento Bee *Collection, Sacramento Archives and Museum Collection Center.*

President Sproul at the UCLA versus Berkeley football game, 1955. In 1955, Sproul had served twenty-five years as president of the University of California (longer than any other president of a major university at that time). Here he is shown symbolically changing sides, with the rooting section marking his tenure. Sproul had helped build a state university of distinctive academic quality. However, his intransigent refusal to recognize the role of the state colleges in California's evolving system of higher education, combined with the expanding political power of these regional colleges, contributed to a corresponding decline in his influence among the regents and legislators. In less than three years, he would retire with the future of California's higher education system in doubt. His replacement would be Clark Kerr. *University of California Archives, Bancroft Library, University of California–Berkeley.*

Kerr and family, 1958. On September 29, 1958, Clark Kerr was inaugurated as president of the University of California after serving more than seven years as chancellor. Kerr would develop a strategy in collaboration with Dean McHenry (a faculty member at UCLA and longtime confidant) that would eventually result in the negotiation of the 1960 Master Plan for Higher Education. The path to the Master Plan reflects Kerr's skills as a labor negotiator and his understanding of the complex political battle with the state colleges and their supporters. Here he is shown with his family shortly after his inauguration held in the Greek Theater on the Berkeley campus. *University of California Archives, Bancroft Library, University of California–Berkeley.*

Assemblywoman Dorothy Donahoe and Senator George Miller, 1959. Dorothy Donahoe became chair of the Assembly Committee on Education when the Democrats gained control of the assembly in 1958. State senator George Miller and Donahoe worked together to discourage legislators from introducing self-serving bills for new public college and university campuses, and they pressured the higher education community to resolve their differences and present a politically acceptable plan for expanding higher education opportunity in California. At the request of university officials, Donahoe would carry Assembly Concurrent Resolution 88 asking for a "master plan" for higher education. *California History Room, California State Library, Sacramento, California.*

The Master Plan Survey Team, 1959. Under a legislative resolution, the team was charged by the Board of Regents and the State Board of Education to develop a master plan for the future of the state's system of higher education. Arthur Coons, president of Occidental College, served as the chair of the survey team and as an arbitrator between the representatives of the university and the state colleges. Front row, left to right: Keith Sexton (aide to Assemblywoman Donahoe), Howard Campion, Arthur Coons, Glenn S. Dumke, and Thomas C. Holy. Back row, left to right: Dean McHenry, Arthur Browne, Henry Tyler, and Robert Wert. *CSU Historical Archives Collection.*

Governor Brown, Dumke, Simpson, and Kerr, April 26, 1960. Governor Edmund "Pat" Brown signed the Donahoe Act, placing major sections of the Master Plan into statute, in the presence of San Francisco State University President Glenn Dumke, State Superintendent of Public Instruction Roy E. Simpson, and University of California president Clark Kerr. State senator George Miller was the principal author of the act. Miller renamed the legislation in honor of Assemblywoman Donahoe, who unexpectedly died prior to final decisions on the act. *University of California Archives, Bancroft Library, University of California–Berkeley.*

Kerr on the cover of *Time* magazine, October 17, 1960. The California Master Plan for Higher Education brought a flood of national and international attention as a blueprint for expanding state systems of higher education. Clark Kerr's pivotal role in the process of negotiating the plan and the preservation of the University of California's primary responsibilities in such areas as research and graduate and professional education resulted in significant national press on his leadership skills. *Time* magazine ran this cover of Kerr in October 1960, six months after the signing of the Donahoe Act. *Time* magazine.

CHAPTER 9

Governor Brown, Clark Kerr, and the Demand for Reform

> It is a theory of government that whenever competition is detrimental to the public welfare, a monopoly should be created, subject to the regulations by the body creating such a monopoly.
>
> —STATE SENATOR GEORGE MILLER, 1959

By late 1957, wartime surpluses were nearly gone. Both the governor and the legislature were unwilling to tackle the politically unpopular problem of reforming an antiquated tax structure. Continued growth in population and demand for services in the midst of recession left California with the largest level of debt since the Great Depression—some $270 million, slightly more than the entire state expenditure for postsecondary education during the previous year. Following the defeat in the legislature of a half-hearted effort by Governor Knight to pass the first major tax increase since 1939, an editorial in the *Sacramento Bee* asked, "How long can the general fund continue to pay out more than it takes in?"[1]

Internal dissent among the higher education segments, external demands for enrollment and program expansion, fiscal problems, and weak political leadership in Sacramento created a sense of crisis among members of the state's higher education community and, more importantly, among lawmakers. California could not, in the words of one legislator, continue to support a hapless jungle of academic programs. It could not "establish fifteen or eighteen state-support universities all competing for the tax dollar."[2] State senator George Miller thought the tripartite system grossly inefficient. California was rapidly growing in population and in the size of its economy. The state would soon surpass New York in total population. The tripartite structure appeared antiquated. However, Miller and other key lawmakers recognized that the disarray should also be blamed on the legislature. "If the practice of adopting special legislation to meet specific problems is continued without a well-defined plan," complained Assemblywoman Dorothy Donahoe, "education in California will 'grow like Topsy.'"[3]

Following the disastrous legislative session in 1957, two major changes in leadership in Sacramento and within the University of California occurred that provide the context for the negotiation of the 1960 Master Plan for Higher Education. The result would be a resolution to the internal conflicts within the higher education community and an end to the entrepreneurial drive of lawmakers.

In November 1957, California voters provided Democratic majorities in the state assembly and senate. They also elected Edmund G. "Pat" Brown as governor over California senator and conservative William Knowland. Democrats controlled state government in Sacramento for the first time in over 100 years. Moderate and liberal Democrats became the majority in the legislative committees key for formulating policy, developing bills, and, along with the governor, ensuring their implementation.

Under the leadership of Brown, Democrats quickly initiated a series of important reforms. The last remaining elements of cross-filing—long the bane of frustrated Democrats and partially weakened in 1952—ended officially in 1959. Brown successfully pushed for an increase in taxes and initiated a flood of bonds to sustain and broaden the progressive programs of the Warren administration and to launch new programs. Brown's finance reform package returned activist state government to California.

The promise of new revenue, however, did not dispel the desire of Brown and the legislature to improve the efficiency of state government. If there was any lesson that came from the postwar period, it was that California would experience even greater growth in population in future years. The policy and budgetary challenges that would accompany such expansion, argued the governor and his staff, required greater efficiency within state government. For Brown, this prospect required a review of the funding and organization of public higher education. The bottom line for Brown was clear: There needed to be a dramatic change in the system, and all options, including a single-board plan, would be considered. The threat of wholesale reform of the state's tripartite system by the new leadership in Sacramento altered the dynamics of policymaking.

A New University President

Robert Gordon Sproul had been president of the university since 1930 and had served as the chief general of the university's persistent battle to contain state college programs and enrollment. Even after conceding a role to the state colleges that went beyond teacher training, Sproul remained a steadfast opponent and symbol of the university's intransigence. The appointment in October 1957 of Clark Kerr as the university's new president marked an important change in leadership. While protective of the university's autonomy and its monopoly in doctoral degrees and research, Kerr accepted the state colleges as an important component of California's evolving higher education system. Kerr also realized that the university needed to take the lead in building a consensus, particularly if the university hoped to maintain its unique role in the tripartite system. Again, time was short. Both the new leadership in the legislature and Governor Brown demanded an end to ad hoc enrollment and program growth.

Supporters of the state colleges represented a disparate group—state college presidents and faculty, community boosters, lawmakers, members of the State Board of Education, and Superintendent of Public Instruction Roy Simpson—whose time and interests were devoted largely to expanding California's school system. Unlike the university, there was no single and powerful advocate for the state colleges. Kerr recognized that the push for a plan and the powerful political position of the university offered an opportunity to end the convoluted process of policymaking. It could solidify and protect the university's unique mission and claim on state resources. In no small part, the regents had chosen Kerr as Sproul's successor because of his background as a labor negotiator. California was at the edge of a major period of transformation in its higher education system. Kerr was perhaps the perfect leader for the university at one of the most critical junctures in its history.

Born in 1911 in Stony Creek, Pennsylvania, the son of Quaker farmers, Kerr graduated from a one-room school and made his way to Swarthmore. There he served as student body president and head of the debate team before graduating in 1932. He planned on entering law school at Columbia. Instead he decided to visit California as part of a Quaker summer peace caravan in support of the League of Nations and to argue the shortcomings of protective tariffs. The plight of the unemployed and the rampant poverty he saw in Depression era California eliminated his interest in law. He entered Stanford to study economics, gaining his master's degree before entering a doctoral program at Berkeley, where he studied self-help cooperatives for the unemployed. While a graduate student, he worked as a field researcher, investigating the causes and problems of the bloody California cotton-pickers' strike. This experience led to his lifelong scholarship and activism in labor relations.[4]

In 1939, Kerr completed his doctorate at Berkeley and the following year became an assistant professor at the University of Washington. During the war, Kerr served as an administrator of regional labor boards in San Francisco and Seattle before he joined the Berkeley faculty in 1945 as an associate professor of industrial relations in the School of Business Administration. He also became the first director of the university's new Institute of Industrial Relations—part of the postwar reconversion effort imagined by Warren and Sproul. Kerr became one of the busiest arbitrators in the West, engaging in over 500 negotiations, including the 1946 West Coast shipping strike.[5]

In early 1952, the regents chose Kerr as the first chancellor at Berkeley, largely because he had proven an articulate advocate for the faculty during the oath controversy. He had signed the oath. But he had also given testimony before the regents calling the oath an infringement on academic freedom and an ineffective measure against Communism. Kerr's moderate stance and principled reasoning impressed several regents, even Francis Neylan, a staunch defender of Senator Joe McCarthy. Sproul found Kerr acceptable as the first chancellor at Berkeley, but for other reasons. Kerr had no administrative experience and little knowledge of the contentious realities of the university's political ordeals in Sacramento.[6]

For six years, Kerr led the Berkeley campus as its first chancellor. Yet he had limited ability to manage its affairs. Sproul had opposed the establishment of chancellors at Berkeley and UCLA because it would, he argued, dilute the concept of a single university and reduce the power of the presidency. Despite the change in the university's organization, Sproul remained a dominant presence. He continued to live in the president's house located in the heart of the Berkeley campus, and his staff remained on the Berkeley campus in the Administration Building, later named Sproul Hall. Most importantly, Sproul managed to retain control over the hiring and firing of faculty and over virtually all major administrative decisions for both the Berkeley and Los Angeles campuses.

As had Raymond White, his counterpart in Los Angeles, Kerr found few outlets for his creative energy. Kerr's most important contribution to the Berkeley campus was his initiation of a comprehensive academic and physical plan. Sproul was obsessed with controlling the day-to-day decisions of the campus and did not mind Kerr's involvement in what appeared to be the esoteric idea of long-range academic planning. After a two-year process of consultation with faculty, Berkeley's first "Long Range Development Plan" was submitted to the regents in 1957. It outlined discipline areas that should grow in faculty and enrollment. It also provided a precedent for future campus and universitywide planning. Henceforth, all UC campuses would develop similar plans as a means to assess a campus's development and as a mechanism for gaining resources.[7]

While Kerr presented Berkeley's plan to the regents, Sproul's tenure was coming to an end. At the age of sixty-seven, Sproul suffered a continuing decline of support among the regents, accentuated by the rise of a contingent of southern California board members, which now included new chairman Edwin Pauley, Edward Carter, and Dorothy Chandler. There was a growing sense among the regents that Sproul's centralized administrative style was no longer appropriate to a multicampus and rapidly growing university. There had also been a series of political failures, including the disastrous Restudy Report and the mixed success of the Additional Center's Report. Many regents felt that the bitter debate over the oath controversy in the early 1950s was largely Sproul's fault. He had assured several regents that the faculty would cause little trouble if the board sanctified the oath. With the 1958 session of the legislature approaching, Sproul announced his retirement.

Assuming his new position in July 1958 at the age of forty-eight, Kerr immediately focused on three tasks: expanding university enrollment and programs, decentralizing the power of the president, and dealing with the political challenges of lawmakers and the state colleges. At the same October 1957 meeting in which the regents chose Kerr as the new president, and reflecting the recommendations of the Additional Centers Report, the Davis, Santa Barbara, and Riverside campuses were redesignated as general campuses of the university. These campuses could now establish doctoral-level programs. The regents also approved the title of chancellor for the administrative head of each of the new campuses.[8] In theory, the University of California would now have five coequal, general campuses.

Kerr recommended a further geographical expansion of the university.

Though the La Jolla campus had initially been designated as a technical and largely graduate-level institution, in early 1959 the regents designated it as a general campus that would have a full breadth of undergraduate programs. Kerr also asked Harry R. Wellman, who occupied the new position of executive vice president, to begin planning for two new, general campuses in the Los Angeles and San Francisco Bay areas and to possibly consider a third in the central valley.

As the chancellor at Berkeley, Kerr had felt Sproul's yoke. Kerr recognized a need for decentralizing decision-making within the university, particularly as it grew in enrollment and the number of campuses. When Sproul began his presidency, the university had just below 20,000 students. It now had nearly 50,000 students, had seven campuses (including San Diego and the medical center in San Francisco), and faced the prospect of tripling its enrollment—a part of what Kerr called a "tidal wave" of students that would enter the state's higher education system. Reflecting the recommendations of earlier reviews of university operations, including the 1955 Restudy Report, Kerr suggested that regents and the president reduce micromanagement of the university and focus on major policy issues. Kerr successfully argued for greater autonomy of the individual campuses and their chancellors, including the abilities to hire and promote faculty below tenure rank.[9] As part of his reorganization of the university, the new president dissolved seventeen statewide university committees and reduced the number of staff in the president's office.

In style and temperament, Kerr stood in sharp contrast to Sproul. Since 1930, Sproul had guided the University of California with a strong hand, helping to create a university of international distinction. His reign of nearly thirty years was the longest tenure of any president of a major research university in the nation. By 1957, though, Sproul seemed to be the autocrat, the vestige of an earlier period of strong-willed university presidents. Kerr appeared to be the diplomat, more mindful of the expanding constituents with a stake and interest in their public university. Perhaps this difference was nowhere more apparent than in Kerr's approach toward the state colleges, the State Board of Education, and lawmakers. In no small measure, the fate of California's higher education system hung on Kerr's ability to fashion a negotiation process. The demands of the new governor and the Democratic leadership in Sacramento added to a new political environment—one in which the university was no longer impervious.

Kerr immediately sought to demonstrate greater flexibility toward the demands of state college supporters and at the same time lock them into a process of negotiations over the future of higher education in California. Legislators such as Miller were demanding a statewide plan and state college supporters were gaining in political strength.

State College Aspirations

For the most ambitious state college presidents, the State Board of Education and State Superintendent Simpson were ineffectual leaders. They capitulated too often to the demands of University of California officials. Roy Simpson, in particular, was viewed as an obstacle for elevating the role of the colleges in California's higher education system. Five presidents, Glenn Dumke at San Francisco State, Arnold Joyal at Fresno, John T. Wahlquist at San Jose, Julian A. McPhee at the California Polytechnic in San Luis Obispo, and Malcolm Love at San Diego, sought the support of key legislators to sanctify a three-part program that would fulfill their aspirations. They looked to the 1959 legislative session as perhaps the best opportunity to make that program a reality.

The first goal was to remove the state colleges from the auspices of the State Board of Education and Simpson. They wanted the colleges placed under a new board with autonomy similar to that of the university. To the great frustration of state college presidents like Malcolm Love, the board, Simpson, and state agencies such as the Department of Finance continued to treat the state colleges as simply one component of the much larger state school system. They were subjected to mounting regulations in the areas of finance and personnel, and they had little freedom in reallocating resources. To reiterate, funding from the state came as line items from the legislature for administrative costs, faculty salaries, and the like. As a result, funds could not be transferred to meet the perceived needs of a college without approval from the Department of Finance. Regulatory restrictions also limited the ability of state college presidents to garner and accept financial gifts. A separate board would, they hoped, result in greater autonomy to manage their campuses.

The second goal was to expand the authority of the state colleges to include professional degrees in engineering and the doctorate in education. Gaining accreditation of state college engineering programs was a major goal for state college presidents. In 1953, the State Board of Education entered an agreement with the regents that the growing number of state college undergraduate programs in engineering would not seek accreditation by the Engineers' Council of Professional Development. Sproul had argued that accredited engineering programs were the distinct purview of the University of California. Further, state college expansion of engineering programs was not needed—the university would expand its engineering programs. For John T. Wahlquist, president of San Jose State, the capitulation of the State Board of Education and Simpson to Sproul's demands was an egregious error. Lack of accreditation severely limited the ability of engineering graduates to enter the job market.

At Wahlquist's request, San Jose State's local assemblyman, Bruce Allen, argued before the regents, the State Board of Education, and the legislature that the 1953 agreement penalized local economies and ultimately jeopardized California's contribution to national defense. A record number of engineers were needed, he argued, particularly in the San Jose area. The agreement "imposes a serious handicap on the ability of these firms to meet their engineering problems," wrote Allen to the regents. Further, their solid opposition to any change in the role of the state colleges "seems particularly vicious in these respects: The state colleges are required to keep their engineering departments at a second rate level, i.e., they are not permitted to apply for professional accreditation, no graduate instruction is permitted, etc."[10]

Corporate leaders at Westinghouse, General Electric, and IBM (all major firms in Allen's district) noted their support for Wahlquist and Allen's position. The lack of accreditation affected the ability of San Jose State to recruit "competent engineering instructors," they argued in a joint letter. It restricted the college's ability to gain moneys from federal agencies and federal scholarships (eligible for only accredited programs), and finally, they concluded, it restricted California's ability to recruit "top grade engineers and scientists" to local industries.[11]

Malcolm Love at San Diego State argued for the granting of the doctorate in education. Love had come to San Diego after serving as the president of the University of Nevada, which had both a doctorate and research function. Teacher training was the historic role of the state colleges, he argued. Now there was increased demand for properly trained administrators in California's schools, and for Love and other college presidents, it was logical that the state colleges should meet this need. There was also a need to fill the expanding ranks of the state college education programs with faculty who had doctorates in education. At the insistence of the state college presidents, a joint study sponsored by the State Board of Education and the regents on "Faculty Demand and Supply" confirmed the significant need for additional doctorate programs in education and other fields.[12]

Finally, the state college presidents argued for state funding for research.

University of California officials had long insisted that the university should be the only state-sanctioned and state-funded agency for research in California. A proposal by Glenn Dumke and Love stated that this placed unnecessary restrictions on the state colleges. There was a need for the state to promote research, particularly in areas that could be beneficial to regional economies. Recognition by the state of the role of research in the mission of the state colleges, they argued, would also help in the recruitment and retention of high-quality faculty.

In the 1950s, state college faculty had been recruited from the same top-level institutions as those captured by the University. Here were Stanford, Berkeley, and University of Washington graduates, all research oriented people.[13] Nearly 53 percent of all college faculty held the doctorate. "They should not be allowed to 'go stale,'" insisted one college president, "but should be encouraged by the most productive type of intellectual environment."[14] In essence, they reiterated an argument made repeatedly by university faculty and administrators: faculty involved in research make better teachers. "While it is recognized that teaching has been and will continue to be a primary function of State College faculties," explained Dumke, "it is futile to insist that teaching at the collegiate level be divorced from research.... The teacher-researcher makes contributions to a body of knowledge, but at the same time he invigorates and vitalizes his own teaching, he stays abreast of, or on occasion moves to the fore-front in new knowledge applicable to the course he teaches."[15]

Four months into Clark Kerr's tenure as the new president of the University of California, the state college presidents circulated their three-point proposal in Sacramento. Due to growing frustration among lawmakers with the lack of leadership by the State Board of Education and Superintendent Roy Simpson, the presidents boldly argued for a separate board for their colleges. The new board proposal reiterated the recommendations of the 1955 Restudy Report and reflected bills submitted in previous legislative sessions by Assemblyman Allen and others, for a reorganization of higher education. The proposal also sought what appeared to be only marginal changes in the mission of the state colleges: accreditation for engineering and the doctorate in education only. The presidents also requested that a mere 1 percent of the state college funding from state government go toward supporting faculty research.[16]

The State Board of Education of Education members and Simpson, cognizant of their declining stock in Sacramento, were reluctant to either support or condemn the proposal openly. Further, there was evidence that the new governor and his two new appointees to the board, Louis Heilbron and Tom Braden, might support the proposal.[17] Simpson privately bristled over the revival of the proposal for a new board, but he was reluctant to take a position. Increasingly, Simpson was driven by political concerns. He had an election approaching and lacked a general strategy on how to handle state college aspirations.

For Kerr and other university officials, the state college presidents had fired an opening salvo that promised more than marginal changes. As Robert Gordon Sproul had long argued, any entrance by the colleges into doctoral training or any recognition of their research role ultimately could lead to a significant expansion of state college programs and the creation of a rival for state funding and public support. Clark Kerr recognized this threat and quickly sought a way to react.

The University's New Strategy

Kerr's presidency initiated the evolution of a new and more conciliatory strategy, one that would protect the university and promote a coordinated system of higher education. The key component of this strategy was to move the public segments—the university, state colleges, and junior colleges—toward a negotiated settlement and to create "an orderly plan" for higher education in California. Mounting a direct attack on the proposals by the state college presidents, as perhaps Sproul would have done, could provide, at best, only a short-term solution. Lawmakers and the new governor had tired of such battles, and, inevitably, new proposals would surface. In the long term, the political power of the state colleges and their supporters was destined to grow.

Kerr believed strongly that California's higher education system needed to keep pace with growing enrollment demand. As an economist, he had written about the need for trained labor and the role of educational opportunity in ensuring economic prosperity. University officials projected that population growth within California's college-age cohort and higher college-going rates meant that enrollments would more than double over the next decade. "Fifty years ago 5 percent of the college-age young people went on to an institution of higher learning," observed Kerr at a meeting with the regents. For the United States as a whole, in 1950 the figure had risen to 27 percent;

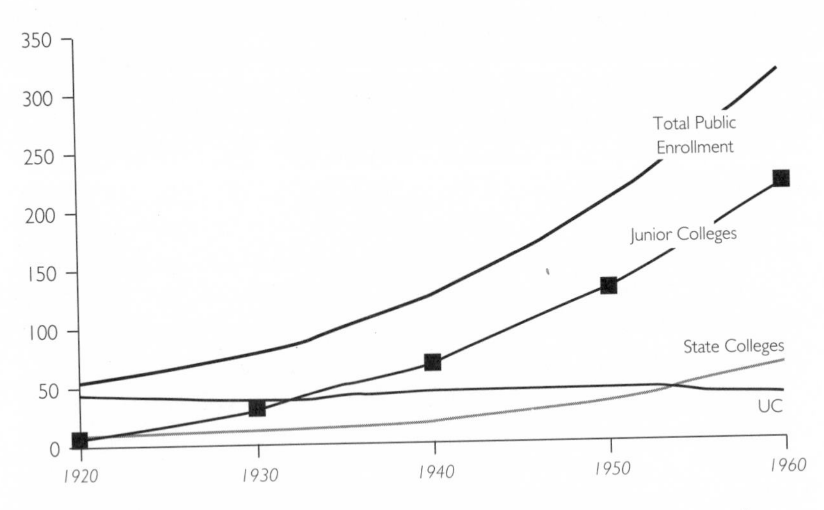

Figure 9. California Public Higher Education Enrollment Per 10,000 of State Population, 1920–1960

SOURCES: *California Statistical Abstract;* California Postsecondary Education Commission

for California, it was 39 percent. "The expectation is that for the entire nation by 1970," Kerr noted, "50 percent of the college-age youth will be entering some college. This 50 percent figure already has been reached in the State of California."[18]

Such growth would result in a dramatic shift in where Californians went to college. In the 1920s, the university enrolled the largest number of students within California's public higher education system—as envisioned by Progressives. The growth of the state colleges, however, had become much more pronounced after 1950. (See Figure 9.) The university's share of enrollment would get progressively smaller. Its political power and ability to hold the line on the functions of the state colleges would decline. As Dean McHenry, a political scientist at UCLA and long-time confidant of Kerr, explained: "The University has an estimated numerical superiority of alumni in the state, but this advantage will soon be gone if the state colleges continue to proliferate. If we are ever going to remold the higher education picture nearer our heart's desire, we ought to strike soon."[19] Thomas Holy, the university's representative on the Liaison Committee, also explained that "[t]he political influence of the university will undoubtedly decline because members of the legislature, including alumni of the university, give their first loyalty to the state colleges if located in their district and secondly to the university."[20]

Kerr wanted a way to transform the ad hoc mode of policy development into a planning process, similar to that of the 1948 Strayer Report, that might favor the university. Kerr, McHenry, and other university officials concluded that the varied interests of the state college presidents, and legislators and their local communities seeking new campuses, could be abrogated or compromised within a planning process oriented toward building an efficient system. By broadening the policy discussion, the university would have allies—specifically, key legislators and possibly Governor Brown, who appeared more concerned with controlling costs than with expanding state college functions. There were also members of the junior colleges and private institutions, who sought greater roles in policy discussions and greater financial support from the state.[21] The key was to gain the agreement of the regents and the State Board of Education for such a planning study and then the acquiescence of lawmakers for a moratorium on new bills.

The path toward such a study and recommendations was well worn. As recounted in earlier chapters, this tactic was used in 1932, 1947, and 1953. The sense of crisis in higher education policymaking, however, was at a new height, and the political environment offered an opportunity. Kerr hoped to formalize and limit the role of the state colleges, possibly in the state constitution. McHenry painted a scenario in which the negotiation of a plan would include junior college and private college representation. By winning their support for the university's point of view, "we can nail our victim in the constitution and end jurisdictional bickering."[22] Any such negotiations would also be extremely risky for the university. A failure to reach a compromise between the university and the state colleges would undoubtedly lead to a solution imposed by legislators with unpredictable results for the university, including possible proposals for a reduction in the university's autonomy.

To signify that he was a substantially different leader than Sproul, Kerr announced a series of possible concessions. He noted his support for the accreditation of engineering programs at San Jose State. He also noted a willingness to support the 1-percent funding scheme for state college research. Such concessions were, of course, conditional. The Liaison Committee was the first stop in Kerr's strategic path toward a planning study. At his first Liaison Committee meeting as the new university president, Kerr explained his general support for these changes in the programs of the state colleges, but only if the regents and the California State Board of Education would agree to complete a long-range study of higher education.[23]

In support of Kerr's proposal, Thomas Holy, the university's staff member for the Liaison Committee, predicted a slew of new campus bills in the next legislative session. "If you don't develop an orderly plan, there is the danger the legislature will authorize new colleges without adequate studies."[24] Harold T. Sedgewick, the new chair of the assembly subcommittee on higher education, had already stated his intention to reorganize the tripartite system. He along with other committee members, including Carlos Bee, expressed support for a new board for the state colleges. Other legislators were drafting bills and constitutional amendments for a new board, new campuses, the election of members of the California State Board of Education, and imposition of tuition on all public higher education.[25]

These bills in Sacramento weighed heavily on the minds of members of the Liaison Committee. Kerr proposed that for only the second time in California history there be a joint meeting of the regents and the State Board of Education. The two boards should meet in about a month and, he hoped, would approve the planning study. As stated in Kerr's resolution, the study would focus on "avoiding unnecessary duplication and greater expense for the taxpayers of California." At the same time, it would allow "all qualified young people of the State of California to obtain the benefits of higher education.[26] Kerr's proposal for the study was approved, and two, not simply one, joint meetings were scheduled for early 1959.[27]

Kerr knew that the proposed study might never be completed. University and state college officials might never agree, and legislators could ignore their efforts. It was also not clear how supportive Superintendent Roy Simpson was. In fact, Simpson hoped the proposed study and plan would falter and die. His support of the Liaison Committee was a matter of political expedience—he did not want the State Board of Education, including Chair William L. Blair, to see him as an obstruction to a possible solution for higher education.

Because of these worries, Kerr secretly contemplated an alternative scheme once considered by Sproul: absorption of the state colleges under the regents. If the negotiations broke down, the university might seek a constitutional amendment that would absorb all the state colleges into the university. Kerr knew the dangers of this scheme were many. Such a blatant attempt to shift control of the colleges would likely generate considerable opposition. There was also risk in pursuing the necessary constitutional amendment. Yet, as

Kerr noted in a confidential memo to McHenry, this might be the last resort to invoke order and specifically to bring "the maverick [state college] presidents in line."[28]

Donahoe's Resolution

Kerr's victory in the Liaison Committee was quickly followed by a campaign for the support of key legislators. The political transition in Sacramento, from Republican domination to a new Democratic leadership, offered new opportunities. Republican Donald Doyle, often a harsh critic of the university and the State Department of Education, was forced to step down from his chairmanship of the Assembly Committee on Education. Democrat Dorothy Donahoe, a second-term assemblywoman from Bakersfield, took his place.[29]

Donahoe was one of only two women in the assembly. Her path to Sacramento began in Bakersfield, where she was a school administrator. After graduating from Bakersfield High School, she refused a scholarship to Stanford, remaining at home to support her invalid mother by working as a secretary in the local high school. Shortly thereafter, Donahoe became the school's registrar and was later a member of the Kern County Council of Community Planning. At the age of forty-one, she won the local seat in the assembly and served on the Education Committee under Doyle. Donahoe had long voiced her concern over the unregulated growth of the state colleges and the open scuffles among the higher education community. At the same time, like so many legislators, she stated her interest, along with the new local state senator from her district, Democrat Walter Stierns, in gaining a state college for Bakersfield.[30]

One day after the approval by the Liaison Committee of Kerr's proposed planning study, Kerr sent James Corley to meet with Donahoe. Corley asked her to support the university's proposal for a "master plan." The term "master plan" had not been used previously in state-level planning for any purpose other than for physical development. In short, it was the terminology of architects and city planners. It conjured images of a comprehensive approach to developing California's beleaguered higher education system, which appealed to Donahoe. Unbeknownst to the regents or the State Board of Education, Corley brought to his meeting with Donahoe a draft resolution that he hoped she might carry in the legislature. The resolution formally asked the regents and the State Board of Education to provide a plan, and it placed a two-year moratorium on all legislation related to higher education in California. If it passed, enormous pressure would be placed on Superintendent Roy Simpson and the State Board of Education, particularly members such as Raymond J. Daba, to acquiesce to the planning study. Daba openly noted his opinion that the proposed study was a university scheme to contain unjustly the state colleges.[31]

Donahoe quickly agreed to support the resolution, but she was uncertain that a woman could carry it through the male-dominated legislature. Lobbying for the measure required the support of key members of the Democrats and Republicans. There was already a flood of bills on the floor and in committees of the legislature. Many lawmakers would be unhappy with anything thwarting their efforts. Donahoe turned to her friend and fellow Democrat, Senator George Miller, for advice, suggesting that perhaps he should sponsor the bill. Miller encouraged Donahoe to take the lead and offered his support.[32]

On March 4, the day after the noted Liaison Committee meeting, Donahoe, along with Assemblyman John Williams and Senator Walter Stierns, introduced Assembly Concurrent Resolution 88 (or ACR 88). The Liaison Committee was to prepare the master plan and report back to the legislature at the opening of its 1960 session (a short seven months away).[33] With ACR 88 pending in the legislature, Donahoe then noted that she, along with several other key legislators, including Miller, would attend the pending joint meeting of the regents and the State Board of Education.[34]

The Joint Meetings of the Boards

In two short months, Kerr had created the political context for a significant reform of California higher education. He had gained the general support of key legislators. Both Donald McLaughlin, the chair of the regents, and William Blair, the long-time chair of the State Board of Education, agreed to the study. Governor Brown, under the advice of the Democratic leadership in the legislature, stated his support for ACR 88. Kerr and university officials now hoped for an agreement by the two boards for the Master Plan and a show of consensus before legislators. The first joint meeting, however, would prove to be a contentious affair.

The two boards and a host of legislators met on the Berkeley campus on March 14. Governor Pat Brown had been invited to chair the meeting. Brown, however, had political business out of the state and instead sent a message insisting that chaos of higher education policymaking in California must end. "Your meeting is a significant one," he wrote. "If California is to meet its responsibilities—and we will—there can be no question that there must be maximum coordination of the several elements that comprise the state's higher education system." He looked to the public segments to provide the "maximum of educational opportunities within the ability of the State's fiscal resources."[35]

In her opening remarks, Dorothy Donahoe reiterated the governor's message. Donahoe hoped the legislature would approve ACR 88. It would give the two boards one last chance to "work out a formula and a pattern which will assist the legislature." Indeed, she suggested that the attitude of the two boards and their progress toward a "Master Plan" might determine the resolution's success in Sacramento. As a clear threat, Donahoe also noted that the Assembly Education Committee had discussed creating a single governing board. The regents might "take the responsibility for all higher education, working closely with the State Board of Education, and having one or two members of the latter board as Regents."[36] The message from Donahoe and other lawmakers: All alternatives were open for discussion, and the legislature and governor intended to be full participants in the final decision.

Kerr recited enrollment projections recently completed by Carl Frisen within the Department of Finance. "We are talking about higher education for a population greater than that of the British Isles at the present time!" Focusing on cold war fears, Kerr noted: "We are not the only people searching for knowledge. All the world, including our chief competitor, is energetically engaged in the search . . . today, high-level skill of the population is essential for the survival of the nation itself." Planned growth and the clear differentiation of functions were the medicine needed in California, according to Kerr. Yet, as a result of the slew of bills over the years in the legislature, he diplomatically noted, there was no integrated and coordinated system. "The differentiation of functions concept presently is not working," proclaimed Kerr. "There is not an adequate definition; it is imprecise and, perhaps, unrealistic."[37]

Superintendent Roy Simpson continued the rallying cry for coordination but with a significantly different approach. He placed before the two boards an aggressive scheme to expand the state colleges. "Public education is considered an inalienable right of California's citizenry," he explained. "Nowhere is the outcropping of this interest more visibly seen than in the large number of bills proposed by the current legislature." There were some forty bills proposed, including those related to elementary and secondary schools.[38]

To the surprise and open frustration of Kerr and university officials, Simpson announced that the state colleges would need to double their enrollment in just over five years. There was a need to act immediately, Simpson proclaimed. The state superintendent then outlined a plan for seven new state colleges. Simpson made no mention of the need for a stronger delineation of functions or for possible changes in governance.[39] Simpson knew that his proposal would reinvigorate the division among the two boards. He was attempting to reassert his leadership and, it appeared to a visibly angry Kerr, to perhaps scuttle the agreement for a master plan study.[40]

With the completion of Simpson's statement, Regent McLaughlin moved that the resolution for a planning study be adopted. State Board of Education member Raymond J. Daba noted his displeasure. In light of Simpson's plan for expansion, Daba proclaimed the two-year moratorium "detrimental to the adequate preparation of plans for handling future State College enrollments." He also complained that, as worded, the resolution would give either board the right to nullify the plans of the other. This might "create a stalemate in future development . . . [and a] great hardship on the state college system."[41]

The joint meeting so carefully orchestrated by Kerr was disintegrating into a bitter debate. Kerr denounced Simpson's priority list of new campuses, insisting that the two-year moratorium, as agreed to at an earlier meeting of the Liaison Committee, was essential. Without it, the idea of the Master Plan as a comprehensive analysis of the needs of the state would collapse. The two boards, Kerr suggested, would simply proceed with their own plans without the concerns for efficiency and the cost to taxpayers. The purpose of their meeting, Kerr concluded, should be to foster coordination, not to announce plans for expansion. State Board of Education Chair Blair retorted that Simpson's new campuses were all identified in the Additional Centers Report, which, Blair reminded the audience, had been approved by the regents.[42]

These and similar exchanges took up much of the afternoon. In the end, both boards agreed to refer the draft resolution back to the Liaison Committee. The same would be done with Simpson's list of seven new state colleges. Both issues would then be brought to the next joint meeting of the boards, which was scheduled for April 15, a month away. Donahoe ended the meeting, noting that the legislature was impatient. The meeting in April, she insisted, needed to launch "a definitive overall program for the development of higher education facilities" for either the 1960 or 1961 legislative session.[43]

The joint meeting reflected decades of conflict between the state colleges and the university. Kerr had hoped for the acquiescence of the State Board of

Education, Simpson, and lawmakers for a planning study, to essentially contain the policymaking process within a forum that might favor the university. Instead, Simpson's proposal essentially launched a preemptive strike to establish seven new campuses and perhaps was an appeal to legislators, particularly with bills pending in Sacramento, to reject ACR 88.

The legislative presence at the next meeting of the Liaison Committee was large. Eleven lawmakers and two staff members appeared, including assembly members Donahoe, John Collier, L. E. Geddes, Lloyd Lowry, and Harold Sedgewick (chair of the Interim Committee on Education), and state senators Miller, Hugh Donnelly, Nathan Coombs, and Fred Farr (the new chair of the Senate Education Committee). They attended not only to hear the discussion between Kerr and Simpson and the eight representatives from the regents and the State Board of Education, but also to promote their own interests. In reviewing the terms of the draft resolution, Senator Gibson chastised the two boards. They had "no right to ask the legislature to endorse any restrictive policy in regard to new institutions." He desired the advice of the boards but no more, and he was bent on providing a new state college in the north San Francisco Bay Area. Senator Coombs agreed. Adopting the proposed resolution, he claimed, was an attempt by the two boards to "take upon themselves an authority which was never intended to be granted them." Two other assemblymen explained that the very existence of the Liaison Committee compromised their constitutionally derived responsibilities.[44]

The concerns of legislators in attendance had a conciliatory effect on the Liaison Committee. As Donahoe had reiterated, the two boards had one more chance to forge their own plan. The regents and the board of education clearly understood the prerogatives and responsibilities of the legislature, explained William Blair. Any plan would come back to Sacramento for approval and legislation. Blair offered a compromise: The State Board of Education could accept the moratorium and oppose all pending legislation for new campuses, but site acquisition should go forward for all potential campus sites thus far approved by the legislature and the two boards. Their ultimate operation would be reviewed in the Master Plan study. The compromise would be brought to the two boards at their second joint meeting, scheduled at UCLA in mid-April, just two weeks away.[45]

University officials worked furiously to make the second joint meeting a success. Regents Edwin Pauley and Samuel Mosher flew key legislators, including Assembly Speaker Ralph Brown, Donahoe, and George Miller, from Sacramento to Los Angeles on their private planes. Also in attendance were Governor Brown, Jesse Unruh, chair of the Assembly Ways and Means Committee, A. Alan Post, the legislative analyst, and Bill Priest, representative of the junior colleges. A dinner at Pauley's home finished a series of social events designed by Kerr and his staff to, according to one observer, "push a still reluctant Roy Simpson and the Department of Education to go along."[46]

Governor Brown chaired the meeting that was held in the Faculty Center on the UCLA campus. He had already proclaimed his strong endorsement for the modified resolution formulated by William Blair. In stark contrast to the first joint meeting, the resolution to proceed with the Master Plan passed with little discussion. Governor Brown called for a reading of Donahoe's ACR 88. The two boards proceeded to endorse it and agreed that the Liaison Committee would coordinate the study and report to the legislature in less than eight months. The governor explained that he would call a special session of the legislature in 1960 to focus primarily on the Master Plan.[47]

Cantankerous lawmakers used the remaining time to lecture the two boards. Senator Miller once again described the pressures on the legislature. The era in which the legislature would simply yield to the higher education community and to the two boards was over. The competition "for the establishment of State Colleges . . . is the result of great local pressures, [and] it is becoming stronger and stronger." Miller was now convinced that a single board for all of California public higher education was a necessity. Bert Levit, the director of the Department of Finance under Governor Brown, concurred and stated: "[E]veryone should recognize that the State is faced with a grave problem. . . . [T]here should not be compromised out of existence the necessity for a radical approach which will place education under a unified direction."[48]

A week after the second joint meeting of the two boards, Donahoe's resolution passed in the legislature. Assemblyman Sedgewick agreed to hold his bill for a new state college board until completion of the Master Plan. However, Sheridan Hegland, author of a bill that would broaden state college functions, protested vehemently. Hegland noted that his bill had the vigorous endorsement of the AFL Teachers Union, the faculty at Fresno State, and the president of the Association of State College Teachers. "Everything is supposed to be held up for this study to be made within the next six months," complained the assemblyman, "which is supposed to solve everything which has not been solved by studies going on for these past fifty years!"[49] However, Hegland and other lawmakers had no choice but to await the results of the study. Kerr's strategy had been successful thus far. Two more steps remained: the successful negotiation of a plan and approval by the legislature and the governor.

CHAPTER 10

Negotiating the Master Plan and the Fate of Higher Education in California

If they don't come up with something, we will do it ourselves . . . we have to move ahead on this Master Plan.

—GOVERNOR EDMUND "PAT" BROWN, 1959

As California struggled to find a common vision for its higher education system in the late 1950s, other states were engaged in a similar debate. Commenting on the lack of state coordination within rapidly growing state systems of higher education, James Conant, the former president at Harvard, described his "sense of horror at the disarray [he] found in a number of large and important states." After touring the nation to assess the future of America's education system, he urged states to "plan more carefully for the development of education beyond the high school."[1]

The post–World War II era was a significant period of reorganization in American higher education. Of the approximately seventeen states during the late 1950s and early 1960s that modified their public and private systems to promote coordination and control costs, most looked toward reducing the autonomy of their public higher education institutions. As Lyman Glenny observed in 1959, state governments found it imperative to develop formal coordinating mechanisms: "Legislatures, in response to the competition for funds, have increasingly turned to superboards or commissions of lay persons with a professional staff for information and recommendations on public higher education. They expect such a board to make the higher educational system more productive, efficient, and economical."[2]

Conscious of the national trend toward centralization of state systems of higher education, and the predilections of powerful political leaders such as state senator George Miller, Clark Kerr and others in California's education community recognized that the Master Plan negotiations might be their last chance to influence reform. Failure to create a politically palatable plan would almost certainly guarantee significant if not radical reform of the tripartite system. For University of California officials, there was a fear that lawmakers might elevate the programs and role of the state colleges; more worrisome, legislators and Governor Brown might attempt a constitutional amendment that would erode the university's autonomy and provide greater regulatory control by both the legislature and state agencies.

State college officials such as San Diego's Malcolm Love imagined another scenario: Kerr might successfully revive the idea of university control of the state colleges, winning the support of the new Democratic leadership in Sacramento. Pressure was building to come to some resolution. An editorial in the *Los Angeles Times* noted, "The patchy development of the State Colleges may reflect regional necessities, but it has become clear that the state must have a master plan for higher education, not only for the state colleges, but for the branching University of California."[3]

Kerr later claimed that the path to the Master Plan was not the end result of a clearly constructed strategic plan either by university officials or other members of the higher education community in California. "We were not on the Acropolis looking back on events," Kerr reflected in 1990, "but down in the Agora, the marketplace, making deals under the discipline of time and deadlines."[4] Yet the ultimate approval of the plan by the two boards and lawmakers was the result of Kerr's efforts and the outcome of a clear, if at times risky, strategy. At the opening of the negotiation process, it was understood that the stakes were extremely high for the University of California and the state colleges, and for the people of California.

The Love Plan

A week after the California Legislature passed Dorothy Donahoe's resolution calling for a Master Plan, Kerr and Simpson agreed that the plan should be completed by a nine-member Joint Advisory Committee (JAC) to the Liaison Committee. The JAC had been established in the early 1950s to assist the

Liaison Committee on key issues. It now consisted of three state college presidents, three university chancellors, and three representatives from the junior colleges. Staff for the JAC included Thomas C. Holy from the university and Arthur Brown from the Department of Education.[5] Both served as staff to the Liaison Committee as well. Kerr and Simpson asked the JAC to immediately negotiate one of the most contested questions facing California public higher education: what was the appropriate function of each segment of the public system? Kerr and Simpson agreed that two other key issues, governance and enrollment expansion, would follow the resolution of segmental functions. However, placing the burden of negotiating the Master Plan on the JAC would prove problematic for the university.

In preparing for the first JAC meeting, Dean McHenry suggested a scheme for Kerr and university officials. Kerr had known McHenry since their days in graduate school at Berkeley, where they had been roommates. McHenry was born in Lompoc, California, and had received his B.A. from UCLA in 1932. Four years later, he had earned his Ph.D. at Berkeley. McHenry then accepted a faculty position at UCLA in the Department of Political Science. After serving in the Navy during World War II, he returned to UCLA and, between 1947 and 1950, served as the dean of the social sciences. McHenry had a scholarly passion about California politics and the workings of state and local government—a passion he then converted into an attempt at a political career. He was an active member of the California Democratic Council and ran unsuccessfully for the State Assembly in the early 1950s. When Kerr became president in 1958, he asked his politically astute and good friend to become an "academic assistant." McHenry accepted, while still retaining his faculty position at UCLA.[6]

McHenry became Kerr's primary strategist and confidant in the difficult days that lay ahead. He told Kerr that the university needed to assess those "areas most vital . . . to the university system, the loss of which would be disastrous, and the sharing of which would lead to the depletion of quality and/or the slow starvation of the portion of functions left with UC." At all costs, argued McHenry, the university must prevent the state colleges from being called universities and should never relinquish doctoral degrees. He was also adamant, as Sproul had been, that the university obstruct any attempt to enlarge the research functions of the state colleges. A change in name or new degrees, noted McHenry, should require legislative action to amend the *Education Code* or, possibly, the state constitution. He advised Kerr that, among legislators, "we must build up such strength that they will fear to propose lest they fail." To do so, the university must "tell them frankly what our vital interests are." In short, he claimed, if a joint agreement fails, "we will fight them in the first house, second house, the governor's office, etc. If they get a bill through we hold it up in referendum."[7] McHenry hoped that, with the help of junior college representatives, the university might "score regular six-to-three victories," in JAC meetings.

The state college presidents had other ideas. They had already circulated their three-point plan for higher education in Sacramento. Now they brought it to the negotiation table with some interesting twists. At the next meeting of the JAC in late March, Malcolm Love offered a radical "redefinition" of state college and university functions. Under the "Love Plan," the state colleges would become universities offering undergraduate liberal arts and occupational and professional curricula, with "specialization continued at the graduate level and culminating in an advanced degree." This would include the Ph.D., a research function with state support for buildings, and a reduction in the teaching loads of faculty. At the same time, the University of California would reduce its admission of undergraduates and focus on the training of advanced research scholars. Terminal master's degrees would cease to be given, and the university would admit students from the top tenth of the high school graduating class—down from approximately the top 15 percent it had accepted since the Progressive Era.[8]

Kerr asked McHenry to attend all the JAC meetings and report their activities to him. He was traumatized by the acquiescence of the university's representatives. Chancellors Glenn Seaborg (Berkeley), Verne Knudsen (UCLA), and Stan Freeborn (Davis) had been appointed to uphold the university's interests. Despite Kerr's instructions, the Love Plan entranced them. The three chancellors—each highly respected scientists, with Seaborg a Nobel Prize winner and one of the discoverers of plutonium—listened intently as Love and his politically savvy colleagues, San Francisco State President Dumke and San Jose State President Wahlquist, explained the advantages of the plan. As McHenry silently watched, deferring to his superiors, the three chancellors immediately noted their general agreement, indeed, enthusiasm, for the proposal. They were attracted to the graduate and research emphasis that appeared to them the true calling of the University of California—an image that had captured the imaginations of Benjamin Ide Wheeler and David Starr Jordan fifty years before.

McHenry reported back to Kerr with alarm. "Having failed to do their homework, these boys have practically given on a silver platter what we have kept from them by force of logic and by power of the legislature," complained McHenry to Kerr. "Deliver us from naive scientists!"[9]

The Love Plan would fulfill the major objectives of the state college presidents. McHenry analyzed President Love's opening move, noting to Kerr: "tactically, it appears that we were outmaneuvered. . . . [T]he state colleges are to take over nearly everything." What remained was a university "pricing itself out of the undergraduate market and living in the stratosphere with Ravel and the Deity . . . shooting [the University of California] into space. Sad thing is that there is little in the way of refueling up there and some solid BTU's and dollars are required to keep such an expensive mechanism operating."[10] Vernon Cheadle, a professor of botany at Davis and chair of that campus' Education Policy Committee, noted that "the University has been beaten to the punch, consciously or unconsciously, and has been thrown into a defensive position."[11] An academic senate committee called Love's proposal "unacceptable." It would create "a second University system in California" and mark the beginning of the end of the university's dominant position in the state's hierarchy of public higher education.[12]

Several days after the Love Plan was unveiled, Chancellor Knudsen innocently sent Kerr an outline of segmental functions that reflected Love's proposal, noting its advantages and conceding doctorate programs to the state colleges as inevitable. Why "give away our heritage," exclaimed an upset McHenry. He urged Kerr to immediately replace Seaborg, Knudsen, and Freeborn on the JAC or to insist that their views represent those of the university president and the regents. Otherwise, McHenry warned, Kerr's presidency would be a black mark in the history of the University of California. "During the Kerr era, the Empire becomes Commonwealth," eulogized McHenry. "Another 'babes in the woods' act like that and Kerr may preside over the liquidation of the new Commonwealth. Or its twilight?"[13]

President Kerr responded by sending a letter addressed to university vice president Harry Wellman and routed to Freeborn, Knudsen, and Seaborg. Kerr noted that he was "disturbed" by the discussion at the JAC. He felt that the "University must have a unified position at this time of great crisis in its external relations. . . . The Love proposals on the functions of the University would make it such an elitist institution that it might no longer endure." Under no circumstances, noted Kerr, should the university accept such a broad definition of the state college mission. Less than a month later, Kerr replaced Knudsen and a retiring Freeborn with the new chancellor at Davis, Emil Mrak, and the new chancellor at Riverside, Herman Spieth. By the end of July, Seaborg had also been replaced on the JAC by the new chancellor at Santa Barbara, Samuel B. Gould. All three replacements were viewed by Kerr and McHenry as more politically adept for the challenges ahead.

Kerr then forcefully told Superintendent Simpson that the Love Plan was unacceptable. At a meeting of the state college presidents, an angry Malcolm Love retorted that Kerr had "prematurely rejected the statement . . . without full study and consideration by everyone concerned." Love noted his worry that Kerr and the university were attempting to forge a consensus among lawmakers in Sacramento toward absorption of the state colleges under the regents. This would presumably end all hope of new graduate programs and make the state colleges second-class citizens within the university system. Glenn Dumke also reported that Governor Brown now seemed to be in favor of this change or a similar reform, joining Senator Miller.[14]

In the wake of the Love Plan, Kerr considered abandoning the Master Plan negotiations. Valuable time had been lost, and the bold and populist demands of Malcolm Love and his compatriots posed a serious challenge to the university. Kerr asked key faculty for their advice. William S. Briscoe, a professor of education at UCLA, advocated the swift absorption by the regents of the state colleges. "I feel we are facing a crisis," he exclaimed.[15] Tom Holy agreed. He had been the university's staff member on the JAC since its creation in 1953 and now warned that the system of voluntary coordination was collapsing. In his opinion, it probably could not be resurrected.[16] It was perhaps time for the university to launch a hostile takeover of the state colleges. "Statements of public officials, legislators and others," he explained, "leave the impression that chaos reigns and that millions of dollars of the taxpayers' money is being wasted in the struggle between the University and the state colleges." This, combined with "the fact that president Kerr is in his 'honeymoon period'" with lawmakers and the public, Holy argued, "offered an opportune time for the University taking control of the colleges."[17]

McHenry thought differently. Reflecting the consternation of former university president Robert Sproul in the 1930s and 1940s, McHenry warned that such a bold move would raise substantial political opposition and result in legislation abhorrent to the university. Even if the university was successful in its conquest, the regents would then face the difficult task of managing two competing groups of institutions. The resolve to protect the university's teaching and research mission might fade over time. There would be pressure for the state colleges to reach some form of parity with the campuses of the university. This pressure might eventually come from within the board as new governors chose new regents with allegiances to the state colleges. He urged Kerr not to abandon the negotiations.

Kerr's legal counsel also advised against absorption of the state colleges: It was bound to raise questions regarding the proper level of autonomy for the university and possibly a movement to end the university's status as a constitutionally protected public trust. Kerr decided to keep with the negotiations but to abandon the JAC as a forum to complete the planning study.[18] Chancellors within the university system appeared consumed by the interests of their own campuses. At the same time, the formidable state college presidents on the committee had a clear agenda that promised little if any compromise. A new forum for negotiating the plan was needed, with new players. At the same time and as a contingency plan, Kerr would keep open the option of a constitutional amendment to place the state colleges under the regents.

Organizing the Plan

In late May of 1959, a little over a month after Love's gambit, Kerr gained Superintendent Roy Simpson's agreement to create a "Master Plan Survey Team." The team would include representatives from the university, the state colleges, the junior colleges, and the addition of private institutions who had been lobbying in Sacramento for a role in the negotiations. Most importantly, it would include as chair an arbitrator without ties to either the university or the state colleges.[19] Though Simpson remained a reluctant supporter of the Master Plan, he was cognizant of the need to complete the plan to maintain, indeed rebuild, his reputation with lawmakers. The Board of Regents and the California State Board of Education then approved the concept of the survey team.

The state college presidents were angry over the abandonment of the JAC and Simpson's capitulation to a new forum for negotiations. University officials, they believed, had created a new negotiating environment by adding a university ally: representatives from the private institutions. However, the key to the negotiations, the state college presidents realized, lay perhaps in the selection of the chair of survey team. Here they found some comfort with the naming of Arthur G. Coons.

Kerr and Simpson considered several people before agreeing on Coons as the survey team chair. A. Alan Post was one candidate, because of his ties with the legislature as the chief budget analyst and his excellent reputation. Another candidate was Wilson E. Lyon, president of Pomona College. Finally, in early June they agreed on Coons, the longtime president of Occidental College and a political scientist who had published in the area of political economy. "It was clear I would be under the necessity of trying to get the 'warring' factions into sufficient agreement fast enough to fulfill the Legislature's demands," reflected Coons in 1968. He agreed to chair the survey team, even though two Occidental trustees strongly opposed his decision. It would take him away from his duties at the small liberal arts college. Friends and trustees at the college told him that any attempt to resolve the fighting within the higher education community on the one side and the reckless abandon of legislators on the other would certainly "ruin his health." Coons had already experienced a heart attack in early 1957.[20]

A native of Los Angeles, Coons began his academic career as a teacher at Fullerton Junior College before becoming a faculty member at the Claremont Graduate School. In 1950 he was named president of Occidental. Glenn Dumke had spent most of his academic and administrative career at Occidental and had served under Coons as a dean before becoming the president of San Francisco State in 1957 at the age of forty. Dumke reported to his fellow state college presidents that Coons could be counted on to provide a fair hearing for their interests.

The other eight members of the survey team were also chosen by Kerr and Simpson and included Glenn Dumke for the state colleges and Dean McHenry for the university. Henry T. Tyler was selected to represent the junior colleges. Tyler was the executive secretary for the California Junior College Association. The Association of Independent Colleges and Universities appointed Robert J. Wert, vice provost at Stanford University. Also appointed to act as staff on the team were Thomas C. Holy for the university, Arthur Browne for the State Department of Education, and retired superintendent of the Los Angeles Public Schools Howard A. Campion.[21]

Coons and the survey team were to consider six major issues. None assumed any major shift in California's commitment to expanding access to higher education; rather they focused on ways to make modifications in the tripartite system that had emerged largely in the Progressive Era. The first concerned enrollment: What was their projection of student enrollment demand from 1960 to 1975, and how might they be distributed among the three public segments?[22] The second issue related to segmental functions—a source of heated debate. "In light of new and changing circumstances," explained the survey team's mandate, "what modifications should be made in the existing agreements on the differentiation of functions among the junior colleges, state colleges and the University of California?" After addressing these two issues, the team needed to provide a priority list and schedule for establishing new campuses, an estimate of the cost of capital and annual operations to the state, and an assessment of the ability of the California government to pay for the expansion plan. The sixth and final challenge of the survey team was to recommend the appropriate model for the governance and coordination of the system.[23]

To assist the work of the survey team, six "technical committees" were established, each focusing on the six planning issues stated in the charge for the survey team.[24] (See Figure 10.) These committees were chaired by faculty and administrators from the public tripartite system and were largely fact-finding groups with representatives from all the public and private segments.[25]

Arthur Coons initially favored a single governing board for all public higher education in California. In his view, it needed to have "inclusive and extensive authority and power" over the tripartite system.[26] In no small part, this position reflected his experience as president of Occidental College. "Coons was one of the old line college presidents," later reflected Glenn Dumke, "who operated very autocratically and with insistence that there be central control. . . . [H]e ran a very tight ship."[27]

Coons saw in California public higher education a level of disarray that needed to be forcefully addressed. This was a viewpoint he brought openly to the first meeting of the survey team on June 16, 1959. Coons' predilection was reinforced by a comparative study of other state higher education governance systems conducted by Tom Holy and Arthur Browne two months earlier.[28] Holy and Browne reported that three general organizational structures could be found in state systems of public higher education in the United States. The first model offered no central governance mechanism and reflected a laissez-faire approach: Each institution, or campus, had its own board that would then report directly to the legislature. Approximately ten states, they noted, functioned in this manner.[29]

The second model, that of a single board with authority over all public higher education, could be found in twenty states. In most of these states, a single board governed all public colleges and universities. In New Mexico, New York, North Carolina, Oklahoma, Texas, and Wisconsin, a superboard was imposed over existing boards for the teachers colleges and the other public colleges and universities in the state. Local boards were subservient to the superboard, whose responsibilities included approving all academic programs, establishing all new campuses, and preparing a single budget for all state-supported higher education.[30] Seven other states were in the process of

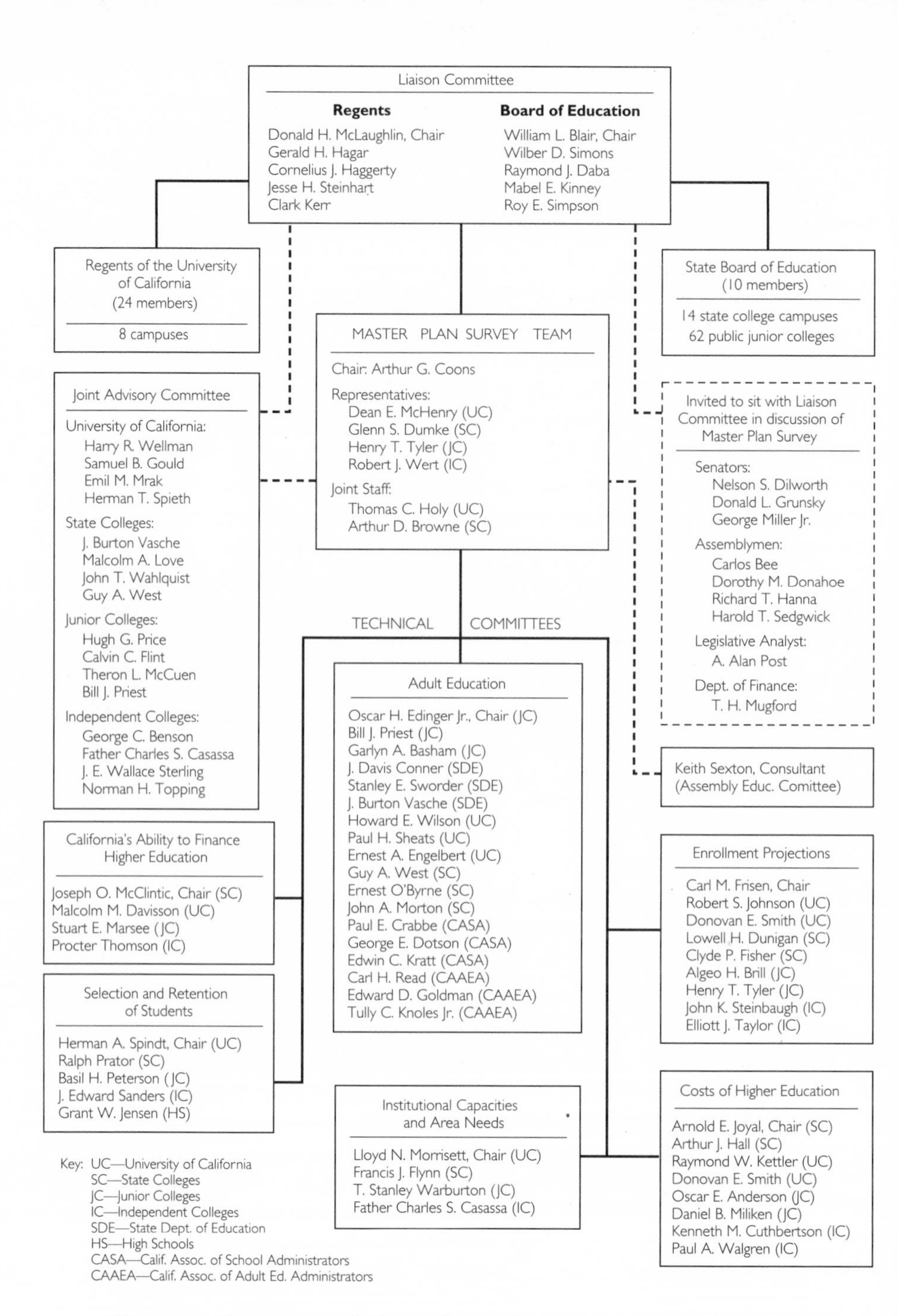
Liaison Committee
Regents
Donald H. McLaughlin, Chair
Gerald H. Hagar
Cornelius J. Haggerty
Jesse H. Steinhart
Clark Kerr
Board of Education
William L. Blair, Chair
Wilber D. Simons
Raymond J. Daba
Mabel E. Kinney
Roy E. Simpson
Regents of the University of California (24 members)
8 campuses
State Board of Education (10 members)
14 state college campuses
62 public junior colleges
MASTER PLAN SURVEY TEAM
Chair: Arthur G. Coons
Representatives:
Dean E. McHenry (UC)
Glenn S. Dumke (SC)
Henry T. Tyler (JC)
Robert J. Wert (IC)
Joint Staff:
Thomas C. Holy (UC)
Arthur D. Browne (SC)
Joint Advisory Committee
University of California:
Harry R. Wellman
Samuel B. Gould
Emil M. Mrak
Herman T. Spieth
State Colleges:
J. Burton Vasche
Malcolm A. Love
John T. Wahlquist
Guy A. West
Junior Colleges:
Hugh G. Price
Calvin C. Flint
Theron L. McCuen
Bill J. Priest
Independent Colleges:
George C. Benson
Father Charles S. Casassa
J. E. Wallace Sterling
Norman H. Topping
Invited to sit with Liaison Committee in discussion of Master Plan Survey
Senators:
Nelson S. Dilworth
Donald L. Grunsky
George Miller Jr.
Assemblymen:
Carlos Bee
Dorothy M. Donahoe
Richard T. Hanna
Harold T. Sedgwick
Legislative Analyst:
A. Alan Post
Dept. of Finance:
T. H. Mugford
Keith Sexton, Consultant (Assembly Educ. Comittee)
TECHNICAL COMMITTEES
Adult Education
Oscar H. Edinger Jr., Chair (JC)
Bill J. Priest (JC)
Garlyn A. Basham (JC)
J. Davis Conner (SDE)
Stanley E. Sworder (SDE)
J. Burton Vasche (SDE)
Howard E. Wilson (UC)
Paul H. Sheats (UC)
Ernest A. Engelbert (UC)
Guy A. West (SC)
Ernest O'Byrne (SC)
John A. Morton (SC)
Paul E. Crabbe (CASA)
George E. Dotson (CASA)
Edwin C. Kratt (CASA)
Carl H. Read (CAAEA)
Edward D. Goldman (CAAEA)
Tully C. Knoles Jr. (CAAEA)
California's Ability to Finance Higher Education
Joseph O. McClintic, Chair (SC)
Malcolm M. Davisson (UC)
Stuart E. Marsee (JC)
Procter Thomson (IC)
Selection and Retention of Students
Herman A. Spindt, Chair (UC)
Ralph Prator (SC)
Basil H. Peterson (JC)
J. Edward Sanders (IC)
Grant W. Jensen (HS)
Enrollment Projections
Carl M. Frisen, Chair
Robert S. Johnson (UC)
Donovan E. Smith (UC)
Lowell H. Dunigan (SC)
Clyde P. Fisher (SC)
Algeo H. Brill (JC)
Henry T. Tyler (JC)
John K. Steinbaugh (IC)
Elliott J. Taylor (IC)
Institutional Capacities and Area Needs
Lloyd N. Morrisett, Chair (UC)
Francis J. Flynn (SC)
T. Stanley Warburton (JC)
Father Charles S. Casassa (IC)
Costs of Higher Education
Arnold E. Joyal, Chair (SC)
Arthur J. Hall (SC)
Raymond W. Kettler (UC)
Donovan E. Smith (UC)
Oscar E. Anderson (JC)
Daniel B. Miliken (JC)
Kenneth M. Cuthbertson (IC)
Paul A. Walgren (IC)
Key: UC—University of California
SC—State Colleges
JC—Junior Colleges
IC—Independent Colleges
SDE—State Dept. of Education
HS—High Schools
CASA—Calif. Assoc. of School Administrators
CAAEA—Calif. Assoc. of Adult Ed. Administrators

Figure 10. Organization of Master Plan Study, 1959

SOURCE: Graphic presented in the *California Master Plan for Higher Education*, 1960

shifting to a single board model (sometimes called a "coordinating agency") with various levels of authority, including Arkansas, Colorado, Illinois, Louisiana, Michigan, Tennessee, and Utah.[31]

The third model, with two separate boards for the state land grant university and state colleges, could be found in approximately eighteen states, including California. Within this model, only three states had a voluntary coordinating mechanism, California, Ohio, and Indiana. In Ohio and Indiana, voluntary boards were formed in the face of a legislative threat to establish a single board.[32]

In Coons' opinion, there was little if any chance to resurrect a workable voluntary mechanism, like the Liaison Committee, in California. In the face of a rising tide of enrollment demand and the often bitter feuds between the university and the state colleges, a single board seemed the most effective and responsible course. He knew that finding an agreement among the survey team was going to be extremely difficult. He hoped to first settle the issue of the function of the various public segments of the public tripartite system before focusing on governance.

The first meeting of the survey team, held on the Berkeley campus, opened with Glenn Dumke, the main spokesman for the state colleges, on the attack. Dumke emerged as the most politically adroit state college president. The other state college presidents hoped that Dumke's personal relationship with Coons might prove a valuable, perhaps decisive, influence on the outcome of the pending negotiations.

At the survey team meeting, Dumke insisted that they take a fresh look at the functions of each of the public segments. He reiterated the complaint of the state college presidents at the outright rejection by Kerr and other university officials of the Love Plan. He then set out a new proposal to extend the doctorate in the field of education to the state colleges. Dumke explained that the "degree would not be a research degree, but a teaching degree." There was a clear and documented need for additional doctoral-level teachers, he insisted. The state colleges were in the best position to provide training in this area, Dumke argued. The state colleges needed the degree for another reason: to "enhance morale and professional advancement" of their faculty. If the colleges were denied this function, he concluded, the effect would be the creation of a permanent "caste system," relegating the colleges to "a second-rate status."[33]

McHenry's response was strong and adversarial. He told Dumke that if he and the other state college presidents continued to "make passes at the Crown Jewels," they could expect "to encounter the firmest resistance" from the university. It was "essential for the well being of the State, and of the institutions themselves," he and Holy stated, to maintain this structure of academic programs that "has been officially and almost universally accepted."[34] They both cited the Restudy Report, which stated that, unless there were "new and compelling factors," doctoral programs at state colleges should not be considered until 1965. According to McHenry, there were no compelling factors. He further insisted that in the "fields in which doctorates are advocated, education, social sciences etc., additional space for students exists in the university and private institutions." The problem in these fields, he claimed, was to recruit students, not to create new programs.

McHenry and Holy told Dumke and Browne that the state college presidents had it all wrong. They should concentrate on improving the quality of their master's degree programs "and achieving eminence within their regular sphere of activity." Sanctioning the doctorate within the state colleges, they concluded, would destroy the concept of differentiation of functions and erode any hope of maintaining a rational public system of higher education.[35] For McHenry, Holy, and other university officials, holding the line on state college functions was the most important goal in the negotiations. The survey team's first meeting, thought Coons, was a disaster.

At the survey team's next meeting in July, Dumke insisted that the state college proposal did not refute the premise of different functions among the three segments of California's higher education system or the basic findings of the previous Strayer and Restudy Reports. Though he did not agree completely with the "flatly vocational concept of education" for the state colleges professed by the Restudy Report, even under this rubric Dumke claimed there was room for innovation. In the field of education and possibly other areas of graduate training, noted Dumke, "clearly it is possible to have each set of institutions doing something different." There already existed this type of differentiation within master's level programs between the University of California and the state colleges in areas such as engineering. The same argument, Dumke explained, could be made to support a research function for state college faculty.[36] The gulf between McHenry and Dumke and their respective institutions was deep and wide.

In the opening months of their negotiations, the survey team found no common ground. A worried Coons abandoned his strategy to tackle the difficult issue of segmental functions first before moving onto other key issues such as governance, admissions standards, enrollment projections, and new campuses. The wrangling at the negotiation table reinforced Coons' view that a single board was the only solution to the vexing problem of creating an ordered system of higher education in California. After numerous meetings, Coons proposed that the survey team move on to the issue of governance and return to the contentious issue of functions at a later date. He was not optimistic about reaching any agreement. "My reaction to the deliberations of the past month," he wrote in his personal diary, "is that I am wasting my time and the State's money. It is evident at this moment to me that no segment of the state supported higher education is willing to retreat. . . . If there is no yielding on major and fundamental issues on each side all along the line, this survey will be doomed."[37]

Debating a Single Board

Meeting on the Berkeley campus in late July and with five months until the legislative deadline for the plan, Arthur Coons offered his proposal for a single governing board. Under this plan, the junior colleges, with their strong link to local districts, would remain under the State Board of Education. Coons explained his view that the lack of "differentiation of functions is forcing California toward a single system." Writing on a blackboard, Coons outlined his plan for a new board to be composed of some forty members, including sixteen former regents, ten lay members from the State Board of Education, five or six new lay members to balance the representation between the university and the state colleges, and eight ex officio members, ranging from the speaker of the assembly to the governor.[38] In form and content, Coons's proposal looked much like the plan forwarded in the 1932 Suzzallo Report.

The monstrous size of the proposed board brought a wince from the rest of the survey team. McHenry and Dumke immediately expressed great reluctance to embrace any proposal for a single board, no matter what its composition. Thomas Holy noted that moving to one board would in fact make it even more difficult to maintain the differentiation of functions between the university and the state colleges—as outlined in his earlier report to Kerr. This differentiation, remarked Holy, was what "made California's system great." McHenry added that the new board would abrogate the existing powers of the university and the regents. This, he insisted, would be rejected by President Kerr.[39]

Dumke protested for different reasons. He explained that even with a balance in representatives on the proposed single board, the political influence of the university would be dominant. Coons' proposed superboard would "so firmly fix their second-class status that it would be unacceptable." Dumke then articulated another objection that would prove a powerful argument against the single board idea. Because of the huge size of the two public segments—the two largest four-year institutions in the nation—Dumke noted the need to retain some form of separate governing boards. How could a single board, he asked, properly manage such a huge conglomeration of campuses? Inevitably, he concluded, the state colleges would suffer a similar level of neglect they now experienced under the State Board of Education.[40]

Although for different reasons, Dumke and McHenry were for the first time standing on common ground. Dumke once again proposed the creation of a new board for the state colleges that could be accompanied by a new "coordinating council" with the power to review the separate budgets of the segments and to approve new degree programs and campuses. Hence, California could create something like a superboard without the direct powers associated with such entities. It might prepare and defend a single statewide budget for higher education, review academic programs to help reduce duplication of programs, and help plan new campuses.[41] Such a system, he noted, could be found in Wisconsin and Utah. Dumke's proposal was, in fact, similar to one that McHenry offered to Kerr two months earlier. For both sides this governance model provided an attractive balance of autonomy and a central coordinating body. It might also distract the interest of influential lawmakers, including state senator George Miller, in forcing a marriage between the University of California and the state colleges.[42]

In the course of the debate over governance, there was some concern over the management of the junior colleges, although, clearly, this was a secondary concern for the survey team. A proposal was offered to create a separate board for the junior colleges, but it was rejected. It implied an infringement on local authority that, in the survey team's opinion, would be wildly unpopular among local communities and their representatives in the California Legislature. A separate board might also require or imply a large increase in the state government's financial responsibility.[43]

For some three months, the survey team debated Dumke's proposal for a new board for the state colleges and a coordinating council with largely advisory powers. Before the survey team, Lyman Glenny, in the midst of his study on state coordination of higher education, warned that the council would likely prove a weak coordinating mechanism,particularly if it had only advisory powers and was largely a reconstituted Liaison Committee. Glenny also assumed that the council would be unattractive to legislators such as Miller. The most significant problem, observed Coons, "was how a legal agency could be established over a constitutionally independent group," such as the regents. A legal structure could exist only if the regents accepted the arrangement, "thus limiting their autonomy in certain respects."[44]

Five months into the deliberations, the survey team finally came to its first major agreement. In October, under a joint proposal offered by Dumke, McHenry, Tyler, and Wert, the survey team agreed to the concept of a separate board for the state colleges and a new coordinating council. The council would need to be established as an amendment to the California Constitution. It would have broad budgetary powers and the final authority to establish new programs and new campuses. The council would review and possibly revise the proposed budgets of the university and the state colleges and would present and then defend the budgets as a package to the legislature. Along with the authority to review new program proposals, this would provide a method for reducing duplication and inefficiencies in the two segments that, it was hoped, legislators would find attractive. Unlike the failed Coordinating Council established in 1933 in California, the council would include primarily members of California's higher education community, and hence it would not be a lay board. The proposal also required the hiring of a research staff and an "executive officer" on the level parallel to that of Superintendent Simpson and President Kerr.[45] (See Figure 11.)

Coons backed away from his insistence on a single board and embraced the idea of the coordinating council. It remained unclear how this proposed "solution" would play in Sacramento. In the legislature, Assemblywoman Donahoe and Senator Miller had already asked Legislative Counsel Ralph N. Kleps to outline the legal wording necessary to create a single board for the University of California and the state colleges, with possible authority over the junior colleges.[46] There was also a diversity of opinion over governance and coordination within the higher education community. State college faculty relished the idea of gaining their own board, relatively free of what was viewed as stifling regulatory controls of state agencies. Among university faculty, however, there remained a strong "con-

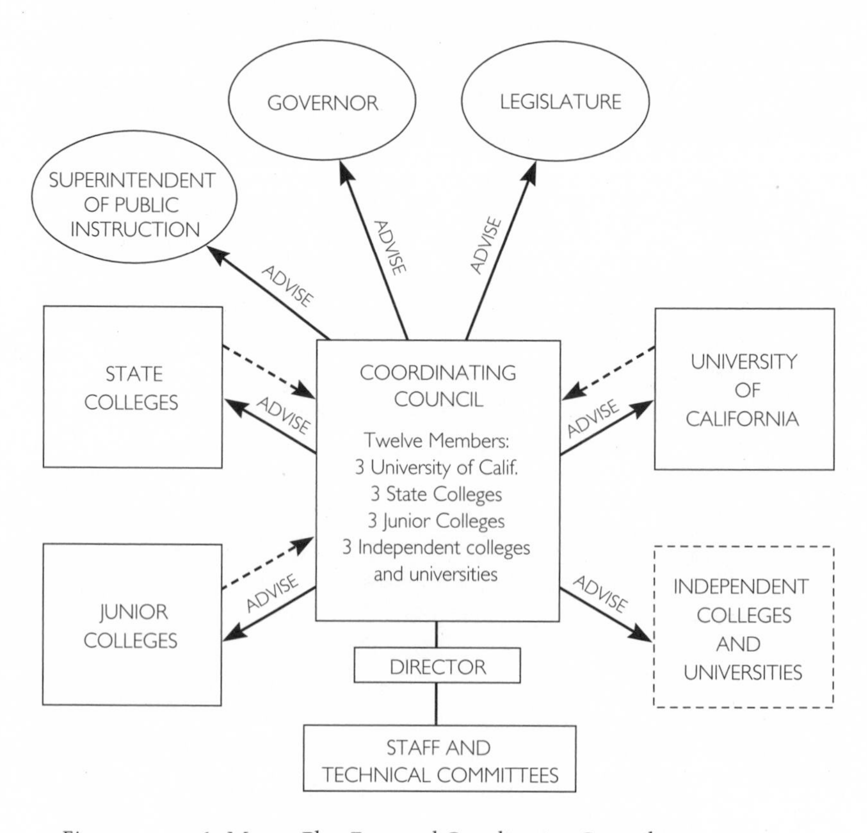

Figure 11. 1960 Master Plan Proposed Coordinating Council
SOURCE: Graphic presented in the *California Master Plan for Higher Education,* 1960

tingent convinced that only a single board could control the thirst of the state colleges for parity with the university.[47]

Students and New Campuses

The agreement on governance was a major achievement. For the first time, Arthur Coons sensed that the completion of the plan was a possibility. With the issue of governance and coordination apparently settled, he hoped that other major agreements would quickly follow. The survey team proceeded to consider the criteria for determining future enrollment demand in California. The flow of students into the respective segments had huge budgetary implications for the state and for the aspirations of the public segments. Since the Progressive Era, the appropriation of state funds for operating costs was directly proportional to student enrollment. Enrollment-driven budgets were the lifeblood of the university, the state colleges, and the junior colleges. Capital costs were also related to projected student enrollment growth.

In yet another surprise move by state college representatives, Arthur Browne presented the survey team with his analysis of how the state might save vast sums of money. California should channel a greater number of the projected freshmen entering the public system into the junior and state colleges, explained Browne, where he claimed that costs per student were much lower. The state, he projected, could save some $45 million by such a shift—a projection later reiterated in the *San Francisco Chronicle* and other newspapers in support of Browne's plan. To accomplish this, Browne proposed raising the admissions requirements of the university. "Why not save money by curbing university expansion?" he asked.[48]

Accompanying Browne's presentation was a large chart displaying the cost of educating a student at each of the public segments. To the great frustration of McHenry and Holy, it showed a huge cost differential between the university and the other two public segments. Browne also implied that California was sinking large sums of public funds into the university while the junior and state colleges did the lion's share of work. Both segments, he noted, had surpassed the university in total enrollments. While the university enrolled only 16 percent of the students in 1958, Browne explained, it received 54 percent of the total state appropriations for higher education. The university also got 62 percent of the capital outlay funds, while the state colleges received only 38 percent. The junior colleges, he explained, received no funds for capital construction from the state. The burden of physical expansion fell solely on local governments.

Browne also presented projections of costs for new campuses. He assumed that each new and planned university campus would cost the state approximately $100 million—an estimate given by Regent Pauley in a speech. However, he remarked, the seven state college campuses proposed by Simpson at the first joint meeting of the two boards would cost a total of only $150 million. Browne was appealing to the members of the legislature. For cost reasons alone, he was implying, state funds needed to be shifted to both the junior and state colleges and away from the university.

McHenry and Holy disagreed sharply with Browne's figures and analysis. For one, they stated, Browne's assessment of costs used head-count numbers, equating the costs associated with part-time students to those with full-time status. Both the junior and state colleges enrolled substantial numbers of part-time students. "I asked whether he would support curbing state college expansion," noted McHenry in his report to Kerr, "if our cost studies showed that we spend less per student on Lower Division then they did. Dumke intervened to try to save him, but Holy read the Lower Division cost figures from Restudy [Report], and we had him nailed."[49] At a subsequent meeting of the survey team, McHenry stated that the university had "modest goals . . . [W]e want to educate about the same proportion of the college age group that we did in 1940 and 1950." This meant maintaining an admissions policy that offered enrollment to approximately the top 15 percent of high school graduating classes.[50]

Browne had argued that the university should reduce its admission pool, while the state colleges should enlarge theirs. In subsequent discussion at the next meeting of the survey team, Dumke noted his concern that the state colleges should, along with the university, reduce their own admission pools. He now distanced himself from Browne's projections and offered this as a formal proposal. The raising of university and state college admissions standards would both reduce costs to the state and increase the overall quality of students attending the state colleges. It would shift prospective students to the junior colleges with the promise that they could matriculate to either the university or the state colleges.[51]

McHenry and university officials agreed with Dumke's proposal. Despite the auspicious opening discussion on eligibility, another general agreement was in the making. Two questions remained regarding future enrollment: What should be the revised admission pool for the university and the state colleges, and how might the state support the subsequent expansion of the junior colleges to accommodate more students? The answer would have a tremendous impact on the flow of students through California's higher education system and on the personal lives of thousands of Californians.

The benefits of diverting more lower-division students to the junior colleges appeared substantial to the survey team. It would certainly make the final Master Plan recommendations more politically attractive. "The probability is that capital outlay for the junior colleges will be much lower than for the other segments," explained McHenry. "[E]ven if instructional costs should prove equal, this fact plus the saving to parents and students through living at home would argue for considerable cost savings to the state and its residents. . . . Further, junior colleges are better able to screen and do remedial work and counseling than are the other segments."[52] In light of the strong sense of competition between the state colleges and the university, Dumke, McHenry, and Coons agreed that the shift of students needed to be equitable and, at the same time, not overburden the junior colleges. To make the plan work, the survey team concluded that state government would need to compensate local districts by providing additional funds for junior college operations and capital costs.

The survey team looked to their technical committee on "Selection and Retention of Students," chaired by Herman A. Spindt, for recommendations on how to accomplish this equitable shift. Dumke proposed that Spindt consider establishing a mandated ratio for both the university and the state colleges of approximately one lower- to two upper-division students within both the university and the state colleges. By establishing this mandate for each campus, it would ensure that state colleges and the university would focus on upper-division courses and students. Spindt's committee, however, returned several weeks later with an unexpected answer. There "should be no attempt to control the size of the lower division in the university and the state colleges on the basis of the 'floor' type of admissions procedure," stated Spindt. The desired enrollment shift could be achieved, he insisted, on a voluntary basis, by having "all public four-year colleges participate wholeheartedly in a 'persuasive guidance' program aimed at increasing the proportion of freshmen and sophomores attending the junior colleges." The survey team rejected this innocuous recommendation. There needed to be a clearly stated policy on admissions and a set percentage of lower- to upper-division students, they concluded. It offered the best method to ensure a shift in students.[53]

In November, less than two months before the Master Plan was due before the legislature, an agreement was reached on admissions. The survey team first determined the current ratio of lower- to upper-division students within state colleges and the university. Taken together, California's public institutions enrolled approximately 180,000 full-time students. Of these students, 88,000 (72,000 undergraduates and 16,000 graduate students) attended the state colleges and the university. In both segments, lower-division students represented approximately 51 percent of the undergraduate population. The survey team agreed that "the percentage of undergraduates in the lower division of each segment [be] reduced to approximately ten percentage points

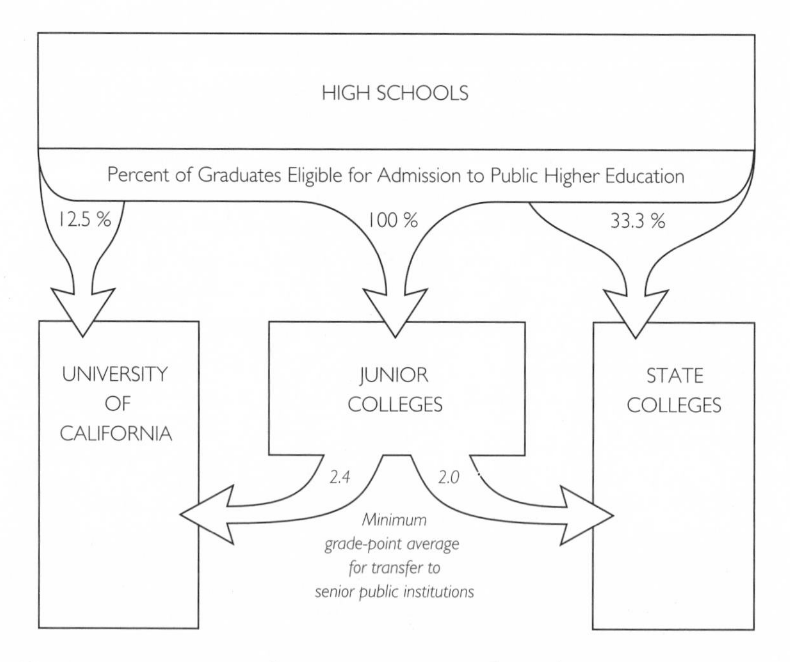

Figure 12. 1960 Master Plan Agreement on Student Admissions
SOURCE: Graphic presented in the *California Master Plan for Higher Education*, 1960

below that [projected] in 1960." This eventually boiled down to a stated policy that would drive new admissions standards and shift students to the junior colleges. The university and the state colleges would have 40 percent lower-division students (freshman and sophomores) and 60 percent upper-division (juniors and seniors).

Based on this shift in ratios for the year 1960, Carl Frisen of the Department of Finance determined that the university should no longer be able to draw from the top 15 percent of California high school graduates but from the top 12.5 percent. Similarly, the state colleges would need to shift from approximately the top 40 percent to the top 33.3 percent.[54] Here was the basis for California's contemporary policy on admission to the state's four-year public institutions—a choice heavily conditioned by the need to reduce costs to taxpayers.

These new admissions standards then allowed Frisen to analyze the impact on future student enrollment between 1960 and 1975. Frisen projected that California could expect to enroll 436,000 additional full-time equivalent students in all higher education institutions, both public and private, by 1975. Of that total, Frisen expected that nearly 94 percent would enter California's public tripartite system, a total of 409,000 additional students. This would represent a 228 percent increase over enrollment in 1958. The change in admissions standards, he estimated, would divert some 50,000 students to locally funded junior colleges where operating costs were lower. In addition, it would reduce the need for state government to fund the construction of new university and state college campuses.[55] Yet how much it would save was subject to unresolved planning assumptions. The need for new campuses was not driven exclusively by projected enrollment demand. It also was contingent on an assessment of the most cost-effective enrollment sizes for existing and planned campuses.

Kerr, McHenry, and other university officials were upset when one of the survey team's technical committees recommended that the maximum enrollment for new state colleges should be 12,000 students, while the goal for all university campuses should be 27,500. Such a low ceiling for the state colleges and a high ceiling for the university implied a potential flood of new state college campuses.[56] McHenry complained that "the political strength of the state colleges will be further accentuated, and the relative influence of the University will decline."[57] McHenry found support from John E. Carr, the new director of finance in the Brown administration. Carr stated that the suggested campus enrollment limits needed to be revised; they would unnecessarily increase state costs. At the request of Coons, the technical committee proceeded to modify their recommendations, creating two categories of state colleges: those in metropolitan areas with a maximum of 20,000 students and those in less densely populated areas at the previous maximum of 12,000 students. Here was another key element of the emerging Master Plan study.

In recommending the location for new campuses of the university and the state colleges, the survey team essentially reiterated the recommendations of the 1957 Additional Centers Report. It was politically expeditious to adopt the findings of this study, completed only two years earlier. The survey team recommended that state funds be provided for three new University of Cali-

	Minimum	Optimum	Maximum
Junior Colleges	400	3,500	6,000
State Colleges			
Densely Populated Metropolitan Areas	5,000	10,000	20,000
Outside Metropolitan Centers	3,000	8,000	12,000
University of California	5,000	12,500	27,500

Figure 13. Master Plan Full-Time Student Enrollment Ranges for Public College and University Campuses

SOURCE: *California Master Plan for Higher Education,* 1960

fornia campuses: in San Diego, the Los Angeles–Orange County area (what would become Irvine), and the south central coast area (what would become Riverside). The list of state college campuses was also familiar. A total of four colleges were proposed, two that already had legislative approval: Northridge, another in the north San Francisco Bay Area (Sonoma), and new campuses at San Bernardino and Dominguez Hills. Each of these campuses, it was explained, should be established before 1965. Beyond 1965, the new coordinating council could conduct "careful studies . . . of the need for additional University facilities in the San Joaquin Valley and the Los Angeles area." They also anticipated the possibility of five other university or state college campuses being built by 1975.[58]

The survey team agreed to a list of twenty-two new junior colleges to be established by 1975. To support the expansion of the junior college system, including the anticipated shift of 50,000 students, they recommended that state government increase its share of the operational budget of the junior colleges from 30 to 42 percent. For the first time, this included a proposed program of state bonds for college construction—capital costs that previously had been borne exclusively by local government.[59]

Reducing Future Costs

Arthur Coons and the survey team members knew that the political appeal of their proposed Master Plan would rest largely on its method of controlling costs. "One of the early issues debated," explained a report by the survey team, "was the extent to which educational policies were to be based on, or determined by, economic factors." There was a great need to make the public system more efficient; but it was not the intention of the team, they argued, simply to make significant adjustments in admissions policies to match a presumed level of state funding in future years. "Good educational planning," they stated, "requires consideration of many factors other than the price tag." Yet the issue of providing a more "efficient" system of higher education, one that promised substantial savings for state government and ultimately for California taxpayers, was clearly a major factor in the survey team's deliberation. Besides shifting students to the junior colleges, the survey team also proposed that all public higher education move to a "full-year calendar."[60] This, it was presumed, would maximize the use of existing campus facilities and lessen the need for new and costly campuses of the university and the state colleges. Improved coordination would, in theory, reduce the unnecessary duplication of programs and would regulate financing to the public segments.

The survey team also recommended a substantial expansion of the state-sponsored undergraduate scholarship program that could be applied at any public or private institution.[61] The scholarship program had been established in 1955 by lawmakers despite the university's opposition, but now university officials saw its advantages. This state scholarship program, it was thought, would encourage some students to attend private colleges and would broaden the political appeal of the Master Plan.

Joseph O. McClintic, chairman of the technical committee that worked on estimating future costs, reported that the shifting of students to the junior colleges and other proposed modifications would provide immediate savings for the state. By 1966, McClintic estimated that the Master Plan would cut the yearly operating and capital costs by $41.5 million. The total amount of savings, however, would decrease in future years. There would be increasing state costs associated with expanding the junior colleges. By 1970, McClintic estimated that the Master Plan would result in substantial yet less spectacular savings: approximately $18 million.[62] (See Figures 14 and 15.)

With the assistance of the Department of Finance, McClintic's committee

Fiscal Year 1965–66	Lower Division (%)	Upper Division (%)	Grad Division (%)	Total (%)
A. Operating Costs				
Junior Colleges	+8.7	—	—	+8.7
State Colleges	−3.7	−1.6	—	−5.3
University of California	−8.2	−7.3	−6.3	−21.8
B. Capital Costs				
State Colleges	−6.0	—	+0.4	−5.6
University of California	−6.1	−6.4	−5.0	−17.5
Total Savings to the State	−15.3	−15.3	−10.9	−41.5
Fiscal Year 1970–71				
A. Operating Costs				
Junior Colleges	+24.5	—	—	+24.5
State Colleges	−11.6	+1.2	+1.0	−9.4
University of California	−12.4	−13.2	−5.8	−31.4
B. Capital Costs				
State Colleges	−7.3	+3.0	+0.6	−3.7
University of California	−4.5	+3.1	+3.5	+2.1
Total Savings to the State	−11.3	−5.9	−0.7	−17.9

Figure 14. Estimate of Annual Savings and Costs for Higher Education Under the Master Plan, 1965–1966 and 1970–1971

SOURCE: *California Master Plan for Higher Education,* 1960

also offered a projection of future state revenues. Would California state government have the funds to pay for the projected price tag of the Master Plan? Even with the proposed methods for saving costs, the available state revenues would be inadequate by as early as 1962. California state government would need to either re-allocate existing revenue to higher education or raise taxes. The survey team concluded that the state should raise revenue. California was a relatively wealthy state, they argued, yet state tax collections represented only a moderate percentage of the state's total income. The percentage of personal income allocated to higher education was comparatively low, only thirty-fifth in the nation. As the survey team later reported

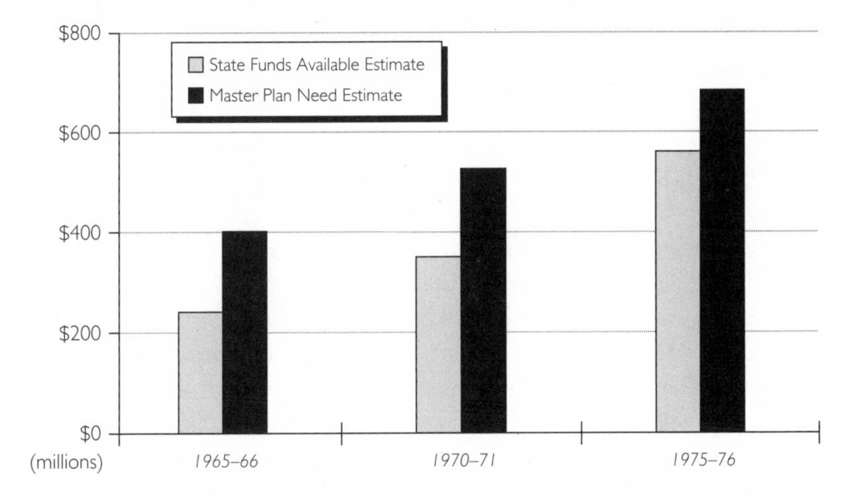

Figure 15. 1960 Master Plan Estimate of State General Funds and Capital Outlay Needed for Expanding Enrollment

SOURCE: *California Master Plan for Higher Education, 1960*

to the legislature, "Even though this state possesses the taxable wealth, a critical question concerns its willingness to use larger proportions of this wealth for its educational welfare."[63]

The Impasse

By November 1959, with the January deadline for submittal to lawmakers approaching, Arthur Coons and the survey team had made progress on governance and coordination, admissions standards, new campuses, and methods for reducing future costs. Yet there remained one unresolved issue: the functions of the state colleges and particularly a resolution to their demand for the doctorate and state funding for research. As Coons readily acknowledged, what had been agreed to thus far by the survey team was tenuous. The months of arduous discussions and agreements could quickly unravel.

When the survey team met with lawmakers to discuss the plan, Coons, appraised them of the unfinished business. Kerr and other members of the

Liaison Committee attended as well. A. Alan Post told Coons, "[F]rankly I don't see how you can do it at this point." A frustrated Coons responded, "You are no more worried than I am." The "warring factions" made it difficult to resolve certain aspects of the negotiations. Coons noted that, indeed, the "team has blocked off just about as much time for chatter as they can." The difficulty, he concluded, was gaining agreement on "whose ox is being gored." With Assemblywoman Donahoe, Senators Miller, Grunsky, and Dilworth, and Donald Leiffer from the governor's office looking on, Kerr insisted that the study would be completed in one form or another. It would be a "plan to end all plans" he remarked, seemingly sending a message to both legislators and state college officials. Kerr's resolve was clear.[64]

Despite the best of Coons's efforts and Kerr's promise, the survey team remained entrenched in a bitter battle over the future of the state colleges. The university, stated Dean McHenry, would not support the desires of the state colleges. Dumke told the survey team that in light of the position of university officials, the state college presidents were now opposed to the proposed changes in admission standards. Dumke and his constituents were raising the stakes, hoping to force Kerr and the university to a compromise.

In the next Liaison Committee meeting in mid-November, Coons begged for an agreement before December 7, the scheduled date for the submittal of the plan. In a fit of frustration and fatigue, Coons told legislators that the Master Plan negotiations were in deep trouble. "We are like Montana," Coons analogized. "Montana is snowed in and so are we. But, whereas Montana happens to be way below zero, we happen to be working at temperatures on occasions that have gone well above a hundred."[65]

At the next meeting of the survey team a week later, the intractable positions were once again highlighted. In earlier meetings, Glenn Dumke and Arthur Browne insisted that the new board for the state colleges should have the freedom to review the appropriate functions of the colleges. McHenry and Kerr had clearly stated that this would be vehemently opposed by the university. In preparing for the meeting, McHenry told Kerr they had perhaps four out of eight votes on the survey team. "The junior college boys will be decisive. I think we have hope for Campion but I think Tyler will side with the state colleges." Dumke now presented a revision: an independent commission made up of nine members from the education and business communities could decide the issue at a later date and after the approval of the other aspects of the Master Plan. The plan, explained Dumke, then could be completed on schedule, and possibly California's public tripartite system could be preserved. It was a brilliant countermove, made before several legislators. Frustrated with the stalemate, junior college representatives stated their support.[66]

McHenry and Holy, however, rejected the idea of a commission. It was clearly a tactic to keep the aspirations of the state colleges alive and to shift the decision to a more favorable forum. McHenry and Holy, based on their earlier consultation with Clark Kerr, used the meeting to insist that there be no delay on decision-making. University officials wanted to fix the functions of the colleges in the state constitution—to create a plan to end all plans.[67]

Superintendent Simpson had deliberately played a low-key role in the negotiations, deferring to Dumke and Browne. He had been asked, however, by McHenry and Kerr several weeks earlier to officially state why the state colleges should enter the world of doctoral training. Simpson replied that the great need for additional doctoral-trained professionals and teachers was amply documented. Several state colleges were more appropriate for providing the doctorate, explained the superintendent, than, for example, was the university campus in Santa Barbara with its small number of faculty.[68]

Armed with Simpson's remarks and a recent State Department of Education study on the need for doctoral programs in the state, Dumke argued before the survey committee: "Those who say there are no new and compelling factors to justify the doctorate in the state colleges are giving opinions based on inconclusive evidence." Specifically, noted Dumke, an earlier university study on the need for doctoral programs and graduates was seriously flawed. For instance, it underestimated the demand for faculty with Ph.D.s in the state colleges by assuming that these institutions would attract the same proportion of out-of-state faculty as in the past. The university study also assumed that only 40 percent of the future faculty hires in the state colleges would have a doctorate. "Not only are there shortages of doctorates to satisfy teaching needs, but also in industry, science, and research throughout the nation," insisted Dumke. "If what has happened in other states is any criterion, sooner or later the doctorate will be given to the state colleges. The University cannot maintain its monopoly point of view forever."[69]

Over the course of the two-day meetings, McHenry and Holy stood their ground, although the tone of their arguments seemed more desperate. They were confronted by a solution, the establishment of an independent commission that might gain political support within the legislature and the governor's office. "The state college's house is not fully in order," McHenry countered. "Before allowing a change in function, the state colleges should be helped to get their freedom" in the form of their own board. Sensing that Coons and the junior and private college members of the survey team were sympathetic to Dumke and Browne's position, McHenry even suggested that "the doctorate in certain state colleges might be favored if these colleges were to become a part of the University system." Perhaps three or four colleges could be transferred, they noted.[70]

Concerned with the impasse in the negotiations, Kerr had already approached four state college presidents, including Dumke, Love, Wahlquist, and Joyal, to see if they would be interested in having their campus become part of the university. In the end, however, Kerr found no takers.[71] Kerr's surreptitious offer simply reinforced the opinion of most state college representatives that, if all failed, the university would attempt to absorb all or a part of the state college system, despite the inherent risks. The veracity of Kerr, McHenry, and the regents was something to fear. Indeed, a bid to absorb the state colleges was a possible course of action for Kerr. The university's contingency plan remained an unstated threat but a threat just the same.

With the November meetings concluded, Coons found the December 7 deadline quickly approaching. There was no plan, and there were no further meetings of the survey team scheduled. McHenry sadly wrote to Kerr, "[I]t now appears that the state colleges are unwilling to accept real differentiation of functions that will keep them out of doctorates and the higher professions." Something had to be done, insisted McHenry. Reaching no agreement would bode poorly for the university, possibly lead either to radical reform by legislators or to the continued proliferation of the state college programs and campuses. McHenry now conceded to Kerr that perhaps the only option was a university-derived constitutional proposition to absorb the state colleges.[72]

The deadlock was not a surprise to most lawmakers. Six months earlier and at the beginning of the survey team negotiations, Governor Pat Brown insisted that the education community had better provide a solid plan for higher education. Failure to do so or the presentation of a plan consisting of "mutual log-rolling by which each approves the projects of the other in order to have license for its own," proclaimed Brown, could compel the state "to consider other structural possibilities."[73] With only days left to resolve basic issues of function and in turn governance, Governor Brown, Assemblywoman Donahoe, and Senator Miller renewed this threat. Brown insisted that he and the legislature would make their own Master Plan. Assemblywoman Donahoe complained that she was tired of the fight: "I keep hearing 'mine, mine, mine.' But what we need to hear is 'our state.'"[74] Senator George Miller thought the survey team's efforts doomed. "We can no longer afford this competition," he told reporters on December 2, "and in light of it, as in public utilities, we must establish a monopoly."[75]

Arthur Coons, however, still sought a last-minute agreement. On December 2, he called a special meeting of the survey team at the Bowman House on the Stanford campus. It was a last ditch effort. For two days, the survey team deliberated. To Coons's joy, a compromised was reached. Under great pressure, Dean McHenry and Tom Holy agreed that the proposed "Coordinating Council" could decide the issue of doctoral degrees in the state colleges. The survey team also agreed to the submittal of a proposed constitutional amendment with three major components: Beyond the issue of the doctorate, it would set segmental functions for the tripartite public system, establish a new and autonomous state college board, and create the Coordinating Council.[76] The proposed constitutional amendment would protect the university's historical mission as the primary graduate training and research institution. The primary function of the state colleges would be undergraduate education, teacher training, and graduate education through the master's degree, with the issue of doctoral training to be decided by the Coordinating Council. While "large-scale" research was not a primary function of the colleges, the survey team agreed, "nothing in the Constitution shall be construed to restrict or preclude the allocation of support and facilities adequate for professional research." No major changes were proposed in the functions of the junior colleges.[77]

Per their discussion on the Stanford campus, the state colleges would be governed by a new Board of Trustees. Like the regents, the new state college trustees would be "a public trust, to be administered by a body corporate . . . with full powers of organization and government, subject only to such legislative control as may be necessary." The Trustees would have six ex officio members: the governor, lieutenant governor, speaker of the assembly, superintendent of public instruction, president of the University of California, and chief executive of the state college system. Similar to the regents, sixteen members would be appointed by the governor for twelve-year terms. The survey team also added the recommendation that the present members of the State Board of Education serve as the first members of the trustees "to assume an orderly transition." New trustees would be appointed as the terms of the board members expired.[78]

Finally, the Coordinating Council would decide on issues of segmental functions, enrollment expansion, and "budget coordination," including the submission to the legislature of a budget for all three public segments. New campuses and the establishment of "any new graduate degrees," the survey team agreed, would require the affirmative recommendation of the council and, when it required additional state funding, the legislature. As noted, the council would include twelve members, each representing a member of the higher education community: three representatives each for the university, state colleges, junior colleges, and the Association of Independent California Colleges. For the university, this included the president and two regents. For the state colleges, representatives on the council included the new chief executive and two members of the new Board of Trustees. Superintendent Simpson would sit along with two members of the State Board of Education as representatives of the junior colleges.[79]

Reflecting the extreme caution of all members of the survey team not to abrogate the authority of the regents or the proposed state college trustees, the power of the council had many serious limitations. In matters related to funding, expansion, and curriculum of the university and state colleges, only their respective representatives could vote. The independent college representatives had no voting authority on any of these matters. In addition, because of the status of both the regents and the proposed state college trustees as "public trusts," the council as constituted seemed to have no more authority than the voluntary Liaison Committee.[80]

Arthur Coons left the two-day meeting at Stanford thinking he had achieved an agreement on all the key points of the survey team's charge. The seemingly impossible was accomplished. He had remained in good health, despite his friends' warnings that the ordeal might very well kill him. Several days later, however, McHenry returned with shocking news. President Kerr did not accept a key aspect of the agreement, specifically, the proposal to have the Coordinating Council decide on the issue of the doctorate in the state colleges. He wanted the proposed constitutional amendment to state that only the university could grant the doctorate. Otherwise, Kerr insisted that the university would not support the proposal for a state college Board of Trustees, and he was considering abandoning the work of the survey team altogether to pursue a constitutional initiative for a single board. Coons was livid. Kerr was holding the compromise hostage. At an emergency meeting with the survey team, he chastised university officials. Their demand for a renegotiation, he warned, would not stop him from presenting the previously agreed-upon plan, or some version of it, to the two higher education boards and lawmakers at a Liaison Committee meeting scheduled in four days.[81]

In University Hall across from the Berkeley campus, Coons opened the long-awaited Liaison Committee meeting. It had been scheduled to last for two days, but Coons requested that it be extended to a third. He hoped that the extra time might help him broker a new compromise. "This is what is commonly called in the novel the 'moment of truth,' when your team is called upon to bring to you certain final recommendations," he stated to a large audience that included regents and board of education members, lawmakers such as Donahoe and Miller, members of Governor Brown's staff, and the press. He and other survey team members spent the day explaining their enrollment projections, the plan to shift 50,000 lower-division students to the junior colleges, and the priority list of new campuses—all of the agreed-upon elements.

On the second day, a presentation was made on utilization and space standards used to assess the need for capital construction. The team also reviewed the projected need for faculty. Coons concluded the day's meeting by stating that the survey team had met the previous evening. He announced bitterly that there was as yet no unanimity on the most important agenda items: segmental functions and, in turn, governance. Notwithstanding, he would present his personal recommendations the next day.[82]

A Last-Minute Compromise

Desperate to find a solution and worried by Coons's increasing hostility to the university, that evening Kerr asked for a meeting in his office on the Berkeley campus. This important summit included Coons, McHenry, Dumke, Board of the Regents Chair Donald McLaughlin, State Board of Education Chair William Blair, and State Superintendent Simpson. Only an hour earlier, Coons had given a press conference despairing that an agreement was elusive. In Kerr's office, a frank discussion ensued. Without an agreement on the issues of the doctorate and state college research, reiterated Kerr, the university would refuse to back the creation of the state college trustees or the Coordinating Council. The Master Plan would be dead. Dumke and Blair knew the likely result: a university or legislatively induced superboard. In either case, the state colleges would lose their bid for an autonomous board. For Dumke and the other state college presidents, gaining a board similar to the university's remained the most important goal. It held the promise of greater independence from legislative caprice and the regulatory world of state agencies. It might gain the political power and influence to expand the scope of state college programs. Dumke did not want to lose the board, and Blair agreed.[83]

Kerr presented a series of "solutions" that offered a method for university faculty to regulate doctoral training in the state colleges. One option was to have state college faculty appointed as adjunct professors at the university. They could then direct doctoral degrees at state college campuses but only as university employees. Dumke complained that the state colleges needed recognition as institutions of advanced learning, not as satellites of the University of California. Based on a program sponsored by Wayne State University in Michigan, Kerr also proposed the creation of "joint doctoral" programs. State college faculty could approach university faculty to codevelop a doctoral program. Faculty at both campuses would participate; but the university would always have the ability to simply disband the doctoral program.[84] Details of the joint doctorate needed work, and it was assumed that initially most programs would be in the field of education.[85] If Dumke, Blair, and Simpson could agree to the joint doctorate in principle, Kerr and McLaughlin promised to support the rest of the Master Plan. They would fight for the creation of the Board of Trustees as a public trust within the state constitution. Dumke and Blair acquiesced, but only if there was a more liberal interpretation by the university of the research role of state college faculty. They agreed to the following language for inclusion in the Master Plan: "Research which stimulates professional and scholarly growth of individual faculty members is appropriate for the state colleges and should be authorized." The deal was struck.[86]

The next day, the Liaison Committee and an audience of more than thirty legislators and government officials heard Arthur Coons describe the compromise. The joint doctorate, he explained, would allow the state colleges to meet an apparent need in California's economy while also retaining the university's historic control of doctoral programs. Coons then stated an important contingency: If either the new state college board or the joint doctorate program failed to gain the endorsement of the two boards or the legislature, the whole deal should be called off. The strategy was to have the Master Plan passed as a package and to discourage its dismemberment in the legislative process.[87]

Coons, Kerr, Dumke, and the other major players in the formulation of the Master Plan were relieved to have finally created a meaningful "compact." It was, they thought, a plan that was politically attractive. While it shifted the university and the state colleges toward a more selective admissions policy at the freshman level, the expansion of the junior colleges promised a dramatic increase in access to higher education.

The proposed Master Plan also reaffirmed California's commitment to a tuition-free public tripartite system. With a largely homogeneous population, the primary barrier to higher education, thought the authors of the plan, was economic class. There was little concern about the role of race and inequities in local schools. Low costs for students and their families and a wide geographic distribution of public institutions, they believed, would provide the primary basis for equitable access to all students who could benefit from a higher education—elements of California's higher education system outlined over fifty years ago by Alexis Lange and other Progressives.

The Master Plan was simply a proposal. There remained the approval by both the regents and the State Board of Education, the legislative process, and a constitutional measure. No state had ever placed in either statute or in its constitution such a comprehensive outline of duties of its state-supported colleges and universities, let alone created two distinct and highly autonomous public trusts to govern them. The proposed Master Plan clearly moved against the tide of centralization and increasing legislative authority found throughout the nation.

CHAPTER 11

Selling the Plan and the Beginning of a New Era

> If the recommendations are carried out and the Constitution is amended as indicated, California's tripartite system of public higher education, long admired by other states, will be saved from destruction by unbridled competition. . . . California will again pioneer in the field of higher education, its system a model of cooperation for the whole nation.
>
> — MASTER PLAN SURVEY TEAM, 1960

The compact known as the *California Master Plan for Higher Education* represented a hard-won agreement. Within a myriad of some sixty proposed recommendations, two stood to gain significant scrutiny by California lawmakers. One proposed the creation of yet another public trust to govern and manage the state colleges (what would eventually become the California State University system). The other insisted that major elements of the plan, including the function of each segment, be placed within the California Constitution. Under the compact, there would be no central authority for higher education policymaking and budgeting found in many other states. The proposed Coordinating Council was, in large part, no more than a replacement for the Liaison Committee. It would have no direct powers, only an advisory function for the higher education community and California lawmakers.

With the last-minute compromises in hand, Glenn Dumke, Arthur Browne, Clark Kerr, and Dean McHenry each sought to inform, persuade, and gauge the reactions of their respective governing boards, faculty, and administrators. After months of arguing for the doctorate, Dumke was undoubtedly disappointed in the final results. Solace could be found, however, in the proposed new board for the state colleges and the hope of substantial autonomy similar to the university's Board of Regents. With such autonomy, there could be later victories for gaining the doctorate, perhaps, and for a greater research function within the state colleges.

Dumke approached his campaign with resolve. He needed to convince his constituents that the compact provided a beginning. "Events have moved rapidly this past week," Dumke stated in a letter to faculty written the morning after the summit meeting in Kerr's office.[1] The benefits of the proposed Master Plan were many. The most important change, he reasoned, was the proposed State College Board of Trustees: it was, he stated, to have "all the powers, rights, and autonomy of the Regents." This was the bargain he had struck, and he hoped its clear advantages would temper opposition among faculty and some college presidents. Dumke insisted: "[T]he implications of this power and autonomy for the State Colleges are tremendous. We should be able to solve, in our own way, such things as faculty travel, research, use of college facilities, relations between instructional and foundation funds, determination of salary levels, and, in fact, all the basic financial and personnel problems that have beset the State Colleges. State College policy will henceforth be made by the State Colleges and their new governing board." He concluded that the new Master Plan was "the greatest step forward we could possibly take at this time."[2]

Many in the state colleges did not agree. Malcolm Love, president at San Diego State, argued that the compact was an opportunity lost. Too many concessions had been made to the university, Love protested in local San Diego papers, with grave consequences for not only the state colleges but for all Californians seeking a higher education. Love insisted that the state colleges attain the doctorate and acquire state funding for research. The proposed Master Plan, he concluded, should be modified or rejected by the California State Board of Education and the Legislature.[3] San Diego Assemblyman Sheridan Hegland joined Love's protest. The plan would reduce access to the state colleges by raising admissions standards. Ultimately, he complained, it could lead to an actual reduction in faculty and students at San Diego State.[4]

President Clark Kerr also found substantial opposition to the plan within the university. Many faculty members did not fully embrace the agreement. Leaders within the Academic Senate still thought that a single board stacked with university regents was the best hope for controlling the state colleges. The campus chancellors favored the single-board plan as well. It was, according to a confidential memo to Kerr from the council of chancellors, the "preferable solution."[5] Kerr argued that the compact was a major victory. It would place in the constitution the university's monopoly on the doctorate and its mission as the state's primary research institution. It would end the thirty-year battle over the appropriate role of the state colleges. The chair of the regents, Donald McLaughlin, worked with Kerr to solidify support among the regents and the State Board of Education. They also appealed to Governor Brown for support. The reluctance on the part of many faculty members and the chancellors could be overcome with support from the regents and governor.

Building Support for the Compact

On December 18, two weeks after the summit in Kerr's office, the regents and the State Board of Education convened a third joint meeting to consider the proposed Master Plan. Governor Brown presided and set the tone. He had been discouraged by the reports from staff and legislators that the negotiations devolved into a bitter feud. "Then last week," he stated, "I heard that out of the darkness had come light." Brown was extremely pleased. The plan represented a victory for the governor, a showpiece of his political skills that would be credited to his administration. Brown led a round of applause for Arthur Coons and the survey team. "Where there is good will and intention to do something, you can do it," he exclaimed.[6]

Accolades followed Brown's public announcement of support for the compact. State Board of Education members and regents complimented each other. Louis Heilbron, a recent Brown appointee to the board, opined that the plan provided an important balance. "First, it recognizes that the State Colleges have come of age as institutions of higher education," he noted. "Secondly, it preserves the integrity and standards of the University as the standard bearer in the pursuit of academic excellence and it safeguards the Golden Fleece of the doctoral degree from unreasonable search and seizure." This comment brought good-natured laughter. The report of the Master Plan survey was approved unanimously "in principle."[7]

Momentum was building for the Master Plan.[8] In a press conference after the joint meeting, Coons stated that it was a "take or leave it" package. The survey team's recommendations "are meant to solve an extremely complex problem and could easily be thrown out of balance," he explained. "[L]et's hold on to it." Most press coverage was favorable, supported and complemented by a flood of university press releases. Kerr attempted to marshal all of the university's lobbying resources to secure the plan in the constitution.

In another press conference, Kerr exclaimed that the plan was "a milestone in the history of California higher education." Hours after the joint meeting adjourned, a university spokesman announced: "The Master Plan approved today will enable us to preserve the best features of the historic tripartite system. Moreover it will increase the spirit of understanding among the segments which make up this system." Stan McCaffrey, the university public information officer, investigated the development of a motion picture on the negotiations and the importance of the resulting plan.[9]

The *San Francisco Chronicle* supported the compact. "It is said that it would be better to put up with two independent boards, than to place the colleges together with the University under one board, because the whole lump would be too big and indigestible for sound administration," explained one article. "This argument has dissuaded us of our previously stated preference for one single board." Two days after the announced approval of the Master Plan by the two boards, the *Los Angeles Times* named Assemblywoman Dorothy Donahoe "Woman of the Year" for her role in initiating the plan and guiding its creation.[10]

The *Herald Examiner* in San Francisco also voiced strong support. Both the *Times* and the *Examiner* had ties to the University of California, specifically to the development of Berkeley and the UCLA campuses. Regent Catherine C. Hearst's family owned the *Examiner*. The Hearst's philanthropic contributions to the university dated back to the 1880s. Similarly, Regent Dorothy B. Chandler's family published the *Times*.

Within the university, Academic Senate members gained greater comfort with the Master Plan, influenced in part by the momentum offered by the governor's support and that of the regents. With the help of both university bulletins and favorable local press, Lloyd Morrisett noted that faculty at UCLA were now supportive. The climate of opinion, he wrote to Kerr, "has changed markedly in the past week. Light has replaced gloom, optimism has replaced pessimism." In addition, the politically influential California Teachers Association vigorously supported most elements of the plan. Murray S. Roddes, CTA president, hoped that the new Board of Trustees would help invigorate the state college credential programs, and he welcomed removing them from the purview of the State Department of Education.[11]

A little more than a month later, on February 1, 1960, Clark Kerr and Roy Simpson forwarded the *Master Plan for Higher Education in California: 1960–1975* to the legislature. They asked that the recommendations be viewed as a package deal and urged lawmakers not to unravel it. In their transmittal letter to Assembly Speaker Ralph Brown and the president of the senate, Glenn M. Anderson, they noted that the report was "unanimously approved in principle" by the two boards. "Because of the enthusiastic endorsements of these recommendations by our two boards and their wide acceptance by our faculties, the press in California, and many informed citizens," concluded Kerr and Simpson, "we are anxious to have them fully implemented."[12]

Within the report itself, Arthur Coons and the survey team explained the symbiotic nature of their recommendations. Only by placing key components into the constitution would the plan work and thereby preserve and strengthen California's celebrated tripartite public system. "Long negotiations and extensive consultation produced a delicately balanced consensus among the three segments," they explained. "The agreement that has been reached is essentially a 'compact'; it must be fostered and refined and care must be exercised that modifications do not emasculate it."[13]

Arthur Coons argued before legislators that the proposed Master Plan reestablished California's leadership role in American higher education. By defining the functions of each segment, he stated, duplication of academic programs could be limited, and by establishing a list of new campus locations, the increasingly chaotic and politicized process of establishing new campuses would cease. California would "once again pioneer in the field of higher education," proclaimed Coons.[14]

Key legislators, including State Senator Miller and Assemblywoman Donahoe, noted their general support for the Master Plan. There was an emerging consensus that strengthening the tripartite system, as opposed to establishing a single board, was now the preferable option. Senator Miller, long an advocate of creating a public "monopoly" (i.e., a single board) to govern the system was now a convert, in part because of intense university lobbying. The political momentum for the plan began with Governor Brown's general endorsement. Miller now announced his agreement with the survey team's argument that California's huge public higher education system—the largest in the nation and quickly growing—was simply too large to be effectively governed by one board. Miller and other legislators also agreed it was time to free the state colleges from the shackles of the State Board of Education and specifically from the regulatory controls of the State Department of Education. One other factor now convinced lawmakers such as Miller that California should retain the tripartite public system. Whatever its organization and powers, the uniting of the university and the state colleges under a single board would create a formidable political power that few legislators, including Miller, found attractive. Keeping them independent, thought Miller, would provide more room for lawmakers to set policy.[15]

Trouble in Sacramento

In spite of the general support for the Master Plan, there were signs that not all of the survey team's recommendations would be endorsed by lawmakers in Sacramento. James Corley, the university's lobbyist in Sacramento, explained that many lawmakers were formulating changes before the legislative session had even begun. "Some compromises will have to be made, in my opinion," he told Kerr. Legislators had three major concerns that would shape the final structure and approval of the Master Plan. Each related to the ability of the legislature to set future policy in higher education.

The first concern related to the proposed Board of Trustees for the state colleges and specifically the idea of creating another public trust. A. Alan Post warned Kerr and others of an unwillingness by legislators to relinquish fiscal and administrative controls over the state colleges. There was even discussion within the legislature of reducing the autonomy of the university—long a source of frustration for lawmakers, including Senator Miller.[16] While Miller understood the importance of a certain level of autonomy for higher education, he and other lawmakers felt that the legislature and the governor had the ultimate responsibility to disperse public funds and decide on issues related to expansion. This required retaining and possibly enhancing their ability to make policy decisions. Miller stated his strong opposition to any effort to grant the level of autonomy proposed by the higher education community.[17]

The second concern of legislators related to placing the Master Plan in the state constitution. Similar to his position on state college autonomy, George Miller argued that fixing the functions of each of the public higher education segments would again reduce the authority of the legislature to modify policy. He and other lawmakers, including Donahoe, were now adamant that placing admission standards and the functions of each public segment in the constitution would destroy the ability, and rightful authority, of the legislature to make changes in the future.[18] Assemblyman Bruce Allen also opposed the notion of a constitutional amendment. Fresh from his battles with university officials over expanding engineering programs in his district, the San Jose lawmaker was not only concerned with retaining the authority of the legislature. He also saw a conspiracy. Allen complained, "The college door will be nailed firmly shut for many thousands of California's youngsters under the so-called 'Master Plan' for higher education." The new admission standards for the university and the state colleges were, he complained, overly restrictive. "The powers have decided that California's youngsters need less education and training in the future—at a time when industry and the state itself demand more and higher levels of training for their employees." Allen was not remiss to blame university officials. The plan, he explained, was a way for the university to "emasculate" the state colleges. It "effectively prohibits any state college from ever giving a doctor's degree . . . 'The Crown Jewels are safe' has been the victory cry of some university officials."[19]

There was one other factor that cast doubt on the political feasibility of the proposed constitutional amendment. The introduction of the proposition in 1911, part of the electoral reforms of California Progressives, contributed to the cavalcade of constitutional amendments in subsequent years. In all, California's constitution had been amended 320 times. Assemblyman John A. Busterud, a Republican from San Francisco, had been appointed to chair a joint committee of the Assembly and Senate to revise the California Constitution. He vowed to simplify what was the longest state constitution in the nation. Busterud argued that the Master Plan's proper place was in statute. California, he and other lawmakers claimed, needed to reduce the litter of constitutional amendments.[20]

The third major concern of lawmakers related to the proposed Coordinating Council. Lyman Glenny had earlier warned that the council needed greater lay and nonsegmental representation if it was to provide effective oversight of the state colleges and the university. The survey team's proposal was for a coordinating agency that would have twelve members, including the president of the University of California, his new counterpart within the state colleges, and a professional educator representative of the junior colleges. All other members would be chosen or approved by the university's Board of Regents, by the proposed Board of Trustees, including the members representing the junior colleges, and by California's Association of Colleges and Universities. "Aren't you putting a fox in charge of the hen house?" asked one reporter about the proposed council. Editors at the *Sacramento Bee* thought so and launched a campaign to alter the council's membership. Arthur Browne reported to Kerr and McHenry that he heard numerous "rumblings from legislators, newspapers, and others, who think our coordinating council is weak because it lacks non-partisans."[21]

The Master Plan's Altered Route

With the beginning of legislative hearings in early March 1960, two key elements of the Master Plan compact appeared to be unattainable: autonomy for the state college trustees and placing the mission and function of the public segments in the constitution. The new Democratic leadership in Sacramento convened joint meetings of the Assembly and Senate Committees on Education, chaired by Assemblywoman Donahoe and Senator Hugh Donnelly, respectively. The goal was to develop Master Plan legislation and to place a number of the survey team's recommendations into statute. In the midst of this deliberative process and without warning to Miller and other key legislative leaders, Senator Donald L. Grunsky presented a proposed constitutional amendment on the Senate floor. It included all the major elements of the survey team's recommendations. Encouraged by university officials, Grunsky was attempting to preserve the "compact" and place his name on the final legislation.[22] In arguing for his amendment, Grunsky stated that fixing the state college functions in the constitution was essential for creating an ordered system of higher education. Without it, he explained, the "state colleges will come before the legislature year after year seeking to expand programs in areas now reserved to the University."

Miller, Donahoe, Hugo Fisher, and other lawmakers quickly worked to destroy Grunsky's bold proposal.[23] They were furious with Grunsky and with university officials, including Kerr, for what they viewed as a blatant political maneuver. In the Senate Education Committee, chair Hugh Donnelly, along with Miller, Fisher, and Walter Stierns, proceeded to erode Grunsky's bill by amending it to death.[24] Miller and Fisher outlined the basic changes they wanted to see in the proposed Master Plan, which were a substantial reduction in the powers of the new Board of Trustees, placing the mission and functions of each segment in the *Education Code*, and the addition of lay members appointed by the legislature to the Coordinating Council.[25]

At the University of California annual Charter Day event, one university official commented that "so many proposals have been made to alter or discard vital features of the master plan that the plan was a corpse."[26] Dean McHenry later explained that at this stage Kerr was "ready to throw in the towel." Once again, Kerr contemplated presenting a university-composed amendment for merging the state colleges under the Board of Regents. Vice President Corley convinced a frustrated Kerr that pulling out now would leave the entire public education system at the mercy of the legislature.[27] Within both the university and the state colleges, suspicion grew that the other was engaged in a plot of sabotage.

In an earlier meeting of the Council of State College Presidents, the council insisted that if the compact was not accepted by the legislature, the "State Colleges will seek the status quo." Julian McPhee, president of San Luis Obispo Polytechnic, protested that "it is a mistake to saddle the new Trustees with restrictions on their autonomy that were not part of the Master Plan Study."[28] It was apparent that the new trustees would gain few freedoms from the rules and restrictions of state agencies, including the State Personnel Board.[29]

The legislative session began in mid-February. In the third week of March, George Miller proposed a new statutory bill. Miller's legislation offered a "drastically watered down version of the proposed master plan for higher education," observed the *San Francisco Chronicle*. Under the measure, the composition of the Board of Trustees would have many similarities to the Board of Regents: a total of sixteen trustees appointed by the governor, a nonvoting chief executive officer called the chancellor, and four public ex officio members. There were important differences, however, between Miller's bill and the proposal offered by the survey team two months earlier. Terms for trustees were set at only eight years, as opposed to sixteen for regents. This was, in fact, an improvement over an earlier proposal by Miller that the appointments should be four years in duration, which was the legal limit under the constitution for elected positions. Most significant, the board would be a statutory provision with authority that was very different from that of the regents. Lawmakers would retain "firm budgetary controls over college operations," reported the *Chronicle*, "and non-academic personnel would remain in the state civil service."[30]

The California State Employees Association (CSEA), representing staff in the state colleges, had lobbied hard to limit the autonomy of the new Board of Trustees and to keep nonacademic personnel of the state colleges under the protective wings of the State Personnel Board. They feared that the new and autonomous board would be, like the regents, anti-union.[31] Under Senator Miller's bill, a constitutional amendment was still required. However, its purpose was singular: to wrest the state colleges from the authority of the State Board of Education and to describe its charter and membership.

Miller's bill also established a fifteen-member Coordinating Council for

Higher Education (CCHE) under statute and not as a constitutional entity, as proposed by the Master Plan survey team. The compact proposed only twelve members on the council, each representing the three public segments and the private colleges and universities. Influenced by Lyman Glenny's and legislative analyst A. Alan Post's criticisms of the proposed council, Miller added three lay appointees to be designated by the governor, with no segmental affiliation. This proposed Coordinating Council was still vested with only limited powers; but Miller was adamant that it have authority to approve any new campuses.[32] Miller also proposed that the "differentiation of functions" be placed in statute. There was no mention in his bill of admissions policies and specifically of the survey team's recommendation that the University of California admit the top 12.5 percent and state colleges the top 33.3 percent of high school graduates. Also absent was any stipulation that California's public higher education system should remain tuition-free. These were operational elements of the tripartite system that might need changing in future years.

On March 23, the Senate Education Committee approved Miller's bill. It now proceeded through the finance committee and received approval by the full state senate on March 30, 1960.[33] President Clark Kerr, Board of Regents Chair Donald H. McLaughlin, Superintendent Simpson, and the State Board of Education Chair Louis H. Heilbron issued a statement expressing "their regrets that the legislature won't put the plan into a constitutional amendment." Nevertheless, they urged the quick adoption of a statutory law by the legislature. Each had reservations about Miller's bill. Kerr and McLaughlin wanted, at a minimum, the mission and function of the state colleges in the constitution. Simpson had been reluctant to see the state college pulled from his and the State Board of Education's purview. Heilbron wanted the new Board of Trustees for the state college to have greater autonomy.[34]

Miller's bill, however, retained the authority of the legislature over higher education in a number of areas. The political attractiveness of these changes was tremendous: Why should California, argued Miller, fix its growing higher education system in stone? There would be, undoubtedly, other problems, and other changes necessary to a system that already enrolled more students than any other higher education system in the nation.

With the special session of the legislature drawing to a close, Donahoe worked with the Assembly Education Committee to make minor adjustments to Miller's bill. Donahoe was also cosponsoring the constitutional amendment that would allow for the creation of the Board of Trustees.[35] The day before her committee's expected approval of the compromise legislation,

Donahoe fell gravely ill. "A chronic asthma patient," reported one paper, "she became ill today in the home she maintains with her mother here during legislative sessions." That evening she was admitted to Sutter Hospital in Sacramento. Forty-five minutes later, she died of pneumonia. Donahoe had a long history of health problems, which occasionally kept her from meetings of the legislature. Still, her death was an unexpected shock for her colleagues in the assembly and senate. She was only forty-nine. She had served in the assembly since 1953, when only one other woman was in the California legislature.[36]

The next day, the Assembly Education Committee, without its chair, passed Miller's bill. The measure then traveled to the Assembly Ways and Means Committee for approval of a $131,000 appropriation required to fund the establishment of the Board of Trustees and the Coordinating Council. The only "major change in the measure . . . will give the trustees of the state college system power to employ private architects for development of any college," reported the *Chronicle*. This was a small concession, yet it briefly held up final approval of the bill in the state senate. Both the governor's office and the CSEA came out against taking this discretionary power away from the State Division of Architecture.[37] The disagreement, symbolic of a reluctance to give the trustees any significant level of autonomy, was quickly resolved. The trustees gained the power to appoint architects.

Donahoe's death added momentum to Miller's bill but was not a decisive influence. The emotional loss of Donahoe and respect for her persistent efforts to bring order to California's higher education system led George Miller to rename his legislation the "Donahoe Higher Education Act." The assembly and the senate proceeded to overwhelmingly approve the compromise bill. A week later, on April 14, 1960, Governor Edmund G. Brown signed the Donahoe Act in a public ceremony that included George Miller, Arthur Coons, Clark Kerr, and Roy Simpson. Six months later, in the November general election, a constitutional amendment passed removing the California State Colleges from the purview of the State Board of Education.

The 1960 California Master Plan for higher education became not a single document, but a set of three different documents. There was the statutory bill, which set the mission and function of the various public institutions in the state. There was also a constitutional amendment, creating the Board of Trustees of the state college. Finally, there were dozens of general agreements that were never officially sanctioned by law, including, most prominently, admissions guidelines and California's historic commitment to a nontuition policy for California residents. (See Figure 16.)

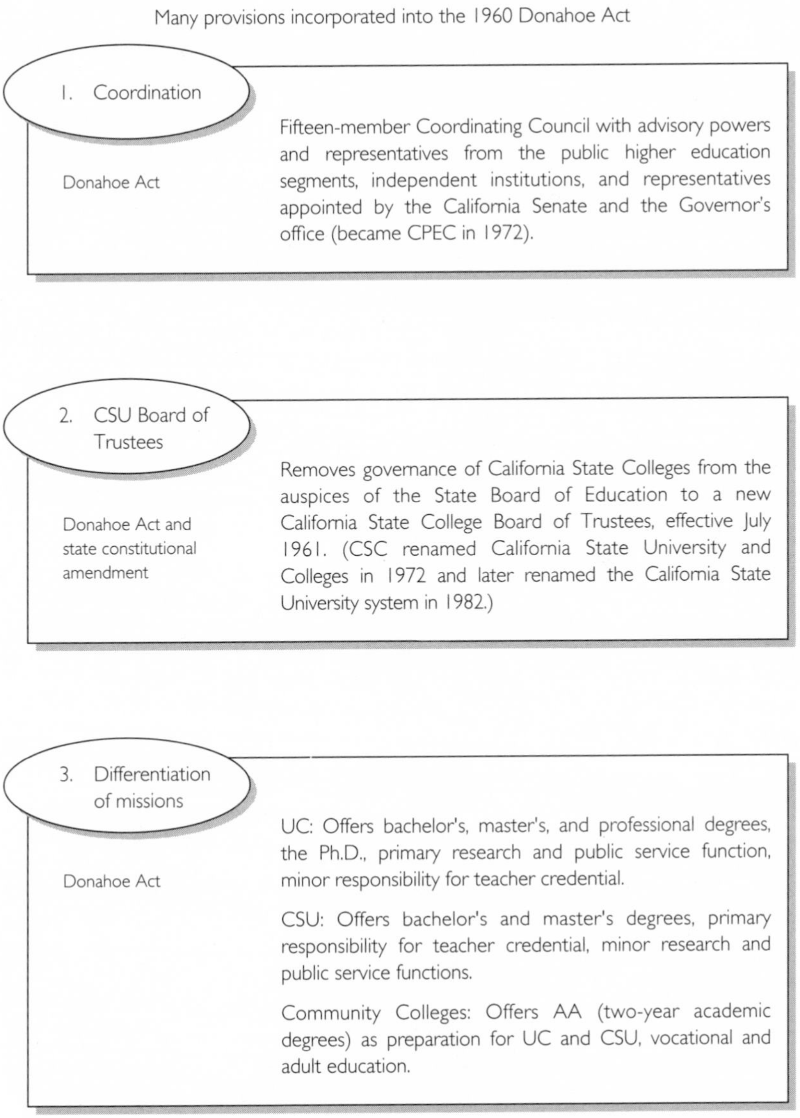

Many provisions incorporated into the 1960 Donahoe Act

1. Coordination	Donahoe Act	Fifteen-member Coordinating Council with advisory powers and representatives from the public higher education segments, independent institutions, and representatives appointed by the California Senate and the Governor's office (became CPEC in 1972).
2. CSU Board of Trustees	Donahoe Act and state constitutional amendment	Removes governance of California State Colleges from the auspices of the State Board of Education to a new California State College Board of Trustees, effective July 1961. (CSC renamed California State University and Colleges in 1972 and later renamed the California State University system in 1982.)
3. Differentiation of missions	Donahoe Act	UC: Offers bachelor's, master's, and professional degrees, the Ph.D., primary research and public service function, minor responsibility for teacher credential. CSU: Offers bachelor's and master's degrees, primary responsibility for teacher credential, minor research and public service functions. Community Colleges: Offers AA (two-year academic degrees) as preparation for UC and CSU, vocational and adult education.

Figure 16. The Heart of the 1960 Master Plan for Higher Education

SOURCE: *California Master Plan for Higher Education: 1960–1975;* Donahoe Act, Senate Bill no. 33, 1960.

4. Policies for Expansion

Admission Standards Not in statute	UC: Admits top 12.5 percent of high school graduates (down from 15 percent), sets minimum community college transfer requirement at 2.4 GPA. CSC: Admits top 33.3 percent (down from approximately 40 percent), sets minimum junior transfer at 2.0 GPA. Community Colleges: Provides open door to all high school graduates, shifts 50,000 prospective UC and CSC students to community colleges between 1960 and 1975.
Increase State Funding of Community Colleges Adopted 1966 statutes	Raises state funding of community colleges from 30 percent to 45 percent of operating budget by 1975; urges first time direct state support of capital construction.
Tuition Free for Californians Not in statute	Maintains student fees only for "incidental costs"; tuition instituted for out-of-state students within the public system.
Proposed Full-Year Calendar Not in statute/1965 joint resolution	Coordinating Council to review proposal and report back to the California legislature. (UC and CSU adopted quarter system in 1965, but with little success in full-time operation.)
New Campuses Adopted in separate statutes	UC: Three new general campuses to be established in San Diego, Irvine, and Santa Cruz (previously approved by regents in the 1957 Additional Centers Report). CSC: Four new general campuses to be established in Stanislaus, Hayward, Northridge, and San Bernardino (previously approved by legislation and/or proposed in the 1957 Additional Centers Report). Community Colleges: Twenty-two campuses proposed for local initiative and partial state funding.
Student Financial Aid 1960 statute	Provides increase in Cal-Grant program (established in 1956) for students attending either public or private institutions accredited by the state of California.

The Focus on California's Achievement

In his effort to sell the Master Plan compact, Arthur Coons argued that its most important goal was to expand access to higher education and to improve the quality of the segments.[38] In 1968, Coons wrote: "Some advocates of what they call the 'Democratic' principle claim to believe, especially in crisis, that quality should be sacrificed in order to keep open for all the doors of opportunity. This is a false dichotomy. It is neither good democracy nor good economy nor good education nor downright good common sense to accept the mediocre in order to achieve inclusiveness." Coons also noted that others, in particular, legislators seeking methods to reduce state expenditures on California public higher education, had argued for limiting enrollments and establishing tuition to avert a "deterioration of quality." The Master Plan rejected both positions. Coons stated that California's Master Plan assured two principles: "The need for opportunity according to ability and willingness, and the availability of education to as high a level of achievement as one may be able to embrace."[39]

William B. Spaulding, the first director of the California Coordinating Council for Higher Education (CCHE), stated that California provided a model for other states. "We can indeed be proud that California's system of higher education, while accommodating more students than any other similar system in the world, has produced and maintained a level of quality in its institutions that is also unparalleled."[40] Accolades for the advent of the Master Plan came from many sources. In October 1960, six months after the passage of the Donahoe Act, *Time* magazine provided a feature article on California's new Master Plan, with University of California President Clark Kerr on the cover. Charged with the task of providing a schedule for major education reform in Great Britain, a committee chaired by Lord Robbins visited California in 1962 to focus on the achievements of the Master Plan.[41] Eight months later, the European Organization of Economic Cooperation Development (OECD) stated at their meeting in Paris that the "development [of] plans of the California type" among the members of the Organization should be undertaken.

> [The Master Plan] represents the most advanced effort to construct a system of mass higher education (for a tripling of enrollment by 1975), while maintaining a quality of research and education at the top which is unsurpassed anywhere among OECD countries and probably in the world. While the contribution of private institutions is not ignored, this emerg-

> ing structural framework provided by [California] may be the appropriate model for higher education in society based on the culture of science and technology.[42]

Articles in popular national publications, such as *Science* and *Readers Digest*, focused on California as the leader in American higher education policymaking. California's Master Plan was "ambitious," a pinnacle of modernist ideals of rationality and efficiency, championing democracy and inclusion and, ultimately, promising prosperity and culture. "Since its earliest days," wrote Ben Hibbs in 1963, "California seems to have been more passionately committed to public education than most states." Hibbs claimed that it was now busily "meeting the skyrocketing needs of tomorrow."[43] California's effort to "plan" the future of its higher education system, and the accompanying publicity and praise, caused a subsequent rush of lawmakers in other states to replicate, if not the edicts of the Master Plan, its organic approach to governance and expansion of public higher education. By the end of the 1960s, twenty-three states completed their own master plans. Eight other states were in this process and seven others were in the planning stages.[44]

More than thirty years after its formulation, the Master Plan has proven an enduring and dominant planning tool. Since 1960, it has undergone few major modifications. Notably, in 1968 a state board was established to guide the loose confederation of what became the California Community Colleges. In 1974, an increase in lay representation on the state's coordinating agency was made, and it was renamed the California Postsecondary Planning Commission. That same year, a bill was passed stating that enrollment in the tripartite system should reflect the ethnic composition of California's high school graduates.

Though suffering the trials of shrinking budgets and growing enrollment demand in the 1990s, California's three public segments are recognized as high-quality college and university systems, still among the best in the world. The Master Plan is viewed appropriately as perhaps the foremost exemplar, nationally as well as internationally, of statewide master planning.[45] In yet another review of California's higher education system, the OECD in 1989 explained that "the past dominates through the famous Master Plan of 1960 which is recognized throughout the OECD world as a blueprint for providing universal postsecondary educational opportunity, while preserving the separate 'missions' of the three types of public institutions."[46] As first articulated by California Progressives and reinforced by the 1960 Master Plan, it is not the individual achievement of one or more segments of the system that distinguishes the tripartite system. Rather, it is what they represent collectively: a symbiotic network of public institutions that balances mass higher education with the concept of a meritocracy.

Epilogue: The Master Plan Legacy

The most notable accomplishment of the Master Plan was not what it invented but what it preserved and, conversely, what it avoided: a centralized governing board. In 1960, the retention of the advisory board model in California was not a unique choice for a state government. It was, however, the exception to a national trend. In 1939, a total of thirty-three states had no form of state coordination of higher education. Thirty years later, only two did not have this structure, Delaware and Vermont, both with relatively small populations and few public postsecondary institutions. More significantly, the number of state governing boards with regulatory powers over all or most public four-year colleges and universities increased from sixteen in 1939 to thirty-three in 1969, including New York, North Carolina, Ohio, Oklahoma, Oregon, Tennessee, Texas, Utah, and West Virginia.

The tendency of colleges and universities to expand their purpose and jurisdiction, in these and other states resulted in a proliferation of doctoral and costly research programs. Lawmakers' reactions were sometimes harsh and simplistic. They wanted to leverage greater control over the academy, both as a matter of principle (i.e., accountability to elected officials) and as a nat-

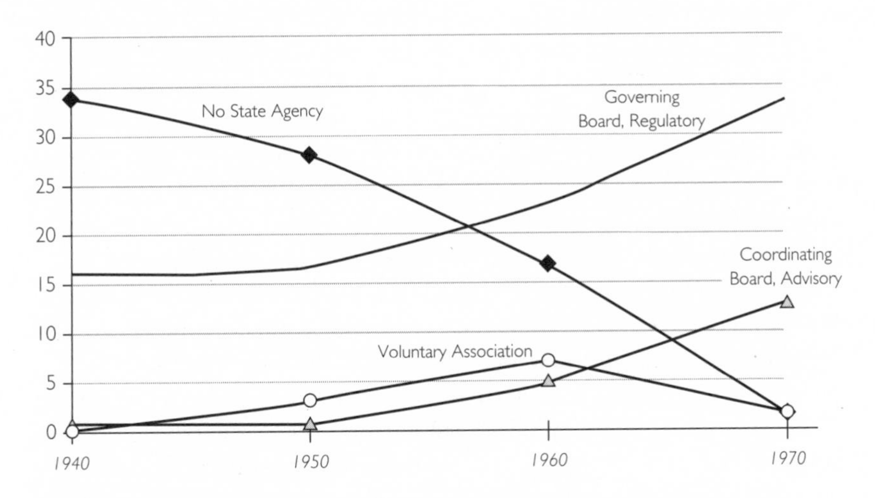

Figure 17. Trends in the Establishment of State Coordinating Agencies for Higher Education, 1940–1970 (by number of states)

SOURCE: Berdahl, *Statewide Coordination of Higher Education*

ural extension of their desire for political influence. The most immediate way to accomplish these ends was to reorganize the governance of public higher education.[1] Legislators created superboards, and in the process they stacked the new boards with political appointees who often had little knowledge of the academy or the historical development of the colleges and universities under their charge. Remarking on this trend, Clark Kerr and Marian Gade stated: "We see a particular threat in the public sector of higher education in the gradual but by now significant shift from independent guardian-type boards to politicized representational boards."[2]

While the general shift was toward superboards in the immediate post–Master Plan era, a number of states kept or established coordinating agencies with only advisory powers. These states grew from five in 1959 to twelve a decade later and included Alabama, Arkansas, California, Kentucky, Maryland, Michigan, Minnesota, Missouri, Pennsylvania, South Carolina, Virginia, and Washington.[3] (See Figure 17.)

In the face of concerns over the spiraling costs of public higher education, California's 1960 Master Plan provided a structure for expansion. In subsequent years, the plan proved successful for two major reasons. First, it provided a rigid definition of the role of each of the public segments that avoided the high cost of all four-year public institutions attempting to provide the same academic programs. The concept was to give each segment a distinct mission that, when combined, would meet the needs of the people of California. The creation of the Board of Trustees for the state colleges (eventually renamed the California State University system) strengthened this objective: It provided a clear charge for managing a quickly growing and massive system of institutions, which totaled twenty-three campuses in 1999.

The forced marriage of the University of California and the California State University systems would have resulted in a hugely complex system. It might have initiated a new and even bloodier turf war that would sap the energy and morale of both segments. The fashioning of an independent board and a revised mission provided a basis for CSU to excel in its own sphere of responsibility and gave some room for maturation. The result was an end to any effective drive of the state colleges to become state-sanctioned research and doctoral-granting institutions. The Master Plan set strict limits on activities that the state would fund, which has resulted in a significant barrier to mission creep.

The second reason for the success of the Master Plan is that it clarified the role of the legislature in policymaking. The open market approach of lawmakers and local communities to create new campuses and to reorganize California higher education ended with the Master Plan. After 1960, lawmakers gained a broader understanding of the functions of each segment and the role of their respective boards in creating new campuses and academic programs. Lawmakers also saw their obligation to fund enrollment expansion, which did not wane to any significant degree until the prolonged economic downturn of the 1990s.

In stark contrast to the political battles and entrenched fighting between the University of California and the state colleges prior to 1960, California proceeded to fund a massive and orderly expansion of higher education. It is a remarkable record unparalleled by any other state. The plan also kept costs (on a per student basis) relatively low for taxpayers. Enrollment in the public segments grew from approximately 227,000 students (full-time equivalent) in 1960 to over 1 million FTE in 1975. In fact, the authors of the Master Plan did not anticipate this rapid pace of growth. They assumed that enrollment in 1975 would be just over 528,000 student FTE within the public tripartite system.[4]

Enrollment projections for the University of California and CSU were

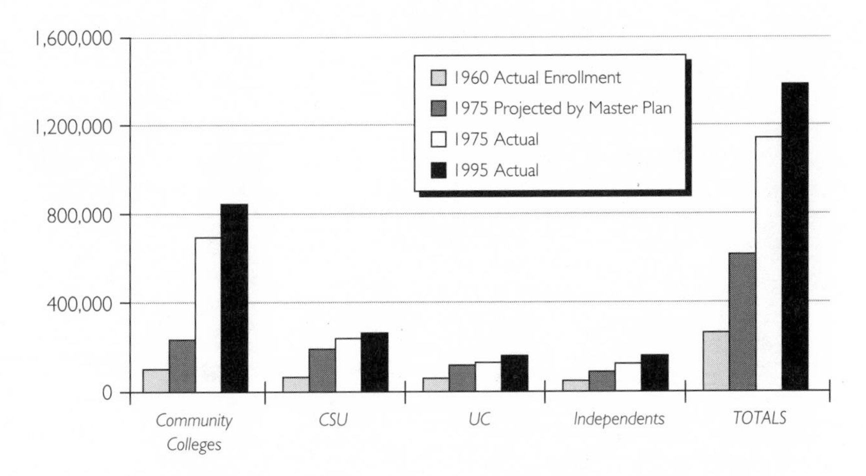

Figure 18. Actual and Master Plan Projected Enrollment in California, 1960–1995

SOURCE: *California Master Plan for Higher Education,* 1960; California Postsecondary Education Commission

fairly accurate. However, enrollment in the California Community Colleges (formerly called junior colleges) dramatically exceeded expectations, driven by market forces that encouraged rapid expansion of courses in the liberal arts, vocational fields, and adult education. (See Figure 18.) This was accompanied by a large increase in part-time students in the community colleges. By 1995, California public higher education had grown to 1.3 million FTE students (a headcount of 1.9 million), with the vast majority in the community colleges.

Part of the Master Plan compact was a commitment by lawmakers to provide additional funding for community colleges to help them cope with the anticipated increase in enrollment demand. Previously, funding for these colleges came primarily from local property taxes (beginning in the 1930s). Post–Master Plan legislation provided state funds for both local college operating costs and capital construction. As a result, by the late 1960s, public two-year colleges for the first time gained more public tax support than either the University of California or the California State University system. Historically, the University of California had secured the majority of public funding. Reflecting its larger research and graduate mission, the University

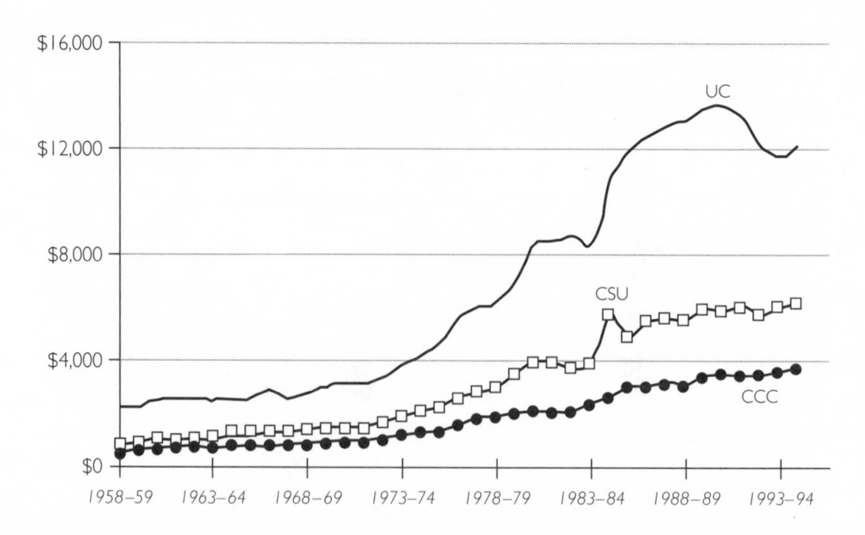

Figure 19. California Public Higher Education: State and Local Funding per FTE, 1958–1995

SOURCE: Pickens, "Financing the Plan"

of California continued to gain the largest public funding support on a per FTE student basis. (See Figure 19.)

Though the tripartite system has more than quadrupled in enrollment, the cost to California taxpayers has remained remarkably steady at around $1,000 per student in 1960 dollars (including both state and local funding). (See Figure 20.) The year the Donahoe Act was passed, California ranked twenty-fifth in costs per student funded by taxpayers, just below Alabama and South Carolina. At the same time, the state led the nation in the college-going rates of high school graduates. Over nearly four decades, the cost of the tripartite system in California has remained at or just below the national average on a cost per student basis.

However, it is important to note a number of caveats. To begin with, many states have significantly increased tuition, shifting more of the burden on students and their families to pay for their educational costs. This has driven down the national average. Similarly, state funding to the California State University and University of California systems on a per student basis also declined significantly during the early 1990s in the wake of a national

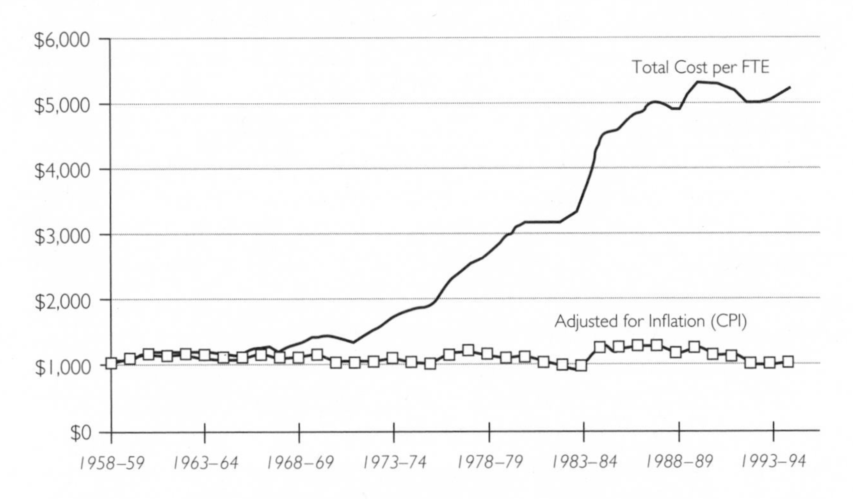

Figure 20. California Public Higher Education: Total Taxpayer Cost per Student FTE, 1958–1995

SOURCE: Pickens, "Financing the Plan"

recession, which hit California's economy particularly hard. Tuition and fees at public education institutions increased in California, breaking a historical commitment to a no-tuition policy that placed the responsibility on state and local governments to fund core costs (such as faculty salaries). However, the increases have been marginal. The cost of attending a public institution in California remains well below those of similar colleges and universities in other highly populated states.

As important as containing costs, the Master Plan provided a framework for increasing the quality of the University of California and the California State University systems. Rankings by the National Research Council and other agencies consistently place University of California campuses such as Berkeley, UCLA, and San Diego among the top institutions in the nation. A 1997 analysis by Hugh Davis Graham and Nancy Diamond is perhaps the most compelling evidence of the overall quality of the University of California system.[5] Their research provides a model for future studies that have, in the past, relied largely on reputational surveys. The Graham/Diamond study analyzed quality measures such as publications in major academic journals. They balance differences between institutions (for example, technically oriented universities such as MIT with campuses with an emphasis on liberal arts such as Berkeley) and the level of equilibrium among sciences, social sciences, and humanities to assess overall quality. The results are significant: Seven of the eight general University of California campuses ranked in the top twenty among public research universities. Four ranked in the top ten, led by Berkeley and followed by Santa Barbara, UCLA, San Diego, Riverside, Santa Cruz, Irvine, and Davis. "This is a stunning tribute to the effectiveness of California's tripartite system," wrote Graham and Diamond, "in raising all boats within the system."[6]

The California State University system also enjoys widespread acknowledgment of the quality of its faculty. This reputation is in part due to the long-standing academic programs at campuses such as San Jose and San Diego that have served important economic interests in the state. The Master Plan bolstered a sense of organizational culture and pride that has proven key for building strong academic departments.

The Master Plan fulfilled its basic promise, fostering ordered growth at a manageable cost to the people of California. Yet policymaking under the plan has not been without problems and significant criticisms. The coordinating board created by the Master Plan (as noted, renamed the California Postsecondary Education Commission in 1974) never developed as a significant source of analysis for the legislature on annual budgets and capital outlay or for developing plans for the orderly growth of higher education. The advisory nature of the board made it a limited partner in California's tripartite system. The rhetoric surrounding the Master Plan's submittal to the California legislature had promised more. It is likely that the higher education community, including Kerr and Dumke, never fully supported the idea of an effective coordination board. Their desire, in the midst of a push for greater public control, was to protect and possibly enhance their autonomy in academic and budgetary decisions. The creation of the Coordinating Council was, in part, a foil to lessen the interest of lawmakers in a centralized board and for greater legislative control. A Coordinating Council with significant powers would have also created significant erosion in the University of California's autonomous status as a public trust.

The Master Plan was also conceived at a time when California was, in fact, a much more homogeneous state. While California has long been the home of a number of minority groups, in the 1950s it was largely a bastion of white Americans who made up nearly 85 percent of the state's population. In 1960, the inequities related to race were not fully recognized. Nor did the plan take into account the uneven quality of the state's system of secondary schools and of high school academic advising, which, in subsequent years, has become significant. The largest hindrances to access, the authors of the Master Plan presumed, were economic and geographic factors.

In contrast to 1960, California's population in 1990 was approximately 58 percent Euro-Americans, 25 percent Hispanic, 10 percent Asian, and 7 percent African-American. By 2010, there are projections that the Euro-American population will make up only 46 percent of California's total population. The demographic mix of students in California high schools is already close to these numbers. At present, there are significant differences in the college-going rates among these different racial and ethnic groups that are reflective of a stratified society never imagined by the authors of the Master Plan. Coping with these issues has been a major challenge and a source of great consternation for Californians and, particularly, for the University of California.[7]

Though a valuable tool for statewide planning, the Master Plan has also been described as an inflexible edict. Strict adherence to the ideal of differentiation of functions bolstered the University of California's ability to acquire state funding within its broad mission of instruction, research, and public service, and it provided an important limit on future costs to state government. The Master Plan also restricted creative initiatives and the ability of California State University campuses to develop new programs and evolve. The effect, critics have argued, is that California's higher education system has not fully met the training and professional needs of certain sectors of the state's economy. No matter what new social and economic needs emerge in California society, complained a report to the California legislature in 1969, the differentiation-of-functions doctrine limits the development of the individual segments. Fourteen years after the passage of the plan, Thomas R. McConnell, coauthor of the Restudy Report, argued: "It is not an overstatement to say that the California Master Plan and the statute which incorporates it have, in effect, engraved the functions [of the public colleges and universities] in tablets of stone. The statute thus brings even orderly and planned evolution to an arbitrary halt."[8]

The compromise reached in Clark Kerr's office in early 1960 included the establishment of a joint doctorate under the supervision and discretion of the

University of California. The assumption was that it would be offered primarily in education and in fields that would be more professional than research oriented. By the 1970s, the joint doctorate program was amended to allow the California State University system to establish a joint doctorate program with accredited private universities in the state that would be subject to the approval of the California Postsecondary Education Committee. However, for a variety of reasons, the program never flourished. Some within the California State University system have viewed this part of the 1960 compact as a ruse.

Indeed, not long after the Master Plan was passed as the Donahoe Act, several California State University presidents attempted to amend the Master Plan to allow the doctorate in education at select campuses. The result would be only a marginal change in the Master Plan, they argued. The concept of differentiation of functions would remain intact. This proposal, as with earlier efforts to expand the role of these regional institutions, was vehemently opposed by University of California officials. It found little support in the highly politicized environment of the 1960s and the decidedly conservative budgets for higher education under Governor Ronald Reagan and then Governor Edmund "Jerry" Brown. Yet some thought that extending the doctorate to the California State University was inevitable. In a 1971 report to the Carnegie Commission on Higher Education, Eugene Lee and Frank Bowen thought it "only a matter of time before one or more of the [California State University] campuses will be granted authority to offer limited doctoral work" beyond the joint doctorate.[9] This did not transpire. In subsequent years, the budgetary implications of new graduate programs, continued hostility of the University of California, and a great reluctance among lawmakers to reopen the issue of segmental functions thwarted the ambitions of the California State University system.

Over time, California State University administrators and faculty have had other frustrations with the content and implementation of the Master Plan. Part of the compact agreed to in Kerr's office included a level of autonomy for California State University's new Board of Trustees similar to that enjoyed by the regents of the University of California. This component of the compact, however, was never fully embraced by lawmakers. Removing the California State University from the purview of the State Board of Education was radical surgery enough, they thought. When Glenn Dumke became the second chancellor of the California State University system in 1962, he and his board found themselves still restricted by a growing labyrinth of personnel and budget controls of state agencies. The first chancellor of the system, Buell Gallagher, the former president of City College of New York, had served for only eight months. After political attacks on his supposed tolerance of Communists and frustration with the limits of the Master Plan, he resigned. Escaping the clutches of the State Board of Education did not prove a salvation. Unlike the highly autonomous University of California, when Chancellor Dumke went to Sacramento to present a proposed budget, he needed not only to negotiate with legislators but also with the Department of Finance and other agencies on the minute details of how money would be spent. The University of California gained block funding for operating costs and retained significant autonomy on how that funding was spent. In contrast, the California State University system gained moneys only for specific programs and faculty, with limited flexibility to change priorities—although the funding process is less restrictive today than in the past.

In the post–Master Plan era, Glenn Dumke and his faculty also complained that there remained a sizable difference in the funding level between the University of California and California State University for support of similar programs at the undergraduate level. The Master Plan, charged Professor Marc R. Tool in a 1967 report to the newly formed California State University faculty senate, "has become a vehicle to be used invidiously to sanction different treatment for programs that are offered in common by the respective systems."[10]

Is the Master Plan simply a political deal, a "peace treaty," as noted by one observer, intended to sustain the University of California's dominant position and its claim on state resources? To a certain extent, the answer is yes. At the time of the Master Plan's formulation and before its submittal to the legislature as a proposed constitutional amendment, Clark Kerr described the plan as a "milestone" in educational policymaking and a "plan to end all plans." Though it found sanction primarily in statute, the plan has obtained a level of durability that is much like a constitutional provision.

In the early 1990s, new doubts arose about the future of higher education in California. A prolonged fiscal crisis, along with relatively new constitutional restraints on state government's ability to tax and spend revenues, contributed to a steady decline in California's college-going rates for the first time since the late 1880s. Public higher education faced significant budget cuts in the midst of a new wave of enrollment demand—one that may surpass the total number of new students that entered California higher education in the boom years of 1960 to 1975. "Whether we choose to recognize it or not," lamented a joint statement by leaders of the state's higher education community in 1993, "for the past several years Californians have been making the decision to slowly dismantle their world-renowned higher education system. Deep budget cuts now occur annually and appear inevitable for the foreseeable future."[11]

Even with the return of a healthy rate of economic expansion in the state, limits on taxation and state appropriations voted in by Californians during the tax revolts of the 1970s and 1980s, and competing demands for tax dollars, including prisons, make the prospect of a sufficient flow of funds to maintain California's post–Master Plan system appear bleak. Yet California stands at the edge of the largest increase in enrollment demand in its history—a demand that relates to projected population growth, the increasing need for skilled and professional labor, and the desire for social and economic mobility among an increasingly diverse population.

Can the tenets of the Master Plan be sustained in California's changing economic and political climate? What does California need from its evolving higher education system, and what can it afford? State lawmakers and the education community have not addressed these fundamental questions in the 1990s nor in other eras of significant change in the economy and perception of societal needs. There has been no dire need to rethink a system of education that, seemingly, has served the state so well. The politics of reform, of revisiting the missions and admission policies of the tripartite system, have been too difficult—particularly during California's relatively healthy post–World War II economic climate.

California, a state that has exuded enthusiasm for public education, has perhaps reached a mid-life crisis. "In the generation immediately following World War II," Peter Schrag notes mournfully in *Paradise Lost*, "California was widely regarded as both model and magnet for the nation—in its economic opportunities, its social outlook, and its high quality public services and institutions." Not the least of California's claims to fame, notes Schrag, was its "nearly free and universally accessible system of public higher education, a well-supported public school system, an ambitious agenda of public works projects, . . . and a wide array of social services and human rights guarantees that had no parallel in any other state."[12] At least at the time of this writing, the political culture of optimism has faded. A significant economic transition is under way, made possible in no small part by the past investment in the state's network of public and private institutions of higher education. State and local government appears impotent to effect change, and the pressures of a rapidly growing and diverse population have set a new stage. Schrag calls the decline the "Mississippification" of California—an era epitomized by the passage of "mad as hell" tax revolts and the plummeting of funding for the state's schools on a per pupil basis from among the top five states to among the bottom five.

Yet a comparison with Mississippi is, perhaps, unfair to Mississippi. Not only does California have its own breed of convoluted politics; it also has an unparalleled accumulation of wealth and affluence that adds special irony to the decline in its infrastructure of roads, buildings, and public institutions.

Adding to the challenges facing California public higher education are significant market shifts that sit on the horizon. The postmodern, global economy and the technological advents that form its foundation are adding fuel to the expanding demand for higher education and for basic and applied research. Markets are opening for new types of instruction, new modes of delivering postsecondary education, and relatively new types of university and private sector cooperative research projects. Throughout the world, the research and training proclivities of the academy are increasingly viewed as key components for economic growth—the land grant vision reprised. Reflecting this trend, American universities are engaged in more applied research and joint industry-university ventures than at any other time in the post–World War II era—a confirmation of the critical role of the academy in the world economy, but also renewing concern over the role of colleges and universities as bastions of free thought and inquiry.

As this history has chronicled, the reality of today is not necessarily that of tomorrow. Californians concerned with the future of the state should look back to debates and innovations of the past to find inspiration and to help place current and future fiscal and social challenges in historical context. The same can be said, of course, for all systems of higher education and, more generally, for the world of policymaking. Certainly, a good dose of history is no panacea. But it is obvious that America's state systems of higher education are not recent inventions. They are organizational structures that have grown and undergone transformation over time. Thoughtful innovation comes from an understanding of the past and thinking about how the future might be different.

APPENDIX 1. CALIFORNIA HIGHER EDUCATION TIME LINE

Year	*California Education Policy History*	*California Political History/ National Events*
1785		First Northwest Ordinance
1787		Second Northwest Ordinance
1803		Louisiana Purchase
1817		Founding of the University of Michigan
1819		Dartmouth College v. Woodward Founding of the University of Virginia
1820		Founding of Indiana University
1822		End of Spanish rule in California; beginning of Mexican rule
1835		Henry Dana arrives in San Francisco Bay
1841		Federal Land Grant Program for Education
1844		Founding of the University of New York (Albany)
1846		Mexican-American War begins
1847		Founding of the University of Iowa Founding of the City University of New York
1848	First California public school and board founded in San Francisco	U.S. acquisition of California and other southwest territories under the Treaty of Guadalupe Hidalgo Founding of the University of Wisconsin American Association for the Advancement of Science established
1849		Gold rush California Constitutional Convention held in Monterey
1850		California accepted into the Union as a state Peter H. Burnett (Dem) elected governor

Year	*California Education Policy History*	*California Political History/ National Events*
1851	First state law authorizing local communities to establish public schools supported by taxes Founding of the University of Santa Clara Founding of the University of the Pacific	John McDougal (Dem) governor First Vigilance Committee—San Francisco Louisa Smith Clapp (Dame Shirley) writes on life in California, published in 1922 as *The Shirley Letters*
1852	First state law allowing for state financial support for schools, providing a state property tax of 5 cents on each $100 of assessed property value Most schools charge "rate-bill" (fees) to subsidize operation costs State Board of Education established along with a general system of local school boards Founding of Mills College	John Bigler (Dem) governor Wells Fargo founded
1853	Contra Costa Academy opened in Oakland by Henry Durant State abolishes state property tax support, relying solely on interest from sales of federal land grants and a new state poll tax	
1855	College of California chartered Founding of the University of San Francisco	Founding of Michigan State University Founding of Pennsylvania State University
1856		J. Neely Johnson (Amer) governor
1857	Minn's Evening Normal School established by the San Francisco Board of Education	
1859		Discovery of the Comstock Load
1860	Berkeley site dedicated by College of California trustees as future site of the college	Milton S. Latham (Lec Dem) governor John G. Downey (Lec Dem) governor First kindergarten in the United States established

Year	*California Education Policy History*	*California Political History/ National Events*
1861	State Superintendent Andrew J. Moulder appoints committee to study state-supported normal school system State legislature funds establishment of yearly "Teachers' Institutes"	Civil War begins Founding of the University of Washington
1862	Legislature establishes State Normal School along with a Board of Trustees in San Francisco John Swett becomes state superintendent of public instruction	Leland Stanford (Rep) governor Federal Morrill Act passed
1863	California Educational Society established	Frederick F. Low (Union/Rep) governor Building of the Central Pacific
1864	California accepts land grant offer under the Morrill Act (150,000 acres) Whitney/Swett report on "Establishing a State University" advocates using federal land grants for a polytechnic school	
1865		Federal Freedman's Bureau established Founding of Cornell University
1866	First Organic Act (or enabling legislation) to establish UC Swett's proposal for free schools enacted in the Revised School Law of 1866 School Law also expands State Board of Education to include professional educators	Founding of the University of Kansas
1867	Benjamin Silliman address at California College commencement	Henry H. Haight (Dem) governor Beginning of the Grange Movement
1868	Second Organic Act establishing UC authored by Assemblyman John Dwinelle	

Year	*California Education Policy History*	*California Political History/ National Events*
1869	UC campus opens on September 20 with thirty-eight students John LeConte named acting UC president	Transcontinental railroad completed Richard Henry Dana's *Two Years Before the Mast* published
1870	Henry Durant named first UC president	California's population increases to 870,000
1871	California State Normal School moved from San Francisco to San Jose	Henry George: *Our Land and Land Policy* Newton Booth (Rep) governor Los Angeles anti-Chinese riot
1872	Daniel Coit Gilman named the second UC president	*Kalamazoo* decision upholds public taxation for high schools Mark Twain's *Roughing It* published Founding of the University of Oregon
1873		National economic depression
1874	Memorial by the California State Grange and the Mechanics Deliberative attacking the management of the university UC Professors Ezra Carr and William Swinton join the protests of the Grange Swinton resigns; Carr is fired by Board of Regents	
1875	Gilman resigns as UC president to help found Johns Hopkins University John LeConte named the third UC president Carr elected State Superintendent of Public Instruction California Teachers Association established (replaces the California Education Society, which disbanded in 1873)	Bank of California falls into bankruptcy Romualdo Pacheco (Rep) governor Governor William Irwin (Dem) governor
1876	Defeat of the Carpenter Bill (sponsored by Assembly Speaker Gidion Carpenter), which would have disbanded the regents and established in its place an elected body with purview over all of public education	Start of two-year severe drought Legislature passes measure calling for a Constitutional Convention Founding of Johns Hopkins University

Year	California Education Policy History	California Political History/ National Events
1877	Professor Eugene W. Hilgard named the new director of UC agricultural programs	Election of delegates to Constitutional Convention Unemployed riot in San Francisco Workingmen's Party formed Federal Hatch Act passed providing funds for agricultural experiment stations
1878	Defeat of Curtis Bill (similar to Carpenter Bill)	Dennis Kearney leads Workingmen's Party Second Constitutional Convention convenes in Sacramento in September
1879	Article IX of new California Constitution elevates UC to a public trust	Constitutional convention completes business in March New California Constitution passed by voters in May
1880	Founding of the University of Southern California	George C. Perkins (Rep) governor Battle of Mussel Slough
1881	Founding of Los Angeles State Normal School	*Los Angeles Times* established Founding of Tuskegee Institute by Booker T. Washington Founding of the University of Texas
1882	William T. Reid named UC president. Reid recommends building California high schools to help create a meaningful system of public higher education	Chinese Exclusion Law passed, suspends immigration for ten years
1883		George Stoneman (Dem) governor
1884	State Board of Education elevated from a statutory to a constitutional provision	
1885	State Supreme Court ruling forbids exclusion of Chinese from public schools; San Francisco builds segregated "Chinese School" Stanford University chartered by state	Sante Fe Railroad to Los Angeles completed Founding of the University of Arizona Harvard adopts elective system under leadership of President Charles Eliot
1886	State legislature provides UC with state funding based on 1 cent per $100 of taxable property (the mill tax).	

Year	California Education Policy History	California Political History/ National Events
1887	Founding of Chico State Normal School Pomona and Occidental Colleges opened	Washington Bartlett (Dem) governor Robert W. Waterman (Rep) governor Founding of Clark University
1890		Second Federal Morrill Act provides annual allocations to states for higher education Union Oil Company formed by Thomas R. Bard
1891	Stanford University opens with an enrollment of 559 students and David Starr Jordan as president Phoebe Apperson Hearst establishes five scholarships for women at UC and provides moneys for the building of the Hearst Mining Building Throop Institute established (later becomes Caltech) Extension program established at UC–Berkeley	Founding of the University of Chicago
1892		Sierra Club founded Edward Doheny discovers major oil field in Los Angeles Federal Geary Act passed, requires all Chinese in the United States to register or be deported
1895	Graduate Council established at UC–Berkeley as part of the Academic Senate	James H. Budd (Dem) governor
1896	Phoebe Hearst funds an international competition for a physical plan for the Berkeley campus (held in 1899–1900)	*Plessy v. Ferguson* decision used to uphold segregated schools
1897	California legislature authorizes another 1 cent levy on taxable property to support UC (now total of 2 cents) Phoebe Hearst appointed to the Board of Regents Founding of San Diego State Normal School	Henry T. Gage (Rep) governor

Year	*California Education Policy History*	*California Political History/ National Events*
1898	Ellwood Cubberley becomes head of Stanford University's Department of Education (one of the first such departments in the nation) Medical Department and Colleges of Pharmacy and Dentistry moved from privately owned buildings in downtown San Francisco to buildings on Parnassus Heights (site of what would become UCSF) Millicent Shinn first woman to be conferred the Ph.D. at UC–Berkeley	Spanish-American War
1899	Founding of San Francisco State Normal School Benjamin Ide Wheeler named president of UC (1899–1919) CTA annual meeting provides progressive education platform	
1900	Education Commission of 1900 established under a proposal by Elmer Brown, professor of education at Berkeley, offered at the previous CTA meeting UC opens first summer school	Percentage of U.S. 18–21-year-olds in college: 4.01 Automobile Club of Southern California founded
1901	Founding of California Polytechnic School (secondary school until 1927; until 1956 enrollment limited to males) Marine Station at La Jolla opened by UC faculty (made part of UC in 1912 and future site of UCSD)	San Francisco's Boss Ruef and Schmitz in power Federal Newlands Reclamation Act passed Frank Norris's *The Octopus: A Story of California* published
1902	Legislation allows for state subsidization of public high schools Normal schools begin transition to postsecondary institutions; most offer two-year programs for high school graduates and four-year programs for graduates of grammar schools	

Year	*California Education Policy History*	*California Political History/ National Events*
1903		George C. Pardee (Rep) governor Los Angeles adopts the initiative, referendum, and recall in new city charter
1905	University Farm School at Davis established by legislature as a branch of UC–Berkeley UC Academic Senate establishes articulation agreements with State Normal Schools and private colleges for students transferring to UC–Berkeley at their junior year	Industrial Workers of the World (IWW) founded Los Angeles voters approve bonds for Owens Valley project
1906	San Francisco builds "Oriental School" (replacing burned "Chinese School") and requires Japanese children to attend UC Professor Elmer Brown named first United States Commissioner of Education by President Roosevelt	Progressives win big in Los Angeles municipal elections San Francisco graft prosecutions
1907	Caminetti Bill provides for nation's first network of public "Junior Colleges" Citrus Experiment Station established at Riverside UC training school for nurses opens in San Francisco UC–Berkeley adopts "lower and upper division" undergraduate curriculum	Lincoln-Roosevelt Republican league founded in Los Angeles James N. Gillett (Rep) governor Federal Japanese Exclusion Act Nelson Amendment to the 1890 Morrill Act
1909	Legislature authorizes a 3 cent levy on taxable property to support UC Founding of Santa Barbara State Normal School, absorbing the Anna Blake School (eventually it becomes UCSB) University of California Farm School opens at Davis First junior high school established in Berkeley	Jack London's *Martin Eden* published California Legislature authorizes bond issue to initiate a system of paved state highways

Year	California Education Policy History	California Political History/ National Events
1910	First public junior college established in Fresno	Percentage of U.S. 18–21-year olds in college: 4.84 *Los Angeles Times* building bombed during major labor strike against metal trades
1911	Founding of Fresno State Normal School SCA proposed by Senator Shanahan. Bill provides for a newly constitutionally elected or appointed State Board of Education The Division of UC Extension established Ishi "discovered"	Hiram Johnson (Rep) governor State constitutional amendments passed providing for the initiative and referendum; recall of officials; women's suffrage, railroad regulation, and workman's compensation
1912	School of Jurisprudence established at UC–Berkeley (now Boalt Law School)	First-year initiatives and referendums offered: all five rejected by voters Governor Johnson runs for vice president with Theodore Roosevelt on the Bull Mouse ticket
1913	Assembly Bill 836 sets four-year terms for Board of Education, appointment of lay members by the governor, and the creation of three commissioners to report directly to the board (creating a "double-headed" system) CTA proposes appointment of the superintendent of public instruction Founding of Humboldt State Normal School David Starr Jordon resigns as president of Stanford, takes ceremonial title of chancellor	Los Angeles Aqueduct completed Alien Land Law passed by California Legislature, prohibiting "aliens ineligible to citizenship" from buying land or leasing it for longer than three years Hetch Hetchy project approved by congress Constitutional amendment establishes "cross-filing" system for statewide and local elections California Legislature passes minimum wage law for women and children

Year	California Education Policy History	California Political History/ National Events
1915	Proposition 11, first voter-approved UC Building Bond Act provides $1.8 million for new construction Ray Lyman Wilbur named the second president of Stanford University	Federal Smith-Lever Act passed providing $10,000 a year to each statelegislature for funding agriculture extension programs at public colleges and universities Hiram Johnson (Progressive Party) serves second term as governor Panama Pacific International Exposition held in San Francisco; Panama Pacific Exposition held in San Diego Gertrude Atherton's *California: An Intimate History* published AAUP's "General Declaration of Principles"
1916	Publication of Ellwood Cubberley's *Public School Administration*	John Dewey's *Democracy and Education* published United States enters World War I
1917	State legislature passes law providing funding for the establishment of junior colleges University of California's new hospital opened in San Francisco (becomes UCSF) Otis Art Institute founded at former home of owner of *Los Angeles Times*	William D. Stephens (Rep) governor Hiram Johnson appointed to the U.S. Senate Federal Smith-Hughes Act passed, providing grants for vocation education, home economics, and agricultural extension.
1918	SCA strengthens the independence of the Board of Regents, eliminating requirement that appointments be confirmed by the state senate and dropping reference to authority granted under the 1868 Organic Act Jessica Peixotto becomes the first woman faculty member to attain status as a full professor at UC–Berkeley.	Thorsten Veblin's *The Higher Learning in America* published, attacking the control of universities and colleges by business interests Four women elected to the California State Assembly
1919	Los Angeles's Normal School transformed into UC's southern campus David P. Barrows becomes UC president	California Legislature passes criminal syndicalism law

Year	California Education Policy History	California Political History/ National Events
1920	Jones Report (chaired by state Senator Herbert C. Jones) Proposition 12, providing a state university tax on property (and circumventing the legislature), rejected by voters Proposition 16 passed, adding kindergartens to public school budgets and creating a state high school fund, sets minimum per pupil expenditures	Percentage of U.S. 18–21-year-olds in college: 8.14
1921	Establishment of the State Department of Education (proposed by Jones Report) Normal Schools renamed State Teachers Colleges (proposed by Jones Report) Teachers colleges and affiliated junior colleges (San Jose, etc.) placed under the State Board of Education (proposed by the 1900 Education Commission and Jones Report) UC enrolls over 14,000 students; largest higher education institution in the nation	
1922		Upton Sinclair's *The Goose-Step: A Study of American Education* published
1923	State Teachers Colleges offer B.A. in education	Friend W. Richardson (Rep) governor
1924		Federal Immigration Act denies entry to most Asians
1925	Founding of the Claremont Graduate School and the "Claremont Plan," guided by the vision of James Blaisdale (president of Pomona College)	
1926		"Federal Plan" of reapportionment adopted by California voters
1927	Bill abolishes the positions of the three commissioners (see 1913) UC regents change name of the southern branch to the University of California–Los Angeles.	Clement C. Young (Rep) governor Upton Sinclair's *Oil!* published

Year	California Education Policy History	California Political History/ National Events
1928	SCA 26 (sponsored by Jones and new Superintendent William Cooper and defeated by the voters) would have given legislature the power to appoint a director of education to supersede the elected position of superintendent of public instruction	Hoover Dam project approved by Congress (opens in 1936)
1929	California Commission for the Study of Educational Problems (to be composed of nine lay members) established by a bill sponsored by Senator Jones Vierling Kersey elected state superintendent (1929–1937) Senator J. M. Inman Bill proposes the conversion of Sacramento Junior College into a four-year program with its own board (thus independent of the State Board of Education and the regents); bill defeated. UCLA moves to Westwood campus from downtown Los Angeles Ernest O. Lawrence invents the cyclotron at UC–Berkeley	Stock market crash First Academy Awards given in Hollywood
1930	Report of the Commission recommends election of Board of Education and appointment of the state superintendent State Board authorizes extension of teacher credential programs to four years for specialized fields at Fresno, San Diego, and San Jose Robert Gordon Sproul named UC president (1930–1958) Founding of the California Junior College Federation (1930–1947)	Percentage of U.S. 18–21-year-olds in college: 12.19 Anti-Filipino riot in Watsonville, California
1931	At the urging of Sproul, the state legislature contracts the Carnegie Foundation to study California higher education, resulting in the 1932 Suzzallo Report	James Rolph Jr. (Rep) governor

Year	*California Education Policy History*	*California Political History/ National Events*
1932	Suzzallo Report recommends that the regents absorb teachers colleges under a new state university system, appoint the state superintendent under the new title of commissioner of education under an appointed Board of Education, and create a State Council for Educational Planning and Coordination	William Randolph Hearst's newspaper empire largest in the nation and includes in California the *San Francisco Examiner*, the *Call-Bulletin*, the *Los Angeles Examiner*, and *Herald-Express*
1933	State Council for Educational Planning and Coordination established (proposed by Suzzallo Report) Sproul creates the Senate Committee on Educational Policy to report on statewide coordination and governance, appoints Professor Joel H. Hildebrand as chair	Central Valley Project Act passed by legislature National Industrial Recovery Act passed by Congress 1.25 million Californians on public relief California sales tax introduced
1934	Proposition 11 rejected, which would have abolished the state superintendent position, created a director of education, and made the State Board of Education elected (reflected Suzzallo Report recommendation)	Upton Sinclair runs for governor (EPIC campaign)
1935	Inman Bill renames State Teachers Colleges to State Colleges and gives them authority in statute to grant the B.A. in select liberal arts fields and only in areas that are applicable to teaching at the secondary level Santa Barbara County Chamber of Commerce proposed the transfer of Santa Barbara State to UC—regents oppose	Frank F. Merriam (Rep) governor California Legislature passes Personal Income Tax Act Social Security Act passed by Congress Hoover Dam completed

Year	*California Education Policy History*	*California Political History/ National Events*
1937	Griffenhagen and Associates report on state government (hired by Governor Merriam) argues for the regents taking responsibility for all public education above the secondary level	First phase of the Central Valley Project begins under the supervision of the Federal Bureau of Reclamation
1939	Bill introduced by Senator Clarence Ward and Assemblyman Alfred Robertson proposes to transfer Santa Barbara and Fresno State Colleges to UC—regents oppose	Culbert L. Olson (Dem) governor Steinbeck's *Grapes of Wrath* published
1940		Percentage of U.S. 18–21-year-olds in college: 15.32
1941	Another bill introduced to transfer Santa Barbara State College to UC—regents oppose Last meeting and report from the State Council (see 1933)	Position of legislative auditor established (Roland Vandegrift appointed); position later becomes the legislative analyst's office (LAO) United States enters World War II
1942	Sproul proposes a superboard or board of "overseers" with a chancellor for higher education and a superintendent for all schools Subcommittee on Postwar Planning created in the state legislature: proposes "Research Foundation"	"Sleepy Lagoon" murder trial Japanese evacuation to "relocation camps" (Executive Order 9066) Congress establishes Bracero Program J. Robert Oppenheimer directs initial investigation into creating an atomic bomb at UC–Berkeley
1943	Sproul and Dexter appoint a Committee of Inquiry, chaired by Ernest Jaqua (president of Scripps College) to review the administration of California higher education—favors Suzzallo Report recommendations, with regents governing UC and state colleges; Board of Education with governing responsibility for public education through the junior college level	Earl Warren (Rep) governor Joint Legislative Committee on Postwar Planning; Warren creates the Postwar Planning Commission UC assumes management of the new Los Alamos National Laboratory and the Manhattan Project Zoot Suit Riots in Los Angeles

Year	*California Education Policy History*	*California Political History/ National Events*
	Regents reject Jaqua proposal (with Sproul, Rowell, and Jordan in favor)	
	Warren signs bill transferring Santa Barbara State College to UC	
1944	Regent accept Santa Barbara at the urging of Sproul and under a plan to absorb one-by-one each of the State Colleges.	*Wartime and Postwar Problems of the States* published by the Council of State Governments
	Proposition 9 passes and provides increase in state funding of local schools from $60 to $80 per child, providing increase in state funding to "tax-poor" districts	Warren calls for a special session of the legislature to focus on postwar planning issues G.I. Bill passed
1945	Creation of the Liaison Committee (at the suggestion of Board of Education member Joseph Loeb and supported by Sproul); both the board and regents support the idea, and the first advisory group to assist in coordination (and negotiations) between the two boards is established	World War II ends United Nations established in San Francisco Vannevar Bush's report *Science — The Endless Frontier* issued
	Strayer Equity Report (part of postwar planning efforts) provides formula for improved state distribution of school funding for K–12	
	College of Engineering and a School of Medicine established at UCLA	
1946	Proposition 3 passed, banning the transfer of any state college to UC	Governor Earl Warren reelected
1947	Douglass Report urges against expanding junior colleges to junior and senior years	Report to President Truman, *Higher Education for American Democracy*, issued
	Founding of the California Junior College Association	House Un-American Activities Committee stages hearings on the "Red Menace in Hollywood"
	Bill passed allowing state colleges to offer M.A. in select fields	Tenney Committee of the California Legislature investigates "infiltration" of Communists in public education
1948	Strayer Report issued Long Beach State College established	

Year	California Education Policy History	California Political History/ National Events
1949		Edward R. Roybal first Hispanic elected to public office in Los Angeles
1950	Regents dismiss thirty-one faculty for not signing the university's Loyalty Oath	Percentage of U.S. 18–21-year-olds in college: 19.27 Establishment of National Science Foundation California Legislature passes Levering Act requiring loyalty oath of all state employees Korean War
1951	College of Letters and Science opened at UC–Davis	
1952	Proposition 2 passes and provides increase in state funding of local schools to $180 per pupil Proposition 3 passes and extends property tax exemption to nonprofit private schools—intended to "help solve the shortage of schools" *Tohlman v. Underhill* decision orders reinstatement of UC faculty fired in the 1950 oath controversy	Lawrence Radiation Laboratory (Livermore) established by the Atomic Energy Commission
1953	State Board of Education and the regents complete agreement on engineering education in the state Bill initiates "restudy" of the previous Strayer Report	Warren resigns as governor to become Chief Justice of the U.S. Supreme Court Goodwin J. Knight (Rep) governor
1954	College of Letters and Science opened at UC–Riverside	*Brown v. Topeka Board of Education* decision requires racial integration of public schools
1955	Restudy Report issued	California repeals its alien land laws
1957	Additional Centers Report issued by Liaison Committee Bill establishes state colleges in Fullerton, Hayward, and Stanislaus	Sputnik I and II launched
1958	Clark Kerr becomes UC president (1958–66)	

Year	*California Education Policy History*	*California Political History/ National Events*
	Bill establishes a state college in Northridge	Federal National Defense Education Act passed Establishment of NASA
1959	State Board of Education and Board of Regents hold two joint meetings Assembly Concurrent Resolution 88 sponsored by Assemblywoman Dorothy Donahoe, Assemblyman Walter Stierns Appointment of the Master Plan survey team	California Legislature passes the Unruh Civil Rights Act, forbidding racial discrimination in business transactions Democratic majority in the state assembly and senate (first time in 80 years) Edmund G. "Pat" Brown (Dem) governor
1960	California Master Plan for Higher Education completed Bills establish California State University campuses at Dominguez Hills, San Bernardino, and Sonoma Board of Regents approve new campus at Irvine	Percentage of U.S. 18–21-year-olds in college: 30.1 California water bonds passed ($1.75 billion)

APPENDIX 2. CALIFORNIA EDUCATIONAL INSTITUTIONS, 1850–1995

TABLE 1. California Public and Private Higher Education Institutions Established Between 1850 and 1979

	University of California	*California State University*	*California Community Colleges*	*Accredited Independent Institutions*
1851				Univ. of Santa Clara
				Univ. of the Pacific, San Jose (in 1871 moves to Stockton)
1852				Mills College, Oakland
1855				University of San Francisco
				College of California (absorbed as part of UC in 1868)
1857		Minn's Evening School for teacher training opened by SF Board of Education		
1861				Chapman College, Orange
1862		State Normal School—San Francisco (absorbs city school moved to San Jose in 1871)		
1863				Saint Mary's College, Moraga
1864				Tollman Medical College (became part of UC in 1873)
1866				Pacific School of Religion, Berkeley
1868	Berkeley			College of Notre Dame, Belmont
				Holy Names College, Oakland
1871				American Baptist Seminary of the West, Berkeley
				San Francisco Art Institute
				San Francisco Theological Seminary, San Anselmo
1873	San Francisco			

TABLE I. *(continued)*

	University of California	*California State University*	*California Community Colleges*	*Accredited Independent Institutions*
1875				Hebrew Union College, Los Angeles
1878	Hastings College of Law, San Francisco (created as an "affiliate" of UC)			
1880				University of Southern California
1881		Los Angeles (absorbed by UC in 1919)		
1882				Pacific Union College, Angwin
1883				Chaffey College (made a public junior college in 1916)
1884				Woodbury University, Los Angeles
1885				Claremont School of Theology
				Stanford University, Stanford (chartered, opened in 1891)
1887		Chico		Pomona College, Claremont
				Occidental College, Los Angeles
				Cogswell College, San Francisco
1889				Dominican College of San Rafael
1891				Throop Institute (renamed California Institute of Technology)
				University of La Verne
1893				Church Divinity School of the Pacific, Berkeley
1894				Saint Patrick's Seminary, Menlo Park
1896				Humphrey's College, Stockton
1897		San Diego		

1898				Saint Joseph's College, Mt. View
1899				Azusa Pacific University
1901		Cal Poly San Luis Obispo		
1902				Point Loma College, San Diego
1904				Southern California College of Optometry, Fullerton Starr King School for the Ministry, Berkeley
1905	Davis (as a agriculture research station)			Loma Linda University National Technical School, Los Angeles
1907	Riverside (as a citrus experiment station)			California College of Arts and Crafts, Oakland University of Redlands
1908				Biola University, La Mirada
1909		Santa Barbara (absorbed in 1944 by UC)		San Francisco Law School West Coast University, Los Angeles
1910			Fresno	
1911		Fresno		Loyola Marymount College, Los Angeles Southwestern School of Law, Los Angeles Cleveland Chiropractic College, Los Angeles Los Angeles College of Chiropractic
1912	San Diego (as a marine research station)			
1913		Humboldt	Bakersfield Fullerton	
1914			San Diego City College Sierra, Rocklin	
1915			Citrus, Azusa Santa Ana	

TABLE 1. *(continued)*

	University of California	*California State University*	*California Community Colleges*	*Accredited Independent Institutions*
1916			Riverside Sacramento Chaffey, Onterio	
1917				San Francisco Conservatory of Music
1918			Santa Rosa	Armstrong College, Berkeley
1919	Los Angeles (absorbing LA State Normal School)		Gavilan, Gilroy	Bethany Bible College, Santa Cruz
1920			Hancock, Santa Maria Hartnell, Salinas	Southern California College, Costa Mesa
1921		[Normal schools renamed State Teachers Colleges, governance given to the State Board of Education]	San Jose Modesto	Simpson College, San Francisco
1922			San Mateo Imperial Valley Taft	
1924			Pasadena	
1925			Los Angeles Trade Sequoias, Vasalia Lassen, Susanville Ventura	Claremont Graduate University Mount St. Mary's, Los Angeles LIFE Bible College, Los Angeles

1926		Marin, Kenfield	Scripps College, Claremont
		San Bernardino	
		Kings River, Reedley	
1927		Compton	Los Angeles Baptist Colleges
		Glendale	Menlo College, Atherton
		Long Beach	
		Porterville	
		Yuba, Marysville	
1928			Pacific Christian College, Fullerton
1929	California Maritime Academy, Vallejo (made part of CSU in 1960)	Antelope Valley, Lancaster	
		Los Angeles	
		Santa Monica	
1930			Art Center College of Design, Pasadena
			Queen of the Holy Rosary College, Mission San Jose
			San Francisco College of Mortuary Science
1931		West Hills, Coalinga	Dominican School of Philosophy and Theology, Berkeley
1934		Mira Costa, Oceanside	Jesuit School of Theology, Berkeley
1935	[Renamed State Colleges]	City College of San Francisco	
1937			Pepperdine University, Malibu
1938	Cal Poly Pomona		
1939			Center for Early Childhood Education, Los Angeles
			Saint John's College, Camarillo
			San Jose Bible College
1940		Napa Valley	Westmont College, Santa Barbara
1942			Northrop University, Inglewood

TABLE I. *(continued)*

	University of California	*California State University*	*California Community Colleges*	*Accredited Independent Institutions*
1944	Santa Barbara (absorbing Santa Barbara State College)			Fresno Pacific College Golden Gate Baptist Theological Seminary, Mill Valley
1945			East Los Angeles Mount San Antonio Solano, Suisun City	Brooks Institute of Photography, Santa Barbara
1946			Palomar, San Marcos	Claremont Men's College (later renamed Claremont McKenna) Holy Family College, Fremont
1947		Los Angeles Sacramento	El Camino, Torrance Pierce, Woodland Hills Monterey Peninsula Orange Coast Palo Verda, Blythe	Fuller Theological Seminary, Pasadena University of Judaism, Los Angeles
1948		Long Beach	Contra Costa Diablo Valley, Pleasant Hill Shasta, Redding	Pacific Oaks College, Pasadena
1949			Los Angeles Harbor—Wilmington Los Angeles Valley, Van Nuys	University of San Diego West Coast Christian University, Fresno

1950				California Baptist College, Riverside Pacific Lutheran Seminary, Berkeley
1951	Davis (College of Letters and Sciences opened)			
1952				Columbia College, Hollywood Grantham College of Engineering, Los Angeles United States International University, San Diego
1953			Laney, Oakland Merritt, Oakland	
1954	Riverside (College of Letters and Sciences opened)			
1955			American River, Sacramento Cerritos, Norwalk	Harvey Mudd College, Claremont Monterey Institute of International Studies Don Bosco Technical Institute, Rosemead Mennonite Brethren Biblical Seminary, Fresno
1957		Fullerton Hayward Stanislaus	Siskiyous, Weed	
1958		Northridge	Desert, Palm Desert Foothill, Los Altos	Bay City College of Dental Medical Assistants, San Francisco California Western School of Law
1959	San Diego (College of Letters and Sciences opened)		Barstow Cabrillo, Aptos	California Lutheran College, Thousand Oaks
1960	Irvine	Dominguez Hills San Bernardino Sonoma State	Victor Valley, Victorville	
1961			Cabot, Hayward Grossmon, El Cajon	Empire College School of Law, Santa Rosa

TABLE I. *(continued)*

	University of California	*California State University*	*California Community Colleges*	*Accredited Independent Institutions*
1962	Santa Cruz		Merced	Graduate Theological Union, Berkeley
			Mount San Jacinto	San Fernando Valley College of Law, Supulveda
			Rio Honda, Whittier	
			San Diego Mesa	
1963			Moorpark	Pitzer College, Claremont
			San Joaquin Delta	Coleman College, La Mesa
			West Valley, Saratoga	West Coast University, Orange
1964			Alameda	California Institute of the Arts, Valencia
			Redwoods, Eureka	John F. Kennedy University, Orinda
			Cuesta, San Luis Obispo	
1965		Bakersfield		
1966			Cypress	University of West Los Angeles School of Law, Culver City
			Huntington Beach	Western State University College of Law, Fullerton
				Whittier College School of Law, Los Angeles
1967			Butte, Oroville	Glendale University College of Law
			De Anza, Cupertino	Maryon Palos Verdes College
			Los Angeles Southwest	
			Ohlone, Freemont	
			Saddleback, Irvine	

1968	Canada, Redwood City	California Institute of Integral Studies, San Francisco
	Columbia	Franciscan School of Theology, Berkeley
	Feather River, Quincy	St. Johns Seminary, Camarillo
	West Los Angeles	The Wright Institute, Berkeley
		Thomas Aquinas College, Santa Paula
1969	Canyons, Valencia	California School of Professional Psychology, Berkeley and Los Angeles
	San Diego, Miramar	Lincoln Law School, Sacramento
	Skyline, San Bruno	San Joaquin College of Law, Fresno
		Fashion Institute of Design and Merchandising, Los Angeles
		Ventura College of Law
		Western State University College of Law, San Diego
1970	Consumnes River	Rand Graduate Institute of Policy Studies, Santa Monica
1971	Indian Valley, Novato	Brooks College, Long Beach
		National University, San Diego
		New College of California, San Francisco
1972	Crafton Hills, Yuciapa	Christ College, Irvine
		Southern California Institute of Architecture, Santa Monica
1973	Cerro Coso, Ridgecrest	Bay Valley Tech, Santa Clara
	Los Medanos	California School of Professional Psychology, Fresno
	Mendocino	
1974	Vista–Berkeley	American Academic of Dramatic Arts, Pasadena
		Heald Institute of Technology, Santa Clara
		The Fielding Institute, Santa Barbara

TABLE I. *(continued)*

	University of California	*California State University*	*California Community Colleges*	*Accredited Independent Institutions*
1975			Evergreen Valley	College of Osteopathic Medicine of the Pacific, Pomona
			Lake Tahoe	
			Los Angeles Mission	
			Oxnard	
1976			Coastline, Fountain Valley	
1977			Mission, Santa Clara	College of Human Services, Oakland
1978			Cuyamaca, El Cajon	
1979				Otis Art Institute of Parsons School of Design, Los Angeles

SOURCES: California Postsecondary Education Commission, *Guide to California Colleges and Universities* (Sacramento: 1997), www.cpec.ca.gov/guide/guide.htm; California Postsecondary Education Commission, *Background Papers to a Prospectus for California Postsecondary Education, 1985–2000* (Sacramento, 1985).

TABLE II. California Public and Partial List of Private Higher Education Institutions Established Between 1980 and 1995

	University of California	*California State University*	*California Community Colleges*	*Partial List of State Approved and Accredited Independent Institutions*
1980				Samuel Merritt College
				Center for Theological Studies
				Southland University
				Pacific National University
				Asian American University
				Center Graduate College
				San Francisco College of Acupuncture
				California Institute of Applied Design
				New School of Architecture
				Simon Greenleaf University
				Western Design Institute
1981				Edwards Inst. for Advanced Studies
				Clinical Psychotherapy Institute
				Saint James College
				Soma University
				Pacific International University
				Hawthorne University
				North American University
				Westlin College
				Bernadean University
				ITT Technical Institute—San Diego
1982				Monterey College of Law
				International College of California
				Charles Dederich School of Law
				Southern Cal Univ. of Prof. Studies
				Pacifica Graduate Institute
				American College of Finance
				Cambridge Grad School of Psychology
				Northwestern Cal University, Law
				California Publishing Institute
				Santa Barbara University
				University of Greater Los Angeles

TABLE II. *(continued)*

	University of California	*California State University*	*California Community Colleges*	*Partial List of State Approved and Accredited Independent Institutions*
1983				America Pacific University Cal Academy of Merchandising Art & Design Univ. of Northern Cal School of Law Institute for Information Management College and Seminary of Southern Cal Bates University Pacific International College CalWest College DeVry Institute of Technology College for Human Services
1984				California College for Health Sciences Southern State University Westminster University City University, Santa Clara European University of America National Schools William Howard Taft University Heald College, Santa Rosa California University of Advanced Studies American Intercontinental University Business College Interior Designers Institute Oakland Law School Northwestern Polytechnical University Criss College California Theological Seminary Americantown University American University of Oriental Studies Balin Institute of Technology American Institute of Hypnotherapy

TABLE II. *(continued)*

	University of California	*California State University*	*California Community Colleges*	*Partial List of State Approved and Accredited Independent Institutions*
				Western Academic University
				California School of Court Reporting
1985				National Education Center
				Laguna Beach College
				The Union Institute
				Kennedy—Western University
				California Paramedical and Technical College
				Irvine Business College
1986			Irvine Valley	ITT Technical Institute, San Diego
1988				Art Institute of Southern California
				ITT Technical Institute, Van Nuys, Sacramento, Carson
				American National University
				August Vollmer University
				Phillips Junior College
				Huffman College of Law
				Foundation College
				Southern California Institute of Law, Ventura, Santa Barbara
				Art Institute of California
1989		San Marcos	Los Pasitos	
1990				
1994		Monterey Bay		

SOURCE: California Postsecondary Education Commission

APPENDIX 3. CALIFORNIA HIGHER EDUCATION ENROLLMENT

TABLE 1. California Public Higher Education Enrollment: Headcount 1920–1995

	University of California	*California State Teachers Colleges/CSU*	*California Junior Colleges/CCC*	*Totals*
1920	13,860	2,721	2,269	18,850
1925	19,036	8,722	6,301	34,059
1930	19,723	9,770	26,961	56,454
1935	23,539	8,131	41,358	73,028
1940	29,423	11,874	86,357	127,654
1945	31,957	7,907	120,685	160,549
1950	44,332	30,502	134,585	209,419
1955	43,619	54,618	211,184	309,421
1960	55,887	95,081	340,049	491,017
1965	79,437	154,927	459,445	693,809
1970	109,033	241,559	652,133	1,002,725
1975	128,486	310,891	1,101,548	1,540,925
1980	135,821	313,850	1,189,976	1,639,647
1985	147,957	324,626	1,142,469	1,615,052
1990	166,547	369,053	1,513,010	2,048,610
1995	163,768	325,604	1,346,000	1,835,372

SOURCES: Stadtman, *Centennial Record of the University of California;* Harris, A *Statistical Portrait of Higher Education;* California State University, *Statistical Abstract 1995;* Lockard, *Watershed Years;* Proctor, *The Junior College;* California Department of Finance, Demographic Research. Most data is for fall enrollment. Junior college enrollment numbers are approximate and reflect a number of sometimes conflicting sources between 1920 and 1960.

TABLE 2. California Higher Education Enrollment: Public and Private Headcount 1920–1990

	Total Public Enrollment	*Total Private Enrollment*	*Total Enrollment*	*Percentage Public*
1920	18,850	9,063	27,913	67%
1930	56,454	28,843	85,297	66%
1940	127,654	30,263	157,917	81%
1950	209,419	62,183	271,602	77%
1960	491,017	75,967	566,984	87%
1970	1,002,725	117,891	1,120,616	90%
1980	1,639,647	156,564	1,796,211	91%
1990	2,048,610	177,077	2,225,687	92%

SOURCES: See previous table; California Department of Finance; Council of State Governments, Higher Education.

NOTES

PREFACE

1. Historians of American higher education have, in general, concentrated on institutional histories, or surveys on the development of the nation's colleges and universities. Examples of the survey approach include Laurence R. Veysey, *The Emergence of the American University*, and John S. Brubacher and Willis Rudy, *Higher Education in Transition*. Roger Geiger's two books, *To Advance Knowledge: The Growth of American Research Universities, 1900–1940* and *Research and Relevant Knowledge: American Research Universities Since World War II*, provide an in-depth analysis of the rise of a class of research institutions. Beyond a series of state surveys completed largely before World War II, there are only two relatively recent studies on how and why states nurtured and developed higher education; they are David G. Sansing, *Making Haste Slowly: The Troubled History of Higher Education in Mississippi*, and Richard M. Freeland, *Academia's Golden Age: Universities in Massachusetts, 1945–1970*. Freeland's study focuses on higher education in Massachusetts after World War II, but, reflecting the powerful influence of private colleges and universities in the state, his account is more of a compilation of histories of varied institutions.

2. The major historical studies on California public higher education include Verne A. Stadtman, *The University of California: 1868–1968*; William Warren Ferrier, *Origin and Development of the University of California, Ninety Years of Education in California, 1846–1936: A Presentation of Educational Movements and Their Outcome in Education Today*, and *Henry Durant, First President University of California: The New Englander Who Came to California with College on the Brain*; Roy W. Cloud, *Education in California: Leaders, Organizations, and Accomplishments of the First Hundred Years*; Charles J. Falk, *The Development and Organization of Education in California*; Donald R. Gerth and Judson A. Grenier, *A History of the California State University and Colleges*; Neil Smelser, "Growth, Structural Change, and Conflict in California Higher Education, 1950–1970" in Smelser and Almond, eds., *Public Higher Education in California*; Diana Northrop Lockard, "Watershed Years: Transformations in the Community Colleges of California, 1945–1960"; Henry F. May,

Three Faces of Berkeley: Competing Ideologies in the Wheeler Era, 1899–1919; Gunther Bard, *California's Practical Period: A Cultural Context of the Emerging University, 1850s–1870s.*

INTRODUCTION

1. Historical data on college-going rates is based on the percentage of 18- to 21-year-olds who are enrolled in higher education. More recent analysis of college-going rates is based on the percentage of the population up to 35 years of age, reflecting the broadening of educational demand and access; see *Historical Statistics of the United States, Digest of Educational Statistics, 1990*. Data on California are based on statistical information compiled by the author.

2. Kerr, "Education for a Free Society."

3. D. O. Levine, *The American College.*

4. In "Schools for Snobbery," 25, historian Paul Fussell explains, "In the absence of a system of hereditary ranks and titles, without a tradition of honors conferred by a monarch, and with no well-known status ladder even of high-class regiments to confer various degrees of cachet," America came to depend "far more than other peoples on their college and university hierarchy."

5. By the turn of the century, a new network of public and private institutions, charted and supported by state government and subsequently complemented by the philanthropy of America's new industrialists, created what Roger Geiger has termed a "national system" of research universities. See Geiger, *To Advance Knowledge.*

6. See Jordan, "University Tendencies in America," 143–44, and Burns, *David Starr Jordan,* 154–158.

7. See *Historical Statistics of the United States: 1960* and *Digest of Educational Statistics: 1990.*

8. D. O. Levine, *The American College,* 7.

9. Trow, "The Transition," 3.

10. Glenny, "State Systems," 86.

11. Graham, "Structure and Governance," 80–107.

12. For a discussion of the development of the idea of mass higher education, see Jencks and Riesman, *The Academic Revolution,* 90–97; Trow, "Reflections on the Transition," "The Democratization," and "Social Class"; and Clark, *The Open Door College,* on the development of the junior college.

13. Technical Committee, *Report on California's Ability to Finance Higher Education, 1960–1975.*

14. McWilliams, *California,* 10.

15. Cited in Schrag, *Paradise Lost,* 28.

16. *Ibid.,* 27.

17. Starr, *Inventing the Dream,* 274.

18. Kerr, *The Uses,* 87–88.

19. For a discussion of these shifts in Europe, see Clark, *Creating Entrepreneurial Universities.*

20. Benjamin, Carroll et al., "The Redesign."

21. For a discussion of the affirmative action debate in California, see J. A. Douglass, "Anatomy of Conflict."

22. V. B. Smith, "The Erosion."

23. Cioffi, "After the Cold War."

CHAPTER 1

1. From this beginning, notes historian Kevin Starr, "California promised much. While yet barely a name on the map, it entered American awareness as a symbol of renewal." See Starr, *California Dream*, vii.

2. Fernham, *In-Doors and Out*, 357.

3. Quoted in Royce, *A Frontier Lady*, 127.

4. Cleland, introduction in *Constitution of the State of California, 1849*, i.

5. Preface offered by the convention delegates entitled "Address to the People of California," ii.

6. Megquire, *Apron*, 39.

7. Hansen, *The Search*, 88.

8. Browne, *Debates*, 25.

9. See Falk, *The Development*, 17, and McWilliams, *California*, 43–44.

10. In *An Historical Introduction*, 51, Gutek notes: "Tax-conscious property owners claimed that it violated the natural sanctity of property rights to tax one man in order to educate another's child. Other opponents [saw] public education as a movement designed to establish the domination of one political power over another." See also Callahan, *Cult of Efficiency*, Cremin, *The Transformation*, Higham, *Strangers*, and Bowles and Gintis, *Schooling in Capitalist America.*

11. H. Mann, *Lectures and Annual Reports*, 151.

12. Ferrier, *Ninety Years*, 29.

13. See Sanchez, *Spanish Arcadia*, 211, Napier, "Origin and Development," 178–88, and Swett, *History*, 170.

14. Browne, *Debates*, 205.

15. See Howell, *Historical Programme*, and Cloud, *Education in California*, 21. Discussion on establishing a healthy public education system took place within the context of a larger, already settled debate over what should be the rights of all California citizens. After much disagreement, the delegates passed a California "Bill of Rights." Sections XVI and XVII of the proposed constitution dealt with issues of civil liberties, including the restrictions and obligations of state government. On September 18, 1849, the *Pacific News* described these developments as "the former [section] opening in the most liberal manner the benefits of our free system to all men who may choose to select California for their future home; and the latter prohibiting forever every form of slavery or

involuntary servitude, except as a punishment for crime" (as cited in Hansen, *The Search*, 117). Within the convention, the deliberations over a California Bill of Rights subsequently provided a basis for establishing a viable common school system and for planning, if not establishing, an institution of public higher education.

16. Preface offered by the convention delegates, "Address to the People of California," ii.

17. *Ibid.*

18. Dana, "Twenty-four years after" in *Two Years Before the Mast*, 485.

19. Browne, *Debates*, 204–5.

20. *Constitution of the State of California, 1849* (San Francisco: Printed at the Office of the *Alta California*, 1849), 18.

21. *Ibid.*, 211. See also Hansen, *The Search*, 140, Ferrier, *Origin and Development*, 93, Stadtman, *The University*, 21–22. As noted in Falk, *The Development*, 19, California was "the first state to receive the benefits of the Oregon Plan, which reserved the sixteenth and thirty-sixth section of land in each township for school purposes."

22. Browne, *Debates*, 204–5.

23. *Ibid.* See also Goodwin, *The Establishment*, 200–202.

24. *Constitution of the State of California, 1849*, Article IX, sections 1 through 4.

25. Duryea, in "The University and the State," 27, notes: "The corporate form in the medieval university created an autonomy from local authority within the sovereignty of the papacy that established its right to existence by means of papal bulls or charters. This conception of corporate association separate from government yet obliged to it for its establishment carried over to the early colleges through precedents associated with the English university and the English legal custom in general. By the eighteenth century in England the corporation had become an accepted legal conception, a distinctive social unit holding designated rights in law similar to those held by individuals. In this regard, English common law set a pattern for similar arrangements in the colonies and served as a starting point for the development of a more indigenous conceptualization in this country." See also Hofstadter and Metzger, *Academic Freedom*, 367–83.

26. Georgia was the first state to charter a public university. In 1785, the legislature stated the need for government to establish and nurture educational institutions. The Georgia Legislature declared: "Where the minds of the people in general are viciously disposed and unprincipled, and their conduct disorderly, a free government will be attended with greater confusions, and with evils more horrid than the wild uncultivated state of nature: It can only be happy where the public principles and opinions are properly directed, and their manners regulated." Higher education offered a primary means to "place the youth under the forming hand of society, that by instruction they may be molded to the love of

virtue and good order." In a typical example of state charters in this early period, the University of Georgia was given a vague governance structure under statutory law, with no statement of the institution's proper relationship to the state.

27. In his brief on the Dartmouth case, Spaeth explains that the decision "dealt with whether corporate charters were contracts within the meaning of the contract clause" (in *Classic and Current Decisions*).

28. A 1933 Carnegie Foundation and U.S. Office of Education study described the importance of the Dartmouth case in this manner: "The history of higher education during the period following the Revolutionary War was characterized by a struggle between those, on the one side, who sought to perpetuate institution control among colonial colleges long established and, on the other, who favored state control. The turning point came in 1819, when the Supreme Court rendered its decision in the Dartmouth College case, to the effect that the charter was a contract secure against violation by either party without the consent of the other. After this decision the institution rather than the state became the center of attention in higher education" (from Kelley and McNeely, *The State and Higher Education*, ix).

29. For further discussion, see Whitehead, *Church and State*. The Northwest Ordinance of 1787 authorized land grants so that new states within the old Northwest Territory could subsidize the creation of state universities and colleges. As noted by John D. Millett, most of the states created after this legislation did just that: "Only the New England and Middle Atlantic states of the original confederation lagged in sponsoring state institutions of higher education," although many provided support for private institutions. The first land grant institutions included Ohio University (1804), Miami University (1809), the University of Michigan (1817), Indiana University (1820), and the University of Wisconsin (1849). See Millett, *Conflict in Higher Education*, 2–3.

30. Jencks and Riesman, *The Academic Revolution*, 91.

31. However, this desire for accountability and control, in California as well as in other states, did not generate the willingness to assume the burden of direct institutional governance. For further discussion, see Berdahl, "Coordination and Governance," and Milstein and Jennings, *Educational Policy-Making*, 4. See also Marsden, *Soul*, and Bailey, "External Forces," 28.

32. Preface offered by the convention delegates, "Address to the People of California," ii.

33. Bean, *California*, 111.

34. See Stanley, "Racism," 171–87, and Bean, *California*, 111–13.

35. See McChesney, *Secondary Education*, 3, and Young, "Anthony Caminetti," 6.

36. Cited in Young, "Anthony Caminetti," 10.

37. Ferris, "Judge Marvin," 50.

38. Quoted in Jones, *Illustrated History*, 31.

39. *Ibid.*

40. Swett, *History*, 170.

41. Ferrier, *Ninety Years*, 309–10, and Stadtman, *The University*, 22–23.

42. Quoted in Ferrier, *Ninety Years*, 8.

43. See King, *Mountaineering*, 287; see also Burich, "Something Newer and Nobler," 234–49.

44. *California Assembly Journal*, 1862, 38.

45. "The Agricultural College Land Act," 503.

46. *Ibid.* See also Gates, "College Lands," 3.

47. Swett, *History*, 170.

48. See Swett, Whitney, and Houghton, "Report."

49. Quoted in Nicholas Polos, *John Swett: California's Frontier Schoolmaster*, 95.

50. In 1866, Swett coauthored legislation that would create this publicly funded system "with the determination to secure for every child in California a right guaranteed by law to an education in a system of free schools based on the proposition that [property] ought to be taxed to educate the children of the State." Polos, "Swett," 17–32.

51. This committee included Henry B. Janes, city superintendent of the San Francisco public schools, along with George W. Minns and Ellis H. Holmes, both administrators of Minns' Evening School. Their report noted the urgent need for a larger normal school program: "[it would] afford to those who design to become teachers that previous training which, for any other business, is deemed indispensable; we need not say more of its importance to California, than to call attention to the fact that the large number of our citizens, male and female, who are looking to the profession of teaching as an employment for life, compete at a great disadvantage with those who come hither educated in the Normal Schools of other states. Our citizens would not be longer subjected to such disadvantages." From *1861 Report to the State Superintendent on the Need for a Normal School*, quoted in Cloud, *Education in California*, 258.

52. Allen, ed., *Historical Sketch*, 11–13. The new Board of Trustees for the Normal School of the State of California received $3,000 from the state for start-up costs. The Normal School was to provide teachers for the entire state. Reflecting this notion and recognizing that the vast majority of the population resided in northern California, the new trustees included the three members of the State Board of Education, in addition to the city superintendents of schools in San Francisco, Sacramento, and Marysville. As noted in Cloud's *Education in California*, 259, the 1862 act "provided that the trustees on or before June 1, 1862, should: (1) arrange for the opening of the normal school; and (2) could, if they saw fit, adopt the private normal school then existing in San Francisco; (3) agree with the [San Francisco] Board of Education to provide an experimental

school; (4) contract with the City Board of Education for the use of buildings, furniture, and equipment for the sessions of the State Normal School for five days of each week for at least five months of each year."

53. Swett, as quoted in Ferrier, *Ninety Years*, 314.

54. Despite the hope of some in the state who desired a replication of Yale or Harvard in California, the commission followed the sentiments of Whitney, who, as early as 1861, insisted that the state not create "an imitation of an Eastern college." Whitney, "An Address."

55. "Announcement of the Mining and Agricultural College, San Francisco, 1863–64." The new mining and agricultural college was a unit of the College of California. William P. Blacke was named director, and the new college briefly occupied a building located at 706 Montgomery Street, San Francisco.

56. "Act to Establish an Agricultural, Mining and Mechanical Arts College," 1866. See also Axt, *The Federal Government*, 59–65.

57. "Act to Establish an Agricultural, Mining and Mechanical Arts College," 1866.

58. Kelley and McNeely, *The State and Higher Education*, ix; Brubacher and Rudy, *Higher Education in Transition*, 64–66; Klein, *Survey of Land-Grant Colleges*, 19–22.

59. As quoted in Gilman, "How Pioneers Began a College," 287.

60. Cited in Ferrier, *Ninety Years*, 181.

61. *Ibid.*

62. *Ibid.*, 184.

63. *Ibid.*, 182.

64. *Ibid.*, 183.

65. Ferrier, *Henry Durant*.

66. Haight had ventured to California in 1850 and, despite his affiliation with the Democratic Party, as governor proved to be a strong supporter of public education.

67. See Kuslan, "Benjamin Silliman, Jr.," 159–205.

68. Silliman, "The Truly Practical Man, " 18. See also Silliman, "Original Papers," 279, 281. Brubacher and Rudy, *Higher Education in Transition*, 292, note that there is much misunderstanding of the Yale Report. "In stating that their aim was both to form and inform the student mind, the Yale faculty were following in the classical tradition of liberal education. They were adhering to its primarily intellectual character. It does not appear, however, that their preference for intellectual studies to the exclusion of practical ones was due, as in Hellenic times, to their regarding the latter as undignified or unworthy of free men." In fact, a place for practical studies existed. On the Yale report, see Hofstadter and Metzger, *Academic Freedom*, 279, 316.

69. Ferrier, *Ninety Years*, 395; Stadtman, *The Centennial Record*, 413.

70. "An Act to Create and Organize the University of California," passed March 23, 1868, *California Statutes of 1867–68*, 248; Stadtman, *University of California*, 32; Constitution Revision Commission, "Article IX, Education: Background Study," 3–7.

71. "The immediate government and discipline of the several colleges shall be entrusted to their respective Faculties . . . for approval by the Regents," noted the act. "[A]ll the faculties and instructors of the University shall be combined into a body which shall be known as the Academic Senate, which shall have stated meetings at regular intervals, and be presided over by the President . . . , and which is created for the purpose of conducting the general administration of the University." *California Statutes of 1867–68*, 248; see also Fitzgibbon, *The Academic Senate*, 17.

72. As cited in Armes, *The Autobiography of Joseph LeConte*, 243, 251.

73. Stadtman, *University of California*, 36.

74. Cited in Ferrier, *Origin and Development*, 302.

75. *Ibid.*, 83.

76. May, *Three Faces of Berkeley*, 8.

77. Cited in Ferrier, *Origin and Development*, 322.

78. Haight, "University Education."

79. Ferrier, *Origin and Development*, 320.

CHAPTER 2

1. Hofstadter and Metzger, *Academic Freedom*, 277.

2. Cited in Ferrier, *Origin and Development*, 285.

3. *Ibid.*, 323.

4. Quoted in Jones, *Illustrated History*, 31.

5. Schulte, "German Standpoint."

6. In his 1871 commencement speech, "University Education," Governor Haight noted that the admission of women "has been settled; and settled wisely, in my judgment." He equated opposition to this policy as outdated and concurring with the "opinion expressed by a writer in the 13th Century, that the education of females should be confined to 'learning to pray to God, to love man, to knit, and to sew,'" 24.

7. Schulte, "German Standpoint."

8. Carr, *The Patrons*, 131–153.

9. Known also as the Agricultural College Land Act, 1862; Bean, *California*, 201–2.

10. "Memorial of the California State Grange and Mechanics Deliberative Assembly on the State University," Sacramento, 1874, in *Pamphlets on the University of California*.

11. Ferrier, *Origin and Development*, 131.

12. "Professor Swinton's Testimony before the Legislature of California Given to the Joint Committee on University Affairs," March 11, 1874, in Carr, "Industrial Education, September 1874," in *Pamphlets on the University of California*, 42, 55.

13. Carr, "Response from the Professor of Agriculture," in *Statements of the Regents*, 18.

14. "Memorial of the California State Grange and Mechanics Deliberative Assembly," in *Pamphlets on the University of California*, 7–8.

15. Carr, "Industrial Education"; Stadtman, *University of California*, 71–74.

16. "Memorial of the California State Grange and Mechanics Deliberative Assembly" in *Pamphlets on the University of California*, 7–8; Swett, *Public Education in California*, 263–64.

17. "Professor Swinton's Testimony before the Legislature" in *Pamphlets on the University of California*, 14.

18. Swinton, "The University and Its Managers before the People and the Law," March 20, 1874, in *Pamphlets on the University of California*.

19. "Statements of the Regents of the University of California, to the Joint Committee of the Legislature, March 3, 1874," San Francisco, 1874, in *Pamphlets on the University of California*, 5, 14–15; Ferrier, *Henry Durant*, 98; Stadtman, *University of California*, 71–74.

20. Gilman, "The Building of the University: An Inaugural Address," Oakland, November 7, 1872, *Pamphlets on the University of California*.

21. *Ibid.*

22. Gilman, *The Launching of a University*, 327.

23. California Legislature, "Resolution of the Senate and Assembly Inquiring Into the Affairs of the University of California," March 3, 1874; *Journals for the Senate and Assembly*, 1874.

24. This attempted deal was exposed in Carr's "Industrial Education," which was issued in reaction to his dismissal.

25. Ferrier, *Origin and Development*, 362; Falk, *The Development*, 32; Franklin, *The Life of Daniel Coit Gilman*, 160–161.

26. California Assembly, "An Act to Reorganize and Simplify the School System and Public Education of the State of California," bill 374, section 3, February 8, 1876; California Senate, "Report of the Senate Special Committee to Whom Was Referred Certain Questions Relative to the Regents of the State University," March 6, 1876.

27. Memorial by the Board of Regents, "The State University, Disastrous Effects of the Passage of the Carpenter Bill—Its Unconstitutionality," April 1876, in *Pamphlets on the University of California*.

28. *Ibid.*

29. California Assembly, "An Act to Reorganize and Simplify the School

System and Public Education of the State of California," bill 198, sections 3, 11, January 16, 1878.

30. Mowry, *The California Progressives,* 11; Bean, "Ideas of Reform" in Knoles, *Essays and Assays,* 13–25.

31. George, "The Kearney Agitation."

32. From the organizing meeting of the Workingmen's Party on October 5, 1977, in which Kearney was elected president; cited in the *Sacramento Bee,* April 24, 1878.

33. See Starr, *California Dream,* 132; Caughey, *California,* 442–50.

34. Mason, "Constitutional History of California," in California State Senate, *Constitution of the State of California,* 299; Bancroft, *History of California,* Vol. XXIV, 370–71.

35. Swisher, *Motivation and Political Technique,* 6.

36. William White in a letter to the *Watsonville Pajoronian,* quoted in Van Houten, "The Development of the Constitutional Provisions," 13.

37. Engelbert and Gunnell, *State Constitutional Revision;* Davis, *History of Political Conventions in California,* 390–93.

38. Kelley, *Battling the Inland Sea,* 325.

39. George, "The Kearney Agitation"; Bancroft, *History of California,* 373, 407.

40. According to the editors of the *Record-Union,* the battle appeared to be between two different camps with sharply defined opinions. "There is the class who hold to the American idea that the attainment of justice is the foundation of government; that the great problem of human government is how to combine the greatest good of the whole with the least practical restraint upon individual liberty. Opposed to this is already seen a class favoring parental government, under which the confiscation of regulation shall be mandatory and constantly operative. . . . The prevailing tendencies of thought [will] place the contest between socialism and legitimate government in the foreground, and will necessarily subordinate all other contests." *Record-Union,* September 30, 1878.

41. *Ibid.*

42. Swisher, *Motivation and Political Technique,* 33–42. Swisher also explains some of the differences between the approach of Grangers and Workingmen delegates. "The farmer delegates distrusted the clannish Kearneyite agitators much too thoroughly to unite them in any case where the effect of doing so was not perfectly clear. They did not vote for the workingmen's candidate for president. It was the workingmen who finally shifted their votes, and by doing so came near to defeating the conservative candidate. Such a combination revealed possibilities for the future, but there seemed small chance for the framing of a workingmen's constitution." See also Scheiber, "Race, Radicalism, and Reform," 35–80.

43. Engelbert and Gunnell, *State Constitutional Revision*, 96.
44. Ferrier, *Origin and Development*, 360.
45. *Debates and Proceedings*, 85.
46. *Ibid.*
47. Brubacher and Rudy, *Higher Education in Transition*, 90–91.
48. A 1969 legislative study of laws affecting the university explains: "The hardy, practical-minded pioneers that peopled the state were much less interested in the life of the mind than they were in developing new techniques for mining and better methods of agricultural production." Constitution Revision Commission, "Article IX, Education: Background Study," 8.
49. *Debates and Proceedings*, 173.
50. In Stadtman, *The Centennial Record*, 293–96.
51. *Debates and Proceedings*, 1110.
52. *Ibid.*
53. *Ibid.*, 437.
54. Wickson, *Rural California*, 33; Hilgard, *Soils*.
55. *Debates and Proceedings*, 438.
56. *Ibid.*, 1087; Peckham, *The Making of the University of Michigan, 1817–1967*, 31. As a result of its 1849 Constitutional Convention, the University of Michigan's Board of Regents were given the unique responsibility to conduct "the general supervision of the university and the direction and control of all expenditures from the university funds" free of legislative interference.
57. *Debates and Proceedings*, 1087.
58. *Ibid.*
59. *Ibid.*, 1089.
60. *Ibid.*, 1113, 1116.
61. *Ibid.*, 1110, 1113.
62. See *Western Homestead*, January 20, 1879.
63. *Debates and Proceedings*, 1123.
64. *Ibid.*, 1401–2.
65. *Ibid.*
66. *Ibid.*
67. *Ibid.*, 1476.
68. In a memorial to Winans after his death in 1887, the Board of Regents noted: "[M]ainly due to Mr. Winans' endeavor we have the present clause in our State Constitution relating to the university." "Memorial to the Late Regent Winans," *Annual Report of the Secretary of the Board of Regents*, 7.
69. Van Houten explains: "The story of his winning over a hostile group of farmers at a meeting shortly after his arrival in California and the statement of one of their leaders that, 'By God, the man knows something,' approaches legendary status." Van Houten, "The Development of the Constitutional Provi-

sions," 166. See also Stewart, "The Development of Constitutional Provisions," 138–44; *California Constitution of 1879*, article IX, section 9.

70. Analysis of balloting by Van Houten shows a more complicated story. "The combination of the lawyers, most of whom were non-partisans, the even split among the farmers, and the sizable minority of Workingmen was sufficient for the eleven vote margin by which the Webster amendment was approved." Van Houten, "The Development of the Constitutional Provisions," 166.

A 1869 Constitution Revision Commission remarked that the political climate during the establishment of the university in 1868 made it virtually impossible to place the institution within any constitutional amendment. Statutory law provided flexibility for legislators to intervene within the affairs of the university or to change the governance system of the institution, as threatened by the Grange in the early 1870s. "But by the time of the convention, the events of the intervening years changed the nature of the debate," notes the commission report. "Article IX, Education: Background Study," 16–19.

71. George, *Progress and Poverty*. In Article XVII, section 2 of the *1879 California Constitution*, it is stated that "the holding of large tracts of land, uncultivated and unimproved, by individuals or corporations is against the public interest and should be discouraged." However, it also noted that any future state policies be consistent "with the rights of private property," which was a far cry from George's insistence that such land be heavily taxed and given to the masses.

72. The *1879 California Constitution* passed by a total vote of 77, 520 to 67, 340; Bean, *California*, 203.

73. *1879 California Constitution*, Article IX, section 9.

74. Gregory, legislative counsel of California, to California Senator Henry J. Mello, January 6, 1989, California Postsecondary Education Commission Library; *1879 California Constitution*, Article IX, section 9; *Regents of the University of California v. City of Santa Monica*, 77 Cal. App. 3d 130, 135; *San Francisco Labor Council v. Regents of University of California*, 26 Cal. 3d 785, 788–89; Joint Committee on Legislative Organization, Constitution Revision Commission, "Article IX, Education: Background Study," January 1969, 16–19, University of California, Santa Barbara, Special Collections.

75. Edmund G. Brown, 30 Ops Attorney General 162 (1957).

76. *Debates and Proceedings*, 1086–1130.

77. *Ibid.*

78. Swisher, *Motivation and Political Technique*, 98. One delegate complained that "we [have] left the whole system without a head." *Debates and Proceedings*, 1088, 1102.

79. William T. Reid to the Board of Regents, *Annual Report of the President* 14; Spindt, "The University of California and William T. Reid."

80. Campbell, *Tenth Report*, 30–32.

81. Office of University Relations, *A Brief History of the University of California*, University of California, 1974.

82. Cited in Starr, *Inventing the Dream*, 225; see also Jordan, *The Strength of Being Clean*.

CHAPTER 3

1. A. Mann, "The Progressive Tradition,"163. For more on California Progressives, see Mowry, *The California Progressives*, Olin Jr., *California's Prodigal Sons* and *California Politics*, Lane, "The Lincoln-Roosevelt League," and Starr, *Material Dreams* and *Inventing the Dream*.

2. Gordon, *Employment Expansion*, 6.

3. John Randolph Haynes to Hiram Johnson, December 17, 1916, cited in Sitton, *John Randolph Haynes*.

4. Quoted in Curti and Carstensen, *The University of Wisconsin*, Vol. II, 90.

5. Brubacher and Rudy, *Higher Education in Transition*, 165.

6. Howe, *Wisconsin*, vii; see also McCarthy, *The Wisconsin Idea*, and Carstensen, "The Wisconsin Idea," 181–87.

7. Because seeking office and power through "the old system of machine control would mean the sacrifice of their integrity," explains Bean, "they overthrew the old system." Bean, *California*, 278.

8. For a discussion of the motivations of liberal reformers and faith in social engineering, see J. Jordan, *Machine-Age Ideology*.

9. "Inaugural Address of Governor Hiram W. Johnson" in Hichborn, *Story of the Session*, appendix, i–xvi.

10. Johnson created the California Social Insurance Commission in his first year in office to study the idea of a state-funded comprehensive health insurance program. Despite the opposition of many in the health profession, in 1918 a constitutional amendment for such a program was placed on the ballot but was defeated. See Numbers, *Almost Persuaded*, 14, and Sinai et al., *Health Insurance in the United States*, 69.

11. On school segregation, see Chan, *Asian Americans*, Daniels, *The Politics of Prejudice*, Wollenberg, *All Deliberate Speed*, and Low, *The Unimpressible Race*. See also Bean, *California*, 287–88, and Heizer and Almquist, *The Other Californians*, 181–83.

12. Starr, *Inventing the Dream*, 236–37.

13. Jordan, *The Days of a Man, Vol. I*, 450.

14. See Lupold, "From Physician to Physicist."

15. *Ibid.*

16. Cited in Ferrier, *Ninety Years*, 319.

17. Veysey, *The Emergence of the American University*.

18. Cited in Ferrier, *Ninety Years*, 226.

19. Cubberly, *School Funds and Their Apportionment*.

20. Cubberley, *Changing Conceptions of Education, The Improvement of Rural Schools, Public School Administration*, and *The History of Education*.

21. See Sears and Henderson, *Cubberley of Stanford*; see also Cremin, *Cubberley*.

22. Cubberley, *Public School Administration*, 11.

23. See Cremin, *The Transformation of the School* (Knopf, 1961), Callahan, *Cult of Efficiency*, Perkinson, *The Imperfect Panacea*, Tyack, *Turning Points*, Katz, *Class, Bureaucracy and the Schools*, and Bowles and Gintis, *Schooling in Capitalist America*.

24. Dewey, "An Undemocratic Proposal," 374–77.

25. Dewey, *Democracy and Education*, 301.

26. Cubberley, *Public Education in the United States*, 527–28.

27. *Ibid.*

28. Justin S. Morrill to Andrew White, May 24, 1883, quoted in Brubacher and Rudy, *Higher Education in Transition*, 164.

29. Jordan, *The Days of A Man, Vol. I*, 77.

30. White, "Evolution and Revolution," 4–5.

31. *Ibid.*, 15. Failure to come to grips with the worst catastrophes, explained White, in the economy could forebode a form of societal extinction. Not developing "better methods is to make the American race a vast body of short-lived, nervous dyspeptics, sure to die out and be succeeded by races of tougher fiber." See also Riesman, *Thorstein Veblen*, for an interesting analysis of the viewpoint of Veblen and his contemporary academics regarding social and economic progress in the age of Darwin.

32. Cited in Elliott, *Stanford University*, 20.

33. See Crothers, *Founding of the Leland Stanford Junior University*, and Jordan, "The Educational Ideas of Leland Stanford."

34. *San Francisco Chronicle*, March 29, 1981; see also Elliott, *Stanford University*, 39–49.

35. Jordan, *The Days of a Man, Vol. I*, 354–55.

36. Cited in Elliott, *Stanford University*, 76.

37. Jane Stanford to David Starr Jordan, September 3, 1898, quoted in Jordan, *The Days of a Man, Vol. I*, 691.

38. As noted in Smith, *Pacific Visions*, 133.

39. Jordan, *The Voice of the Scholar*, 39.

40. Swett, *Public Education in California*, 267.

41. Jordan, *The Days of a Man, Vol. I*, 80–81.

42. Jordan, "The College of the West," 33, and "The University and the Common Man," 320–21.

43. See Jordan, *The Religion of a Sensible American*.

44. Jordan, "University Tendencies in America," 143–44; see also Burns, *David Starr Jordan*, 154–158.

45. The steel giant's interest in promoting education resulted in a huge philanthropic program to build libraries in hundreds of communities and to build colleges and university campuses. Libraries were Carnegie's ideal form of perpetuating democracy, as well as social and economic mobility. Later, he established numerous funds to study and support education, including the Carnegie Foundation for the Advancement of Teaching. This offspring of Carnegie's boosterism would come to wield great influence on the development of public education in California.

46. Veysey, *The Emergence of the American University*, 2, notes: "[T]he American university of 1900 was all but unrecognizable in comparison with the college of 1860. Judged by almost any index, the very nature of higher learning in the United States had been transformed."

47. *Utica Observer*, October 4, 1901.

48. Robinson, *The Hearsts*, 263.

49. Cited in Ferrier, *Origin and Development*, 474–78; see also Stadtman, *The Centennial Record*, 47–48.

50. *Ibid.*

51. Ferrier, *Ninety Years*, 320.

52. "Ingratitude to Mrs. Hearst," *San Francisco Argus*, February 15, 1899.

53. Quoted in L. Gordon, *Education and Higher Education*, 58. See also Nerad, *The Academic Kitchen*.

54. *Ibid.*, 8.

55. Elliott, *Stanford University*, 123.

56. Wheeler's publications include *Analogy and the Scope of Its Application in Language*, *Die Organisation des Hoheren Unterrichts in den Vereinigten Staaten von Nordamerika*, *Dionysus and Immortality: The Greek Faith in Immortality as Affected by the Rise of Individualism*, and *Alexander the Great: The Merging of the East and West in Universal History*.

57. Slosson, *The Great American Universities*, 148–49.

58. Bowman, "Reminiscences," 31.

59. Robinson, *The Hearsts*, 300.

60. Cited in Ferrier, *Origin and Development*, 478.

61. Stadtman, *The Centennial Record*, 214.

62. Jones, *Illustrated History*, 138.

63. Cited in Kerr, "Remarks by President Kerr."

64. "Report of the Citizen's Tax Committee to the California Legislature," 845–52; Krueger, "The California Property Tax System," 1–2.

65. Wheeler speech, Charter Day, published in the *University of California Chronicle*, XIII: 2 (1911), 201–6.

66. University of California, Biennial Report of the President: 1910–1912,

Berkeley: University of California, 1912; University of California, Annual Report of the President: 1914–1915, Berkeley: University of California, 1915.

67. *Ibid.*

68. Merritt, *Controller's Report and Financial Statement, 1914–15*. This board was one of many new agencies created in 1911 to reorganize and bring professionalism (and aspects of Taylorism) to California government. It was presumed that the Board of Control would develop a coherent system of supervision over state finances. John Francis Neylan, a reporter for the *San Francisco Bulletin* and a founding member of the Progressive Party, had proposed the idea during the 1911 campaign. Johnson liked it and appointed Neylan the first chairman. Neylan then led the way to developing the first comprehensive budget and inventory of state property. His work with Merritt and his role in the Johnson administration eventually led to Neylan's being named a regent in the late 1920s.

69. Based in part on these detailed budget requests presented in 1912, the university also gained for the first time a state bond for capital construction. The first came in 1914 as a result of a petition drive by alumni, which, based on the Progressive Era advent of the initiative, resulted in a general election victory that gave the Board of Regents $1.8 million for permanent improvements. These improvements included Agriculture Hall, Hilgard Hall, Gilman Hall, and Wheeler Hall. By the 1950s, enrollment-based budgeting would evolve into a direct budget formula to cover teaching expenses that were based on a calculation of full-time equivalent students and their associated costs, thereby creating a relatively predictable method for estimating the university's budget from year to year. It was both a promise for funding by the state (although the rules were, on key occasions, changed) and a necessary element to help the university plan its future.

70. Stadtman, *The University of California*, 211–13.

71. Quoted in Muto, "A Voice from the Wilderness," 222–23.

72. Wickson, *Rural California*, 355.

73. *Ibid.*

74. See Stadtman, *The Centennial Record.*

75. Cited in Elliott, *Stanford University*, 123.

76. Roosevelt, "Charter Day Address," 131–45.

CHAPTER 4

1. See Dunbar, *The Michigan Record*, 239–48.

2. Lange, "The Junior College," *Sierra Educational News* (October 1920), 483–86.

3. Cited in Elliott, *Stanford University*, 522.

4. Harper, speech before the National Education Association in *Journal of Proceedings and Addresses of the Thirty-Ninth Meeting*, Charleston, S.C., July 1900, 80–84.

5. Jordan, "Lines of Distinction."

6. Cited in Elliott, *Stanford University*, 526–27.

7. Jordan quoted in *Yale News*, February 26, 1909.

8. *Ibid.*

9. Jordan to Andrew D. White, August 31, 1903, cited in Elliott, *Stanford University*, 518. See also Herbst, "Liberal Education and the Graduate Schools," 244–58.

10. Cited in Elliott, *Stanford University*, 518.

11. *Ibid.*, 528.

12. Lange, "The Junior College with Special Reference to California, 1–8.

13. Lange, "Introduction to the Study of the Rise and Development of the University Idea," address before the California Union, October 12, 1897, in Lange Collection, UCA.

14. *Ibid.*

15. Lange, "Our Adolescent School System,"2–14.

16. Lange, "The Junior College—What Manner of Child This Be!" 211–16; see also Eells, "What Manner of Child This Be?" 309–28.

17. Lange, "The Junior College," 1915, Lange Collection, UCA.

18. Lange, "The Unification of Our School System," 346.

19. Hichborn in *Story of the Session*, 21, explains the bifurcation of the Democratic Party during California's Progressive Era. "The Democratic minority was important. Ten members of the Senate and twenty-five members of the Assembly had been elected as Democrats. But the Democrats were divided into two groups, the Progressive Democrats constituting one group and the Reactionary Democrats the other. The line of division between these two groups was as sharply drawn as the line between the Progressive majority and the Republican minority. Logically, the Progressive Democrats and the Progressives belong in the same group . . . such is the real division in the 1913 Legislature."

20. *San Francisco Chronicle*, January 17, 1907. Caminetti's accomplishments and regard within political circles is described by his old friend Silas Penry in the *Amador Dispatch*, September 7, 1906. See also Young, "Anthony Caminetti."

21. Young, "Anthony Caminetti."

22. *Sacramento Bee*, January 31, 1907.

23. McLane, "The Junior College," 161–62.

24. Alexis F. Lange, address to the Northern California Teachers Association, Sacramento, October 24, 1907, published in Chamberlain, *The Lange Book*, 37.

25. As cited in Lockard, "Watershed Years," 21. Caminetti was also a leader in attempting to provide funding for high schools in the 1890s and in amending the constitution for that purpose.

26. "The Fresno Junior College," *The California Weekly*, July 15, 1910, 539; Hill, "The Junior College Movement," 254.

27. "Fundamentally, the junior college was intended to embrace two years of work as an extended secondary school," reflected a 1930 study of California's innovative junior college movement. "Subsequent demands for courses suited to students not aspiring to pursue higher cultural and technical studies have caused the broadening of these institutions by introducing various vocational courses of a more or less technical, practical and unprofessional nature." "Report of the California Commission for the Study of Educational Problems," 62. See W. W. Campbell, "The Junior Colleges," 117, and D. O. Levine, *The American College*, 174–75.

28. "It was to supply such a need that at the second session of the legislature in 1851 Senator Thomas J. Green [representative from Eldorado County] . . . introduced a bill providing for a higher institution modeled after the Colegio de Minora (Mining College) of New Mexico," observed Peter Conmy in 1940. Conmy, "The Development of Vocational Education in California," in *Proceedings of the American Vocational Association Meeting*, December 1940, UCA.

29. Snyder, "Report of the Commissioner on Vocational Education, California State Board of Education, Biennial Report, 1916–1918," UCA; Conmy, "The Development of Vocational Education in California."

30. Cited in Cloud, *Education in California*, 130.

31. Bowles and Gintis, *Schooling in Capitalist America*, 199.

32. For discussion of the innovation of the junior college that "had little to do with the democratization of higher education," see Brint and Karabel, *The Diverted Dream*; Zwerling, *Second Best*. For critique of "revisionist" studies on the junior college, see Gallagher, "Revisionist Nonsense" and "Jordan and Lange."

33. See Proctor, *The Junior College*, vi; Lindsay, "California Junior Colleges," 137–42. "The public junior college is entirely a twentieth-century phenomenon," observes Clark in *The Open Door College*, 3. "None existed at the turn of the century; nineteen units that could be considered public junior colleges were in existence by 1915, but their total enrollment did not exceed 600 students. Rapid growth occurred after World War I; there were 178 colleges with 45,000 students by 1930, 261 colleges with 168,000 students in 1940, and 329 schools with more than 450,000 students in 1950."

34. Mowry, *The California Progressives*, 156, 195; Cloud, *Education in California*, 141; Gerth and Grenier in *A History of the California State University and Colleges*, 10, note: "During World War I, the normal schools lost much of their sparse male enrollment; for example, San Diego had no men students in 1918." In "Watershed Years," 30, Lockard notes that in "two years the number of junior college students dropped nearly 30 percent, from 1,561 in 1918–1919 to 1,096 in 1919–1920. Eight new junior college departments had been founded between 1917 and 1919. Two of these survived only a year, a third two years, and six others founded earlier closed their doors as well."

35. Stadtman, *The University of California*, 215–19.

36. Cited in Stadtman, *The University of California*, 216.

37. University of California, "President's Report on the Relations of the Teachers College at Los Angeles to the University of California," 2.

38. Sears and Cubberley, *The Cost of Education in California.*

39. Sears and Cubberley, *The Cost of Education in California*, 17, 116.

40. This theme was a reiteration of his book *The Human Harvest: A Study of the Decay of Races Through the Survival of the Unfit.*

41. Cited in Elliott, *Stanford University*, 530.

42. "Report of the Secretary of the Regents, 1917–18," UCA.

43. See Fitzgibbon, *The Academic Senate*, 23–31.

44. Pettitt, *Twenty-Eight Years in the Life of a University President*, 31.

45. The "faculty revolution" at Berkeley, in which the Board of Regents assigned significant powers to the Academic Senate, came at the time of Barrows' elevation from a professor in the Department of Political Science to the presidency, and it was in large part a reaction to problems presented by Wheeler's administration and the confusing leadership provided by the short-lived Council of Deans.

CHAPTER 5

1. Kerr, "Governance and Functions," 111.

2. Initial local and state efforts to reduce costs included drastic reductions in funding, cutting teacher salaries and moneys for school supplies, reducing or eliminating funding for new construction and building maintenance, and action by Governor Rolph that cut a major part of the state school fund to help balance an ailing state budget.

3. William M. Proctor, quoted in *The Junior College Journal* (April 1936), 12.

4. "Report of the Education Commission"; "Report of the Special Legislative Committee on Education," 71.

5. See Cloud, *Education in California*; Swett, *History of the Public Schools.*

6. Report of the Education Commission; Cloud, *Education in California*, 264.

7. See the *Report of the Special Legislative Committee on Education.*

8. California Legislature, *Report of the Special Legislative Committee on Education*, 20.

9. Sproul, inaugural address as president of the University of California, October 22, 1930, Berkeley, California, UCA.

10. Sproul, "Address to the California Alumni Association" March 23, 1934, Sproul Papers, UCA.

11. Quoted in Stadtman, *The University of California*, 269.

12. *Los Angeles Examiner*, September 27, 1938; *Riverside Press*, February 27, 1933; "One Great University," *Daily Bruin*, January 31, 1933.

13. Sproul to the Board of Regents Committee on Educational Policy, August 20, 1935, UCA; see also J. A. Douglass, "A Brief on the Historical Development."

14. Stadtman, *The University of California*, 258.

15. Pettitt, *Twenty-Eight Years*, 29.

16. California Senate, Senate bill 48, 1929. "An act to provide for the creation of a commission for the study of the problem of public education in California and making an appropriation therefore."

17. In response to the commission's criticism, Sproul tried to dispel the perception that the university was limiting enrollment. Sproul and Vice President Deutsch wrote: "May this be taken to correct a false impression, which may be rather widespread. The admission standards of the University of California have at no time been established for the purpose of limiting enrollments." The university, they insisted, "is a genuinely democratic institution, and welcomes to its privileges all who are properly qualified on the basis of scholarship, without regard to wealth, prominence, social standing, or athletic ability." Sproul and Deutsch to the California Commission for the Study of Educational Problems, November 6, 1930, CSA.

18. Sinclair, *The Goose-Step*.

19. *Ibid.*, 127–28. Sinclair also explained that "William H. Crocker, whose father looted the Southern Pacific railroads . . . is a 'social leader,' and active head of the Republican political machine, which runs the government and is run by the finance of the state. . . . Associated with Mr. Crocker in the running of the University of California is Mortimer Fleishacker, the biggest banker in San Francisco, president of the Anglo-California Trust Company, and first vice-president of the Anglo and London National Bank. . . . Mr. Fleishacker is also vice-president of the Alaska Canning Company, whose workers are hired by a Chinese contractor for $34 a month and board—which consists of two meals a day of scurvy diet, and only one cup of water a day."

20. Pettitt, *Twenty-Eight Years*, 29–30.

21. Sproul, inaugural address.

22. Stadtman, *The University of California*, 260.

23. Sproul, "Certain Aspects," 276–77; Lockard, "Watershed Years," 54–56.

24. Quoted in Stadtman, *The University of California*, 262.

25. *Ibid.*, 264.

26. A. J. Cloud, "A Summarized History of the California Junior College Federation."

27. As cited in Stadtman, *The University of California*, 261.

28. Kersey, "A Review of Public Education," 5.

29. Deutsch, "A Point of View," 117–21.

30. *Ibid.*. See also Coons, *Crises*, 26–27; Robert Sproul to Earl Warren, May 13, 1943, UCA.

31. California Senate, "Senate Bill 895," Chapter 493, passed by the legislature and approved by the governor on May 29, 1931.

32. Suzzallo Report, 13–14; Deutsch, "A Point of View," 121, lists the members. "The chairman was Samuel P. Capen, chancellor of the University of Buffalo, who for five years (1914–19) was the specialist in higher education for the United States Bureau of Education; another member was George F. Zook, now president of the municipal University of Akron and who was also for five years (1920–25) specialist in higher education for the United States Bureau of Education. Teachers colleges were represented by James E. Russell, Dean Emeritus of Teachers College, Columbia University, New York, and Orval R. Letham, president of Iowa State Teachers College. The only state university official in the group was President Lotus D. Coffman of the University of Minnesota. The remaining two were Dean Charles H. Judd of the School of Education in the University of Chicago, and Professor Albert B. Meredith, Professor of Education and Head of the Department of Administration in the School of Education of New York University."

33. Sproul, address given at the Annual Charter Day Dinner, March 23, 1932, quoted in Pettitt, *Twenty-Eight Years*, 201–3.

34. Carnegie Foundation, *State Higher Education in California*, 15 (Suzzallo Report).

35. *Ibid.*

36. Kelly and McNeely, *The State and Higher Education*, VIII–IX.

37. Suzzallo Report, 29.

38. *Ibid.*, 21–23.

39. *Ibid.*, 42, 47.

40. Board of Regents, Minutes, September 13, 1932, UCA; Cloud, *Education in California*, 176.

41. Suzzallo Report, 65.

42. Jensen, "An Analysis," 58–67.

43. *Ibid.*; Thomas, "The Carnegie Foundation Report," 122–30; Morgan, "An Appraisal," 131–38.

44. University of California, Academic Senate Committee on Educational Policy, "Report on Four Year Teachers Colleges," April 21, 1933, UCA.

45. Board of Regents, Minutes, September 13, 1932, UCA; Academic Senate Committee on Educational Policy, "Report on Four Year Teachers Colleges," April 21, 1933, UCA.

46. As quoted in Pettitt, *Twenty-Eight Years*, 45; Board of Regents, Minutes, September 13, 1932, UCA.

47. *University of California Clip Sheet*, September 20, 1932, UCA.

48. Deutsch, "A Point of View," 121.

49. "Education Code, 1933," Article 8, Section 20201.

50. Smelser, "Growth, Structural Change, and Conflict," 116.

51. Pettitt, *Twenty-Eight Years*, 44.

52. Suzzallo Report, 45. It was noted in the report: "This development has been without sanction from the traditional intent of teachers colleges, from the long established subdivision of function between the university and the State teachers colleges, from the university regents who have controlled senior college work, or from the Legislature of the State." Further, it was noted: "The other four teachers colleges (Arcata, Chico, San Francisco, Santa Barbara) have not enrolled many pre-secondary students in their divisions. Nevertheless, all four of these have been given permission by the State Board of Education to add various fields of specialization, academic training, which offer the student opportunity to concentrate on some academic field under the legal guise of taking at the teachers college four years of work preliminary to securing a secondary credential through a fifth year at the university."

53. Burkman, "The State Colleges."

54. *Statutes of California of 1935*, Chapter 261, Sections 1–6.

55. Pettitt, *Twenty-Eight Years*, 44; Gerth and Grenier, *A History of the California State University and Colleges*, 13.

56. Regents Committee on Educational Policies and Relations, Minutes, November 2, 1935, UCA.

57. *Ibid.*

58. "The functions of the State Board of Regents for the University of California," stated their report, should "be expanded to include the establishment and the coordination and determination of the scope and activities of the various public educational institutions engaged in educational work above the secondary level." As quoted in Holy and Browne, "Material Presented to the Joint Meeting of the State Board of Education and the Regents of the University of California." See also McPhee, "California State Polytechnic College."

59. Robert G. Sproul to Governor Earl Warren, May 13, 1943, UCA.

60. Storke, *California Editor*, 431–36.

61. Ellison, "Antecedents of the University of California, Santa Barbara"; Sproul to Warren, May 13, 1943, UCA, 170; Board of Regents, Minutes, March 9, 1939, and March 19, 1939, UCA; Robert Kelley, *Transformation*, 7–15.

62. J. Herchel Coffin, State Department of Education survey as cited by Ellison, "Antecedents of the University of California, Santa Barbara," 165.

63. "Report of the State Council of Educational Planning and Coordination to the Legislature of the State of California," March 24, 1941, UCA.

64. Committee of Inquiry, "Recommendations Respecting the Adminis-

tration of Public Education in California," September 7, 1942, UCA. Henceforth cited as the Jaqua Report.

65. Jaqua Report, 10.

66. Deutsch to Sproul, March 22, 1943, UCA; Regents Committee on Educational Policies and Relations, Minutes, March 26, 1943, UCA.

67. Dean McHenry to Clark Kerr, February 19, 1959, UCA; G. P. Adams to Sproul, January 3, 1941, UCA; T. C. Holy, "Summary of the Work of the Liaison Committee of the Regents of the University of California and the State Board of Education, 1945–1960," March, 1961, California State Archives, Sacramento; University of California Academic Senate, "Proposed Reorganization of State Education System," UCA; Stadtman, *University of California*, 342–44.

68. Quoted in the University of California Second All-Faculty Conference, "The Relation of the University and the State," 18–21.

69. Regents Committee on Educational Policies and Relations, Minutes, March 26, 1943, UCA.

70. *Ibid.*

71. Sproul to Warren, May 13, 1943, UCA; State of California, *California Assembly Journal*, 2 (1948), 3345–46. According to Sproul's biographer, George A. Pettitt, "the Regents were not at all certain that additional campuses of the University should be provided while the United States was at war, and enrollments on existing campuses were dropping sharply." Pettitt, *Twenty-Eight Years*, 47.

72. Sproul to Warren, May 13, 1943, UCA.

73. *California Statutes of 1943*, Chapter 1130, section 3, 3073–75.

74. Douglass, "On Becoming an Old Blue," 6–11.

75. Ellison, "Antecedents of the University of California, Santa Barbara."

76. Regents Committee on Educational Policies and Relations, Minutes, September 23, 1943, UCA; Stadtman, *University of California*, 345.

77. Board of Regents, Minutes, October 22, 1943, UCA; Board of Regents, Minutes, August 25, 1944, UCA.

78. The CTA had helped to draft the proposition and lobbied vigorously for its passage. It was passed November 5, 1946. Proposition 3 amended Article IX, section 6, to read: "No school or college or any other part of the Public School System shall be, directly or indirectly, transferred from the Public School System or placed under the jurisdiction of any authority other than one included within the Public School System." See Cloud, *Education in California*, 228–29, for a description of the major elements of the proposition.

CHAPTER 6

1. Warren, "We Have Sniffed Our Destiny," 432.

2. See Nash, *The American West Transformed*, 17–19. "If before 1941

the federal government had been a junior partner with private business in financing new enterprises in the West," notes Nash, "during World War II it became a dominate influence."

3. Warren, speech before the California State Reconstruction and Reemployment Commission, March 22, 1944, cited in *Postwar California*, 2.

4. California State Chamber of Commerce, "Economic Survey of California and its Counties," 823.

5. See Arnold et al., *The California Economy*, 247–60; Southern California Associates of the Committee for Economic Development, National Defense and Southern California, 1961–1970, Los Angeles, December 1961.

6. Mervyn Rathborne (secretary of the Congress of Industrial Organizations in California) to Governor Earl Warren, October 20, 1944, Warren Papers, Reconstruction and Reemployment Commission Files, California State Archives. Henceforth known as the Warren Papers.

7. M. I. Gershenson, Division of Labor Statistics and Law Enforcement, State Department of Industrial Relations, presentation to the Citizens Tax Committee, San Francisco, February 5, 1943.

8. The National Resources Planning Board published a series of pamphlets intended to address postwar planning: "After Defense—What?" (August 1941), "After the War—Full Employment" (January 1942), "Better Cities" (April 1942), "Post-War Planning" (September 1942), and "Demobilization and Readjustment" (June 1943). Council of State Governments, *Wartime and Postwar Problems*.

9. Warren, speech before the first meeting of the California State Reconstruction and Re-Employment Commission, March 22, 1944, *Postwar California*, 2.

10. *Ibid.*

11. *Sacramento Bee*, January 28, 1946, 1; Office of the Director of Planning and Research, *California Reports on Planning* (Sacramento, February 1948).

12. "Report of the Citizen's Tax Committee to the California Legislature," *California Assembly Journal* (March 15, 1943), 851.

13. Earl Warren, 1943 Inaugural Address, 11–12.

14. Julian McPhee to the California Assembly Interim Committee on Postwar Rehabilitation, October 18–19, 1944, Berkeley.

15. See also Sexson, "Postwar Problems of Education," 163–66; Lounsbury, "Postwar Planning for the Junior Colleges," 188–90; Lounsbury, "Some Problems in Postwar Planning," 360–66; "Preliminary Report of the Armed Forces Committee on Postwar Educational Opportunities for Service Personnel," Washington, D.C., October 27, 1943, submittal to Congress.

16. *Ibid.*

17. Warren, *Memoirs*, 226.

18. "Crowded California," *Newsweek*, October 11, 1948, 36.

19. Warren, *Memoirs*, 215–17; Pettitt, *Twenty-Eight Years*, 34.

20. "House Resolution No. 186," *California Assembly Journal* (May 15, 1941), 3109.

21. "Report of the Subcommittee on Postwar Planning," *California Assembly Journal* (May 3, 1943), 3162; see also "House Resolution No. 78, pursuant to HR 186," January 30, 1943; Charles W. Weber, *California Assembly Journal* (May 3, 1943), 3167.

22. "Report of the Committee on Legislative Organization: The Procedure of Planning in State Government," *California Assembly Journal* (May 3, 1943), 3167–72.

23. *Ibid.*, 3169. Despite earlier legislation, the findings of the report explained that there "is no organized procedure in government to provide for both land use planning and economic planning." To effectively shape the postwar period, California needed new legislation and a more formal structure for ensuring planning by state entities such as the State Board of Education and the University of California. The committee noted that if California was to truly "enter the field of economic planning, the legislative and executive branches of government must have available correlated research material pertinent to the problems which confront government."

24. *Ibid.*, 3171.

25. *Laws Relating to the State Reconstruction and Reemployment Commission*; Warren, speech before the first meeting of the California State Reconstruction and Re-employment Commission, March 22, 1944, *Postwar California*, 2.

26. *Sacramento Bee*, January 28, 1946, 1; Office of the Director of Planning and Research, *California Reports on Planning*; Tompkins, "Recent Trends in State Planning and Development," 7.

27. Using moneys allocated by the legislature, Dr. Simpson conducted the "Study of a Method of Equalization of the Burden of Supporting the State's Program of Education," and Dr. Hanna completed the "Study of the Supply and Demand for Teachers in California." Both received the help of Superintendent Odell and faculty and administrators at the University of California, Stanford, and the University of Southern California. In turn, Strayer presented his recommendations in *The Administration, Organization and Financial Support of the Public School System, State of California*, which was then incorporated into the *Report of the Citizens Advisory Committee on Readjustment Education* to the Reconstruction and Reemployment Commission, dated January 12, 1945, and dubbed the Strayer Equity Report.

28. Strayer Equity Report, 2–3.

29. "The same principles of equalization that apply in the field of state aid for the educational program are equally valid in the field of capital outlay," noted the State Reconstruction and Re-employment Commission. "In the State's post-

war building program, schools should have a high priority" and should take into account the need and ability of local districts to pay. As explained by a State Department of Education study: "The plants in rural schools and those in relatively poor districts are the ones most in need of replacement, modernization and enlargement. But under present conditions they are the districts doing the least planning for needed construction." Charles Bursch, "Memoranda from the State Department of Education Concerning State Aid for Schoolhousing in Rural Areas and in Other School Districts with Low Financial Ability," State Department of Education, December 18, 1944.

30. The report also suggested that secondary schools and junior colleges serve a similar function to that of the Conservation Corps camps and the Youth Administration of the New Deal, which was to provide "a program of work experience. . . . Every secondary school program in the State of California should include productive work. This will require cooperation with industry, with agriculture, with forestry, and with business and commerce." Strayer Report, 5–6.

31. See Falk, *The Development*, 107–41.

32. "Registration Data for California Institutions of Collegiate Grade, 1940, 1941, 1942 and 1943," *California Schools* 15:5 (May 1944), 115–26.

33. Sexson, "Postwar Problems of Education," 163–66; Robert Gordon Sproul to Deans E. T. Grether, Gordon S. Watkins, and C. B. Hutchison, 1943, cited in Pettitt, *Twenty-Eight Years*, 77.

34. Eells, "The Junior College in the Postwar Period," 52.

35. State Reconstruction and Reemployment Commission, "Postwar Objectives of Public Education in California," a report of the Project Committee on Postwar Objectives of Public Education, chaired by Gilbert H. Jertberg (State Board of Education), to the Citizens Advisory Committee on Readjustment Education, February 1945.

36. William Blair, long-time chair of the State Board of Education, noted this within the minutes of the Joint Meeting, March 14, 1959, Berkeley.

37. Joint Staff for the Committee and the Technical Advisory Committee, "The Origin and Functions of the Liaison Committee of the State Board of Education and the Regents of the University of California," August 1957, Liaison Committee Minutes and Reports, California State Archives, Sacramento (henceforth CSA).

38. *Ibid.* As noted in the Joint Staff Report, the creation of the Liaison Committee would allow for discussion between the two boards "without intervention by a third organization such as a committee or a commission created by the legislature."

39. Board of Regents, Minutes, January 19, 1945; Pettitt, *Twenty-Eight Years*, 48.

40. Not until late 1947 were all the new associate superintendents ap-

pointed under legislation passed in 1946. Five appointments were made as part of the reorganization scheme: Aubrey Douglass was appointed associate superintendent of the Division of State Colleges and Teacher Education; Ralph R. Fields became associate superintendent of the Division of Instruction; Frank M. Wright became associate superintendent of the Division of Public School Administration; George E. Hogan become deputy superintendent of the Division of Departmental Administration; and Herbert R. Stolz, M.D., was appointed deputy superintendent of the Division of Special Schools and Services. Simpson, "Reorganization of the California State Department of Education," 1946, CSA.

41. Governor Earl Warren, Address to the Joint Convention of the California Legislature, January 7, 1946.

42. Governor Earl Warren, Address to the Joint Convention of the California Legislature, February 4, 1946.

43. Monroe E. Deutsch, Aubrey A. Douglass, and George D. Strayer, "A Report of a Survey of the Needs of California in Higher Education," report to the Liaison Committee of the Board of Regents and the State Board of Education, March 1, 1948, 2.

44. "Report of the Regents of the University of California and the State Board of the Education and Recommendations Made Pursuant to Senate Concurrent Resolution No. 12 of the First Extraordinary Session of the Fifty-Sixth Legislature," *California Assembly Journal* (January 28, 1947), 794–96. Other members of the Survey Committee included university Deans Frank N. Freeman (one of the attendees at the meeting at Sproul's home that helped to create the Liaison Committee) and Edwin A. Lee. Representing the Department of Education were Frank B. Lindsay and Alfred E. Lentz.

45. The final report of the Douglass subcommittee was "Emergency Needs of California for Higher Education: A Report of the Subcommittee Appointed by the Liaison Committee," *California Assembly Journal* (May 15, 1947), 3352–79.

46. *Ibid.*, 3366–67, 3371; see also Lockard, "Watershed Years," 130.

47. "Report of the Regents of the University of California and the State Board of Education and Recommendations Made Pursuant to Senate Concurrent Resolution No. 12 of the First Extraordinary Session of the Fifty-Sixth Legislature," January 27, 1947. A draft charge for the study was also offered by the Douglass subcommittee, noting that the proposed survey "shall analyze the present and future needs." To do this, the draft requested $50,000 to support the study.

48. "The Relation of the University to the State," 10, 62.

49. "Assembly bill 2273: "An act to provide for a comprehensive survey of the system of publicly supported higher education in California, including the junior colleges, the state colleges and the university of California and making an appropriation therefore, declaring the urgency thereof, to take effect immediately," passed April 12, 1947, Statutes of 1947, chapter 1349. Lawmakers also put

in provisions to accelerate the deadline of the larger survey and to have two members of both the assembly and the senate "meet and advise with the person or persons under whose immediate supervision the survey is conducted."

50. *California Senate Journal* (February 4, 1947), 786–87; "Survey of Higher Education," 282.

51. Liaison Committee Minutes and Reports, June 10, 1947, CSA.

52. *Ibid.*

53. Washington State Survey of Education Institutions, "Public Education in Washington: A Report of a Survey of Public Education in the State of Washington," directed by George Strayer, submitted to Governor Wallgren, September 5, 1946. Shortly after the 1947 California study, Strayer went on to conduct a review of Georgia's university system in 1949 and Iowa's higher education system in 1950.

54. Deutsch, Douglass, and Strayer, *Survey of the Needs of California in Higher Education.* According to Kent Halstead in a 1974 report to the Department of Health, Education, and Welfare, the Strayer Report was the first state study that could truly be classified as a master plan. "The national attention received by this comprehensive report did much to dramatize the obsolescence of the state survey." Halstead, *Statewide Planning in Higher Education,* 10.

55. Liaison Committee Minutes and Reports, February 16, 1948, CSA.

56. *Ibid.* Summaries of the Strayer Report were also presented in various publications, including Strayer, "California's Needs in Higher Education," and A. A. Douglass, "Report on the Survey of the Needs of California in Higher Education."

57. Deutsch, Douglass, and Strayer, "Survey of the Needs of California in Higher Education," 7–8.

58. *Ibid.*, 26. The state colleges should continue to develop "a wide variety of curricula" to meet regional needs, including occupational or professional training that "lies between the level that can be supplied by the two-year training of the junior colleges and the professional schools of the University." The report also noted that there should be official recognition of the state colleges as regional institutions. "Whatever the legal and administrative ethics of the situation," noted the Survey Committee, "the fact remains that the state colleges have developed into institutions responsive to the educational problems and demands of the areas they serve. Although the student body of a state college will contain students from outside the local area, and although training will be offered which has general as well as local appeal, a state college is primarily concerned with the area or region it serves."

59. Statutes of California, chapter 367, sections 20301 and 20429 of the Education Code. Assembly Bill 1530 was sponsored by Assemblywoman Kathryn T. Niehouse and Assemblymen Frank Luckel and Howard K. Cramer—all Republicans from San Diego.

60. The specific language for a proposal of a master's degree "had been withdrawn at the request of the University," complained an angry Malcolm Love, president of San Diego State College, at the January 24, 1947, meeting of the Liaison Committee. "Laws of 1946 and 1947 Relating to the California Public School System," *Bulletin of the California State Department of Education* 16 (November 1947).

61. Deutsch, Douglass, and Strayer, "Survey of the Needs of California in Higher Education," 48–49.

62. *Ibid.*, 29.

63. *Ibid.*, 35–36. "Anyone acquainted with the capabilities of high school graduates is aware of the fact that those lowest in ability and scholarship are incapable of doing college work of good quality," explained the report.

64. *Ibid.*, 39–40.

65. *Ibid.*, 38–40.

66. National Resources Planning Board, *National Resources Development Report, Part 1*, 69–70. Not until the 1930s, and as part of the New Deal relief effort, was federal aid extended to individual students under the National Youth Administration. Between 1935 and 1945, scholarships were provided for students to attend either public or private institutions. Under this program, various studies showed unequal and varied opportunities to attend institutions of higher education among the states.

67. Brubacher and Rudy, *Higher Education in Transition*, 236.

68. National Policies Commission, *Education for ALL American Youth*, 246.

69. The report of the United States President's Commission on Higher Education, issued in six volumes, was entitled *Higher Education for American Democracy*.

70. Commission on Higher Education, "Higher Education for American Democracy, Vol. I," 56–61.

71. Deutsch, Douglass, and Strayer, "Survey of the Needs of California in Higher Education," 58–63, 78–92.

72. *Ibid.*, 78, 80–92. When compared to the other two public segments, expanding the enrollment capacity of the university was recognized as the most expensive. As part of the Survey Committee's attempt to assess projected state costs for expansion, for the first time a unit cost for each student was calculated using a simple formula that divided total operating costs of a segment by the number of full-time equivalent students. The unit cost of one student enrolled at the university for a full year was $666, as compared to $361 at the state colleges and $278 at the junior colleges. University growth, it was explained, should include a shift in its instructional program, with greater focus on upper-division graduate and professional training. Higher standards for freshmen admission would reduce the flow of lower-division students into the university and allow expanding junior and state colleges to absorb the vast enrollment growth.

73. *Ibid.*, 112, 115, 118–119. For this proposed voluntary coordinating system between the Board of Educaton and the State Board of Education to work, it would require both state "funds and authority to secure professional and technical staff necessary to carry forward the inquiries" and expansion of staff within the Department of Education for administration and control of the state colleges. State support for the activities of the Liaison Committee should be at least $50,000 annually. Under the provisions of the 1945 Strayer Equity Report, the Department of Education had created and appointed a new associate superintendent, Aubrey Douglass. However, this reorganization of the Department of Education was not sufficient in itself to ensure these changes. Additional staff and financial support were required to manage and coordinate activities of the different state colleges. "It is obvious that efficiency in the utilization of the moneys made available to these institutions requires competent thinking and most careful planning," noted the 1948 Strayer Report. "The current programs of the several state colleges suggest that there has been a lack of proper coordination among the several institutions and inadequate planning from the state standpoint." The system needed additional support in directing finance and administration, further curricular development, teacher's credentials requirements, and more support staff.

74. Martinez, "700 Join in UCR's Second Founder's Day Celebration."

75. *California Statistical Abstract, 1961*, 61.

76. *Ibid.*

77. *1960 Statistical Abstract of the United States*, 205.

78. *California Statistical Abstract, 1961*, 157–58, 168.

79. *Ibid.*

80. Statistics from annual enrollment reports in *California Schools*, 1942–1950.

81. *California Statistical Abstract, 1961*, 157–58, 168.

82. Pomeroy, *The Pacific Slope*, 299.

CHAPTER 7

1. Glenny, "State Systems," 86.

2. Wolfle, *America's Resources of Specialized Talent*; see also Fine, "Education in Review," *New York Times*, October 10, 1954.

3. Lederle, "The State and Higher Education," 327.

4. Hofstadter and Metzger, *Academic Freedom*, x.

5. Chambers, *Freedom and Repression in Higher Education*, 10, 20; see also Chambers, *The Campus and the People*.

6. Committee on Government and Higher Education, *The Efficiency of Freedom*.

7. California Legislature, "Building Needs for State Colleges and Schools: Fifteenth Report of the Senate Investigating Committee on Education," 1957.

8. *Ibid.*

9. *Saturday Evening Post*, April 14, 1956.

10. Interim Committee on Education, *Report of the Subcommittee on School District Tax and Bonded Indebtedness*, March 1957; see also California Department of Finance, "Digest of the California State Budget for the Fiscal Year July 1, 1954 to June 30, 1955," 9.

11. Semans and Holy, *Report of the Joint Staff on the Proposal for a Four-Year State College in the Modesto Area*.

12. A. Alan Post, interview by author, Sacramento, April 1989.

13. For discussion of this phenomenon, see Coons, *Crises*, 5.

14. California Legislature, "Joint Budget Message by Governor Earl Warren: 1953–54 Budget," *California Assembly Journal* (January 12, 1953), 181–88.

15. Post, "Extent of Junior College Courses Above the 14th Grade," 411–13; Liaison Committee, Minutes, February 11, 1953, CSA.

16. Paraphrased by Hubert Semans in an interview with author, May 10, 1989, Los Altos Hills, California. Semans was a member of the Liaison Committee's Joint Staff for the State Department of Education and was a coauthor of the Restudy Report.

17. *Ibid.* According to Hubert Semans, a member of the Liaison Committee's Joint Staff at the time, Assemblyman Bower's question reflected a general desire by legislators "to provide more information about the budget . . . they were really interested in the long-term problem of costs."

18. *Ibid.*

19. The subsequent California oath controversy generated significant national publicity and has received extensive study by a host of historians, most importantly, David P. Gardner, *The California Oath Controversy*; see also Russell H. Fitzgibbon, *The Academic Senate of the University of California*, and Verne Stadtman, *The University of California: 1868–1968*.

20. Bean, *California*, 394.

21. Cited in Stadtman, *University of California*, 320.

22. Board of Regents, Minutes, January 1, 1946, UCA.

23. Ellis et al., "Attitudes and Reactions of the Public Toward the University," *The Relation of the University*, 46.

24. *Ibid.*; Mowat et al., "Obligation of the University to the Nation and the World," *The Relation of the University*, 64–65.

25. California Legislature, "Report of the Joint Fact-Finding Committee to the Fifty-Seventh California Legislature," 95; California Legislature, "Fourth Report of the Senate Fact-Finding Committee on Un-American Activities."

26. Subcommittee No. 6, "Attitudes and Reactions of the Public Toward the University" in "The Relation of the University and the State," 46.

27. Gardner, *California Oath Controversy*, 73–105, provides a detailed account of these events.

28. *San Francisco Chronicle*, February 25, 1950.

29. Board of Regents, Minutes, March 31, 1950, UCA; White, *Earl Warren, A Public Life*, 114–26.

30. Gardner, *California Oath Controversy*, 169.

31. *Ibid.*, 245.

32. Fitzgibbon, *The Academic Senate*, 41–42.

33. As explained by Bean, led by Tolman, the nonsigners brought "a suit against the board as represented by its secretary and treasurer, Robert M. Underhill, and in 1951 a state district court of appeals ruled that the special oath violated the state constitutional provision protecting the freedom of the university against political influences." The state supreme court disagreed with this interpretation in its final ruling in *Tolman v. Underhill* in 1952. But the supreme court also invalidated the oath and ordered the professors reinstated. See Bean, *California*, 396.

34. Clark Kerr, interview by Amelia Fry, 1969, Regional Oral History Office, Bancroft Library, Berkeley.

35. *Ibid.*

36. California Legislature, "Tenth Report of the Senate Fact-Finding Committee on Un-American Activities."

37. *Ibid.*; California Legislature, "Ninth Report of the Senate Fact-Finding Committee on Un-American Activities," 155, "Seventeenth Report of the Senate Investigating Committee on Education: Report of Activities in 1958," 87, "Report of the Subcommittee on Constitutional Rights of the Committee on Judiciary Pertaining to Loyalty Oaths."

38. Dilworth sponsored the School Building Aid Program in 1949 (chapter 1389) providing $250 million, an unprecedented amount at that time. According to Dilworth's own committee report in 1957, over an eight-year period the bond program had provided a quarter of all classrooms built in the state, which amounted to a total of 16,836, with the intent to "provide schools who could not finance them with their own bonding resources." California Legislature, "Building Needs for State Colleges and Public Schools," "Fifteenth Report of the Senate Investigating Committee on Education."

39. Robert E. McKay (former California Teachers Association lobbyist), interview by James H. Rowland, Regional Oral History Office, Bancroft Library, Berkeley, 1979.

40. Liaison Committee, Minutes, February 27, 1953, CSA.

41. Liaison Committee, "Proposal for a Survey on Curricula and Costs of Public Higher Education in California," submitted to the California Legislature, Subcommittee on Education, Assembly Ways and Means Committee, March 9, 1953, Liaison Committee Minutes and Reports, CSA.

42. *Ibid.*; *A Restudy of the Needs for California in Higher Education*, pre-

pared for the Liaison Committee of the Regents of the University of California and the California State Board of Education, 2, issued Feb. 7, 1955 (Restudy Report); Liaison Committee Minutes and Reports, CSA.

43. Liaison Committee Minutes and Reports, April 22, 1954, Los Angeles, CSA.

44. Semans interview, May 1989; Restudy Report, 3–5.

45. Strayer Report, 19–20, 107.

46. Restudy Report, 39.

47. *Ibid.*, 47.

48. *Ibid.*, 39–40, 47–50.

49. Allen, "The New York State System," 110–16.

50. Restudy Report, 67–68.

51. *Ibid.*, 65, 69–70.

52. *Ibid.*, 16.

53. Liaison Committee Minutes and Reports, December 18, 1954, Los Angeles, CSA.

54. At a later meeting of the Liaison Committee, university Vice President Harry R. Wellman protested the report's encouragement of state college research in professional fields such as public administration. In a Liaison Committee meeting, McConnell retorted that by law the "state colleges are permitted to make studies related to work of civic, industrial, and business agencies and enterprises in their communities and such service involves research." The issue of both professional training and research within the state colleges remained a touchy issue, with Sproul reluctant to give any ground. As a prelude to the conciliatory position he would take in future negotiations, at that same meeting, Kerr noted that it was "inevitable that an increasing amount of research will be done by the state colleges, and this is probably desirable because there is a great deal of research that can be done in the field." Liaison Committee Minutes and Reports, February 17, 1955, Los Angeles, CSA.

55. McConnell, *Restudy: Summary Analysis*, April 27, 1956, CSA, Liaison File. To reinforce these concerns, several national reports were cited noting the difficulty of cost comparisons. A 1935 report contended that: "A source of great dissatisfaction with cost studies in the past has been the frequent attempts to compare the costs of one institution with those of another. . . . Costs computed for a small liberal-arts college, in which the instruction of students is practically the only function of the institution, should not be compared indiscriminately with those computed for a university in which the instruction of students supplemented to a great extent by such functions as research, extension, and other service activities." National Committee on Standard Reports, *Financial Reports for Colleges and Universities*, 177.

The categories of expenses used by the restudy staff were a modification to those developed by the National Committee on the Preparation of a Manual on College and University Administration found in *College and University Business Administration*, 82.

56. For instance, within the University of California, the expense per student credit hours (SCH) varied from only $15.03 at Hastings to $201.96 at the University of California medical school in San Francisco. There were other important disparities: "The unit expense at Santa Barbara, which in 1953–54 was primarily an undergraduate campus, with fewer specialized fields of instruction than the two large campuses, was $46.12." At Los Angeles it was $51.97, at Berkeley $64.84, and at Davis, "reflecting the heavy research emphasis in agricultural fields," it was a total of $181.82. Restudy Report, 425.

57. Liaison Committee Minutes and Reports, December 18, 1954, Los Angeles, CSA.

58. *Ibid.*

59. *Ibid.*

60. *Ibid.*

61. A. Alan Post, interview, May 1990.

62. Hubert Semans, interview, May 1989; Liaison Committee Minutes and Reports, December 18, 1954, Los Angeles, CSA.

63. Hubert Semans, interview, May 1989.

64. Roy E. Simpson and Robert G. Sproul to L. H. Lincoln, speaker of the assembly, and Harold J. Powers, president of the senate, February 7, 1955, in Restudy Report.

65. T. C. Holy, "Summary of the Work of the Liaison Committee of the Regents of the University of California and the State Board of Education, 1945–1960," March 1961, CSA, Liaison Files.

CHAPTER 8

1. Liaison Committee Minutes and Reports, January 6, 1956, Los Angeles, CSA. "From the standpoint of certain influential legislators," lamented one Liaison Committee member, the report's plan for enrollment expansion "was not popular."

2. Lyman Glenny, interview, June 1, 1989.

3. Hubert Semans, interview, May 1989.

4. California Legislature, Assembly bills 24 and 881, *Assembly Bills, Original and Amended*,1955; California Legislature, Senate Bill 1039, *Senate Bills, Original and Amended*, 1955.

5. *Ibid.*; California Legislature, Senate Bill 1039; Lockard, "Watershed Years," 209.

6. *Ibid.*; California Legislature, Senate Bill 1981.

7. *Ibid.*

8. Liaison Committee Minutes and Reports, January 6, 1956, Los Angeles, CSA.

9. Liaison Committee Minutes and Reports, January 6, 1956, Los Angeles, CSA.

10. *Ibid.*

11. Liaison Committee Minutes and Reports, January 6, 1956, Los Angeles, CSA; Additional Centers Report, 3. Approval for a new campus needed to be retained by the Liaison Committee and the respective governing boards. The subsequent joint resolution of the state board and the regents stipulated that the new report would provide "a priority list for use of the Liaison Committee and the two boards . . . [in] the order in which new institutions may be needed in the several areas of the state. . . . The purpose of such a list is to have pertinent data available as a basis for reaction of the two boards to specific legislative proposals in the future."

12. Semans and Holy, *A Study of the Need for Additional Centers of Public Higher Education in California*, 2–3 (Additional Centers Report).

13. Superintendent Simpson and President Sproul to L. H. Lincoln and Harold J. Powers, December 17, 1956, as cited in Restudy Report, vi–vii.

14. Additional Centers Report, 109–10; California State Board of Education, Minutes, January 2 and 3rd, 1957, Los Angeles, CSA.

15. Additional Centers Report, 1, 3–4.

16. *Ibid.*, 41–42.

17. *Ibid.*, 34.

18. *Ibid.*, 49.

19. *Ibid.*, 94.

20. See Liaison Committee Minutes and Reports, May 15, 1956, San Francisco, CSA.

21. Additional Centers Report, 84–87.

22. *Ibid.*

23. California Senate bill 2680 proposed new campuses; Senate resolution 138, also sponsored by Dilworth, created the Senate Investigating Committee on Education.

24. Stadtman, *University of California*, 387; Liaison Committee Minutes and Reports, February 9, 1957, Los Angeles, CSA.

25. Superintendent Roy E. Simpson, speech before the California Junior College Association, "The Need for State College–Junior College Cooperation," October 28, 1959, CSUA.

26. Allen (Assembly concurrent resolution 111) and Far (senate resolution 120) asked the Board of Regents to study the feasibility of a University of California campus in Santa Clara valley and on the Monterey peninsula, respectively. Crown (assembly concurrent resolution 191), House (house resolution 244), and Kilpatrick (house resolution 283) asked the Department of Education

to investigate the establishment of the new state college in Alameda on a temporary basis on a U.S. Maritime Station, and to study the need for a new state college in the Imperial Valley and in Los Angeles County, respectively.

27. Liaison Committee Minutes and Reports, October 14, 1959, CSA.

28. Post, interview, May 1989; Council of State College Presidents, Minutes, February 10–11, 1958, CSUA; Gilbert G. Lentz, assistant legislative analyst, to J. Burton Vasche, chief of the Division of State Colleges and Teacher Education, August 24, 1958, CSUA.

29. See *A Master Plan for Higher Education in California, 1960–1975*, 68–70.

30. California State Board of Education, Minutes, May 9–10, 1957, CSA. At a joint meeting of the State Board of Education and the state college presidents, Simpson and board Chairman Blair attempted to placate those college presidents who favored a new board. The chair established a subcommittee of two state college presidents and three board members to seek ways to improve the governance of the colleges and possibly to give the presidents more freedom in financial matters.

31. Liaison Committee Minutes and Reports, November 5, 1957, CSA.

32. Arnold et al., *The California Economy*, 347. See also Schechner, "The Cold War and the University of California."

33. Caughey, *California*, 372.

34. Bonner, "Sputniks and the Educational Crisis in America," 177–84.

35. "A Time for Greatness," 105.

36. Salisbury, "The Soviet Educational System," 462–64.

37. DeWitt, *Soviet Professional Manpower*, 3–4. Though DeWitt's study was made before Sputnik, it was highly influential. Other studies and reports included such books as George S. Counts, *The Challenge of Soviet Education*, Division of International Education, U.S. Department of Health, Education, and Welfare, *Education in the USSR*, and Alexander G. Korol, *Soviet Education for Science and Technology*.

38. California Legislature, "Preliminary Progress Report of the Joint Interim Committee on the Public Education System," 1959.

39. Cited in California Legislature, "Report of Activities in 1958: Seventh Report of the Senate Investigation Committee on Education," 1959, 23.

CHAPTER 9

1. "Knight Funds Plea is Solon's Big Problem," *Sacramento Bee*, January 16, 1957; "Knight Favors CTA Proposal to Boost School Aid," *Sacramento Bee*, January 18, 1957. Knight proved a reluctant supporter, giving way to pressure from members in his own party to let his measure die in the legislature. "Knight Denies Commitment to Beer, Cigarette Tax Bill," *Sacramento Bee*, February 19, 1957.

2. Joint Meeting, Minutes, March 14, 1959.

3. *Ibid.*

4. A. Levine, "Clark Kerr: The Masterbuilder at 75," 12–30, 35.

5. A. Levine, "Clark Kerr."

6. Clark Kerr, interview by author, August 7, 1992, and February 11, 1994.

7. *Ibid.*

8. University of California, Office of the President, "Administrative Changes and Developments at the University of California: Progress Report," April 23, 1965, UCA; Office of the President, *University Bulletin,* August 31, 1958, 5.

9. At the University of California Fourteenth Annual All-Faculty Conference, "Autonomy and Centralization in the Statewide University," April 1959 (p. 5), Kerr asked leading senate members to focus on reorganizing the university. An important conclusion of the conference was that Berkeley, UCLA, and the new campuses needed to manage their own affairs within the confines of statewide policy. Kerr agreed to alter the hands-on management style of the regents and the president.

10. Quoted in Joint Staff of the Liaison Committee, "Outline of a Study of the Engineering Agreement Between the Regents of the University of California and the State Board of Education," December 12, 1957, CSUA.

11. Council of State College Presidents, Minutes, May 8, 1957; Liaison Committee, Minutes, November 5, 1957, San Francisco.

12. Holy and Semans, "Faculty Demand and Supply in California Higher Education, 1957–1970," January 1958; Council of State College Presidents, Minutes, January 2–4, 1958.

13. Lyman Glenny, interview, June 1, 1989.

14. "Statement of Proposed Policy on Research in the State Colleges," March 1, 1958, CSUA.

15. *Ibid.*

16. Council of State College Presidents, Minutes, April 8–9, 1958.

17. Dorothy Knoell (former staff member, State Department of Education), interview with author, November 8, 1988.

18. Joint Meeting, Minutes, March 14, 1959, Alumni House, Berkeley, CSA.

19. Dean McHenry to Clark Kerr, March 17, 1959, UCA, McHenry File.

20. Holy, "Some Factors Indicated the Need for Overhaul in the Control of Public Higher Education in California," April 22, 1959, UCA, LCF.

21. See Coons, *Crises,* 21–22.

22. Dean McHenry to Clark Kerr, March 17, 1959, UCA, McHenry File.

23. Liaison Committee, Minutes, December 11, 1958, Berkeley.

24. *Ibid.*

25. Post, interview, May 1990; California Legislature, "Report of the Subcommittee on Higher Education Beyond the Twelfth Grade of the Assembly Interim Committee on Education," March 1959.

26. *Ibid.*

27. Liaison Committee, Minutes, March 3, 1959, Sacramento.

28. Dean McHenry to Clark Kerr, March 9, 1959, UCA, McHenry File, includes notes by Kerr in margins.

29. Keith Sexton, interview with author, May 3, 1989. Clark Kerr, interview with author, February 11, 1994.

30. "Assemblywoman Donahoe Dies at 49—Pneumonia," *San Francisco Chronicle*, April 5, 1960.

31. Sexton, interview, 1989.

32. *Ibid.*

33. The resolution asked for a master plan "for the development, expansion, and integration of the facilities, curriculum, and standards of higher education, in junior colleges, state colleges, the University of California, and other institutions of higher education of the State, to meet the needs of the State during the next ten years and hereafter. . . . That in preparing such a master plan, the Liaison Committee is requested to do all things necessary to make such master plan comprehensive. . . . That the Liaison Committee is requested to report on the subject of this resolution to the Legislature at its 1961 Regular Session." Assembly Concurrent Resolution 88, introduced by Donahoe and Williams in the assembly and cosponsored by Stierns in the state senate on March 4, 1959.

34. Donahoe to Donald McLaughlin, chair of the regents, February 27, 1959, copy provided in Liaison Committee, Minutes, March 3, 1959, Sacramento.

35. Joint Meeting, Minutes, March 14, 1959.

36. *Ibid.*

37. *Ibid.*

38. *Ibid.*

39. *Ibid.*

40. Clark Kerr, interview with author, August 7, 1992. Kerr, interview, February 1994.

41. Joint Meeting, Minutes, March 14, 1959.

42. *Ibid.*

43. *Ibid.*

44. Liaison Committee, Minutes, April 2, 1959, State Board of Education Building, Sacramento.

45. *Ibid.* Blair also suggested that the two boards request from the legislature almost a quarter of a million dollars to complete the Master Plan study. What exactly this dollar figure covered was not clear, for the plan itself was not fully defined. The Joint Staff was already instructed to make a "long-range study of financing in higher education in California." Should this study be folded into

any pending Master Plan study or continued separately? No one at this meeting was quite sure what the proper approach should be.

46. Rowland, interview, 1978. Sexton, interview, 1989. According to Sexton, at this stage the superintendent was brought into the fold "kicking and screaming."

47. Joint Meeting, Minutes, April 15, 1959, Los Angeles, CSA.

48. *Ibid.*

49. Assemblyman Collier, sponsor of a similar bill, also showed reluctance to do the same. Stan E. McCaffrey, public information officer at the University of California, presented to Clark Kerr a *Report on Assembly Education Committee Hearing*, April 29, 1959, UCA, LCF. Clark Kerr to Assemblymen Sheridan N. Hegland and Harold T. Sedgewick, May 22, 1959, UCA, LCF.

CHAPTER 10

1. Conant, *Shaping Policy*, 15, 48.

2. Glenny, *Autonomy of Public Colleges*, 18.

3. Budgetary considerations, noted the editorial, were paramount. There was no room to increase the $232 million budgeted by the Brown administration for higher education. "A Master Plan for Colleges," *Los Angeles Times*, April 24, 1959.

4. Kerr, "The California Master Plan of 1960 for Higher Education: An Ex Ante View," speech delivered at a meeting of the Organization of Economic Cooperation and Development, May 21, 1990, Berkeley, 20–21.

5. They included university Vice President Wellmen, Chancellors Seaborg, Allan, and Freeborn, and state college Presidents Love, Dumke, and Wahlquist. The other three members were junior college Presidents Calvin Flint from Foothill College, Bill Priest at American River Junior College, and Theron L. McCuen from Kern County Junior College. After the April 2 meeting, the new group would be called the "Joint Advisory Committee" and, for the purposes of the up-coming Master Plan study, would include an equal representation from the private colleges and universities. "Constitution of the Technical Advisory Committee to the Joint Staff for the Liaison Committee," January 15, 1959, CSA.

6. Dean E. McHenry, interview with author, March 29, 1989, McHenry Library.

7. Dean McHenry to Clark Kerr, March 17, 1959, UCA, McHenry File.

8. Malcolm Love, "Functions of the Three Segments of Public Higher Education in California," March 26, 1959; Robert S. Johnson to Clark Kerr, "Analysis of President Love's Proposal for Redefinition," March 31, 1959, UCA, LCF.

9. Dean McHenry to Clark Kerr, March 31, 1959.

10. Dean McHenry to Clark Kerr, "How Much was Lost at the JAC Meeting Last Week," March 31, 1959, UCA, McHenry File.

11. Vernon I. Cheadle (chair EPC–Davis) to C. W. Jones (chair EP–northern division of the Academic Senate), April 10, 1959, UCA, LCF.

12. Dean McHenry to Harry Wellman, May 19, 1959, UCA, LCF.

13. *Ibid.*

14. Council of State College Presidents, Minutes, May 6–7, 1959.

15. William S. Briscoe to Chancellor Vern O. Knudsen, May 22, 1959, UCA, LCF.

16. T. C. Holy to Clark Kerr, Harry Wellman, Jim Corley, and Stan McCaffrey, April 27, 1959, UCA, LCF; T. C. Holy, "Some Factors Indicated the Need for Overhaul," April 22, 1959, UCA, LCF.

17. *Ibid.*; see also "It'll Be Tougher to Get Into College," *San Francisco Chronicle*, April 13, 1959; "Coordinating Higher Education," *San Diego Union*, April 15, 1959.

18. Clark Kerr to Harry Wellman (copies to S. B. Freeborn, V. O. Knudsen, and G. T. Seaborg), April 9, 1959; Clark Kerr to Herman Spaeth, June 5, 1959; Joint Advisory Committee, Minutes, July 29, 1959, UCA, JACF.

19. T. C. Holy to Clark Kerr, May 14, 1959. Holy and Browne provided the general proposal for a Master Plan survey team, although they had different ideas on how it should be structured. Browne suggested a fifteen-member commission directed possibly by John W. Gardner, head of the Carnegie Foundation for the Study of Higher Education. Holy argued that there was no time to form such a large group of outsiders, which would be "too unwieldy."

20. Coons, *Crises*, 33–34; Dean McHenry to Clark Kerr, May 27, 1959, UCA, McHenry File. As it turned out, "I had my second [heart attack] in January 1960," explained Coons.

21. *Master Plan*, 21–22; T. C. Holy to Clark Kerr, May 14, 1959; Liaison Committee, Minutes, June 3, 1959; Bill J. Priest of the California Junior College Association and a representative on the JAC, requested the addition of another junior college representative in his June 11, 1959, letter to Roy Simpson (UCA, LCF). Wert was added after R. J. Wig, president of the Association of Independent California Colleges and Universities, requested representation in a letter to Roy Simpson and Clark Kerr, June 25, 1959, UCA, LCF.

22. Browne and Holy, "Plan Recommended to the Liaison Committee for the Master Plan Study Authorized by ACR 88," May 26, 1959, CSA, LCF.

23. *Ibid.*

24. Coons, *Crises*, 42. In addition, while three state senators, four assembly members, A. Alan Post, and T. H. Mugford from the Department of Finance were all invited to attend subsequent Liaison Committee meetings, it was thought wise to have only one legislative representative attend the survey team meetings. Keith Sexton, Donahoe's young assistant, was assigned to keep "selected persons of the two legislative houses informed, and to [maintain] contact with the governor's staff, channeling back to the team reactions to ideas as pro-

posed." Sexton was part of the first group of "legislative interns" hired to staff several legislative committees, which included Jack Smart (future vice chancellor for the California State University system), Stan Anderson, and Jan Stevens. Sexton, interview, May 3, 1989.

25. All Technical Committee reports, stated Coons, "will be forwarded to the Liaison Committee, the two executive officers [Kerr and Simpson], and the JAC two weeks before discussion in the Liaison Committee."

26. Coons, *Crises*, 43.

27. Dumke, interview by Judson A Grenier, July, 1981, Oral History Pilot Project on the Origins of the CSU System, CSA.

28. Holy and Browne, "Materials Presented to the Joint Meeting of the State Board of Education and the Regents of the University of California," March 14, 1959, CSA, LCF.

29. *Ibid.*

30. *Ibid.*

31. Working with the help of T. R. McConnell at Berkeley, Glenny was completing the first detailed survey of the varied governing systems for higher education employed in the states. "Without exception," observed Glenny, "since 1950 [most] state surveys of higher education conducted by recognized experts have recommended coordinating some or all of the major activities of the colleges and universities." Lyman Glenny, as quoted by Holy and Browne from his pending book, *State Coordination and Control of Higher Education.*

32. Stanley B. Freeborn to Clark Kerr, August 13, 1959, UCA, JACF. The Ohio plan was created in 1935 and included an "inter-university council," consisting of one member of the Board of Trustees and the president and business manager of each of the state's six public higher education institutions. In 1940, the council said of the functions of doctoral-level work: "Specialized technological and professional training should be the sole property of the main land grant campus at Columbus." The other state universities were to be limited, much like California's state colleges, to "liberal arts (including fine arts), education, business and commerce through undergraduate curricula leading to the Bachelor's degree and in graduate work for the Master's degree."

33. Master Plan survey team, Minutes, June 16, 1959, California Postsecondary Education Commission Library.

34. *Ibid.*; Dean McHenry to Clark Kerr, June 24, 1959, UCA, McHenry File. "Past experience reveals the ineffectiveness," argued a university senate committee, "once authorization to grant a given degree has been given to the state colleges, of even direct prohibitions against its extension to unauthorized fields, under the most detailed conditions, restrictions, and procedures."

35. Master Plan survey team, Minutes, June 16, 1959.

36. Glenn Dumke to the Joint Advisory Committee, July 9, 1959, UCA, JACF.

37. Arthur G. Coons Papers, Binder 1, Occidental College Library.

38. Master Plan survey team, Minutes, July 27–28, 1959.

39. *Ibid.*; Dean McHenry to Clark Kerr, July 28, 1959, UCA, McHenry File.

40. Master Plan survey team, Minutes, July 27–28, 1959.

41. Stanley B. Freeborn to Clark Kerr, August 13, 1959, UCA, JACF.

42. Dean McHenry to Clark Kerr, July 28, 1959, UCA, McHenry File.

43. Presley C. Dawson to Arthur G. Coons, "Junior Colleges and the Master Plan for Higher Education in California," December 10, 1959; Master Plan survey team, Minutes, Regents Room, UCLA, September 29–30, 1959.

44. Master Plan survey team, Minutes, President's Conference Room, San Francisco State College, July 6–8, 1959.

45. Master Plan survey team, Minutes, October 12, 1959; Master Plan survey team, Minutes, November 23–24, 1959; Dean McHenry to Clark Kerr, October 23, 1959, UCA, LCF; Glenn Dumke to the Master Plan survey team, "Coordination of Higher Education in California," October 10, 1959, UCA, LCF.

46. Dean McHenry to Clark Kerr, July 28, 1959, UCA, McHenry File.

47. Dean McHenry to Clark Kerr, October 23, 1959, UCA, LCF.

48. It was estimated in a Joint Staff study, made prior to the survey team's establishment, that some 50,000 students could be channeled into the junior colleges by a change in the admission policies of the university and the state colleges. As reported in the *San Francisco Chronicle*, cost savings over a ten-year period or more could come to approximately $45 million because of their lower operating costs. Dean McHenry to Harry Wellman, March 22, 1959, UCA, JACF.

49. Master Plan survey team, Minutes, July 27–28, 1959; Dean McHenry to Clark Kerr, July 28, 1959, UCA, McHenry File.

50. Dean McHenry to Clark Kerr, July 28, 1959, UCA, McHenry File.

51. Master Plan survey team, Minutes, July 29–30, 1959.

52. *Ibid.*

53. "Major Recommendations of the Technical Committee on Selection and Retention of Students, with Comments by the Master Plan Team," as presented to the Liaison Committee, October 14, 1959.

54. Master Plan survey team, Minutes, Occidental College, November 2–4, 1959; Master Plan survey team, Minutes, University Club, Los Angeles, November 16–18, 1959; Master Plan survey team, Minutes, Occidental College, November 23–24, 1959.

55. Master Plan survey team, Minutes, Occidental College, November 23–24, 1959; *Master Plan*, 51–63. As later stated in the final Master Plan report, "under this plan, lower division enrollments in the state colleges in 1975 are 67,400 as compared with 91,750 under the status quo projections. For the University of California, comparable figures are 28,800 and 45,900." Junior college enrollment could jump from 246,350 to 288,950 under the proposed change in admissions.

56. Dean McHenry to Lloyd N. Morrisett, November 10, 1959, UCA, McHenry File.

57. *Ibid.*

58. *Master Plan*, 111–14.

59. *Ibid.*

60. *Ibid.*, 97.

61. *Ibid.*, 189.

62. *Ibid.*, 192–93.

63. *Ibid.*, 188–91.

64. Liaison Committee, Minutes, State Education Building, October 14, 1959, Sacramento.

65. Liaison Committee, Minutes, Los Angeles State College, Dining Room, November 18, 1959.

66. Joint Advisory Committee, October 13, 1959; "Functions of a Commission to Investigate the Potentialities for Increasing the Number of College and Universities Programs at the Doctoral Level," October 9, 1959, CSUA; Master Plan survey team, Minutes, November 23–24, 1959.

67. Dean McHenry to Clark Kerr, November 13, 1959, UCA, McHenry File.

68. Lloyd D. Bernard, Lowell H. Dunigan, and Charles E. Young, "Faculty Demand and Supply: Preliminary Report of the Technical Committee on Institutional Capacities and Area Needs," November 4, 1959, CSA, LCF; Roy Simpson to Arthur G. Coons, "Doctoral Programs," October 29, 1959, UCA, LCF; Master Plan survey team, Minutes, October 12–14, 1959.

69. Master Plan survey team, Minutes, November 23–24, 1959.

70. *Ibid.*

71. Clark Kerr, interview with author, February 11, 1994; Coons, *Crises*, 33–34.

72. Dean McHenry to Clark Kerr, November 29, 1959, UCA, LCF.

73. Op-Ed, *San Francisco Chronicle*, April 15, 1959.

74. "Brown Asks Action on College Issue," *Berkeley Daily Gazette*, November 30, 1959.

75. "Master Plan on College Policy Due," *Berkeley Daily Gazette*, December 2, 1959; "Higher Education Program Still Faces Many Hurdles," *Berkeley Daily Gazette*, December 1, 1959.

76. Master Plan survey team, Minutes, December 2–3, 1959.

77. *Ibid.*

78. *Ibid.*

79. *Ibid.*

80. Master Plan survey team, Minutes, December 2–3, 1959.

81. Coons, *Crises*, 56.

82. Liaison Committee, Minutes, December 7–8, 1959.

83. Kerr, interview, February 11, 1994.

84. Master Plan survey team, Minutes, December 8, 1959; Coons, *Crises*, 57–60.

85. After the meeting, Kerr called key senate members. Later that evening, he then called Coons and stated that sufficient support was available to allow a tentative commitment on the joint doctorate.

86. However, there was no direct statement supporting state funding for this college function placed in the Master Plan. Further, the plan would state: "The superiority and supremacy of the University of California as the state-sponsored research agency should be recognized." Liaison Committee, Minutes, December 9, 1959.

87. *Ibid.*

CHAPTER 11

1. Glenn Dumke and Arthur Browne to the presidents and faculty representatives of the state colleges, December 11, 1959, CSUA.

2. *Ibid.*

3. James H. Corley to Clark Kerr, January 12, 1960, UCA, LCF.

4. James Corley to Clark Kerr, January 15, 1960, UCA, LCF; James Corley to Dean McHenry, January 21, 1960, UCA, LCF.

5. Verne O. Knudsen to Clark Kerr, "Chancellor's Advisory Council," December 16, 1959, UCA, LCF.

6. Joint Meeting, University Hall, Berkeley, December 18, 1959, CSA, LCF.

7. *Ibid.*

8. Op-Ed, *Los Angeles Times*, December 20, 1959; "Brown Will Tackle Smog, Education," *San Francisco Chronicle*, January 6, 1960; "Chessman Battle Opens Assembly: Row Puts Budget in Rear Seat," *San Francisco Chronicle*, March 1, 1960.

9. Clark Kerr, University of California press release, December 18, 1959; Stanley E. McCaffrey to Ralph S. Gordon (Ford Motor Company, northwest public relations office), "A Motion Picture on the Making of the Master Plan," December 18, 1959, UCA, LCF.

10. Op-Ed, *Los Angeles Times*, December 20, 1959; "This World," *San Francisco Chronicle*, March 6, 1960.

11. Lloyd Morrisett to Clark Kerr, December 18, 1959, UCA, LCF; *CTA Legislative Letter*, April 4 and 25, 1960; *San Francisco Chronicle*, April 9, 1960.

12. *Master Plan*, xii.

13. *Master Plan*, 27.

14. *Master Plan*, xii.

15. Sexton, interview, May 3, 1989.

16. *Ibid.*; Sexton, Rowland interview, 1978.

17. Assemblyman Samuel R. Geddes, statement before the Assembly Committee on Education, March 1, 1960, UCA, LCF.

18. Sexton, Rowland interview, 1978.

19. Assemblyman Bruce F. Allen, February 11, 1960, press release, UCA, LCF.

20. James Corley to Clark Kerr, January 29, 1960, UCA, LCF; Assemblyman John Busterud, chair of the Joint Committee on Constitutional Amendments, cited in Dean McHenry to Clark Kerr, March 2, 1960, UCA, LCF.

21. Press Conference, Governor Pat Brown, Arthur Coons, Clark Kerr, Dean McHenry, and Glenn Dumke, December 20, 1959, Berkeley, UCA, LCF; Arthur Browne to Dean McHenry, January 15, 1960, UCA, LCF; Stan McCaffrey to Clark Kerr and Dean McHenry, January 14, 1960, UCA, LCF.

22. Coons, *Crises*, 64.

23. Sexton, Rowland interview, 1978.

24. *Ibid.*

25. *Ibid.* In the assembly, both Donahoe and Bee reportedly became upset with Glenny's aggressive attempt to influence legislators. Sexton reports that they asked "How's this guy getting in here?" and noted that he should be at Sacramento State teaching classes. Glenny, interview by author, June 1, 1989.

26. "U.S. Education is in Danger Conant Warns at UC Rites," *San Francisco Chronicle*, March 22, 1960.

27. Dean McHenry, interview with author, McHenry Library, UCSC, March 23, 1989; Sexton, interview, 1978; "Senators Strip College Plan," *San Francisco Chronicle*, March 17, 1960.

28. Julian McPhee to Harry Wellman, March 3, 1960, UCA, LCF.

29. Coons, *Crises*, 64. With the hope of a board similar to the regents slipping away, it would not seem far-fetched that several key state college presidents would urge placing in statute the *Master Plan*'s edict on functions. Statutory status for this element of the plan was in fact the view of President Malcolm Love before the legislative hearings even began. One can only conjecture that Senator Hugo Fisher of San Diego may have listened to his local state college president in seeking the final amendment to Grunsky's bill.

30. *San Francisco Chronicle*, March 17, 1960; "State Employees Hit the Jackpot," *San Francisco Chronicle*, April 3, 1960.

31. Dean McHenry to Harry Wellman, "CSEA Attitudes Toward MP," February 9, 1960, UCA, LCF; "CSEA Merit System Proposal," Master Plan survey team, Minutes, February 1, 1960.

32. As stated in Miller's bill: "It is hereby declared to be the policy of the Legislature not to authorize or to acquire sites for new institutions of public higher education unless such sites are recommended by the Co-Coordinating Council for Higher Education and not to authorize existing or new institutions

of public education . . . to offer instruction beyond the fourteenth grade level." Senate bill 33, to section 1, division 16.5 of the *California Education Code.*

33. "Senate OKs Master Plan for Colleges," *San Francisco Chronicle,* March 30, 1960.

34. "College Master Plan Can Work," *San Francisco Chronicle,* March 29, 1960.

35. "Legislature in Closing Days—Two Bid Issues," *San Francisco Chronicle,* March 28, 1960.

36. "Legislature Heads for Adjournment," *San Francisco Chronicle,* April 4, 1960; "$275 Million State College Building Plan," *San Francisco Chronicle,* April 5, 1960; "Assemblywoman Donahoe Dies at 49—Pneumonia," *San Francisco Chronicle,* April 5, 1960; Sexton, interview, May 3, 1989.

37. "Legislature Snags on School Bonds, Doesn't Adjourn," *San Francisco Chronicle,* April 7, 1960.

38. *Master Plan,* xi.

39. Coons, *Crises,* 85.

40. *Ibid.,* 86.

41. [Robbins] Committee on Higher Education, *Higher Education.*

42. Organization of Economic Cooperation Development, "Review of Higher Education," January 1963, 18.

43. Cited in Coons, *Crises,* 87.

44. Halstead, *Statewide Planning in Higher Education,* 10.

45. California Postsecondary Education Commission, "Background Papers to a Prospectus for California Postsecondary Education," Report 85–20, March 1985, 19.

46. Organization of Economic Cooperation Development, "Review of Higher Education Policy in California: Examiners' Report and Questions," February 1989, 9.

EPILOGUE

1. See Callan, "Government and Higher Education," 3–19.

2. Kerr and Gade, *The Guardians.* Corson, *Governance of Colleges and Universities,* 270.

3. Berdahl, *Statewide Coordination of Higher Education,* 35.

4. California Postsecondary Education Commission, "Data Abstract Series, 1990"; California State University, Office of the Chancellor, "Statistical Abstract: To July 1990."

5. See Graham and Diamond, *The Rise of American Research Universities.*

6. *Ibid.,* 212.

7. See Douglass, "Anatomy of Conflict."

8. McConnell, "Flexibility, Quality, and Authority in Coordinating Systems of Higher Education," 170–71.

9. Lee and Bowen, *The Multicampus University*, 408.

10. Tool, "The California State Colleges Under the Master Plan," 60; "Prof Group Wants State Colleges on Par with UC," *Sacramento Bee*, March 25, 1966.

11. "The Golden State at Risk: A Joint Statement on the Crisis Facing California Higher Education Prepared by the Higher Education Members of the Education Roundtable," press release, Sacramento, March 28, 1993, 2–3.

12. Schrag, *Paradise Lost*, 7.

BIBLIOGRAPHY

ABBREVIATIONS

CDE	California State Department of Education
CPEC	California Postsecondary Education Commission Library
CSA	California State Archives, Sacramento
UCA	University of California Archives, Berkeley
LCF	Liaison Committee File
JACF	Joint Advisory Committee File
The Warren Papers	Warren Papers, Reconstruction and Reemployment Commission Files, California State Archives

PERIODICALS

San Francisco Chronicle, San Francisco, April 1959–April 1960.
Berkeley Daily Gazette, Berkeley, November–December 1959.
Sacramento Bee, Sacramento, January–February 1957.
San Diego Union, San Diego, April 1959.
California Weekly, July 1910.
San Francisco Argus, San Francisco, February 1899.
Los Angeles Times, Los Angeles, April 1959.
Daily Bruin, UCLA, January 1933.

MINUTES, REPORTS, AND GOVERNMENT DOCUMENTS

Bernard, Lloyd D., Lowell H. Dunigan, and Charles E. Young. "Faculty Demand and Supply: Preliminary Report of the Technical Committee on Institutional Capacities and Area Needs." November 4, 1959, CSA, LCF.

Browne, Arthur D., and T. C. Holy. "Plan Recommended to the Liaison Committee for the Master Plan Study Authorized by ACR 88." May 26, 1959, CSA, LCF.

Browne, J. Ross. "Report of the Debates in the Convention of California." CSA.

Burkman, J. A. "The State Colleges" in the "Biennial Report of the California State Department of Education: 1936." California State Library.

Bursch, Charles. "Memoranda from the State Department of Education Concerning State Aid for Schoolhousing in Rural Areas and in Other School Districts with Low Financial Ability." CDE, December 18, 1944.
California State Department of Education. "Biennial Report of the California State Department of Education: 1936." Sacramento: California State Library.
California State Department of Finance. "Digest of the California State Budget for the Fiscal Year July 1, 1954 to June 30, 1955." Sacramento: State Department of Finance.
——— "Report of Total and Full-Time Enrollments in California's Institutions of Higher Education," 1961–1999. Sacramento: State Department of Finance.
California Legislature. Assembly Concurrent Resolution 88, March 4, 1959.
——— "Report of the California Commission for the Study of Educational Problems," 1931.
——— Constitution Revision Commission. "Article IX, Education: Background Study." CSA, 1968.
——— *Education Code, 1933*, Article 8, section 20201.
——— "An Act to Create and Organize the University of California," March 23, 1868. *California Statutes of 1867–68.*
——— "Act to Establish an Agricultural, Mining and Mechanical Arts College," March 31, 1866. *California Statutes of 1866.*
——— "Resolution of the Senate and Assembly Inquiring into the Affairs of the University of California," March 3, 1874. Appendix, *Journals for the Senate and Assembly*, 1874.
——— "An Act to Reorganize and Simplify the School System and Public Education of the State of California," Bill 374, February 1876.
——— "Report of the Senate Special Committee to Whom Was Referred Certain Questions Relative to the Regents of the State University," March 1876.
——— *Debates and Proceedings of the Constitutional Convention of the States of California, 1878–79*. Sacramento: State Office, 1880.
——— "Report of the Education Commission." Sacramento: State Printing Office, 1900.
——— "Report of the Special Legislative Committee on Education." Sacramento: State Printing Office, 1920.
——— Senate Bill 895, May 1931.
——— *Statutes of California of 1935*, Chapter 261, Sections 1–6, 948.
——— House Resolution 186, May 1941.
——— "Report of the State Council of Educational Planning and Coordination to the Legislature of the State of California." UCA, Sacramento, March 1941.

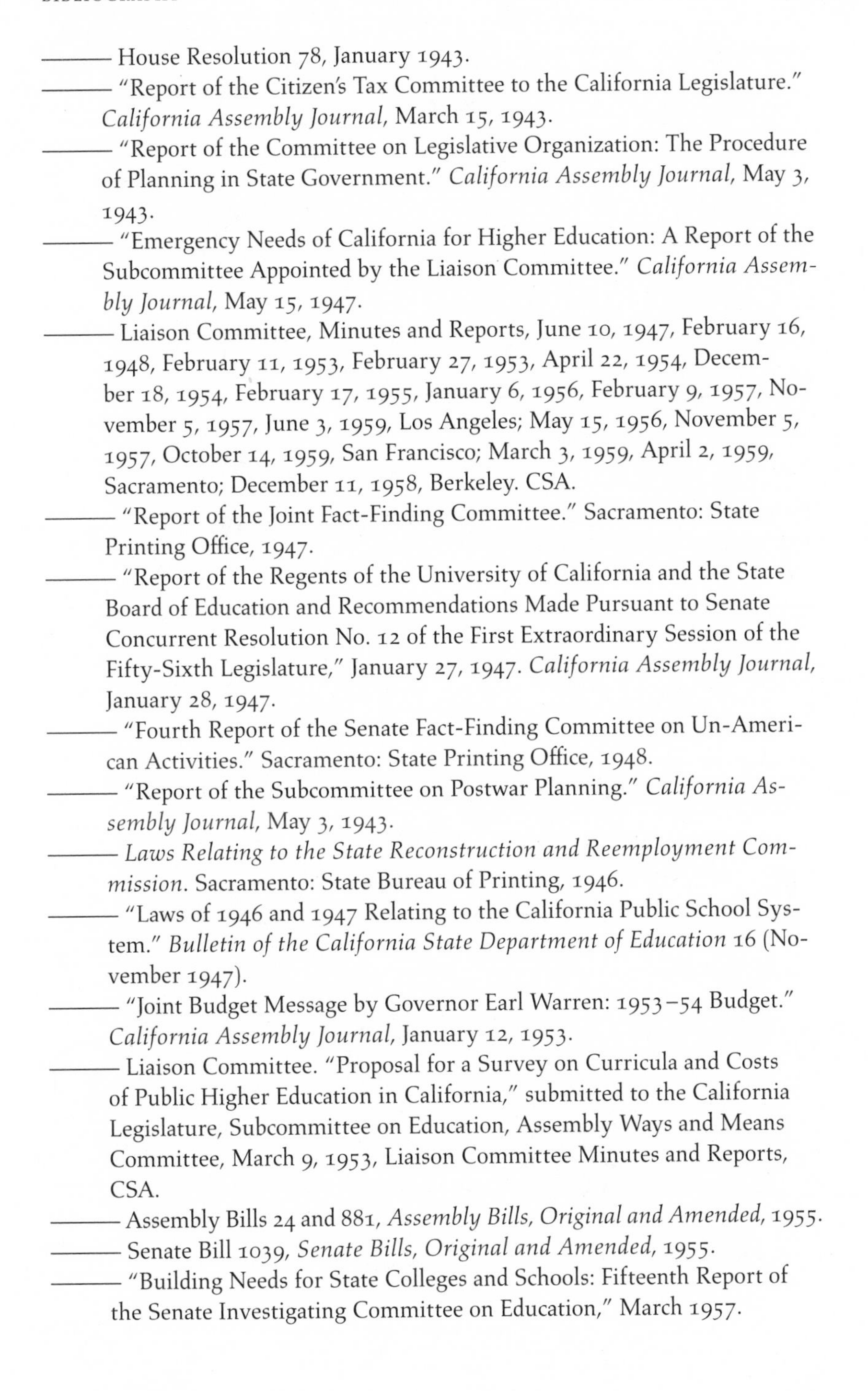

——— House Resolution 78, January 1943.

——— "Report of the Citizen's Tax Committee to the California Legislature." *California Assembly Journal,* March 15, 1943.

——— "Report of the Committee on Legislative Organization: The Procedure of Planning in State Government." *California Assembly Journal,* May 3, 1943.

——— "Emergency Needs of California for Higher Education: A Report of the Subcommittee Appointed by the Liaison Committee." *California Assembly Journal,* May 15, 1947.

——— Liaison Committee, Minutes and Reports, June 10, 1947, February 16, 1948, February 11, 1953, February 27, 1953, April 22, 1954, December 18, 1954, February 17, 1955, January 6, 1956, February 9, 1957, November 5, 1957, June 3, 1959, Los Angeles; May 15, 1956, November 5, 1957, October 14, 1959, San Francisco; March 3, 1959, April 2, 1959, Sacramento; December 11, 1958, Berkeley. CSA.

——— "Report of the Joint Fact-Finding Committee." Sacramento: State Printing Office, 1947.

——— "Report of the Regents of the University of California and the State Board of Education and Recommendations Made Pursuant to Senate Concurrent Resolution No. 12 of the First Extraordinary Session of the Fifty-Sixth Legislature," January 27, 1947. *California Assembly Journal,* January 28, 1947.

——— "Fourth Report of the Senate Fact-Finding Committee on Un-American Activities." Sacramento: State Printing Office, 1948.

——— "Report of the Subcommittee on Postwar Planning." *California Assembly Journal,* May 3, 1943.

——— *Laws Relating to the State Reconstruction and Reemployment Commission.* Sacramento: State Bureau of Printing, 1946.

——— "Laws of 1946 and 1947 Relating to the California Public School System." *Bulletin of the California State Department of Education* 16 (November 1947).

——— "Joint Budget Message by Governor Earl Warren: 1953–54 Budget." *California Assembly Journal,* January 12, 1953.

——— Liaison Committee. "Proposal for a Survey on Curricula and Costs of Public Higher Education in California," submitted to the California Legislature, Subcommittee on Education, Assembly Ways and Means Committee, March 9, 1953, Liaison Committee Minutes and Reports, CSA.

——— Assembly Bills 24 and 881, *Assembly Bills, Original and Amended,* 1955.

——— Senate Bill 1039, *Senate Bills, Original and Amended,* 1955.

——— "Building Needs for State Colleges and Schools: Fifteenth Report of the Senate Investigating Committee on Education," March 1957.

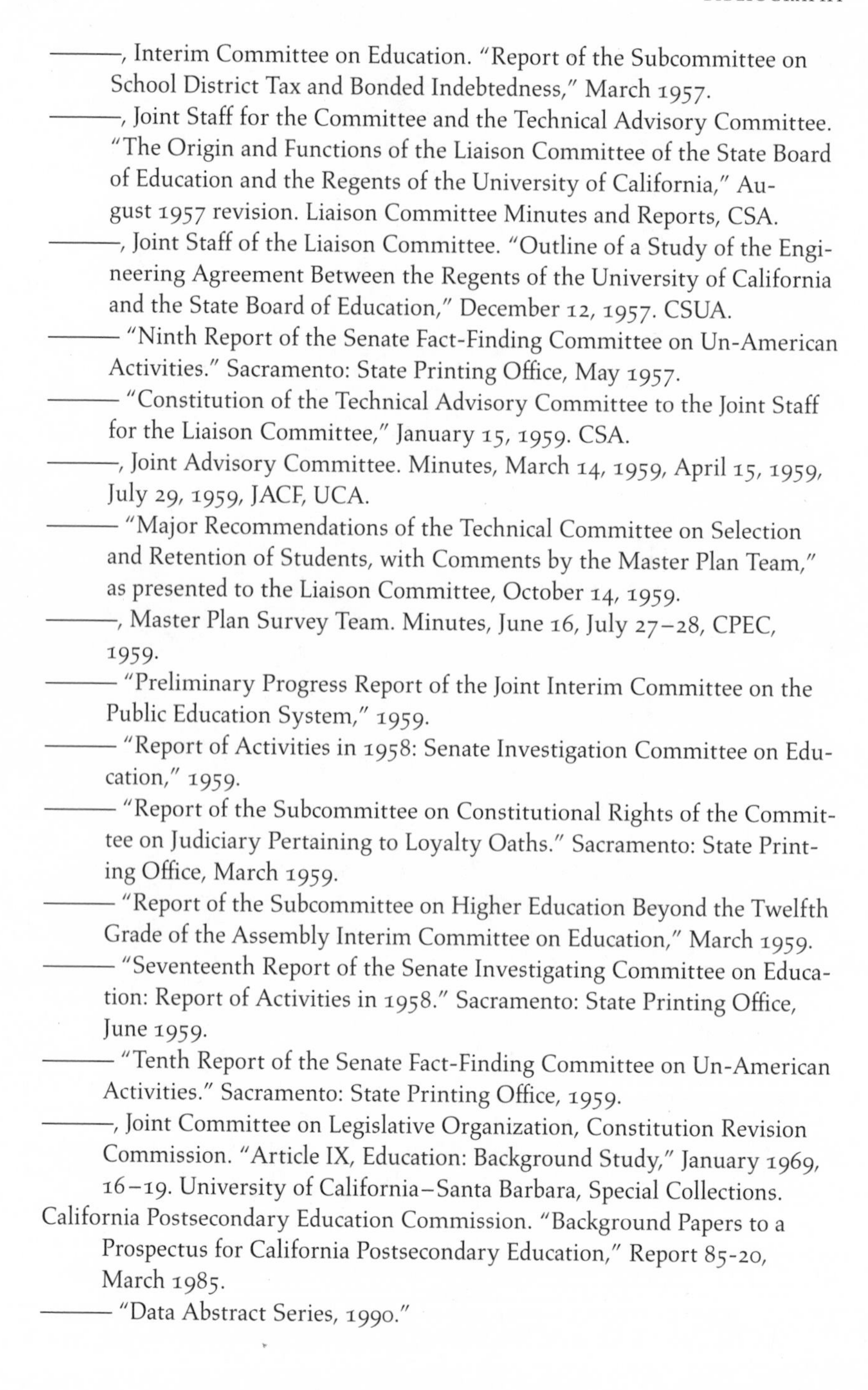

———, Interim Committee on Education. "Report of the Subcommittee on School District Tax and Bonded Indebtedness," March 1957.
———, Joint Staff for the Committee and the Technical Advisory Committee. "The Origin and Functions of the Liaison Committee of the State Board of Education and the Regents of the University of California," August 1957 revision. Liaison Committee Minutes and Reports, CSA.
———, Joint Staff of the Liaison Committee. "Outline of a Study of the Engineering Agreement Between the Regents of the University of California and the State Board of Education," December 12, 1957. CSUA.
——— "Ninth Report of the Senate Fact-Finding Committee on Un-American Activities." Sacramento: State Printing Office, May 1957.
——— "Constitution of the Technical Advisory Committee to the Joint Staff for the Liaison Committee," January 15, 1959. CSA.
———, Joint Advisory Committee. Minutes, March 14, 1959, April 15, 1959, July 29, 1959, JACF, UCA.
——— "Major Recommendations of the Technical Committee on Selection and Retention of Students, with Comments by the Master Plan Team," as presented to the Liaison Committee, October 14, 1959.
———, Master Plan Survey Team. Minutes, June 16, July 27–28, CPEC, 1959.
——— "Preliminary Progress Report of the Joint Interim Committee on the Public Education System," 1959.
——— "Report of Activities in 1958: Senate Investigation Committee on Education," 1959.
——— "Report of the Subcommittee on Constitutional Rights of the Committee on Judiciary Pertaining to Loyalty Oaths." Sacramento: State Printing Office, March 1959.
——— "Report of the Subcommittee on Higher Education Beyond the Twelfth Grade of the Assembly Interim Committee on Education," March 1959.
——— "Seventeenth Report of the Senate Investigating Committee on Education: Report of Activities in 1958." Sacramento: State Printing Office, June 1959.
——— "Tenth Report of the Senate Fact-Finding Committee on Un-American Activities." Sacramento: State Printing Office, 1959.
———, Joint Committee on Legislative Organization, Constitution Revision Commission. "Article IX, Education: Background Study," January 1969, 16–19. University of California–Santa Barbara, Special Collections.
California Postsecondary Education Commission. "Background Papers to a Prospectus for California Postsecondary Education," Report 85-20, March 1985.
——— "Data Abstract Series, 1990."

——— "The Condition of Higher Education in California," Report 98-6, October 1998.

California State Board of Education. Minutes, January 2 and 3, 1957, Los Angeles; May 9 and 10, 1957, CSA.

California State Chamber of Commerce. "Economic Survey of California and its Counties." Sacramento: California State Chamber of Commerce, 1948, 823.

California State Department of Education. "Laws of 1946 and 1947 Relating to the California Public School System." In *Bulletin of the Calif. State Department of Education* 16 (November 1947).

California State University, Office of the Chancellor. "Statistical Abstract: To July 1990," Long Beach.

California Statistical Abstract. Sacramento: State Printing Office, 1961.

Council of State College Presidents. Minutes, May 8, 1957; January 2–4, February 10 and 11, April 8 and 9, May 6 and 7, 1958.

Council of State Governments. *Higher Education in the Forty-Eight States,* Chicago: Council of State Governments, 1952.

Council of State Governments, Interstate Committee on Postwar Reconstruction and Development. *Wartime and Postwar Problems and Policies of the States.* Chicago: Council of State Governments, 1944.

McPhee, Julian A. "Engineering Programs in California." Report to the Senate Investigating Committee on Education, 1958, CSA.

Office of the Director of Planning and Research. *California Reports on Planning.* Sacramento, February 1948.

Organization of Economic Cooperation Development. "Review of Higher Education," January 1963.

——— "Review of Higher Education Policy in California: Examiners' Report and Questions," February 1989.

Simpson, Roy E. "Reorganization of the California State Department of Education," 1946, CSA.

——— "The Need for State College–Junior College Cooperation." Speech before the California Junior College Association, October 28, 1959, CSUA.

Snyder, Edwin R. "Report of the Commissioner on Vocational Education, California State Board of Education, Biennial Report, 1916–1918." UCA, Sacramento.

Southern California Associates of the Committee for Economic Development. National Defense and Southern California, 1961–1970. Los Angeles, December 1961.

State Reconstruction and Reemployment Commission. "Postwar Objectives of Public Education in California," a report of The Project Committee on Postwar Objectives of Public Education, chaired by Gilbert H. Jertberg

(State Board of Education), to the Citizens Advisory Committee on Readjustment Education, February 1945.
"Statement of Proposed Policy on Research in the State Colleges." March 1, 1958, CSUA.
Tompkins, Dorothy C. "Recent Trends in State Planning and Development." Bureau of Public Administration, University of California–Berkeley, April 25, 1949.
Tool, Marc R. "The California State Colleges Under the Master Plan: A Report to the Academic Senate of the CSC." March 1967, CSA.
United States Legislature. "The Agricultural College Land Act, July 2, 1862." *United States Statutes at Large*, Article VIII, section 4, 503.
University of California, Board of Regents. "Statements of the Regents of the University of California to the Joint Committee of the Legislature." San Francisco: Excelsior Press, March 3, 1874.
——— "Annual Report of the President, 1882–82." Sacramento, 1882, UCA.
——— Board of Regents, *Annual Report of the Secretary of the Board of Regents of the University of California*, Sacramento: State Office, 1887.
——— "Biennial Report of the President: 1910-1912." Berkeley: University of California, 1912
——— "Annual Report of the President: 1914-1915." Berkeley: University of California, 1915.
——— "Report of the Secretary of the Regents, 1917–1918," UCA.
——— "President's Report on the Relations of the Teachers College at Los Angeles to the University of California." Berkeley: University of California Press, 1928.
———, Board of Regents. Minutes, September 13, 1932, March 9, 1939, March 19, 1939, January 19, 1945, January 1, 1946, and March 31, 1950, UCA.
———, Academic Senate Committee on Educational Policy. "Report on Four Year Teachers Colleges." April 21, 1933, UCA.
———, Regents Committee on Educational Policies and Relations. Minutes, November 2, 1935, March 26, 1943, UCA.
———, Second All-Faculty Conference. "Proceedings of the University of California Second All-Faculty Conference, February 8–10, 1947." Berkeley: University of California, 1947.
———, Second All-University Faculty Conference. "The Relation of the University and the State," February 8–10, 1947. Berkeley: University of California, 1947.
———, Fourteenth Annual All-University Faculty Conference. "Autonomy and Centralization in the Statewide University," April 1959. Berkeley: University of California, 1959.

———, Office of the President. "Administrative Changes and Developments at the University of California: Progress Report," April 23, 1965, UCA.

Warren, Earl. Address to the Joint Convention of the California Legislature, January 7, February 4, 1946.

Whitney, Josiah Dwight. "An Address Delivered at the Celebration of the Sixth Anniversary of the College of California," Oakland, Calif., June 6, 1861. UCA, Sacramento.

ADDITIONAL SOURCES

Adams, Stephen B. *Mr. Kaiser Goes to Washington: The Rise of a Government Entrepreneur*. Chapel Hill, N.C.: University of North Carolina Press, 1997.

Allen, Charles H., ed. *Historical Sketch of the State Normal School at San Jose*. Sacramento: State Printing Office, 1889.

Allen, James E., Jr. "The New York State System." In Wilson, *Emerging Patterns*, 110–16.

Almond, Gabriel, and Neil J. Smelser, eds. *Public Higher Education in California*. Berkeley: University of California Press, 1974.

"Announcement of the Mining and Agricultural College, San Francisco, 1863–64," December 1863. In *Pamphlets on The College of California*, UCA.

"Annual Enrollment Reports." In *California Schools*.

Armes, William Dallam, ed. *The Autobiography of Joseph LeConte*. New York: Appleton and Company, 1903.

Arnold, Robert K., et al. *The California Economy, 1947–1960*. Menlo Park, Calif.: Stanford Research Institution, 1960.

Axt, Richard G. *The Federal Government and Financing Higher Education*. New York: Columbia University Press, 1952.

Bailey, Stephen. "External Forces Affecting Higher Education." *NACUBO Professional File*, 1975.

Bancroft, Hubert Howe. *History of California*. Seven vols. San Francisco: A. L. Bancroft, 1884–1890.

Bard, Gunther. *California's Practical Period: A Cultural Context of the Emerging University, 1850s–1870s*. Berkeley: Center for Studies in Higher Education and Institute of Governmental Studies, 1994.

Beals, R. L., et al. "Obligation of the University to the Nation and the World." University of California All-Faculty Conference, 1947, UCA.

Bean, Walton E. "Ideas of Reform in California." In George H. Knoles, ed., *Essays and Assays: California History Reappraised*. San Francisco: California Historical Society, 1973.

——— *California: An Interpretive History*, 3rd ed. New York: McGraw-Hill, 1978.

Benjamin, Roger, Stephen Carroll et al. "The Redesign of Governance in Higher Education." Santa Monica: Institute on Education and Training, RAND, 1993.

Berdahl, Robert O. "Coordination and Governance of Postsecondary Education: The U.S. Experience." Paper delivered at the Association for the Study of Higher Education, San Diego, 1984. Berkeley: Center for Studies in Higher Education Library.

——— *Statewide Coordination of Higher Education*, Washington, D.C.: American Council on Education, 1971.

Bonner, Thomas N. "Sputniks and the Educational Crisis in America." *Journal of Higher Education* 29: 4 (April 1958), 177–84.

Bowles, Samuel, and Herbert Gintis. *Schooling in Capitalist America: Educational Reform and the Contradictions of Economic Life*. New York: Basic Books Publishers, 1976.

Bowman, Jacob Neibert. "Reminiscences of the University of California, 1906." Bancroft Library, UCA.

Brint, Steven, and Jerome Karabel. *The Diverted Dream*. New York: Oxford University Press, 1989.

Brubacher, John S., and Willis Rudy. *Higher Education in Transition: A History of American Colleges and Universities, 1636–1968*. New York: Harper & Row, 1968.

Burich, Keith R. "Something Newer and Nobler Is Called into Being: Clarence King, Catastrophism, and California." *California History*, 72: 3 (Fall 1993), 234–49.

Burns, Edward McNall. *David Starr Jordan: Prophet of Freedom*. Stanford: Stanford University Press, 1953.

Callahan, Raymond. *Education and the Cult of Efficiency*. Chicago: University of Chicago Press, 1962.

Callan, Patrick M. "Government and Higher Education." In Arthur Levine, ed., *Higher Learning in America: 1980–2000*. Baltimore, Md.: Johns Hopkins University Press, 1993, 3–19.

Campbell, Fred M. *Tenth Report of the Superintendent of Public Instruction of the State of California*. Sacramento: State Printing Office, 1882.

Campbell, William Wallace. "The Junior Colleges in Their Relationship to the University." In *California Quarterly of Secondary Education*. Society for the Study of Education, January 1927, 117.

Carnegie Foundation for the Advancement of Teaching. *State Higher Education in California*. The Suzzallo Report. Sacramento: California State Printing Office, June 24, 1932.

Carr, Ezra S. "Professor Swinton's Testimony Before the Legislature of California Given to the Joint Committee on University Affairs." In Ezra S. Carr,

The University of California and Its Relations to Industrial Education (September 1874), in *Pamphlets on the University of California*. UCA, Sacramento, 42, 55.
——— "Response from the Professor of Agriculture." In *Statements of the Regents of the University of California to the Joint Committee of the Legislature*. San Francisco: Excelsior Press, 1874.
——— "The University of California and Its Relations to Industrial Education, September 1874." In *Pamphlets on the University of California*. UCA, 42, 55.
——— *The Patrons of Husbandry on the Pacific Coast*. San Francisco: A. L. Bancroft, 1875.
Carstensen, Vernon. "The Origin and Early Development of the Wisconsin Idea." *Wisconsin Magazine of History*, Spring 1956, 181–87.
Caughey. *California: History of a Remarkable State*. New York: Prentice-Hall, 1940.
Census Bureau. *1960 Statistical Abstract of the United States*. Washington, D.C.: U.S. Government, 1960.
Chamberlain, Arthur H. *The Lange Book*. San Francisco: Trade Publishing, 1927.
Chambers, Marritt Madison. *The Campus and the People: Organization, Support and Control of Higher Education in the United Sates in the Nineteen Sixties*. Danville, Ill.: The Interstate, 1960.
——— *Freedom and Repression in Higher Education*. Bloomington, Ind.: Bloomcraft, 1965.
Chan, Sucheng. *Asian Americans: An Interpretive History*. Boston: Twayne, 1991.
Cioffi, Denis F. "After the Cold War: University Reformation in a Global, Networked Marketplace." George Mason University, 1997.
Clark, Burton R. *The Open Door College: A Case Study*. New York: McGraw-Hill, 1960.
——— *Creating Entrepreneurial Universities: Organizational Pathways of Transformation*. Paris: Pergamon, 1998.
Cleland, Robert Glass. Introduction in a special Huntington Library edition of the *Constitution of the State of California, 1849*. San Marino, Calif.: Ward Ritchie Press, 1949.
——— *From Wilderness to Empire: A History of California*. New York: Alfred A. Knopf, 1959.
Cloud, Archibald Jeter. "A Summarized History of the California Junior College Federation (1930–1947) and of Its Successor the California Junior College Association (1947 to date)." California Junior College Association, April 1955.

Cloud, Roy W. *Education in California: Leaders, Organizations, and Accomplishments of the First Hundred Years.* Stanford: Stanford University Press, 1952.

College and University Business Administration. Washington, D.C.: American Council on Education, 1952.

Commission on Higher Education. *Higher Education for American Democracy.* Washington, D.C.: U.S. Printing Office, December 1947.

Committee of Inquiry. "Recommendations Respecting the Administration of Public Education in California." The Jaqua Report. September 7, 1942, UCA.

Committee on Government and Higher Education. *The Efficiency of Freedom.* Baltimore, Md.: Johns Hopkins University Press, 1959.

Conant, James Bryant. *Shaping Policy.* New York: McGraw-Hill, 1964.

Conmy, Peter T. "The Development of Vocational Education in California." American Vocational Association Meeting, Sacramento, December 1940, UCA.

——— "Some Opportunities for the Junior Colleges." In *Proceedings of the Tenth Annual Meeting of the American Association of Junior Colleges,* November 1929.

The Constitution of the State of California as Adopted in 1879. San Francisco: Sumner Whitney, 1879.

Coons, Arthur G. Coons Papers, Occidental College Library, Occidental, Calif.

——— *Crises in California Higher Education.* Los Angeles: Ward Ritchie Press, 1968.

Corson, John J. *Governance of Colleges and Universities.* New York: McGraw-Hill, 1975.

Counts, George S. *The Challenge of Soviet Education.* New York: McGraw-Hill, 1957.

Cray, Ed. *Chief Justice: A Biography of Earl Warren.* New York: Simon & Schuster, 1997.

Cremin, Lawrence A. *The Transformation of the School: Progressivism in American Education, 1876–1957.* New York: Alfred K. Knopf, 1961.

——— *Transformation of the Schools: Progressivism in American Education.* New York: Vintage, 1961.

——— *The Wonderful World of Ellwood Paterson Cubberley.* New York: Bureau of Publishing, Teachers College, Columbia University, 1965.

Crothers, George E. *Founding of the Leland Stanford Junior University.* San Francisco: A. M. Robertson, 1932.

——— *Public Education in the United States.* Boston: Houghton Mifflin, 1934.

"Crowded California." *Newsweek,* October 11, 1948.

Cubberley, Ellwood. *School Funds and Their Apportionment*. Teachers College, Columbia University, 1905.

——— *Changing Conceptions of Education*. Boston: Houghton Mifflin, 1909.

——— *1912 Public School Administration: A Statement of the Fundamental Principles Underlying the Organization and Administration of Public Education*. Boston: Houghton Mifflin, 1916.

——— *The History of Education*. Boston: Houghton Mifflin, 1920.

——— *The Improvement of Rural Schools*, Boston: Houghton Mifflin, 1912.

Curti, Merle Eugene, and Vernon Carstensen. *The University of Wisconsin: A History, 1848–1925*. Vol. 2. Madison, Wisc.: University of Wisconsin Press, 1949.

Dana, Richard Henry. *Two Years Before the Mast*. Boston: Houghton Mifflin, 1911.

Daniels, Roger. *The Politics of Prejudice: The Anti-Japanese Movement in California and the Struggle for Japanese Exclusion*. Berkeley, Calif.: University of California Press, 1962.

Davis, Winfield J. *History of Political Conventions in California, 1848–1892*. Sacramento: California State Library, 1893.

Deutsch, Monroe E. "A Point of View Concerning the Report of the Carnegie Foundation." In *California Quarterly of Secondary Education* 8: 2 (January 1933), 117–21.

Deutsch, Monroe E., Aubrey A. Douglass, and George D. Strayer. "A Report of a Survey of the Needs of California in Higher Education." Report to the Liaison Committee of the Regents of the University of California and the State Board of Education, March 1, 1948.

Dewey, John. "An Undemocratic Proposal." *Vocational Education* 2 (1913), 374–77.

——— *Democracy and Education: An Introduction to the Philosophy of Education*. New York: Macmillan, 1916.

DeWitt, Nicholas. *Soviet Professional Manpower*. Washington, D.C.: U.S. Government Printing Office, 1955.

Division of International Education, U.S. Department of Health, Education, and Welfare. *Education in the USSR*. Washington, D.C.: U.S. Government Printing Office, 1957.

Douglass, Aubrey A. "Report on the Survey of the Needs of California in Higher Education." *California Schools* 19: 4 (April 1948), 81–89.

Douglass, John A. "On Becoming an Old Blue: Santa Barbara's Controversial Transition from a State College to a Campus of the University of California." *Coastlines* (Spring 1994), 6–11.

——— *A Brief on the Historical Development of the UC Academic Senate and the Universitywide Administration*. Berkeley: Center for Studies in Higher Education, 1997.

——— "Anatomy of Conflict: The Making and Unmaking of Affirmative Action at the University of California." *American Behavioral Scientist* 41: 7 (April 1998), 938–59.

Dumke, Glenn S. Interview by Judson A. Grenier, July, 1981. Oral History Pilot Project on the Origins of the CSU System, CSA.

Dunbar, Willis F. *The Michigan Record in Higher Education*. Detroit, Mich.: Wayne State University Press, 1963.

Duryear, E. D. "The University and the State: A Historical Overview" in Philip G. Altbach and Robert O. Berdahl, eds., *Higher Education in American Society*. Buffalo, N.Y.: Prometheus, 1981, 20–33.

Eells, Walter Crosby. "What Manner of Child This Be?" *Junior College Journal* 1 (February 1931), 309–28.

——— "The Junior College in the Postwar Period." *Junior College Journal* 14: 2 (October 1943), 52.

Elliott, Orrin Leslie. *Stanford University: The First Twenty-Five Years*. Stanford: Stanford University Press, 1937.

Ellis, Harold, et al. "Attitudes and Reactions of the Public Toward the University." *The Relation of the University and the State*, University of California All-Faculty Conference, February 1947, UCA.

Ellison, William H. "Antecedents of the University of California, Santa Barbara, 1891–1944." Unpublished manuscript, UCA, 1950.

Engelbert, Ernest A., and John G. Gunnell. *State Constitutional Revision in California*. Los Angeles: University of California Bureau of Governmental Research, 1961.

Falk, Charles J. *The Development and Organization of Education in California*. New York: Harcourt, Brace & World, 1968.

Fernham, Eliza. *California In-Doors and Out, or, How We Farm, Mine, and Live Generally in the Golden State*. New York: Dix, Edwards, 1856.

Ferrier, William Warren. *Origin and Development of the University of California*. Berkeley: Sather Gate Book Shop, 1930.

——— *Ninety Years of Education in California, 1846–1936: A Presentation of Educational Movements and Their Outcome in Education Today*. Berkeley: Sather Gate Book Shop, 1937.

——— *Henry Durant, First President University of California: The New Englander Who Came to California with College on the Brain*. Berkeley, published by author, 1942.

Ferris, David Frederic. "Judge Marvin and the Founding of the California Public School System." Ph.D. dissertation, University of California–Berkeley, 1962.

Fine, Benjamin. "Education in Review." *New York Times*, October 10, 1954.
Fitzgibbon, Russell H. *The Academic Senate of the University of California*. Berkeley: Office of the President, 1968.
Foster, Mark S. *Henry J. Kaiser: Builder in the Modern American West*. Austin, Tex.: Univ. of Texas Press, 1989.
Franklin, Fabian. *The Life of Daniel Coit Gilman*. New York: Dodd, Mead, 1910.
Freeland, Richard M. *Academia's Golden Age: Universities in Massachusetts, 1945–1970*. New York: Oxford University Press, 1992.
"Functions of a Commission to Investigate the Potentialities for Increasing the Number of College and Universities Programs at the Doctoral Level." October 9, 1959, CSUA.
Fussell, Paul. "Schools for Snobbery." *New Republic*, October 4, 1982, 25.
Gallagher, Edward A. "Revisionist Nonsense and the Junior College: Early California Development." *Michigan Academician* 26 (1995), 215–28.
——— "Jordan and Lange: The California Junior College's Role as Protector of Teaching." *Michigan Academician* 27 (1994), 1–12.
Gardner, David P. *The California Oath Controversy*. Berkeley: University of California Press, 1967.
Gates, Paul W. "California's Agricultural College Lands." *Pacific Historical Review*, 30 (May 1961), 103–22.
Geiger, Roger. *To Advance Knowledge: The Growth of American Research Universities, 1900–1940*. New York: Oxford University Press, 1986.
——— *Research and Relevant Knowledge: American Research Universities Since World War II*. New York: Oxford University Press, 1993.
George, Henry. *Progress and Poverty: An Inquiry into the Cause of Industrial Depressions and of Increase of Want with Increase of Wealth*. San Francisco: W. M. Hilton, 1879.
——— "The Kearney Agitation in California." *Popular Science Monthly* 17 (August 1880).
Gershenson, M. I. Division of Labor Statistics and Law Enforcement, State Department of Industrial Relations, presentation to the Citizens Tax Committee. San Francisco, February 5, 1943.
Gerth, Donald R., and Judson A. Grenier. *A History of the California State University and Colleges*. Long Beach: California State University, 1970.
Gilman, Daniel Coit. "The Building of the University: An Inaugural Address." *Pamphlets on the University of California*. Oakland, November 7, 1872, UCA.
——— "How Pioneers Began a College." *Overland Monthly* 8 (March 1875), 287.
——— *The Launching of a University and Other Papers: A Sheaf of Remembrances*. New York: Dodd, Mead, 1906.

Glenny, Lyman A. *Autonomy of Public Colleges*. New York: McGraw-Hill, 1959.
——— "State Systems and Plans for Higher Education." In Wilson, *Emerging Patterns*, 86.
——— Interview by author, June 1, 1989.
Goodwin, Charles. *The Establishment of State Government in California, 1846–1850*. New York: Macmillan, 1914.
Gordon, Lynn. *Education and Higher Education in the Progressive Era*. New Haven, Conn.: Yale University Press, 1990.
Gordon, Margaret. *Employment Expansion and Population Growth: The California Experience, 1900–1950*. Berkeley: University of California Press, 1954.
Graham, Hugh Davis. "Structure and Governance in American Higher Education: Historical and Comparative Analysis in State Policy." *Journal of Policy History* 1: 1 (1989), 80–107.
Graham, Hugh Davis, and Nancy Diamond. *The Rise of American Research Universities: Elites and Challengers in the Postwar Era*. Baltimore, Md.: Johns Hopkins University Press, 1997.
Graubard, Stephen R., and Geno A. Ballotti, eds. *The Embattled University*. New York: George Braziller, 1970.
Gutek, Gerald Lee. *An Historical Introduction to American Education*. New York: Crowell, 1970.
Haight, Henry H. "University Education: An Address Delivered at the Commencement Exercises of the University of the State of California," 1871, UCA.
Halsey, A. H. "The Changing Functions of Universities in Advanced Industrial Societies." *Harvard Educational Review* 30: 2 (Spring 1960), 118–27.
Halstead, D. Kent. *Statewide Planning in Higher Education*. Washington, D.C.: U.S. Printing Office, 1974.
Hansen, Woodrow James. *The Search for Authority in California*. Oakland: Biobooks, 1960.
Harper, William Rainey. Speech before the National Education Association. *Journal of Proceedings and Addresses of the Thirty-Ninth Meeting*, Charleston, S.C., July 1900, 80–84.
Harris, Seymour E. *A Statistical Portrait of Higher Education: A Report for the Carnegie Commission on Higher Education*. New York: McGraw-Hill, 1972.
Harvey, Richard. *Earl Warren: Governor of California*. New York: Exposition Press, 1969.
Heizer, Robert F., and Alan Almquist. *The Other Californians: Prejudice and Discrimination Under Spain, Mexico, and the United States to 1920*. Berkeley: University of California Press, 1974.

Herbst, Jurgen. "Liberal Education and the Graduate Schools: An Historical View of College Reform." *History of Education Quarterly* 11: 4 (December 1962), 244–58.

Herman Miles Somers. *Presidential Agency: Office of War Mobilization and Reconversion.* Cambridge, Mass.: Harvard University Press, 1950.

Hichborn, Franklin. "Inaugural Address of Governor Hiram W. Johnson." In Hichborn, *Story of the Session,* 1911.

——— *Story of the Session of the California Legislature of 1911.* San Francisco: James H. Barry, 1911.

——— *Story of the Session of the California Legislature of 1913.* San Francisco: James H. Barry, 1913.

Higham, John. *Strangers in the Land.* New York: Athenaeum, 1969.

Hilgard, E. W. *Soils: Their Formation, Composition and Relations to Climate and Plant Growth,* New York: Macmillan, 1906.

Hill, Merton E. "The Junior College Movement in California." *Junior College Journal* 16: 6 (February 1946), 254–57.

Hofstadter, Richard, and Walter Metzger. *The Development of Academic Freedom in the United States.* New York: Columbia University Press, 1955.

Holy, T. C. "Some Factors Indicated the Need for Overhaul in the Control of Public Higher Education in California," April 22, 1959, UCA, LCF.

——— "Summary of the Work of the Liaison Committee of the Regents of the University of California and the State Board of Education, 1945–1960," March 1961, CSA, LCF.

Holy, T. C., and Arthur D. Browne. "Materials Presented to the Joint Meeting of the State Board of Education and the Regents of the University of California," March 14, 1959, CSA, LCF.

Holy, T. C., and Hubert Semans. "Faculty Demand and Supply in California Higher Education, 1957–1970." Report to the Liaison Committee, January 1958.

Howe, Frederic C. *Wisconsin: An Experiment in Democracy.* New York: Charles Scribner's and Sons, 1912.

Howell, John. *Historical Programme, Century of Commerce Celebration.* San Francisco, October 1935, CSA.

Janes, Henry B., George W. Minns, and Ellis H. Holmes. "1861 Report to the State Superintendent on the Need for a Normal School." Quoted in Cloud, *Education in California,* 258.

Jencks, Christopher, and David Riesman. *The Academic Revolution.* New York: Doubleday, 1968.

Jensen, George C. "An Analysis of the Report of the Carnegie Foundation Survey and Recommendations." *California Quarterly of Secondary Education* 8:1 (October 1933), 58–67.

Jones, William Carey. *Illustrated History of the University of California*. San Francisco: Frank H. Dukesmith, 1895.

Jordan, David Starr. "The Educational Ideas of Leland Stanford." *The Sequoia* 3 (September 13, 1893).

——— "The University and the Common Man." *The Independent* 51 (February 2, 1899), 7–10.

——— *The Strength of Being Clean: A Study of the Quest for Unearned Happiness*. Boston: American Unitarian Association, 1900.

——— "University Tendencies in America." *The Popular Science Monthly* 63 (June 1903), 143–44.

——— *The Voice of the Scholar*. San Francisco: P. Elder, 1903.

——— "The Actual and the Proper Lines of Distinction Between the College and University Work." In *Proceedings of the Association of American Universities*, February 1904, Special Collections, Stanford University Library, Stanford.

——— "The College of the West." *The Popular Science Monthly* 65 (May 1904).

——— *The Human Harvest: A Study of the Decay of Races Through the Survival of the Unfit*. Boston: American Unitarian Association, 1907.

——— *The Religion of a Sensible American*. Boston: American Unitarian Association, 1909.

——— *The Days of a Man: Being Memories of a Naturalist, Teacher and Minor Prophet of Democracy*. Yonkers-on-Hudson, N.Y.: World Book Company, 1922.

Jordan, John M. *Machine-Age Ideology: Social Engineering and American Liberalism, 1911–1939*. Chapel Hill, N.C.: University of North Carolina Press, 1994.

Katz, Michael. *Class, Bureaucracy and the Schools: The Illusion of Educational Change in America*. New York: Praeger, 1971.

Kelley, Fred, and John H. McNeely, Carnegie Foundation for the Advancement of Teaching. *The State and Higher Education: Phases in Their Relationship*. Pittsburgh: Carnegie Foundation, 1933.

Kelley, Robert. *Transformation: UC Santa Barbara 1909–1979*. Santa Barbara: University of California–Santa Barbara, 1981.

——— *Battling the Inland Sea: American Political Culture, Public Policy, and the Sacramento Valley, 1850–1986*. Berkeley: University of California Press, 1989.

Kerr, Clark. "Education for a Free Society: The California Experience." Speech before the Convention of the California Labor Federation, AFL-CIO, August 11, 1959, Balboa Park Convention Hall, San Diego, UCA.

——— "Remarks by President Kerr: Ninety-Second Charter Day Ceremonies," University of California–Berkeley, March 21, 1960, UCA.

——— *The Uses of the University*. New York: Harper Torchbook, 1963.

——— Interview by Amelia Fry, 1969. Regional Oral History Office, Bancroft Library, Berkeley.

——— "Governance and Functions." In Geno A. Ballotti, ed., *The Embattled University*. New York: American Academy of Arts and Sciences, 1970, 111.

——— "The California Master Plan of 1960 for Higher Education: An Ex Ante View." Speech delivered at a meeting of the Organization of Economic Cooperation and Development, May 21, 1990, Berkeley, 20–21.

——— Interview by author, August 7, 1992, and February 11, 1994, Berkeley.

——— *The Gold and the Blue: A Personal Memoir of the University of California (1949-1967)*. Berkeley: University of California Press, forthcoming.

Kerr, Clark, and Marian Gade. *The Guardians: Boards of Trustees of American Colleges and Universities*. Washington, D.C.: American Council on Education, 1989.

Kersey, Vierling. "A Review of Public Education in California for the Year 1933." *California Schools* 5 (1935), 5.

King, Clarence. *Mountaineering in the Sierra Nevada*. Lincoln, Neb.: University of Nebraska Press, 1970.

Klein, Arthur J., ed. *Survey of Land-Grant Colleges and Universities*, vol. 1. Washington, D.C.: Government Printing Office, 1930.

Knoell, Dorothy. Interview with author, November 8, 1988, Sacramento.

Knoles, George H., ed. *Essays and Assays: California History Reappraised*. San Francisco: California Historical Society, 1973.

Koos, Leonard V. *The Junior College Movement*. Boston: Ginn, 1925.

Korol, Alexander G. *Soviet Education for Science and Technology*. New York: MIT Technology Press/John Wiley and Sons, 1957.

Krueger, DeWitt W. "The California Property Tax System," CSA, 1943, 1–2.

Kuslan, Louis I. "Benjamin Silliman, Jr.: The Second Silliman." In Leonard G. Wilson, ed., *Benjamin Silliman and His Circle: Studies on the Influence of Benjamin Silliman on Science in America*. New York: Science History Publications, 1979.

Lane, J. Gregg. "The Lincoln-Roosevelt League: Its Origin and Accomplishments." *Quarterly of the Historical Society of Southern California* 25 (September 1943).

Lange, Alexis F. "Introduction to the Study of the Rise and Development of the University Idea." Address before the California Union, October 12, 1897. In Lange Collection, UCA.

——— Address to the Northern California Teachers Association, Sacramento, October 24, 1907, published in Chamberlain, *The Lange Book*, 37.

——— "Our Adolescent School System." *University of California Chronicle* 1 (1908), 2–14.

——— "The Unification of Our School System." *Sierra Education News* 5 (June 1909), 346.

——— "The Junior College." Lange Collection, 1915, UCA.

——— "The Junior College with Special Reference to California." *Educational Administration and Supervision*, January 1916, 1–8.

——— "The Junior College—What Manner of Child This Be!" *School and Society* 7 (February 23, 1918), 211–16.

——— "The Junior College." *Sierra Educational News*, October 1920, 483–86.

Lederle, John W. "The State and Higher Education: A Report from Michigan." In Moos and Rourke, *The Campus and the State*, Appendix A.

Lee, Eugene, and Frank Bowen. *The Multicampus University: A Study of Academic Governance*. New York: McGraw-Hill, 1971.

Levine, Arthur. "Clark Kerr: The Masterbuilder at 75." *Change* 19:2 (March/April 1987), 12–35.

Levine, David O. *The American College and the Culture of Aspiration*. Ithaca, N.Y.: Cornell University Press, 1986.

Lindsay, Frank B. "California Junior Colleges: Past and Present." *California Journal of Secondary Education* 22:3 (March 1947), 137–42.

Lockard, Diana Northrop. "Watershed Years: Transformations in the Community Colleges of California, 1945–1960." Ph.D. dissertation, Claremont Graduate School, 1986.

Lotchin, Roger W. *Fortress California 1910–1961: From Warfare to Welfare*. New York: Oxford University Press, 1992.

Lounsbury, John L. "Postwar Planning for the Junior Colleges." *California Journal of Secondary Education* 19: 3 (April 1944), 188–90.

——— "Some Problems in Postwar Planning." *Junior College Journal* 14:8 (April 1944), 360–66.

Love, Malcolm. "Functions of the Three Segments of Public Higher Education in California." CSUA, March 26, 1959.

Low, Victor. *The Unimpressible Race: A Century of Educational Struggle by the Chinese in San Francisco*. San Francisco: East/West, 1982.

Lupold, S. "From Physician to Physicist: The Scientific Career of John LeConte, 1818–1891." Ph.D. dissertation, Columbia, S.C.: University of South Carolina, 1970.

Mann, Arthur. "The Progressive Tradition." In John Higham, ed., *The Reconstruction of American History*. New York: Harper Torchbooks, 1962, 163.

Mann, Horace. *Lectures and Annual Reports on Education*. Ithaca, N.Y.: Cornell University Press, 1867.

Marsden, George M. *The Soul of the American University: From Protestant Establishment to Established Nonbelief*. New York: Oxford University Press, 1994.

Martinez, Richard. "700 Join in UCR's Second Founder's Day Celebration." *Press Enterprise*, October 7, 1987.
Mason, Paul. "Constitutional History of California." In California State Senate, *Constitution of the State of California and the United States and Other Documents*. Sacramento: State Printing Office, 1949.
Master Plan survey team. *A Master Plan for Higher Education in California, 1960–1975*. Prepared for the Liaison Committee of the State Board of Education and the Regents of the University of California, Sacramento: CDE, 1960.
May, Henry F. *Three Faces of Berkeley: Competing Ideologies in the Wheeler Era, 1899–1919*. Berkeley: Center for Studies in Higher Education and Institute of Governmental Studies, 1993.
McCarthy, George. *The Wisconsin Idea*. New York: Macmillan: 1912.
McChesney, J. B. *Secondary Education in California*. San Francisco: California Louisiana Purchase Exposition Commission, 1904.
McConnell, T. R. *Restudy: Summary Analysis*, April 27, 1956, CSA, LCF.
——— "Flexibility, Quality, and Authority in Coordinating Systems of Higher Education." In Neil J. Smelser and Gabriel Almond, *Public Higher Education in California*. Berkeley: University of California Press, 1974.
McHenry, Dean E. Interview with author, March 29, 1989, McHenry Library.
McKay, Robert E. Interview by James H. Rowland, 1979, Regional Oral History Office, Bancroft Library, Berkeley.
McLane, Charles L. "The Junior College, or Upward Extension of the High School." *School Review* 21 (March 1913), 161–62.
McPhee, Julian A. "California State Polytechnic College: Pioneer in Occupational Education." In *The California State Colleges*, Sacramento: CDE, 1955.
McWilliams, Carey. *California: The Great Exception*. New York: Current Books, 1949.
Megquire, Mary Jane. *Apron Full of Gold: The Letters of Mary Jane Megquire, 1849–1856*. San Marino, Calif.: The Huntington Library, 1849.
"Memorial of the California State Grange and Mechanics Deliberative Assembly on the State University," Sacramento, 1874. In *Pamphlets on the University of California*, UCA.
Merritt, Ralph P. *Controller's Report and Financial Statement, 1914–15*, UCA.
Millett, John D. *Conflict in Higher Education: State Government Coordination Versus Institutional Independence*. San Francisco: Jossey-Bass, 1984.
Milstein, Mike M., and Robert E. Jennings. *Educational Policy-Making and the State Legislature: The New York Experience*. New York: Preager, 1973.
Moos, Malcolm, and Frank Rourke. *The Campus and the State*. Baltimore, Md.: Johns Hopkins University Press, 1959.

Morgan, Walter E. "An Appraisal of the Financial Recommendations Contained in the Carnegie Foundation Report on State Higher Education in California." *California Quarterly of Secondary Education* 8:2 (January 1933), 131–38.

Mowat, Charles L., et al. "Obligation of the University to the Nation and the World." *The Relation of the University and the State*. University of California All Faculty Conference, February 1947, UCA, 64–65.

Mowry, George E. *The California Progressives*. Berkeley: University of California Press, 1951.

Muto, Albert. "A Voice from the Wilderness: The Early University of California Press." *California History* 72: 3 (Fall 1993), 222–23.

Napier, John H. "Origin and Development of the Public High School in California." *California Quarterly of Secondary Education* 8: 2 (January 1933), 178–88.

Nash, Gerald D. *The American West Transformed: The Impact of the Second World War*. Bloomington, Ind.: Indiana University Press, 1985.

National Committee on Standard Reports for Institutions of Higher Education. *Financial Reports for Colleges and Universities*. Chicago: University of Chicago Press, 1935.

——— *College and University Business Administration*. Washington, D.C.: American Council on Education, 1952.

National Policies Commission. *Education for ALL American Youth*. Washington, D.C.: National Education Association, 1944, 246.

National Resources Planning Board. *National Resources Development Report*, Part 1. Washington, D.C.: Government Printing Office, 1943.

Nerad, Maresi. *The Academic Kitchen: A Social History of Gender Stratification at the University of California, Berkeley*. Albany: State University of New York Press, 1987.

Numbers, Ronald L. *Almost Persuaded*. Baltimore, Md.: Johns Hopkins University Press, 1978.

Office of University Relations. *A Brief History of the University of California*. Berkeley: University of California, 1974.

Olin, Spencer C., Jr. *California's Prodigal Sons: Hiram Johnson and the Progressives, 1911–1917*. Berkeley: University of California Press, 1968.

——— *California Politics, 1846–1920: The Emerging Corporate State*. San Francisco: Boyd and Fraser, 1981.

Partridge, Loren W. *John Galen Howard and the Berkeley Campus: Beaux-Arts Architecture and the "Athens of the West."* Berkeley: Architectural Heritage Association, 1978.

Peckham, Howard H. *The Making of the University of Michigan, 1817–1967*. Ann Arbor, Mich.: University of Michigan Press, 1967.

Penry, Silas. Article in *Amador Dispatch*, September 7, 1906.

Perkinson, Henry J. *The Imperfect Panacea: American Faith in Education, 1865–1965*. New York: Random House, 1968.

Pettitt, George A. *Twenty-Eight Years in the Life of a University President*. Berkeley: University of California Press, 1966.

Pisani, Donald. *From the Family Farm to Agribusiness: the Irrigation Crusade in California and the West, 1850–1931*. Berkeley: University of California Press, 1984.

Polos, Nicholas C. "John Swett: The Horace Mann of the Pacific." Ph.D. dissertation, University of California, Berkeley, 1962.

——— *John Swett: California's Frontier Schoolmaster*. Washington, D.C.: University Press of America, 1978.

Pomeroy, Earl. *The Pacific Slope*. New York: Alfred K. Knopf, 1965.

Post, A. Alan. Interview with author, April 1989, Sacramento.

——— "Extent of Junior College Courses Above the 14th Grade," March 11, 1954. *California Assembly Journal* (January 14, 1955), 411–13.

"Preliminary Report of the Armed Forces Committee on Postwar Educational Opportunities for Service Personnel." Submittal to Congress, Washington, D.C., October 27, 1943.

Proctor, William Martin, ed. *The Junior College: Its Organization and Administration*. Stanford: Stanford University Press, 1927.

"Registration Data for California Institutions of Collegiate Grade, 1940, 1941, 1942 and 1943." *California Schools* 15:5 (May 1944), 115–26.

Reid, William T. *Annual Report of the President, 1882–82*. UCA, 1882.

Restudy Survey Team. *A Restudy of the Needs for California in Higher Education*. Study prepared for the Liaison Committee of the Regents of the University of California and the California State Board of Education, Liaison Committee Minutes and Reports, CSA. Sacramento: CDE, 1955.

Riesman, David. *Thorstein Veblen: A Critical Interpretation*. New York: Charles Scribner's and Sons, 1953.

Rhode, Paul. "The Nash Thesis Revisited: An Economic Historian's View." *Pacific Historical Review* 62: 3 (August 1994), 363–92.

Robbins, Committee on Higher Education. *Higher Education*. London: Her Majesty's Stationary Office, 1963.

Robinson, Judith. *The Hearsts: An American Dynasty*. New York: Avon Books, 1991.

Roosevelt, Theodore. "Charter Day Address," March 23, 1911. *University of California Chronicle* 13: 2 (1911), 131–45.

Rothblatt, Sheldon. *The Modern University and Its Discontents: The Fate of Newman's Legacies in Britain and America*. Cambridge: Cambridge University Press, 1997.

Royce, Sarah. *A Frontier Lady: Recollections of the Gold Rush and Early California*. New Haven, Conn.: Yale University Press, 1932.
Salisbury, H. E. "The Soviet Educational System." *Journal of Higher Education* 29:8 (November 1958), 462–64.
Sanchez, Nellie Van De Grift. *Spanish Arcadia*. Los Angeles: Powell, 1929.
Sansing, David G. *Making Haste Slowly: The Troubled History of Higher Education in Mississippi*. Jackson, Miss.: University Press of Mississippi, 1990.
Schechner, Mark. "The Cold War and the University of California." In Dennis Hale and Jonathan Eisen, eds., *The California Dream*. New York: Collier Books, 1968.
Scheiber, Harry N. "Race, Radicalism, and Reform: Historical Perspective on the 1879 California Constitution." *Hastings Constitutional Law Quarterly* 17:1 (Fall 1989), 35–80.
Schrag, Peter. *Paradise Lost: California's Experience, America's Future*. New York: The New Press, 1998.
Schulte, Gustavus. "A Glance from a German Standpoint at the State University of California." *Pamphlets on the University of California*. January 2, 1871, UCA.
Schwartz, Bernard. *Super Chief: Earl Warren and His Supreme Court*. New York: New York University Press, 1983.
Sears, Jesse B., and Ellwood P. Cubberley. *The Cost of Education in California*. New York: Macmillan, 1924.
Sears, Jesse B., and Adin D. Henderson. *Cubberley of Stanford and His Contribution to American Education*. Stanford: Stanford University Press, 1957.
Semans, Hubert H. Interview with author, May 10, 1989, Los Altos Hills.
Semans, Hubert H., and T. C. Holy. *Report of the Joint Staff on the Proposal for a Four-Year State College in the Modesto Area*. Sacramento, 1953.
——— *A Study of the Need for Additional Centers of Public Higher Education in California*. Sacramento: California State Department of Education, 1957.
Sexson, John A. "Postwar Problems of Education." *California Journal of Secondary Education* 19:3 (April 1944), 163–66.
Sexton, Keith. Interview with author, May 3, 1989, University Hall, Berkeley.
——— Interview with James Rowland, 1978. Regional Oral History Office, The Bancroft Library, University of California, Berkeley.
Silliman, Benjamin, Jr. "Original Papers in Relation to a Course of Liberal Education." *The American Journal of Science and Arts* 15 (January 1829). Cited in Richard Hofstadter and Wilson Smith, *American Higher Education: A Documentary History*, vol. 1. Chicago: University of Chicago Press, 1961.
——— "The Truly Practical Man, Necessarily an Educated Man: Oration De-

livered at the Commencement of the College of California," June 5, 1867. *Pamphlets on the College of California*, 18, UCSA.
Sinai, Nathan, et al. *Health Insurance in the United States*. New York: The Commonwealth Fund, 1946.
Sinclair, Upton. *The Goose-Step: A Study of American Education*. Pasadena, Calif.: Published by the author, 1922.
Sitton, Tom. *John Randolph Haynes: California Progressive*. Stanford: Stanford University Press, 1992.
Slosson, Edwin E. *The Great American Universities*. New York, 1910.
Smelser, Neil. "Growth, Structural Change, and Conflict in California Higher Education, 1950–1970." In Smelser and Almond, eds., *Public Higher Education*, 9–141.
Smith, Michael I. *Pacific Visions: California Scientists and the Environment, 1850–1915*. New Haven, Conn.: Yale University Press, 1987.
Smith, Virginia B. "The Erosion of Educational Monopolies." *CrossTalk* 6:1 (Winter 1998), 8.
Spaeth, Harold J. *Classic and Current Decisions of the United States Supreme Court*. New York: W. H. Freeman, 1977.
Spindt, Herman A. "The University of California and William T. Reid." UCA, Sacramento.
Sproul, Robert Gordon. Inaugural Address as President of the University of California, October 22, 1930, Berkeley. UCA, Sacramento, 1930.
——— "Certain Aspects of the Junior College." *Junior College Journal* (February 1931), 276–77.
——— Address given at the Annual Charter Day Dinner, March 23, 1932. Quoted in Pettitt, *Twenty-Eight Years in the Life of a University President*, 201–3.
——— "Address to the California Alumni Association," March 23, 1934. Sproul Papers, UCA.
Stadtman, Verne A., ed. *The Centennial Record of the University of California: 1868–1968*. Berkeley: University of California Press, 1967.
——— *The University of California: 1868–1968*. New York: McGraw-Hill, 1970.
Stanley, Gerald. "Racism and the Early Republican Party: The 1856 Presidential Election in California." *Pacific Historical Review* (May 1974), 171–87.
Starr, Kevin. *Americans and the California Dream: 1850–1915*. New York: Oxford University Press, 1973.
——— *Inventing the Dream: California Through the Progressive Era*. New York: Oxford University Press, 1985.
——— *Material Dreams: Southern California Through the 1920s*. New York: Oxford University Press, 1990.
Stewart, David Barrows. "The Development of Constitutional Provisions Per-

taining to Education in California." Ph.D. dissertation, University of California, Berkeley, 1958.

Storke, Thomas M. *California Editor*. Los Angeles: Westernlore, 1958.

Strayer, George D., director, Washington State Survey of Education Institutions. "Public Education in Washington: A Report of a Survey of Public Education in the State of Washington." Submitted to Governor Wallgren, September 5, 1946.

——— "California's Needs in Higher Education." *California Journal of Secondary Education* 23: 4 (April 1948), 236–38.

"Survey of Higher Education." *California Schools* 17 (December 1947), 282.

Swett, John. *History of the Public School System of California*. San Francisco: A. L. Bancroft, 1876.

——— *Public Education in California: Its Origin and Development, with Personal Reminiscence of Half a Century*. New York: American Book Co., 1911.

Swett, John, Josiah Dwight Whitney, and J. F. Houghton. "Report Relative to Establishing a State University: 1864." In *Pamphlets of the University of California, Vol. 1 (1861–75)*. UCA, The Bancroft Library, Berkeley.

Swinton, William. "The University and Its Managers Before the People and the Law," March 20, 1874. In *Pamphlets on the University of California*, UCA.

Swisher, Carl Brent. *Motivation and Political Technique in the California Constitutional Convention: 1878–79*. Claremont, Calif.: Pomona College, 1930.

"A Time for Greatness." *Journal of Higher Education* 29: 2 (February 1958), 105.

Thomas, Frank W. "The Carnegie Foundation Report from the Standpoint of the Teachers Colleges." *California Quarterly of Secondary Education* 8:2 (January 1933), 122–30.

Trow, Martin. "The Democratization of Higher Education in America." *European Journal of Sociology* 3:2 (1962), 231–62.

——— "The Transition from Mass to University Higher Education." In Stephen R. Graubard and Geno A. Ballotti, eds., *The Embattled University*. New York: George Braziller, 1970, 1–42.

——— "Social Class and Higher Education." *American Behavioral Scientist* 25:4/5 (1992), 585–605.

Tyack, David. *Turning Points in American Educational History*. Waltham, Mass.: Blaisdell, 1967.

U.S. Government. *1960 Statistical Abstract of the United States*. Washington, D.C.: 1960.

Van Houten, Peter. "The Development of the Constitutional Provisions Pertaining to the University of California in the California Constitutional

Convention of 1878–1879." Ph.D. dissertation, University of California, Berkeley, 1973.
Veysey, Laurence R. *The Emergence of the American University*. Chicago: University of Chicago Press, 1965.
Warren, Earl. 1943 Inaugural Address, CSA.
——— Speech before the California State Reconstruction and Re-employment Commission, March 22, 1944. Cited in *Postwar California*. Berkeley: Bureau of Public Administration, University of California, 1:2 (April 1944), 2.
——— *The Memoirs of Earl Warren*. New York: Doubleday, 1977.
——— "We Have Sniffed Our Destiny." *Vital Speeches* 10 (May 1, 1944), 432.
Weber, Charles W., "Report of the Committee on Legislative Organization: The Procedure of Planning in State Government." *California Assembly Journal* (May 3, 1943), 3167.
Wheeler, Benjamin Ide. *Analogy and the Scope of Its Application in Language*. Ithaca, N.Y.: J. Wilson and Son, 1887.
——— *Die Organisation des Hoheren Unterrichts in den Vereinigten Staaten von Nordamerika*. Munich: C. H. Beck'sche Verlagsbuchhandlung, 1897.
——— *Dionysus and Immortality: The Greek Faith in Immortality as Affected by the Rise of Individualism*. New York: Houghton, Mifflin, 1899.
——— *Alexander the Great: The Merging of the East and West in Universal History*. New York: G. P. Putnam's Sons, 1900.
——— Charter Day speech. In the *University of California Chronicle* 13:2 (1911).
——— *The Abundant Life*. Monroe E. Deutsch, ed. Berkeley: University of California Press, 1926.
White, Andrew Dickson. "Evolution and Revolution." *An Address Delivered at the Annual Commencement of the University of Michigan: June 26, 1890*. Ann Arbor, Mich.: University of Michigan, 1890.
White, G. Edward. *Earl Warren: A Public Life*. New York: Oxford University Press, 1982.
Whitehead, J. S. *The Separation of Church and State: Columbia, Dartmouth, Harvard and Yale, 1776–1786*. New Haven, Conn.: Yale University Press, 1973.
Wickson, E. J. *Rural California*. New York: Macmillan, 1923.
Wilson, Logan, ed. *Emerging Patterns in American Higher Education*. Washington, D.C.: American Council on Education, 1965.
Wolfle, Dael. *America's Resources of Specialized Talent*. New York: Harper and Brothers, 1954.
Wollenberg, Charles. *All Deliberate Speed: Segregation and Exclusion in California Schools, 1855–1975*. Berkeley: University of California Press, 1976.

Young, Miriam Elinor. "Anthony Caminetti and His Role in the Development of a Complete System of Free Public Education in California." Ph.D. dissertation, Denver: University of Denver, 1966.

Zwerling, L. S. *Second Best: The Crisis of the Community College*. New York: McGraw-Hill, 1976.

INDEX

In this index an "f" after a number indicates a separate reference on the next page, and an "ff" indicates separate references on the next two pages. A continuous discussion over two or more pages is indicated by a span of page numbers, e.g., "57–59," and *passim* is used for a cluster of references in close but not consecutive sequence. Page numbers in italics represent illustrative material, with the letter "c" indicating a chart.

Library of Congress Cataloging-in-Publication Data

Douglass, John Aubrey.

The California idea and American higher education: 1850 to the 1960 master plan / John Aubrey Douglass.

p. cm.

Includes bibliographical references and index.

ISBN 0-8047-3189-6 (alk. paper)

1. Education, Higher—California—History. 2. Higher education and state—California—History. I. Title.

LA243.5 .D68 200
378.794 21—dc21

99-045668

⊗ This book is printed on acid-free, archival quality paper.

Original printing 2000
Last figure below indicates year of this printing:
08 07 06 05 04 03 02 01 00

Designed by Janet Wood
Typeset in Aldus 10.5/13 by G&S Typesetters